Hospitality & Tourism

An Introduction to the Industry

Eleventh Edition

Robert A. Brymer
Florida State University

KENDALL/HUNT PUBLISHING COMPANY
4050 Westmark Drive   Dubuque, Iowa 52002

Book Team
President & Chief Executive Officer   Mark C. Falb
Vice President, Director of National Book Program   Alfred C. Grisanti
Assistant Director of National Book Program   Paul B. Carty
Editorial Development Manager   Georgia Botsford
Developmental Editor   Angela Willenbring
Assistant Vice President, Production Services   Christine E. O'Brien
Prepress Project Coordinator   Sheri Hosek
Prepress Editor   Charmayne McMurray
Permissions Editor   Renae Heacock
Design Manager   Jodi Splinter
Designer   Suzanne Millius
Senior Vice President, College Division   Thomas W. Gantz
Managing Editor, College Field   Paul Gormley
Associate Editor, College Field   Jeanette Laessig

Cover image © Digital Vision

To my other parents
Bob & Virginia Smith, Dorothy & Art Tattersall,
Wayne & Lorraine Shook

Growing up in Toledo, Ohio, I had several homes. Besides the wonderful home provided by my parents, I also had my "other parents." These were my aunts and uncles who cooked meals for me, taught me how to blow bubbles, coached my teams, laughed with me, trusted me, always encouraged and supported me—even when I didn't deserve it. They gave me time, love, and understanding. They have provided that extra foundation, stability, and continuity in my life that is so important to who I am today. They were always there and always will be.

Contents

Acknowledgments

The 11th edition of this book is a collection of readings written by 48 authors representing 38 colleges and universities across the United States. These authors have written papers specifically for this book, and without their generous contributions the publication of this edition would have been impossible. They have truly created an outstanding edition, and I am very grateful for the special role each and every author played.

The following alphabetical list of authors includes their mailing addresses, phone numbers, FAX, and e-mail addresses at the time of publication.

John L. Avella
School of Hotel, Restaurant, & Tourism
Fairleigh Dickinson University
1000 River Street
Teaneck, NJ 07666
201-692-7271
FAX: 201-692-7279
e-mail: spechtavella@email.msn.com

Bradley Beran
Nutrition and Hospitality Management
Syracuse University
34 Slocum Hall
Syracuse, NY 13244-1250
315-443-2735
FAX: 315-443-2795
e-mail: bcberan@syr.edu

Francis X. Brown
Hospitality Management Program
St. John's University of New York
8000 Utopia Parkway
Jamaica, NY 11439
718-990-6137
FAX: 718-990-1882
e-mail: brownf@stjohns.edu

John C. Crotts
School of Business & Economics
College of Charleston
9 Liberty Street
Charleston, SC 29424-0001
843-953-6916
FAX: 843-953-5697
e-mail: crottsj@cofc.edu

Duncan R. Dickson
Rosen School of Hospitality Management
University of Central Florida
Orlando, FL 32816-1450
407-823-4406
FAX: 407-823-5696
e-mail: ddickson@mail.ucf.edu

Daryl V. Georger
Department of Hotel, Restaurant and
    Institutional Management
Mercyhurst College
501 East 38th St.
Erie, PA 16546
814-824-2340
FAX: 814-824-2107
e-mail: dgeorger@mercyhurst.edu

T. C. Girard
Hospitality and Tourism
Southern Illinois University
Carbondale, IL 62901-4317
618-453-7515
FAX: 618-453-7517
e-mail: tcgirard@siu.edu

Frank B. Guadagnolo
School of Hotel, Restaurant and
    Recreation Management
201 Mateer Building
Pennsylvania State University
University Park, PA 16802
814-863-8987
FAX: 814-863-8992
e-mail: fbg@psu.edu

Catherine M. Gustafson
School of Hotel, Restaurant and
    Tourism Management
University of South Carolina
Columbia, SC 29208
803-777-7720
FAX: 803-777-1224
e-mail: cgustafson@sc.edu

John C. Hartley
Department of Hotel, Restaurant and
    Tourism Management
New Mexico State University
Las Cruces, NM 88003-8003
505-646-3271
FAX: 505-646-8100
e-mail: johartle@nmsu.edu

Kathryn Hashimoto
The Lester E. Kabacoff School of Hotel,
    Restaurant, and Tourism Administration
University of New Orleans
210 Business Building, Lakefront
New Orleans, LA 70148
504-280-3157
FAX: 504-280-3189
e-mail: khashimo@uno.edu

Rob Heiman
Hospitality Foodservice Management
100 Nixson Hall
Kent State University
Kent, OH 44242
330-672-2075
FAX: 330-672-2194
e-mail: rheiman@kent.edu

Clark Hu
School of Tourism and Hospitality Management
Temple University
Philadelphia, PA 19122-0840
215-204-1994
FAX: 215-204-1455
e-mail: clark.hu@temple.edu

Joe C. Hutchison
Department of Hospitality Management
University of Southern Mississippi,
    Gulf Coast Campus
Long Beach, MS 39560
228-214-3226
FAX: 228-214-3223
e-mail: joe.hutchison@usm.edu

Joan M. Janson
College of Hospitality and Tourism
Niagara University
Niagara University, NY 14109-2012
716-286-8653
FAX: 716-286-8277
e-mail: jmj@niagara.edu

Doug Kennedy
Hotel, Restaurant and Tourism Management
University of Wisconsin—Stout
Menomonie, WI 54751-0790
715-232-5061
FAX: 715-232-2588
e-mail: kennedyd@uwstout.edu

Stephen W. Litvin
School of Business and Economics
College of Charleston
66 George St.
Charleston, SC 29424
843-953-7317
FAX: 843-953-5697
e-mail: litvins@cofc.edu

Stuart H. Mann
William F. Harrah College of
    Hotel Administration
University of Nevada, Las Vegas
Las Vegas, NV 89154-6013
702-895-3308
FAX: 702-895-4109
e-mail: shmann@ccmail.nevada.edu

Lincoln H. Marshall
Tourism and Hospitality Management
George Washington University
600 21 Street, NW
Washington, DC 20052
202-994-3327
FAX: 202-994-1630
e-mail: lincolnm@gwu.edu

Karl J. Mayer
William F. Harrah College of
   Hotel Administration
University of Nevada, Las Vegas
Las Vegas, NV 89154-0623
702-895-4841
FAX: 702-895-4870
e-mail: karl.mayer@ccmail.nevada.edu

Michael J. McCorkle
Hospitality Management
Richard Stockton College
P.O. Box 195
Pomona, NJ 08240
609-748-6020
FAX: 609-652-4858
e-mail: michael.mccorkle@stockton.edu

Robert A. McMullin
Hotel, Restaurant and Tourism Management
East Stroudsburg University
East Stroudsburg, PA 18301
570-422-3290
FAX: 570-422-3777
e-mail: mcmullin@po-box.esu.edu

Richard G. McNeill, Jr.
School of Hotel and Restaurant Management
Northern Arizona University
Flagstaff, AZ 86011
928-523-1713
FAX: 928-523-1711
e-mail: richard.mcneill@nau.edu

Richard J. Mills, Jr.
Hospitality and Tourism
Seton Hill University
Seton Hill Drive
Greensburg, PA 15601
724-830-1863
FAX: 412-262-8494
mills@setonhill.edu

Albert J. Moranville
Hotel, Restaurant, and Tourism Management
East Stroudsburg University
East Stroudsburg, PA 18301
570-422-3511
FAX: 570-422-3198
e-mail: moranville@po-box.esu.edu

Gail J. Myers
Hotel, Restaurant and Institutional Management
University of Minnesota, Crookston
Crookston, MN 56719
218-281-8200
FAX: 218-281-8250
e-mail: gmyers@mail.crk.umn.edu

Ken W. Myers
Hotel, Restaurant and Institutional Management
University of Minnesota, Crookston
Crookston, MN 56719
218-281-8200
FAX: 218-281-8250
e-mail: kmyers@mail.crk.umn.edu

Michael J. Oliver
Hotel, Restaurant, and Institution Management
Iowa State University
Ames, IA 50011-1120
515-294-7575
FAX: 515-294-6364
e-mail: moliver@iastate.edu

Radesh Palakurthi
Hospitality Management
San Jose State University
One Washington Square
San Jose, CA 95192-0058
408-924-3186
FAX: 408-924-3114
e-mail: rpalakur@online.sjsu.edu

Robert Alan Palmer
Collins School of Hospitality Management
California State Polytechnic University
3801 West Temple Avenue
Pomona, CA 91768
909-869-4283
FAX: 909-869-4805
e-mail: raplamer@csupomona.edu

William R. Petersen
School of Hospitality, Tourism and
   Culinary Management
Southern New Hampshire University
Manchester, NH 03106-1045
603-644-3128
FAX: 603-644-3166
e-mail: w.petersen@snhu.edu

Catherine H. Price
Department of Hospitality Management
University of Southern Mississippi
Box 5176
Hattiesburg, MS 39406
601-266-5008
FAX: 601-266-6707
e-mail: catherine.price@usm.edu

Paul D. Rompf
Rosen School of Hospitality Management
University of Central Florida
Orlando, FL 32816-1450
407-823-1120
FAX: 407-823-5696
e-mail: prompf@mail.ucf.edu

Mary Jo Ross
Rosen School of Hospitality Management
University of Central Florida
Orlando, FL 32816-1450
407-823-1112
FAX: 407-823-5696
e-mail: mross@mail.ucf.edu

Denis P. Rudd
Hospitality and Tourism
Robert Morris University
881 Narrows Run Road
Moon Township, PA 15108-1189
412-262-8636
FAX: 412-262-8494
e-mail: rudd@rmu.edu

Denver E. Severt
Hotel and Restaurant Management
Eastern Michigan University
Ypsilanti, MI 48197
734-487-0483
FAX: 734-487-7087
denver.severt@emich.edu

Janet Sim
Department of Hospitality Management
San Francisco State University
San Francisco, CA 94010
415-338-2673
FAX: 415-405-0492
e-mail: jsim@sfsu.edu

Paul Sorgule
Hospitality Management
Paul Smith's College
Paul Smiths, NY 12970
518-327-6215
FAX: 518-327-6369
e-mail: sorgulp@paulsmiths.edu

John M. Stefanelli
William F. Harrah College of
    Hotel Administration
University of Nevada, Las Vegas
Las Vegas, NV 89154-0623
702-895-4841
FAX: 702-895-4870
e-mail: stefan@ccmail.nevada.edu

Nancy Swanger
School of Hospitality and Business Management
Washington State University
Pullman, WA 99164-4742
509-335-2443
FAX: 509-335-3857
e-mail: swanger@wsu.edu

Marcia H. Taylor
Cecil B. Day School of Hospitality
    Administration
Georgia State University
MSC 4A1267, 33 Gilmer St. SE #4
Atlanta, GA 30303
404-651-4253
FAX: 404-651-3670
e-mail: mhtaylor@gsu.edu

Michael Terry
Rosen School of Hospitality Management
University of Central Florida
Orlando, FL 32816-1450
404-823-1114
FAX: 407-823-5696
e-mail: mterry@mail.ucf.edu

Patrick T. Tierney
Department of Recreation and Hospitality
    Management
San Francisco State University
San Francisco, CA 94132
415-338-1818
FAX: 415-338-0543
e-mail: ptierney@sfsu.edu

Ronald A. Usiewicz
International College of Hospitality Management
   "Cesar Ritz"
101 Wykeham Road
Washington, CT 06793
860-868-9555
FAX: 860-868-2124
e-mail: ronaldu@ichm.cc.ct.us

C. E. Vlisides
Tagliatela School of Hospitality and Tourism
University of New Haven
West Haven, CT 06492
203-932-7412
FAX: 203-932-7086
e-mail: cvlisides@newhaven.edu

David B. West
School of Tourism and Hospitality Management
Temple University
Philadelphia, PA 19122
215-204-1474
FAX: 215-204-1455
e-mail: dbwest@temple.edu

John M. Wolper
College of Business, Hospitality Management
University of Findlay
Findlay, OH 45840
419-434-6949
FAX: 419-434-4082
e-mail: wolper@findlay.edu

Paula Wolper
College of Business, Hospitality Management
University of Findlay
Findlay, OH 45840
419-422-4625
FAX: 419-434-4082
e-mail: pwolper@findlay.edu

Alina Zapalska
Division of Finance and Economics
Lewis College of Business
Marshall University
Huntington, WV 25755
304-696-3234
FAX: 304-696-3662
e-mail: zapalska@marshall.edu

Part I
Hospitality and Tourism Industry

1
Welcome to Hospitality and Tourism

2
The Past: Hospitality and Tourism "Yesterday"

3
The Present and Possible Future: Hospitality and Tourism "Today and Tomorrow"

4
Information Resources: Periodicals and the Web

5
Industry Associations and Rating Services

6
Career Realities and Opportunities

Chapter

1

Welcome to Hospitality and Tourism

Castle in Germany

POSTAGE
PAID

Robert A. Brymer
Florida State University

John L. Avella
Fairleigh Dickinson University

Corbis

This book is about one of the fastest growing industries in the world. It comes to you at a time when the wonderful world of hospitality and tourism has never been more exciting. The authors in this book will introduce you to an industry that truly is a "people" business. Chapter after chapter will reaffirm that, in the world of hospitality, taking good care of the guest is the single most critical element for success.

Hospitality and tourism is systematically organized for the introductory student. The book begins with a broad overview of the industry and gradually narrows the focus to include an introduction to companies and operations. The final section reviews many specific career options available to prospective managers. Please see Figure 1.1 for a graphic view of how the book is organized. The goal is to provide a survey approach to hospitality and tourism, while offering the information needed to help students proceed into more advanced courses and readings.

FIGURE 1.1   **ORGANIZATION OF THE BOOK**

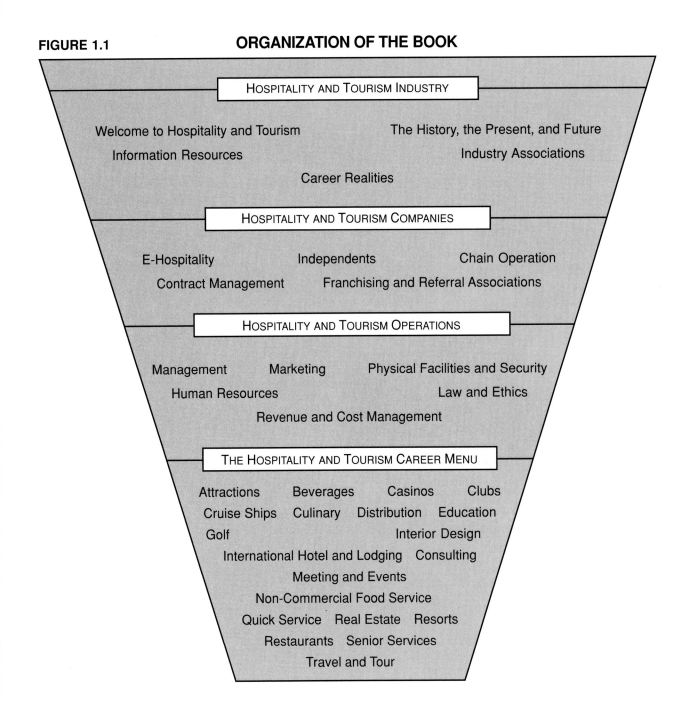

HOSPITALITY AND TOURISM INDUSTRY

Welcome to Hospitality and Tourism   The History, the Present, and Future

Information Resources   Industry Associations

Career Realities

HOSPITALITY AND TOURISM COMPANIES

E-Hospitality   Independents   Chain Operation

Contract Management   Franchising and Referral Associations

HOSPITALITY AND TOURISM OPERATIONS

Management   Marketing   Physical Facilities and Security

Human Resources   Law and Ethics

Revenue and Cost Management

THE HOSPITALITY AND TOURISM CAREER MENU

Attractions   Beverages   Casinos   Clubs

Cruise Ships   Culinary   Distribution   Education

Golf   Interior Design

International Hotel and Lodging   Consulting

Meeting and Events

Non-Commercial Food Service

Quick Service   Real Estate   Resorts

Restaurants   Senior Services

Travel and Tour

When we think of tourism, we envision a family traveling, sightseeing, and relaxing together.

The Service-Tourism-Hospitality Connection

For a better understanding of where the industry fits in the economy, please refer to Figure 1.2. Starting at the top of that chart—The Economy—you will see that the economy is made up of agriculture, manufacturing, and service. They are three separate parts of the economy, yet each plays a role in the service part of the economy. In the past, agriculture and manufacturing contributed the most to the economy. Now the service sector is the most dominant contributor. This shift of dominance from agriculture and manufacturing to service has required people to acquire different skills. In an agricultural economy, people were engaged in growing products for consumer consumption. In a manufacturing economy, people were occupied with producing a product. In today's service economy, there is no tangible product—the product is service, and the quality of that product rests in the mind of the guest. Herein lies the difficult and exciting part of this industry: forecasting the guests' service expectations. The skills necessary to survive in an agricultural economy and manufacturing economy are physical and mental. In the service economy, they are more interpersonal and intellectual. For many people, this is quite a change and a difficult transition.

Figure 1.2 illustrates the relationship between the economy, service, and the hospitality and tourism industry.

Hospitality and Tourism

The hospitality and tourism industry includes many different segments, as can be seen in Figures 1.1 and 1.2, including recreation, entertainment, travel, food service, lodging, and many others. We will devote a little more time in this chapter to food service and lodging, the two single largest sectors. Even though they are the largest, however, they're closely related and work hand-in-hand with many other vital segments of this vast industry.

Food Service

This part of the hospitality industry is growing at a dramatic rate. The reason for this growth is that more people are consuming meals out of their homes. The increase in second-income families and the inadequate time to prepare meals is a significant factor in this growth.

This industry is about far more than just food and service. Although serving great food and delivering exceptional service is very important, food service is more about creating an exceptional dining experience for the guest: great food,

FIGURE 1.2   THE SERVICE-TOURISM-HOSPITALITY CONNECTION

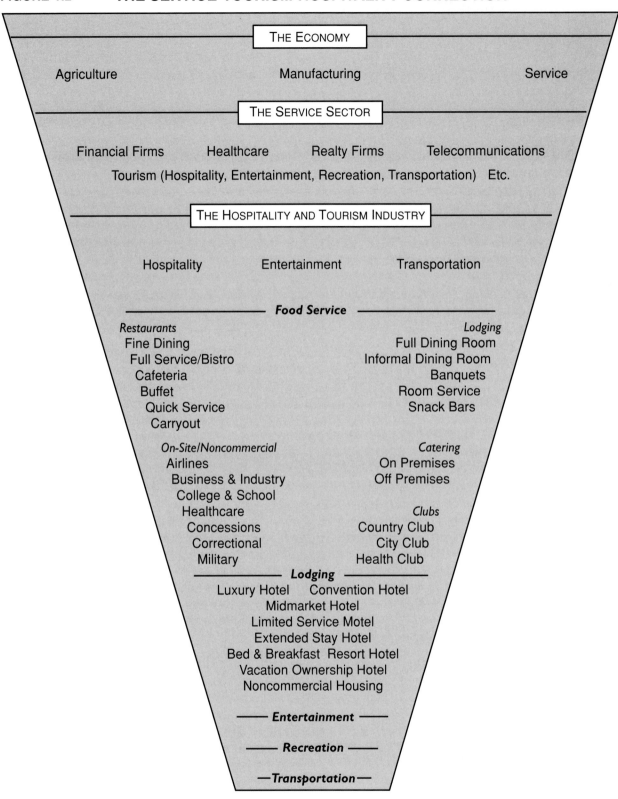

On any given day, almost half of all adults eat a restaurant meal.

their conversation and laughter—and the clanking of dishes and silverware.

When Windows on the World reopened in 1996, the president of Windows, Joe Baum, announced at the employee orientation, "We are not in the restaurant business, we are in the entertainment business because we are creating a unique experience." He took the notion of a dining experience to the next level. Windows on the World went on to become the highest volume restaurant in the United States. Unfortunately, that ended on September 11, 2001, when the industry and the world lost many good people.

The restaurant segment of the food service industry can be a trip around the world. In any major city, you can experience food from almost any country in the world. Chefs are blending different cuisines to produce what is called "fusion" cuisine. For example, the blending of the flavors from Chinese cuisine and French cuisine produces a unique taste. Creative themes and décor can transport the guest to any country in the world and make them feel like they are in the eighteenth or the twenty-third century. The diversity of the restaurant segment is immense. As a customer, you can spend five dollars for dinner or you can spend one hundred dollars for dinner. You can select from an assortment of five beverages or a selection of one thousand varieties of wine. You can also experience an operation that is owned by an individual who has one restaurant and works at it all the time or a

exceptional service, and ambiance. Ambiance is made up of the décor, the sound level, the lighting, the furniture, and the symphony of dining sounds created by both the diners themselves—

Buffet restaurants are just one of the vast and diverse elements of the food service industry.

restaurant that is one of a thousand restaurants owned by a corporation, where the owners are never around. For the employee, both entrepreneurial properties and franchises have advantages and disadvantages.

The food service industry is made up of more than just restaurants. The non-commercial food service industry feeds students—elementary, secondary, and college—as well as patients and corporate employees. The challenge is to offer food they will eat and that is nutritious. In some college dining programs, a cafeteria is set aside just for vegetarians. That goes a long way to meet and exceed the expectations of the customer. There will be many students who will choose that university because they have a vegetarian cafeteria. Hospital food service is challenging in that meals must be suitable for all kinds of diets that are required by patients. Many institutional dining facilities (hospitals, schools, companies) have gone to branding. Branding is taking a known brand like McDonald's and opening that facility in a hospital or a school. This trend brings to the operation the name recognition and appeal that goes with it, as well as the standards of operation for that brand.

An often overlooked segment of the food service industry is the private club segment. These operations can provide an exciting, interesting place to work, especially if the club has a large food service facility that serves a la carte and has catering for special events. In addition to the food service operation, a manager could end up managing the challenges of the golf course and tennis courts.

Probably the largest segment of this industry is the quick-service or fast food restaurants. As you know, you can eat in or drive through, which affords a variety of eating options. Quick-service restaurants are continually trying to reinvent themselves, but the eating public continues to go for that hamburger, fried chicken, and pizza.

Another subdivision of the food service business is found in special events and catering. Special events include food service at outdoor concerts, golf tournaments, tennis tournaments, and huge events like the Olympics. These events are intense and many times more difficult to operate because the dining tents and kitchens are normally temporary. During the Winter 2002 Olympics, the food service people were providing one hundred thousand meals per day. The dining tent in the Olympic Village housed thirteen hundred seats, a huge kitchen and a full-service McDonald's. Working in stadiums and arenas is a unique challenge because they contain almost every segment of the food service industry: concession stands, private clubs, luxury sky boxes, a la carte restaurants, and catering for special events. As a free bonus, you get the excitement of watching a major sporting event.

The sale of rooms represents the primary revenue source of lodging properties.

Lodging

If you were to ask ten people to give you an example of the lodging industry, you might get answers like: a resort in the Bahamas or Hawaii; a small inn in Vermont; a bed and breakfast in Cape May, New Jersey; a small exclusive converted castle in France; a roadside motel in Akron, Ohio; a 1200-room luxury hotel in New York; a 100-room budget motel in Fresno, California; an all suite hotel in Memphis; a mega hotel in Las Vegas; and an apartment hotel in London. All these answers, although different in some ways, represent examples of the lodging industry. The common bond is that they all have sleeping rooms. However, the amenities and quality of service will vary from concept to concept. Some lodging facilities will have .5 employees per room, while others will have two or more employees per room. Some will have extensive food service with two or three restaurants with different cuisines and twenty-four hour room service. Some will have one restaurant that serves breakfast, lunch, and dinner. An apartment or residential hotel may provide the guests with a fully equipped kitchen. A bed and breakfast will serve only breakfast. Some will have no food service except for a vending machine with snacks and soft drinks. It is amazing that there are over 50,000 lodging operations in the United States. What incredible opportunity.

The lodging industry is very broad and varied, with each segment requiring a different skill set. Can you imagine the amount of experience you would need to run one of those mega properties in Las Vegas? You would actually be running a medium sized corporation. You would need to have experience in all facets of hotel operations, excellent interpersonal and leadership skills, extensive food and beverage experience, plus excellent knowledge of the gaming industry. Obviously, to run a hundred room, or less, property without food and beverage would require much less experience than the Vegas property. Some managers of these properties have less than five years experience in the lodging business.

The basic strategy in the lodging business is to sell rooms; that is pretty obvious. The challenge for marketing is to bring people in to buy rooms. Once the guest is at the property, a challenge might be to sell them the kind of room they desire at a price that represents value to the guest. Value, like quality, is determined by the guest, not the management of the property. A guest room is a perishable product. If it is not sold on any one night, that revenue is lost, so the challenge is to know how to sell that room based on the guests' expectation and their perception of value.

The profitability percentage of a sold guest room is usually higher than the profitability percentage of selling a meal. Many owners make the decision not to have food service in their properties because of the profitability picture and the difficulty of operating that food service facility. In some cases, lodging owners want to provide food service for their guests and will lease the food service facility.

Conclusion

The bottom line in the hospitality business is managing the "moments of truth." A "moment of truth" is any time the guest comes in contact with anything that represents the operation. The perception of that contact could be positive or negative. Those contacts could be the condition of the parking lot, the friendliness of the voice on the phone when the reservation was made, the cleanliness of the entrance way, the greeting by the front desk person or a hostess, the speediness of the elevator, and so on. In a one-night stay or the time it takes to enjoy a meal, the guest could experience one hundred "moments of truth." The greatest challenge in the industry is to manage those "moments of truth" so that they are positive for the guest who then wants to return and tell their friends how wonderful that facility is.

Hospitality, tourism, and service are interwoven in this exciting worldwide industry. Enjoy your exploration into the industry, companies, operations, and careers. Welcome!

Chapter One Review Questions

1. Why is the hospitality industry referred to as a "people" business?

2. What are the three separate parts of the economy described by the author? Define each.

3. Describe the major shift in the economy concerning the manufacturing industries and the service industries.

4. What is the product in a service economy?

5. Who judges the quality level of service?

6. What are the skills necessary to survive in the service economy?

7. Describe the various segments of the hospitality industry.

8. Describe the current trends in the food service industry. How and why are they changing?

9. List 3–5 factors which influence decisions concerning a meal away from home.

10. What is fusion cuisine?

11. What is a challenge of the non-commercial food industry?

12. Describe the different attributes of the private club segment of the hospitality industry.

13. What are the common menu choices of fast food restaurants?

14. What types of venues are likely to cater to or hold special events?

15. What makes working in stadiums and arenas a unique challenge?

16. Give six examples of different types of lodging.

17. What is the range of employees per guest room ratio? How does that vary within the lodging industry?

18. What are the different types of food services you will find in many hotels?

19. What type of lodging management skills would be needed to run a mega-property in Las Vegas?

20. What is meant by the concept that a guest room is perishable?

21. List five examples of "moments of truth" in a hospitality setting.

22. What is one of the greatest challenges related to managing moments of truth?

Chapter 2

The Past: Hospitality and Tourism "Yesterday"

Victorian Architecture

Corbis

POSTAGE PAID

Michael Terry

Mary Jo Ross
University of Central Florida

Introduction

Hospitality and tourism is the largest, fastest growing industry in the world. The World Travel and Tourism Council (WTTC) estimates that consumer-driven travel and tourism as a part of the global economy are directly and indirectly responsible for 10 percent of gross domestic product, 200 million jobs, 7.5 percent of total employment, and 5.0 million new jobs per year until 2010. The sheer size, however, does not do justice to the comprehensive nature of the interrelated components of products and services.

Whether for business or leisure, for luxury or economy, people have traveled since the beginning of time. As a result, tourism entrepreneurs have seized this opportunity to provide accommodating products and services throughout the world. From the biblical story of the inn in Bethlehem, to the European Medieval Castle feasts, to the Orient Express, to the Titanic maiden voyage, to the transatlantic Supersonic Concorde, to Las Vegas's 5,500 suite MGM Grand Resort, hospitality is inarguably the most fascinating field on the planet. The diversity of the industry includes stadium hot dog stands, underwater hotels, trips to the Grand Canyon or Niagara Falls, gambling cruises to nowhere, military facilities, colleges, health care facilities, and business/industrial facilities.

In order to truly gain an appreciation for the industry, it is important to understand the historical roots of hospitality and tourism. The great sages agree that there is little way of projecting the future without understanding the past. Tim Garvey says it another way: "Knowledge is telling the **past**. Wisdom is predicting the **future**." In keeping with this philosophy, we now explore the history of this incredible field called hospitality and tourism.

Scope

In order to gain an understanding of the evolution of hospitality and tourism, we need to apply an organized perspective that defines the various segments of the industry. Therefore, the historical scope will reflect the following four major subdivisions:

Lodging: Hotels, motels, resorts, and vacation ownership

Food/Beverage: Taverns, restaurants, bars, catering, and vending

Travel: Railroads, automobiles, cruise ships, and airlines

Recreation: Festivals, parks, gaming, and attractions

Eras of Hospitality and Tourism

Volumes of pertinent history can be (and have been) written about the literally millions of lodging, food/beverage, travel, and recreational aspects and facilities surrounding the business. This diary of events is but a thumbnail sketch of the highlights. It is meant to educate the reader from a "big picture" point of view, and will not, by definition, cover every moment of the world's illustrious hospitality history. In order to create the best "word video," this author has divided "the past" into six convenient segments. These periods are outlined by significant travel or tourism milestones and outstanding industry "players" who defined their eras.

Enjoy this accelerated stroll down hospitality's memory lane. . . .

Prior to 1700

The Phoenicians were among the first real travelers. In both the Mediterranean and the Orient, travelers were motivated by trade, commerce, and food supplies. The excavated ruins of the Roman town Pompeii, which was buried by an eruption of Mt. Vesuvius, yielded several restaurants, taverns, and inns that tourists visit even today. Medieval travel was mostly confined to religious travel, such as the Crusades (1095–1300). Later, aristocrats undertook grand tours of Europe, stopping at major cities for weeks or months at a time. It was considered a necessary part of "rounding out" a young lady's or gentleman's education. During the seventeenth century, pineapples were brought back to Europe from the West Indies by early European explorers. It became the favored fruit to serve the royalty and the elite and was later introduced into the North American hospitality culture. The pineapple is now recognized as the international symbol of hospitality: friendliness, warmth, cheer, graciousness, and conviviality.

The ancient Egyptians and Babylonians recorded the fermentation process, and the very first records of wine making date back about 7,000 years. The Greeks received the vine from the Egyptians, and later the Romans contributed to the popularization of wine in Europe by planting vines in the territories they conquered. As far back as the year 1000, the Roman soldiers tasted *picea* and thought it lacked *focus* (the Latin word for hearth). On a hearth, along with oil, herbs and cheese . . . the modern precursor to what we call pizza was born in pre-Renaissance Naples. Poor housewives had only flour, olive oil, lard, cheese, and herbs with which to feed their families, so combining them in a tasty and delicious manner became the goal. All of Italy proclaimed the Neapolitan pies to be the best. In 1637, the first European coffee-house opened in England; within thirty years, coffee houses had replaced taverns as the islands' social, commercial, and political melting pots.

As early as 300 B.C., ancient Egyptians sailed up and down the Nile River, carrying huge rocks with which to build pyramids as tombs for their leaders. The Roman Empire provided safe passage for travelers via a vast road system that stretched from Egypt to Britain. The wealthy Romans traveled to Egypt and Greece to experience the Pyramids, the Sphinx, as well as baths, shrines, and seaside resorts. In North America, the first racetrack was built on Long Island in 1665.

The 1700s

A half-dozen lotteries sponsored by prominent individuals such as Ben Franklin, John Hancock, and George Washington operated in each of the thirteen colonies to raise funds for building projects. Early hotels in North America began as inns or taverns. In 1794, the City Hotel on Broadway in New York City opened as the first hotel in the U.S. During the 1770s, taverns sprang up in the colonies and became a focal point of the community. In Boston, these eating and drinking establishments were called "the candles of liberty" by Patrick Henry.

The 1800s

Tourism first appeared in the English language in the early nineteenth century. At the time, tour was associated with the idea of a voyage or theatrical tour. Today, the WTTC's definition is: "comprising the activities of persons traveling to and staying in

Industry "Players" Mini-Case

Ellsworth Statler is considered to be the finest hotelier of modern times. The hotel business fascinated Statler, and at 15, he took a job as a head bellboy at the McClure in Wheeling, Ohio; he eventually became clerk, and by the time he was 16, he could handle the hotel books. At 19, he was the untitled manager. Enterprising and innovative, he leased the McClure billiard room and made it a profitable venture. He set up a railroad ticket booth, which was the first transportation department in a U.S. hotel. He bought out a company that had been operating the Musee Bowling Lanes. He also opened a lunchroom, The Pie House, in the Musee building, and his mother and sister were soon baking there. Statler's own formal schooling ended with the second grade, but he valued education. The terms of his will established the Statler Foundation. The major beneficiary is the School of Hotel Administration at Cornell University, Ithaca, N.Y., and large grants have gone to other colleges and universities. Ellsworth Statler's dream was to have his own hotel, and in 1907, that dream became a reality. He opened the Buffalo, N.Y., Statler and offered "a room and a bath for a dollar and a half." He proceeded to establish a chain of middle-class hotels, which set standards for comfort and cleanliness at moderate prices. Seeking a competitive edge, he designed a plumbing shaft that permitted bathrooms to be built back to back, providing two baths for little more than the price of one, and allowing him to offer many private rooms with adjoining baths. He became the first to put telephones and radios in every guest room, along with full-length mirrors, built-in closets and a special faucet for ice water.

Eventually, Statler opened hotels in Boston, Cleveland, Detroit, and New York. Emphasizing that "the guest is always right," he demanded top performance from employees, but was also caring about their needs. His program of job and retirement security was unique in its time.

The arrival of trains in the mid-1800s made travel easier, faster, and more comfortable.

places outside of their usual environment for not more than one consecutive year for leisure, business, and other purposes." The oldest U.S. travel agency began in 1888 when Ward Grenelle Foster opened a "travel information office" in St. Augustine, Florida. In the 1890s, the legendary agency expanded to all three Sunshine State coasts, New York, and other metropolitan centers.

The bed and breakfast and inn concept started in Europe in the early 1800s as overnight stays in private homes, bud did not become popular in the United States until nearly a century later. Since the hotel opened its doors on June 1, 1898, the Ritz Paris™ has been a symbol of opulence, luxury, and lavish attention to detail. And for more than a century, the hotel has played host to royalty, society mavens, Hollywood stars, literary lions, and fashion giants. Cesar Ritz, the son of an alpine shepherd, made his profession out of catering to the tastes of European high society and devoted his life to defining the deluxe hotel business we know today. When his career began in 1886, the hotel industry was in its infancy. By making hotels a fashionable and acceptable part of society, Cesar Ritz's reputation was assured. He developed his craft working in the company of some of the industry's great pioneers, including the chef, Auguste

Escoffier. A Ritz hotel syndicate was formed and the Ritz in Paris opened in 1898. The first hotel to have bellpersons, front desk persons, locks on guest room doors, and free soap for guests opened in 1829. In 1859, N.Y. Fifth Avenue Hotel installed the first hotel elevators, and hotels began using electricity. Auguste Escoffier, the first chef at the Ritz Paris™ and friend of the hotel's founder, Cesar Ritz, is largely responsible for developing haute gastronomy, a high style of cooking: elegantly prepared and served. Escoffier, considered by many to be the greatest chef of the 20th century, created some of the most legendary dishes of all time, including the dessert Peach Melba, created to honor the great soprano Nellie Melba. In 1818, the Black Ball Line in New York was the first shipping company to offer regularly scheduled service from the United States to England and to be concerned with the comfort of their passengers (rather than cargo, which had been the norm). The first railroad was built in the United States in 1830, and by 1869, the transcontinental connection was completed. Thomas Cook, recognized as the first professional travel agent, chartered a train in 1841 to carry 540 people to a temperance convention in Loughborough, England. In 1872, Cook hosted an around-the-world trip that took the 10 member group 222 days. Mark

Twain was a passenger on the 1867, first cruise originating in America. Automobiles evolved from steam engines in the late 1800s, and in 1891, Karl Benz and Gottlieb Daimler built a factory for internal combustion engines, which is now Mercedes (Daimler) Benz Foster. The demise of the riverboat gambler had more to do with the emergence of railroads and the outbreak of the Civil War than direct action by the people. Travel by steamboats declined as railroads started to supplant steamboats as the more reliable and faster method of transportation.

During the early 1800s, the parks movement expanded rapidly as a responsibility of government and voluntary organizations. Lotteries and casinos were initiated, but gambling came under increasing attack and was outlawed. The prohibition also led to the creation of illegal lotteries. The Civil War interrupted virtually all river travel and abruptly diminished gambling in that area. The expansion of the western frontier spurred the second wave. As the country moved westward, the frontier spirit continued to spread. Mining booms lured by the promises of easy and abundant riches, personified the frontier spirit and increased the rush to the Far West. Mining was a gamble, and these risk-takers were restless and ambitious people who had high expectations. Probably nowhere was this more apparent than in California. Laws against gamblers and gambling began to be enacted in California. Gambling was legal in Nevada between 1869 and 1910. As a result, gaming activity moved from California to places such as Virginia City, Nevada.

1900–1950

More than 60 agents in 1931 formed the American Society of Travel Agents (ASTA), the world's largest travel trade association, which promised to protect and promote the mutual interests of travel agents and the traveling public members. In 1941, the Travel Industry of America (TIA) became the established national association for the common interests and concerns of all components of the U.S. travel industry. The American Hotel Protective Association was founded in Chicago in 1910 when the lodging industry consisted almost entirely of hotels situated in urban centers and resorts near the principal vacation destinations. Electricity began to be installed in new hotels for cooking purposes, as well as for light-

Industry "Players" Mini-Case

Howard Johnson began franchising his hotels and restaurants in 1927, as he was the pioneer of brand leveraging. The year was 1925; the financial health of the nation was sound. Economists talked about "an era of prosperity" and the future seemed nothing but bright. However, the outlook for 27-year-old Howard Deering Johnson was not so bright. Johnson owed $40,000. He had voluntarily assumed business obligations left by his deceased father and had gone deeper in debt by borrowing $500 and taking over the operation of a small patent medicine store, soda fountain, and newsstand, located in Wollaston, a section of Quincy, Massachusetts. The store was a money loser. Still, Johnson felt he could make it work. The first thing he did was send out delivery boys to sell newspapers in nearby communities. Sales went up, and then Johnson turned his attention to the soda fountain. The store sold just three flavors of ice cream: vanilla, chocolate, and strawberry. Johnson believed the number of flavors should be expanded, but first, he was determined to improve the quality of the ice cream he was selling. Using an old-fashioned freezer in the basement, he began cranking away by hand and experimenting to develop the best product possible. By doubling the butterfat content and using only natural ingredients, Johnson came up with what he thought was a superior ice cream. His customers thought so, too, and soon they were standing in lines outside his establishment. The demand led to expansion, and soon he was selling his ice cream at stands on nearby beaches and other locations. In three years, his debts were overcome and his business was a success. He added frankfurters, hamburgers, and other foods, carefully making sure of the best quality of content and preparation. His little store had become a restaurant, and Johnson then decided that the food business was a way to greater success. In 1929, he opened another restaurant, in downtown Quincy, Massachusetts, and began planning further expansion.

Industry "Players" Mini-Case

Because the only business that they had seen succeeding in the current economy was a little hot dog stand, the McDonald brothers, Maurice and Richard, decided to open a small drive-in restaurant in 1940. To their own surprise, their business was an instant success, making $40,000 profit in its first year. Desiring greater speed in serving customers, the brothers shut the store down for a few months to restructure. The first step was getting rid of all the carhops. Next, the menu was cut down from 25 items to 9, which mostly consisted of hamburgers. They replaced their old grills with larger, more efficient ones. The plates and silverware were replaced by paper, taking away the need for a dishwasher and constant replacements. The size of the burgers was cut down, and the workers, not the customers, put the condiments on the burger. In an effort to further increase speed and efficiency, the McDonald brothers ordered 8 milkshake machines that made 5 shakes at the same time, from a man named Ray Kroc. Intrigued by a business that would need so many milkshake machines, Kroc decided to give McDonald's a visit of his own. Liking what he saw, Ray Kroc offered to run the franchising for McDonald's and offered them a percentage of profits in return. Eventually, the brothers simply sold the business (for much less than they could have asked for) and got out. Ray Kroc changed the size of the burgers and standardized the burger process. The burger patty was to be 3 5/8 inches in diameter. The fat content was between 17 and 20 percent. He demanded employee cleanliness and exact uniforms. Starting in 1955, there were 7 McDonald's stores. In 1956, 12 more were added. There are currently over 7,000 McDonald's restaurants in over 25 countries around the world. McDonald's, a simple restaurant, started by two brothers who had failed in every business they had tried, has set the standard for fast-food restaurants and for franchising.

ing. Franchising began in 1907 when Ritz Development Company franchised the Ritz-Carlton name in New York City. Conrad Hilton bought his first hotel in 1919, the Mobley, in Cisco, Texas. He was a shrewd, cautious bargainer and believed in hiring the best managers available. He built the first Hilton Hotel in 1925 in Dallas, Texas, the Sir Francis Drake in San Francisco in 1938, and the Waldorf Astoria in New York City in 1949. The first motel, allowing guests to drive right up to the doors of their rooms or to an adjacent garage, was designed by California architect Arthur Hinneman and opened in 1925 in San Luis Obispo, California. Hilton became the first international hotel chain with the opening of the Caribe Hilton in San Juan, Puerto Rico in 1949. Belgian diamond cutter and water polo champion, Gerard Blitz, conceived the first Club Med Village in 1950 on the Balearic Islands, Spain. It was created for people from diverse backgrounds, to encourage them to share a good time, and to offer a unique escape from the stress of post World War II Europe.

The widest-reported "first" appearance of the hamburger most commonly cited in the lore of food service was that the product appeared at the World's Fair in St. Louis in 1904. With the growing affluence of America after World War II and customer demand for automobiles, food service operators turned to the drive-in as the preferred format for serving the hamburger. While drive-ins were conceived as early as the mid-1930s, the concept exploded phenomenally during the war and after. California and Texas were particularly active enclaves for drive-ins, where the hamburger, fries, and shakes were the dominant menu offerings, served by a carhop, who often delivered the meal on roller skates. The man who gave the hamburger its contemporary look, while he sought to expand the product's appeal through chain operations, was J. Walter Anderson, a Wichita, Kansas resident who went on to co-found the White Castle Hamburger system, the oldest continuously running burger chain. Helped by the marketing savvy of Edgar Waldo "Billy" Ingram, White Castle reach five units by the 1920s, selling a standardized product for five cents. Later White Castle would pioneer the concept of chain marketing with the advertising tag line "Buy 'em by the sack." Another early pioneer in chain development through burgers was the Wimpy Grills chain, launched in 1934, in homage to J. Wellington Wimpy, the chubby, mustachioed cartoon character who hung around with Popeye. Wimpy was ground-breaking in two respects: It was the first chain that attempted to court an upscale diner with 10 cent hamburgers, and it was the first to go overseas. At age 26, J. Willard Marriott, with his new bride Allie, entered the business world with the opening of a nine-seat root beer stand in Washington, D.C. Hot food was added, the name was changed to The Hot Shoppe, and eventually the Hot Shoppe drive-in was created. By 1937, Marriott had pioneered in-flight catering at Washington's old Hoover Airfield (current site of the Pentagon) serving Eastern, American and Capital airlines. In 1939, Colonel Harland Sanders first gave the world a taste of his most famous creation, original recipe Kentucky Fried Chicken, featuring that secret blend of 11 herbs and spices in Cobin, Kentucky. *ARAMARK* traces its history back to 1926, when the Slater Corporation was founded in a fraternity house on the University of Pennsylvania campus. Slater Corporation initially managed dining service programs in colleges and then expanded to business and industry, vending, and hospitals. As Slater Corporation was expanding its manual food service business, two other companies, which were to join later as the founding companies of *ARAMARK*, were also developing in the late 1930s and '40s. Davidson Brothers Inc. and Automatic Retailers Merchandising Company merged and formed Automatic Retailers of America.

The Wright brothers tested their thirteen-horsepower engine in 1903. The year 1907 saw the beginning of air passenger service between London and Paris. Railroads continued to extend their lines at the turn of the century in the United States, upgrading to excellent dining cars and sleeping berths. However, the industry was not able to adapt and compete with the automobile in the 20th century and eventually faltered during the Great Depression of the 1930s and World War II. Advent of the railroad led to the founding of Las Vegas on May 15, 1905. The Union Pacific auctioned off 1,200 lots in a single day in an area which today is casino-lined Glitter Gulch. Henry Ford was producing one Model-T every 24 seconds in 1914 on the newly created assembly line, as automobiles created a wave of hotel and motel construction in the 1940s, 1950s, and 1960s. The Kelly Airmail Act of 1925 provided airlines the opportunity to function as mail carriers through involvement in a competitive bidding system. Charles Lindbergh's 1927

flight across the Atlantic Ocean spurred oceanic flights in the 1930s. In 1944, seventy airlines and forty countries (American and European) ratified an agreement to form the International Air Transportation Association (IATA).

The Great Depression led to a much greater legalization of gambling. The antigambling mood changed as tremendous financial distress gripped the country, especially after the stock market crash of 1929. In 1931, the Nevada Legislature was motivated to build on the tourism boom that was expected in the wake of the completion of Boulder, now Hoover, Dam. Nevada had a flourishing, albeit illegal, gambling industry prior to the legalization. The move for making gambling legal also grew out of concerns that the flourishing illegal gambling was corrupting law enforcement and prohibition was unenforceable. Gaming in Nevada struggled from its inception until after World War II, when the prosperity of post-war America started a boom in the fledgling industry. In 1978, New Jersey became the second state to legalize casino gambling in an attempt to revitalize the rundown resort area of Atlantic City.

1951–1975

In the 1950s, disposable income increased, and society became more mobile (cars, railroad, and airlines). As Americans began to travel the countryside, they learned to enjoy the convenience of roadside accommodations. The air transport also served to entice travelers to resort destinations and city hotels. During the 1960s, tour wholesaling (consolidated travel accommodation "package" sold through a sales channel) came into prominence.

Prior to the 1950s, a few referral chains developed, consisting of all independent owners. These chains—Best Western is an example—helped travelers identify lodging and making a reservation in a distant town or city through the referral process. Referral chains served a purpose, but they did not address the inconsistency among motels. The idea for Holiday Inns came to Kemmons Wilson in the early 1950s, in a now-famous trip with his family from Memphis to Washington, D.C. Wilson didn't like the inconsistency of the mom-and-pop motels. He decided to create a consistent product in many parts of the country so families could be comfortable when taking trips. This led to franchising in the 1950s and '60s, where a "prepackaged" motel identity was sold to an entrepreneur for a fee. What franchises did better than the referral chains was create consistency in room design and operational standards. The cookie-cutter architecture employed by franchises literally enveloped the concept. Wilson felt the industry was ready for changes, so with his own resources, he created Holiday Inns over several years at gateway locations in Memphis. Wilson, a devoted family man, introduced Holiday Inn innovations, such as children staying free, swimming pools, free ice, chaplains on call, and pet kennels. He insisted that guests all be treated the same way. In 1962, Wilson built the 400th Holiday Inn in Vincennes, Indiana. One of Wilson's trademarks was his involvement in the business, even flying in his private plane to review proposed Holiday Inn sites. He knew the importance of location to a motel's success, insisting that new properties be located on the right-hand side of inbound lanes of a major commercial highway at a city's gateway. This is well known by commercial property developers as "the right-turn rule," allowing motorists easy access from highways.

The year of 1957 saw the opening of the first luxury Hyatt Hotel by Nicholas Pritzker. Isadore Sharp opened the first Four Seasons Hotel on Jarvis Street in Downtown Toronto, Canada in 1960. The hotel company that Sharp built over 40 years has grown from its humble beginnings to become a unique, multimillion-dollar, international hotel empire that continues to spread its reach around the world. Desegregation in hotels began in 1963 and coincides with the changing of the name of the AHA to the American Hotel & Lodging Association. In 1970, Hilton became the first billion-dollar lodging and food service company and the first to enter the Las Vegas market. This was the same year that Cecil B. Day opened the first Days Inn on Tybee Island, Georgia. Franchising was rampant during the 1960s and 1970s with companies such as Motel 6, Days Inn, Sheraton, and Hilton. Other developmental financing arrangements followed such as: partnerships, leasing, syndicates, and management contracts. This time of improved prosperity resulted in tourists flocking to beaches, hot springs, mountainsides, and other special locations. The net result of this expanded economy and desire to travel within the states was the rapid development of vacation homes and condominiums in popular tourist destinations. The organization now known as the American Resort De-

velopment Association (ARDA) began in 1969 as the American Land Development Association.

At age 10, Norman Brinker started his own rabbit farm, and the opportunities never stopped multiplying. After college, Brinker went into the restaurant business in a small way, before founding Steak and Ale in 1966. In 1961, Automatic Retailers of America (then doing approximately 65 million dollars in vending sales) merged with Slater Corporation (doing approximately 65 million dollars in manual service sales) and the company was renamed ARA Services, Inc. Since 1961, ARA has grown from a company managing 130 million dollars of food service to a company managing nearly 5 billion dollars of diversified services, including the management of services in the food and refreshment, health care, environmental and janitorial services, uniform and clothing rental, and magazine and book distribution industries. In Wichita, brothers Frank and Dan Carney opened the first Pizza Hut restaurant on June 15, 1958. The Carneys borrowed $600 from their mother, located John Bender, an airman from McConnell Air Force Base who had worked as a pizza cook, purchased some secondhand equipment and opened for business. The first night, they gave away pizza to interest potential customers. Pizza Hut became incorporated in 1969—the same year that the first franchise unit opened in Topeka, Kansas. In 1952, Pete Harman in Salt Lake City became the first Kentucky Fried Chicken franchisee. Four years later, the Colonel signed his first international franchisee in Canada. KFC sold to a group of investors, including John Y. Brown, Jr. and Jack Massey for $2 million in 1964. The first T.G.I. Fridays opened in 1965. In 1966, the Robert Mondavi Winery was established as one of the world's top wineries. Bill Darden founded Red Lobster in 1968, a key component of what is now Darden Restaurants, and expanded in 1971 with Olive Garden. A&W Restaurants, Steak n' Shake, and Sonic Drive-in became the major players in the burger field. While Steak n' Shake later abandoned the carhop format by the early 1970s, Sonic and A&W Restaurants remain today the only active descendants of a once-thriving segment. Snapping at McDonald's heels the closest was Burger King, followed by Wendy's and Hardee's. All four chains underwent tremendous growth during the mid '60s to late '70s, expanding with the massive teenage baby boom. At one point in the late 1970s, the four chains together accounted for as much as 37 cents of every dollar

Americans spent to eat out. Carlson Properties was founded in 1972, and the name was changed to Carlson Companies in 1973, TGIF in 1975, and Country Kitchens International in 1977.

The Boeing 727 was built in 1964 to carry 145 passengers, followed by the 737 and 747 (500 passengers) in 1970. The U.S. government created and subsidized AMTRAK (semi-public), which faced a total collapse due to the popularity of the automobile in 1971. (It should be noted that rail travel in Europe and Asia is more successful, cost effective, efficient . . . and faster.) Las Vegas city and county community leaders realized in the 1950s the need for a Las Vegas convention facility. The initial goal was to fill hotel rooms with conventioneers during slack tourist months. A site was chosen one block east of the Las Vegas Strip and a 6,300-seat, silver-domed rotunda with an adjoining 90,000-square-foot exhibit hall opened in April, 1959, on the site of the current Las Vegas Convention Center. In 1955, Walt Disney opened the first major American theme park, Disneyland, in Anaheim, California. The 1970s marked the first serious creation of EcoTourism Societies across the globe, dedicated to the preservation and sustainable development of the environment for the wellbeing of the local people. In 1971, Disneyworld opened in Orlando, Florida.

1975–1990

During the 1970s, the concept of timesharing took root and flourished as a direct result of the affordability and the offering of exchange services. As we moved into the 1980s, the lodging giants began adding timesharing to their portfolio of business units, adding credibility and visibility to the industry, while infusing improved product and service standards. Marriott joined the vacation ownership industry in 1984, followed quickly by Disney and Hilton. The most ambitious resort project in the history of Las Vegas is located at the intersection of the Las Vegas Strip and Tropicana Avenue. It is the MGM Grand Hotel & Theme Park—the largest resort hotel in the world and the dream of pioneer Las Vegas hotel developer and multimillionaire entrepreneur Kirk Kerkorian. The $1 billion, 112-acre resort hotel, casino, and theme park highlights the MGM Hollywood image. The Ritz-Carlton Hotel Company, formed in 1983 under the direction of Horst Schultz, Founding President and CEO, is the only hospitality organization to be awarded the prestigious Malcolm Baldridge National Quality Award, given by the U.S. Department of Commerce. Schultz's commitment to excellence is based on a trained, fully-empowered workforce, schooled in the company's Gold Standards, which include a credo, motto, three steps to service, and

Industry "Players" Mini-Case

Marriott, with his new bride Allie, entered business with the opening of a nine-seat root beer stand in Washington, D.C. in 1927. Hot food was later added, and the name changed to the Hot Shoppe, followed by the drive-in Hot Shoppe. Marriott pioneered in-flight catering at Washington's old Hoover Airfield (current site of the Pentagon), serving Eastern, American, and Capital Airlines in 1937. Marriott's highway division began in 1955 with several shops on the New York State Thruway, the opening of the first hotel, the Twin Bridges Marriott Motor Hotel in Arlington, Virginia, and acquisition of the 22-shop Big Boy restaurant chain. Marriott began the Roy Rogers fast food restaurant division in 1967. The first pizza restaurant may have appeared in the United States in the 1930s. The first Courtyard by Marriott, moderate price segment hotels, open near Atlanta, Georgia in 1982, which was the same year that Marriott entered the vacation timesharing business with acquisition of American Resorts Group. In 1987, Marriott entered the all-suite/extended stay, economy and assisted living markets by acquiring the Residence Inn Company, opening the first Fairfield Inn in Atlanta, and announcing plans for Brighton Gardens as part of their Senior Living Services Division. In 1982, Marriott began to build its travel mega-conglomerate, as it acquired Host International and became the country's largest operator of airport terminal food, beverage, and merchandise facilities. Marriott acquired Saga Corporation, a diversified food service management company in 1986, making Marriott the largest company in food service management in the United States.

twenty Ritz-Carlton basics. The company is also the leader in customer data collection, which is used to ensure the ultimate in customer relationship building. And finally, Ritz-Carlton sets the standards in the industry for guest recognition programs, luxury amenities, and architectural design. In the 1980s, Real Estate Investment Trusts (REITS) began to own property outright, and focus turned to physical assets like hotels, office buildings, malls, nursing homes, and apartments, which reaped significant tax advantages. At this time, the Japanese economy was robust, and their wealthy companies turned to the U.S. to buy real estate in the form of hotels. The timeshare industry experienced a temporary flourish of activity as independent start-ups opened new or, in many cases, converted existing buildings as timeshare offerings. Unfortunately, most of these attempts failed due to marketing "over-promises" and facility "under-deliveries."

As the recession kicked in during the late 1980s to early 1990s, the burger boys found that their customers were abandoning them for value and broader menu diversity. Taco Bell rolled out the 39-cent taco while cash-strapped families begin eating more and more at dinner houses where their dollars stretched farther in a table service setting. Pressuring the traditional burger chains as well was the fantastic growth of the double-drive-through burger segment, led by such chains as Rally's, Checker's, Hot 'n Now, Juicy Lucy's, and at least a dozen more, all promising delivery to the customer in less than 40 seconds. In 1976, after Brinker built S&A to 100 restaurants, the company was acquired by the Pillsbury Company, and he was made a member of the Board and the largest individual shareholder. He continued to head S&A Corporation and developed another casual-dining concept, Bennigan's. In 1982, Brinker became Chairman of the Pillsbury Restaurant Group, the world's second-largest restaurant organization, which included Burger King, with total sales approaching $4 billion. In 1983, he resigned and bought Chili's, a Dallas-based restaurant company operating 23 units with $35 million in sales. This visionary inspirational leader has added other successful creations, including On the Border, Romano's Macaroni Grill, Cozymel's, Corner Bakery, Big Bowl, Eatzi's, and other chains. Starbucks Coffee Company was founded in 1971, opening its first location in Seattle's Pike Place Market. Today, Starbucks, named after the first mate in Herman Melville's *Moby Dick*, is the world's leading retailer, roaster, and brand of specialty coffee with coffeehouses worldwide. Outback Steakhouse, Inc., formerly Multi-Venture Partners, Inc., continued to develop full-service restaurants in addition to the Outback Steakhouse, including Carrabba's Italian Grill, Fleming's Prime Steakhouse & Wine Bar, Roy's, and Bonefish Grill brand names.

This era was marked by the deregulation of the airline industry, which resulted in the growth of smaller carriers and the mergers of larger carriers. Major U.S. airlines launched financial expansions, interest rates increased, and price wars followed, resulting in major losses. The new cruise line image was solidified with the popularity of the TV series "Love Boat," which aired from 1977 to 1983. In 1988, Indian Gaming Regulatory Act passed to protect both the tribes and the general public. With both parents working full-time in most U.S. households, theme parks became competitive in the 1980s and 1990s, as Universal Studios, Six Flags, Dollywood, Branson, Missouri, Williamsburg, Virginia, and many other parks recognized the need for Baby Boomers and children to enjoy "quality time." Tokyo Disneyland opened in 1983. In 1976, when casino-style gaming was legalized in Atlantic City, New Jersey, it became apparent to Las Vegas casino owners that Nevada no longer could claim exclusive rights to gambling casinos. It, perhaps, hastened the beginning of another era for the Strip—the megaresort. Hotel-casinos began the race to become full-blown destination resorts for travelers, vacationers, gamblers, conventioneers, and all members of the family.

References

See Chapter 3, which includes a list of all references used in Chapters 2 and 3.

Chapter Two Review Questions

1. How does travel and tourism affect the global economy?

2. Why is it important to know the past/history of the hospitality industry?

3. What are the four major subdivisions in the hospitality and tourism industry?

4. What motivated the first travelers?

5. Who first recorded the fermentation process? When? For what was it used?

6. What is the history of today's pizza?

7. Summarize the key points in hospitality history that occurred prior to the 1700s.

8. Discuss the varying countries of origin in food and beverage history. How has this cultural diversity affected the foods we eat today?

9. What is the WTTC?

10. Restate in your own words the WTTC's definition for tourism.

11. Trace transportation's impact on hospitality in the 1800s.

12. Name three of the trade associations that have been established to service the hospitality and tourism industry professionals.

13. Trace the development and success of the "drive thru" concept used in restaurants.

14. What other types of businesses in your area are experimenting with the "drive thru" concept?

15. Who opened the oldest hamburger restaurant? What was the price of a hamburger?

16. What major event brought down (hampered) the train industry?

17. Draw a time line, note on one side the increase in hotel/motel construction, and note on the other side the advances in the transportation industry. What conclusions can you make?

18. Describe a referral chain. What are the advantages and disadvantages associated with referral chains?

19. What is the "right turn rule?"

20. What was the first billion-dollar lodging and food service company?

21. When did the following companies open for business? Describe one interesting, historic fact on each.

    a. Pizza Hut:

    b. Kentucky Fried Chicken:

c. ARA:

d. Steak and Ale:

e. TGI Fridays:

22. What is the historic background of timeshare properties?

23. What are some of the service/training standards used by the Ritz-Carlton properties?

24. What were the results on the tourism industry after airline deregulation?

Chapter 3

The Present and Possible Future: Hospitality and Tourism "Today and Tomorrow"

POSTAGE PAID

Corbis

Michael Terry
University of Central Florida

Introduction

Whether for business or travel, luxury or economy, people have traveled since the beginning of time. As a result, tourism entrepreneurs have seized this opportunity to provide accommodating products and services throughout the world. From the biblical story of the inn in Bethlehem to the European Medieval Castle feasts to the Orient Express to the Titanic maiden voyage to the transatlantic Supersonic Concorde to Las Vegas's 5,000 suite MGM Grand Resort, hospitality is arguably the most fascinating field on the planet. The diversity of the industry includes stadium hot dog stands, underwater hotels, trips to the Grand Canyon and Niagara Falls, gambling cruises to nowhere, military facilities, colleges, health care facilities, and business/industrial facilities.

The Present: 1990–9/11/2001; Hospitality and Tourism "Today"

The hospitality environment of today began to take shape in 1990, as the country emerged from yet another recession—this time riding the coattails of the World Wide Web. The evolution of the Internet shifted the power to the consumer in this information age. The public began to research their own tour and travel places, prices, and promotions, much to the chagrin of travel agents, who were forced to broaden their services or perish. By the end of the century, the end-user was beginning to shop online direct with the airline, rental car agency, hotel, etc. for the best possible rates available. Choice Hotels International and Promus Corporation, for example, became the first companies to offer guests "real-time" access to its central reservations system in 1995. Choice and Holiday Inn were the first to introduce online booking capability.

Three other industry trends framed this dozen years of modern history: consolidation, branding, and globalization. Beginning in 1990, the country's major airlines, rental car agencies, and hotels followed the economy out of the recession, which resulted in a dramatic increase in the number of consumers, including first-time customers. However, the supply for all three segments of the industry grew as fast as demand, resulting in price cuts and aggressive movement toward market share

growth. Travel and tourism masked the country, but nowhere was it more successful than in the two U.S. vacation resort anchors: Orlando and Las Vegas would become the heavyweight, bi-polar, mega-resort vacation center competitors at the turn of the millennium.

The big hotel companies got bigger via takeovers and brand leveraging. Merger-mania continued throughout the 1990s as Hilton, Six Continents, Marriott, Hilton Hotels, Starwood Hotels & Resorts Worldwide, and Choice Hotels International became hotel/motel conglomerates, taking their businesses global, as Europe and Asia were ripe for branding. Marriott, for example, added three brands (Renaissance, Ramada International, and New World), while doubling its presence overseas. This industry strategy was implemented to help diversify geographically, thereby protecting stakeholders' financial interests.

The vacationer in the 1990s sent a clear message to the hospitality industry—"we want permanent or temporary accommodations with plenty of space; and on-site food and beverage services are not required." These customers opened their pocketbooks to rent limited services, all-suite and extended-stay accommodations, and purchase time share/vacation ownership facilities. Consumers in the new millennium favored these new products; as the majority of newly-constructed properties built from 1998–2001 were from this segment. The extended-stay hybrid bridged the gap between the hotel and apartment/corporate housing industry, which boasted their own Accommodations America, CRS Corporate Housing, California Suites, ExecuStay, Oakwood, and Preferred Living. The growth of U.S. timeshare/vacation ownership sales volume in the 1990s ($1.4 billion dollars in 1992 increased to $4.0 billion in 2000) exceeded 285 percent.

A first for the industry occurred in 1990, when Cendant Corporation's Henry Silverman, a 20th century travel empire builder, created a diversified global travel, business, consumer, and real estate services conglomerate. Cendant accumulated integrated holdings of three national real estate brokerage businesses, nine major national hotel chains; one national car rental business; global distribution and computer reservation services to airlines, hotels, car rental companies; and the world's leading global referral/exchange provider of products and services to the timeshare industry.

Consolidation and branding were also a way of life for quick service (QSRs) and casual dining res-

Business travel grew rapidly in the 1960s, since airlines could deliver a traveler anywhere in 24 hours.

taurants, as recissionary times improved during the early 1990s. With both parents working, time was of the essence and fast-food became the norm. The so-called "burger boys" found that their customers were abandoning them for value and broader menu diversity. Taco Bell rolled out the 39-cent taco while cash-strapped families began eating more and more at dinner houses where their dollars stretched farther in a table service setting. Pressuring the traditional burger chains as well was the fantastic growth of the "double-drive-through" burger segment, led by such chains as Rally's, Checker's, Hot 'n Now, Juicy Lucy's and at least a dozen more, all promising delivery to the customer in less than 40 seconds. Additional pressure came from Pizza Hut, which delivered, for example, more than 1,349,000 pizzas on Superbowl Sunday in 1990.

Casual dining and drinking were the mantra of the times, as themed venues were popular. By 2000, Brinker International operated over 750 creative restaurants. Darden Restaurants increased to 630 Red Lobster restaurants and 480 Olive Garden restaurants. Applebee's, TGI Friday's, and Outback Steakhouse continued to develop full-service restaurants. The beverage trends in the 1990s were the coffeehouse concept and microbreweries. Starbucks Coffee International's locations totaled over 3,500. Under the direction of Howard Schultz, more than 11 million customers visited a Starbucks coffeehouse each week. Hometown breweries cropped-up in every region of the country.

The cruise ship market increased more than 800 percent from 1970–2000, as North American cruise passenger numbers reached 6.5 million, up half a million from 1995's figures. Since major cruise lines' port and itinerary differentiation became minimal, new ships began to incorporate a variety of entertainment venues (bars, lounges, libraries, spas, workout facilities, and business centers) in order to appeal to wider audiences. As more facilities were incorporated, ship sizes increased; and this additional capacity provided by the new mega-ships helped the industry expand its passenger loads by nearly 60 percent between 1990–1999. The average passenger capacity of ships jumped from 800 during the 1980s to over 2000 at the end of 1999. The "Big Three," Carnival, Royal Caribbean and Princess Cruises, acquired fleets to the point that they enjoyed a combined market share of over 85 percent.

Airlines created their own regional "baby airlines," such as American (Eagle) and Delta (Express and COMAIR) to compete with the smaller regional carriers. However, the pure regional carriers such as Southwest and Airtran remained powerful. Throughout the booming 1990s, business travelers paid as much as five times more than leisure travelers for the same seat. While they made up 8 to 10 percent of the major carriers' passengers, they accounted for as much as 40 percent of their revenues. The entire hub-and-spoke system, developed after deregulation, was designed to attract and keep business travelers. But there was a price. It cost more to run and maintain such a system than a destination-to-destination structure—the kind instituted with great success by low-cost carriers such as Southwest. It's the only major carrier that continued to make money through these tough times.

The Future: 9/11/2001 and Beyond; Hospitality and Tourism "Tomorrow"

When the hospitality industry budgeted for 2001, it was expecting a moderate slowdown in growth as the Silicon Valley's electronics "gold rush" of the mid and late 1990s tumbled in late 2000. The future changed on 9/11/2001, however, with the terrorist attacks on New York City and Washington, D.C. Due to the unforseeable events and volatility of 2001, the hospitality industry experienced the largest single-year deterioration in tourism and travel performance ever. Hotel and rental car business declined by as much as 30 percent in major metro-politan areas (New York, Orlando, Las Vegas), as international and domestic travel halted for business, leisure, and group travel! International competition and 9/11 became the undoing of several U.S. airlines, which sustained losses in the billions and were forced into global alliances.

The industry's woes actually started a year before the terrorist attack. The airlines' entire financial structure is based on the premise that business passengers will pony-up far more to fly on the spur of the moment than leisure fliers who book well in advance. When the recession first hit in late 2000, business travelers started to balk at paying high prices. They flew far less frequently, and when they did travel, they looked for lower-priced options, using everything from the Internet to discount airlines to Amtrak's high-speed train in the Northeast. The major carriers' revenues plummeted, but they were still left with the higher costs associated with their network systems. Additionally, regional carriers, such as Southwest, Jet Blue, and Frontier, with lower operating costs and consequently lower fares, took a toll on the larger operators. After 8 percent growth rates the previous five years, the nation's top airlines saw passenger traffic decline. The slowing economy and the terrorist attacks caused businesses to pull back on travel spending;

During the 1970s, the cruise industry began to shed its image of "only for the rich."

and since business travelers were the highest paying customers, this reduction had an enormous effect on the industry.

The nation's top airlines saw passenger traffic decline nearly 10 percent in 2002, compared to the previous year. Enormous financial losses caused by this low demand and operational problems resulted in U.S. Airways and United Airlines filing for bankruptcy in 2002. Increased travel costs, the global economic slowdown, and new security concerns caused corporations to cut spending, tighten travel policies, and redefine supplier relationships. Trying to match lower demand levels, many airlines cut back on routes, number of flights, and aircraft. Yet low-fare airlines like Southwest, Frontier, and Jet Blue experienced increased passenger traffic, in part because the corporations looked for cheaper alternatives to the major airlines. In addition, corporations experimented with air charter services and company-owned aircraft as other alternatives to the high business fares offered on the nation's major carriers. The airline industry faces many challenges in 2003–2005, including a slow economy and the conflicts in the Middle East, which could slow travel even more and raise fuel prices. Speculating about the next five years: In the 1990s, the Concorde became the first supersonic aircraft, developed jointly by the British and French at a cost of $3 billion. With a cruising speed of 1336 m.p.h., the Atlantic travel time was halved. Unfortunately, a crash outside Paris in 2000 temporarily grounded the project. Indication is that a safer model will prevail in the next several years. Peering a little farther, commercial space travel has already begun as several private individuals and organizations have committed funds to underwrite such projects.

In the short term, hotels, to great degree, are dependent on the international and domestic airlines. Low occupancy rates will force hotel companies to become more flexible on rate negotiations—particularly for the gateway cities serving more air travelers. Since supply is a big concern, lodging companies are scaling back construction plans to prevent profitability problems. This means rates will be favorable for corporations as hoteliers reduce supply to meet demand. Hotels in big cities were affected most by the downturn. While the upper end of the market has been impacted to a larger degree than mid-scale and economy hotels, both the limited-service and full-service hotel segments are expected to move to-ward recovery in 2003–2005. Despite the frustrations that many are feeling about securities, market performance, and slow growth of lodging demand, the prospects look quite favorable for chain-affiliated hotels. The unanticipated consequences of a war in Iraq, however, shifts hotel revenue forecasts noticeably downward.

In the mid-term, hotels will refocus on regional feeder cities in order to become a bit less dependent on air travel. They will begin to establish strong Web sites and may soon act as their own electronic travel agents by packaging/aligning/partnering themselves very closely with rental car agencies, cruise lines, etc., a la Cendant Corporation and Disney World.

Car rental firms will also be affected by a decline in demand in 2003–2005. Unlike airlines, car rental firms will have a more difficult time obtaining profits by reducing capacity, which will have a significant impact on pricing. If airline demand remains stagnant, car rental firms will either attempt to increase rates or create additional service charges. In 2002, car rental demand rebounded from the low levels seen at the end of 2001. However, car rental firms were hit with the same negative economic conditions as the airlines and hotels. The average car rental rate has risen throughout the year, yet smaller fleets will provide these companies with less revenue. As corporations and travelers have become more price-sensitive about car rentals, they have turned to alternative and economy suppliers. Through cost-cutting efforts and increases in demand, the U.S. car rental industry should see the beginnings of recovery in 2003.

With only 5–6 percent of the cruise market tapped to date, and with an estimated market potential of billions, the cruise industry gives all indications of a bright future. Only 11 percent of North Americans have ever set sail, and cruising still attracts only 2 percent of the entire leisure travel industry—a statistic that suggests an extraordinary growth potential for this industry.

There are now over three million timeshare owners in the United States with domestic sales in 1998 at $4.0 billion (1,600 resorts representing more than 33 percent of the worldwide inventory). The continued improvement of the timeshare product, increased flexibility through the exchange networks and points-based ownership, participation of respected hospitality brands, influx of public capital, and added consumer confidence each contribute to the ongoing success of the industry. The aftermath of 9/11 will favor the purchase of a time-share "home feel" (that can be passed along to other family members) rather than a hotel room.

Business meals are still considered necessary to the business traveler, so there will not be a dramatic reduction in cost resulting from the slow-down, and meal prices will continue to rise in 2003–2005. But meal service providers will be forced to create marketing and service solutions to attract business travelers. Any increase in the minimum wage, as proposed in many of the economic stimulus plans currently before Congress, will have a direct impact on meal prices. Casual dining restaurants are forecast to be the fastest-growing segment of the restaurant industry for the next 5 years and will become global in nature.

As we look to the future, consider that the World Travel and Tourism Council forecasts travel and tourism growth at 40 to 50 percent in real terms in the next ten years. This astronomical increase presents tremendous challenges and career opportunities for today's hospitality and tourism graduates. The futurist, John Naisbitt, says that the global economy of the twenty-first century will be driven by three super-service industries: telecommunications, information technology, and travel and tourism. The following hospitality and tourism items are but a few examples of the wave of the future: Increased speed and shopping-use of the Internet in developed countries; extended reach in less-developed countries; improved security of personal information; robotic labor sources; reservation systems with more sophisticated, voice activated, artificial intelligence; improved navigational systems for rental cars; electronic entertainment venues in rental cars and on planes and cruise ships; upgraded Internet personal digital assistants for operations; marketing mass customization; comprehensive branding campaigns for large and small operators; virtual online customer communication; just-in-time seats/rooms/cars inventories; electronic travel agents; blended hybrid accommodations; global anti-terrorist micro-chip security systems; more nutritional fast-food offerings, emphasis on eco-tourism, and improved customer relationship marketing information.

References

A. J. Butkarat and S. Meddick, *Tourism: Past, Present and Future*. London: Hinneman, 1974, p. 3.

American Economics Group, Vacation Ownership Sales Volumes, http://www.arda.org/consumer/stats/stats.htm#1.

Donald E. Lundberg, *The Tourist Business*, 6th ed. New York: Van Norstrand Reinhold, 1990, pp. 9–16.

Edward J. Mayo and Lance P. Jarvis, *The Psychology of Leisure Travel*: *Effective Marketing and Selling of Travel Services*. Boston: CBI Publishing Company, 1981, p. 5.

Hilton Hotels' Internet Travel Center, Hilton Press Releases, http://www.hilton.com.

Jan Van Harssel, *Tourism: An Exploration*, 3rd ed. Englewood Cliffs, New Jersey: Prentice Hall, 1994.

John R. Walker, *Introduction to Hospitality*, 3rd ed. Englewood Cliffs, New Jersey: Prentice Hall, 2002.

Richard Kelly, "To Create Jobs, Sumitears Should Take a Breath of Rocky Mountain Air and Promote Tourism," http://www.wttc.org, July 20, 1997.

Rosa Songel, "Statistics and Economical Measurement of Tourism," World Tourism Organization, http://www.world-tourism.org/omt/wtich.htm.

Sara Perry, *The Complete Coffee Book*. San Francisco: Chronicle Books, 1997, p. 8.

World Travel and Tourism Organization, http://www.wttc.org.

Colonel Harland Sanders, http://KFC.com.

Joan Cook, "Conrad Hilton, Founder of Hotel Chain, Dies at 92," *The New York Times*, January 5, 1979, sec. 11, p. 5.

Hospitality Optimism and Budgeting, http://www.hotel-online.com/NewsPR2002_4thOptimismBudgeting.html.

Norman Brinker, http://www.rimag.com/501/int.htm.

Outback Steakhouse, Inc., http://www.osi.com.

Southwest Airlines, http://www.southwest.com

History of ARAMARK, http://bluehawk.monmouth.edu/~dining/history.html.

History of Cendant Corporation, http://biz.yahoo.com/p/c/cd.html.

History of Howard Johnson's, http://hojoland.homestead.com/history.html.

History of Gambling, http://www.library.ca.gov/CRB/97/03/Chapt2.html.

Tim Garvey quote, http://www.quoteworld.org/docs/phgiv328.php.

History of Club Med, http://www.clubmedjobs.com/history.htm.

Do Tell About Motels, http://pr.tennessee.edu/alumnus/spring98/motel.html.

Ellsworth Milton Statler Inducted into Wheeling Hall of Fame, http://wheeling.weirton.lib.wv.us/people/hallfame/1984stat.htm.

Life of Cesar Ritz, http://www.londonreservation.com/Ritz.htm.

Isadore Sharp, http://www.lodgingnews.com/lodgingmag/2000_08_93.asp.

History of McDonald's, http://www.geocities.com/mcdonaldization/history.html.

Nations Restaurant News, Milford Prewitt, Story of the Mighty Hamburger, http://www.geocities.com/NapaValley/Kitchen/1493/history.html.

History of American Hotel & Lodging Association, http://www.ahma.com/infocenter/lodging_history.asp.

Brief History of the Passenger Ship Industry, http://scriptorium.lib.duke.edu/adaccess/ship-history.html.

Brief History of the U.S. Airline Industry, http://scriptorium.lib.duke.edu/adaccess/airline-history.html.

History of Rental Car Industry, http://www.ma.org/History/WhoOwnsWhat/Pages/Barry_Wenger/RentalCarhistory.html.

History of Best Western Hotels, http://www.travelreport.dk/articl/art_all/01111502.htm.

Avis Rent-a-Car System Corporate Web Site, www.avis.com.

Greyhound Bus Company Corporate Web Site, www.greyhound.com.

Scott Heil, and Terrance W. Peck, eds. *The Encyclopedia of American Industry, 2nd ed.* Detroit: Gale Research, 1998.

Hertz Rent-a-Car Corporate Web Site: History of Rental Cars, www.hertz.com.

Statistics regarding extended-stay hotels, http://www.str-online.com.

All-suite concepts, http://str-online.com/news/articledir/Lodging/1996/11/ALLSTE96.htm.

Carlton Jackson. *Hounds of the Road: A history of the Greyhound Bus Company.* Bowling Green, Ohio: Bowling Green University Popular Press, 1984.

Jack Rhodes. *Intercity Bus Lines of the Southwest.* College Station, Texas: Texas A&M University Press, 1988.

Oscar Schisgall. *The Greyhound Story: From Hibbing to Everywhere.* Chicago: J. G. Ferguson Publishing Company, 1985.

Chapter Three Review Questions

1. What are three major trends of the 1990s–present which are impacting the hospitality industry?

2. What was considered a "primary demand" of the 1990 vacationer?

3. Describe the cruise industry growth. Who are the three major leaders in this industry segment?

4. What impact did the terrorist attacks of 9/11/01 have on the travel and tourism industry?

5. Describe the changes seen in the airline industry over the last decade. What are your predictions for the next decade?

6. What are your predictions for the hotel industry over the next decade? How do they compare to the research reported?

7. What are the industry projections for the cruise industry?

8. What are the current plans/proposed legislation concerning minimum wage?

9. What impact would an increase in minimum wage have on the restaurant industry?

10. What are the three super-service industries Naisbitt estimated would have a major impact on the future?

Chapter **4**   *Information Resources: Periodicals and the Web*

Space Needle, Seattle

Corbis

POSTAGE
PAID

Paul Sorgule
Paul Smith's College

State of Affairs

Things change! We are all fully aware of how fragile our economy is and now the country is vividly aware of the significant role that hospitality plays in defining the health of the economy. Interesting was how clear the issues of customer service and attentiveness came to the surface immediately after the tragic events of September 11. Those hotel and restaurant companies that responded to the evolving needs of their customers are fairing reasonably well, in the face of a definitive economic turndown. Just as was the case a few short years ago, we continue to be part of a new, exciting, unpredictable, and unnerving economy that is heavily influenced by customers with a strong taste for customization, new products, exceedingly attentive service, and recognition by the business of the customers' value.

New words and phrases continue as part of our vocabulary: real-time, paradigm, paradigm shift, empowerment, self-managed teams, 7 steps to this, 12 parts to that, etc., etc. Everyone seems to have their own theory of management, leadership, strategic planning, business organization, the future of our economy, and so on. The fastest growing sections for books at your local Barnes and Noble continue to be business management and self-help. Management periodicals and industry journals number in the dozens and Websites dealing with the management of business and, in particular, the hospitality industry, have grown exponentially. Keeping track of all of these insights and facts can be mind boggling, yet this task is not only essential for success, it is quickly becoming a core competence. Some may refer to this phenomena as "information overload," while others hunger for as much information as possible. In the end, these tools will help each individual form their own style of leadership. Managing these tools becomes as essential to today's leaders as those critical skills; accounting and cost control, principles of marketing, staffing and human resource management, design, food preparation, yield management, etc. that have been the focus of formal education for years.

A great misconception among those in business and education is that ideas, innovations, and guiding principles of management are best resourced from those actively involved in those industries specific to a field of application: hospitality from hospitality people, food service from food professionals, etc. To take a lead from industries not directly related would seem illogical to many, yet today's benchmarks may have those core competencies right and could thus provide any business professional with a model for improvement. To coin a slightly overused phrase, "thinking out of the box" has become a mantra for companies who have made the leap from good to great and from great to extraordinary. Tom Peters, one of America's most admired business consultants and management author, refers to this transition as "WOW." Thinking out of the box can often lead to evaluation of your true business.

Many companies have changed their focus from specific products to markets. As an example, General Motors became enlightened when they realized that staying an automobile manufacturer would not prepare them adequately for the future. Their current focus is to be a leader in people movement. This new strategic focus opens a world of future opportunities for this great company. Hospitality and tourism, in a similar fashion, is not just involved in selling rooms; and booking flights; they are involved in a market known as "service." The ramifications of this move are tremendous. As examples, refer to Macaroni Grill, Hard Rock Cafe, extravagant casinos in Las Vegas, Four Seasons' exemplary service, Ritz-Carlton's customer profiling, priceline.com, travelocity.com, hotels.com, and hundreds of other "breakthrough organizations."

How do these "WOW" companies think out of the box? Simple, they access, research, and analyze data from any and all sources that they can in an effort to go beyond knowing what people want. They are able to anticipate what people will want in the future. Stan Davis, management author, gave us significant pause for thought in his recent book, *Blur,* when he defined the new business environment through a formula of speed, connectivity, and intangibles. He states the following: SPEED: Every aspect of business and the connected organization operates and changes in real time. CONNECTIVITY: Everything is becoming electronically connected to everything else: products, people, companies, countries, everything. INTANGIBLES: Every offer has both tangible and intangible economic value. The intangible is growing faster. Davis did not limit his "blur" theory to any one business or type of business. He includes everyone and everything in this theory. Rarely, if ever, has there been a time when how we approach business management and the service of customers has been blurred more. If we are to "blur" the hospitality industry, we must stay in touch with the intangible needs that customers and employees have and will have in the future.

What Is Required

The word education is derived from a concept of "drawing forth" from the individual. In some cases, education has evolved into a "giving to" process, a far cry from the original intent. Today's "new economy" requires education to change as it never has before. Education must be an open loop process that takes into account a multitude of concepts, including drawing forth, giving to, seeking out, networking, exploring, and interacting. What has become the most significant asset for any organization and in any individual is their base of knowledge. In fact, volumes have been written on the rise of the "knowledge worker." The knowledge worker is not necessarily one who has immense capacity for retaining information, but rather, a person who knows how to access, where to search, and how to get to this base of knowledge in real time. Sometimes referred to as "intellectual capital," this new definition of knowledge is what makes good companies "WOW" and what allows them to maintain that remarkable position in customers' minds.

Frances Horibe, in his book, *Managing the Knowledge Worker,* describes this person as one who uses his/her head more than their hands to produce value.[1] Estimates demonstrate that nearly 59 percent of the workforce will be knowledge workers as we enter this new century.[2] Knowledge workers have an uncanny ability to assess situations based on access to information drawn from multitudes of resources and experiences. This, by the way, is your real value to companies seeking to add your name to their roster. Interestingly enough, this knowledge is what defines you as an individual employee, and wherever you go, it goes with you.

Think of this incredible example: McDonald's is the largest restaurant chain in the world, with sales that are difficult to comprehend. What is most interesting is that more than 60 percent of their annual sales come from an idea that a knowledge worker pitched more than two decades ago. The basic concept of McDonald's is and always has been convenience and value. They may have been the first to promote the concept of "real time" by defining what fast food was to become. They successfully convinced the American public to find an alternative use for their most important tool, the automobile. McDonald's convinced us that this symbol of freedom could also serve as a dining room. The drive-thru window now accounts for the lion's share of their annual sales. Thinking out of the box!

If these observations and predictions are true, it becomes imperative for individuals to transition into knowledge workers and for organizations to teach their employees how to make this transition. Horibe goes on to state, "the most effective way to ensure that knowledge workers use their intellectual capital in service of the organization is to convince them that they want to."[3] As managers, you will need to not only access and manage information, but to encourage your staff to want to do the same. Developing the ability to do this certainly goes beyond the limitations of this article, but will nevertheless become a key responsibility that you will assimilate in the near future.

Where to Begin

Building a learning organization, full of active knowledge workers, is not easy. You cannot assume that simply knowing that it must happen is enough, nor is having a list of great resources (like the one that follows). To be effective as a hospitality knowledge worker, you must have a plan. Lewis Carroll summed it up in *Alice in Wonderland* when he stated, "If you don't know where you are going, any road will take you there."[4] If you do not have a plan

[1] Horibe, F. 1999. *Managing Knowledge Workers,* New York: John Wiley and Sons, preface xi

[2] Barley, S. 1994. *The Turn to a Horizontal Division of Labor. On the Occupationization of Firms and the Technization of Work. The Office of Educational Research and Improvement,* U.S. Dept. of Education.

[3] Horibe, F. 1999. *Managing Knowledge Workers* New York, John Wiley and Sons, page 3

[4] Carroll, L. 1946. *Alice in Wonderland,* Grosset and Dunlap
Other:
Peters, T. 1994. *The Pursuit of WOW* New York, Vintage Books
Davis, S. & Meyer, C. 1998. *BLUR, The Speed of Change in the Connected Economy* Reading, MA, Perseus Books
Stewart, T. 1997. *Intellectual Capital, The New Wealth of Organizations Currency* New York Doubleday
Berry, L. 1999. *Discovering the Soul of Service* New York, Free Press
Seybold, P. 2001. *The Customer Revolution* New York, Crown Business
Albrecht, K. 2001. *Service America in the New Economy* New York, McGraw Hill

for accessing, analyzing, and using information, then any process will lead you to a point of utter frustration. If you have ever taken part in a blind search on the Internet, you are well aware of this reference. A plan becomes your map for accessing information that is appropriate and that allows you to move forward with the speed that stakeholders in your organization have come to expect.

One approach would be to truly buy into the learning organization concept and look at your hospitality firm as a network of knowledge workers, each with a specific area of "learning expertise." This network can come together in various forms as a "taskforce team" to solve a problem or innovate a product or service and then dissolve when the task is finished. Different networks form for different issues. To make the process even more effective, look to the network as borderless. By this I am referring to the true definition of an open-loop business. Taskforce team members can come from within or outside the business. Peers, friends, customers, and even competitors can take part. This brings a limitless amount of insight and knowledge to the table in an effort to create "WOW." Regis Philbin would call it a "life line."

The inevitable question is "why would people participate in this process?" Here come the intangibles. Self-fulfillment, being part of something great, the human need for discovery, a thirst to know, and the gratification that comes from winning are all ways that people can self-actualize. Abraham Maslow would refer to these as ultimate motivators. On the tangible side, very few things are free, including knowledge. If knowledge is the value that you or others bring to the table, then some form of tangible compensation will need to be part of the formula.

If I seemed to stray from the topic, I apologize; however, it cannot be adequately addressed without presenting the scope of the need and the process that must be followed to fulfill this need. Here are some key resources to get you started. Note that textbooks cannot adequately address the need for real-time knowledge in a business environment that changes daily. Periodicals, Web sources, journals, and books of contemporary theory are the best, unless, of course, you find a book comprised of contemporary thought from various authors. This can be your first map.

Table 4.1	Resources—Periodicals, Journals, Web Sites
Topical Area Resource

1. *Creative Thought Fast Company Magazine,* P.O. Box 421196, Palm Coast, Florida 32142, 800-542-6029, www.fastweb.com. The premier periodical for the knowledge worker.
2. *Strategy and Management Business 2.0 Imagine Media,* 150 North Hill Drive, Brisbane, California 94005, www.imaginemedia.com. New rules for the new economy.
3. *Strategy and Management Strategy and Business,* P.O. Box 548, Lewiston, New York 14092, 888-557-5550, www.Sbsubscriber.com, www.strategy-business.com. Strategic planning and leadership insight solid case studies.
4. *Service Management Journal of Service Research,* Sage Periodicals Press, Sage Publications, Inc., 2455 Teller Road, Thousand Oaks, California 91320, 805-499-9774. Statistical and qualitative research on service economics.
5. *Business Management Harvard Business Review,* 60 Harvard Way, Boston, Massachusetts 02163, 800-274-3214, www.hbsp.harvard.edu. Leading authority on management theory, great case studies.
6. *Hotel Marketing Hospitality Sales and Marketing Association International,* www.hsmai.org. Club management, Club Managers Association of America, www.cmaa.org.
7. *Hospitality Management, Cornell Quarterly,* Elsevier Science, Inc., P.O. Box 945, New York, New York 10010, 212-633-3730, http://hotelschool.cornell.edu/pub2/pub.html. Leading authority on hospitality management, great case studies.
8. *Hotel Operations Lodging, American Hotel Association Directory,* 1201 New York Ave., NW #600, Washington, DC 20005, 202-289-3100, www.lodgingmagazine.com. State of the industry, new products and services.

Table 4.1 (continued)

Topical Area Resource

9. *Hospitality Education Journal of Hospitality & Tourism Education,* CHRIE International, 1200 17th Street, NW, Washington, DC 20036, 202-331-5990, www.chrie.org.

10. *Cahners Business Information,* 8773 South Ridgeline Boulevard, Highlands Ranch, Colorado 80126, 303-470-4445.

11. *Restaurant Management Restaurants USA,* The National Restaurant Association Member Subscriptions Only, www.restaurant.org. Annual demographic and statistical data about the industry.

12. *Industry Lobbyists in Washington, Restaurants and Foodservice Restaurants and Institutions,* Cahners Publications, Cahners Plaza, 1350 East Touhy Ave., P.O. Box 5080, Des Plaines, IL 60017, 312-635-8800.

13. *Business Performance, Fortune Magazine, Time Life,* Time Life Building, Rockefeller Center, New York, New York 10020, www.fortune.com. Business performance.

14. *Forbes,* Forbes Subscriber Service, P.O. Box 5471, Harlan, IA 51593, 800-888-9896, www.forbes.com. Business current events.

15. *Business Week,* McGraw Hill, The McGraw Hill Companies Building, 1221 Avenue of the Americas, New York, NY 10020, 800-635-1200, www.businessweek.com.

16. *Culinary Trends Food Arts,* M. Shanken Communications, 387 Park Avenue South, New York, New York 10016, 212-684-4224, www.foodarts.com.

17. *American Authority on Cooking,* The National Culinary Review, The American Culinary Federation (available to members only), 10 San Bartola Drive, St. Augustine, Florida 32086, 800-624-9458, www.acfchefs.org.

18. *Culinary Artistry, Art Culinaire,* Culinarie, Inc., P.O. Box 9268, Morristown, New Jersey 07960, 800-SO-TASTY, www.getartc.com.

19. *Food and Beverage Nations Restaurant News,* 800-944-4676, www.nrn.com. The most current periodical on the market, conference and convention meetings and conventions management, www.meetings-conventions.com.

20. *Travel and Tourism Trade,* travel.koreantown.com/travelMag.htm. *Magazine List Hospitality and Tourism,* www.islandnet/~htm/home4.html. *Resources List Travel and Tourism,* www.nacta.com/trades.html.

21. *Trade Publications List Wines and Beverages,* American Institute of Wine and Food, 304 West Liberty Street, Suite 201, Louisville, Kentucky 40202, 502-992-1022, www.aiwf.com.

22. *Wines and Beverage Wine Spectator,* P.O. Box 37367, Boone, Iowa 50037, 800-752-7799, School and College Foodservice, American School Foodservice Association, www.asfsa.org.

23. *National Association of College & University Foodservice,* www.nacufs.org, *Hospitality Magazines List,* www.restaurantresults.com/hospitalitymag/002.html.

24. Over 50 magazines linked: Hospitality Exchange, Internships, Research Collaboratives, www.gsu.edu/global.

25. SEARCH ENGINES:
    a. www.hotbot.com
    b. www.yahoo.com
    c. www.google.com
    d. www.inktomi.com
    e. www.FAST.com

Chapter Four Review Questions

1. Give an example of a hospitality business that expanded from "product" to "market."

2. How do the three elements of *Blur* (speed, connectivity, and intangibles) relate to the hospitality industry?

3. Describe a "WOW" experience you have had in a hospitality setting. What made it special?

4. What is a learning organization?

5. As a leader, what is an effective way to create a learning organization?

6. List five characteristics of a learning organization.

7. Give three examples of tasks that could be addressed by a "task force team."
   a. Restaurant (1)

   b. Hotel (1)

   c. Tourism and travel (1)

Industry Associations and Rating Services

St. Mark's Square and San Marco Basilica
Venice, Italy

Corel

POSTAGE
PAID

William R. Petersen
Southern New Hampshire
University

You may have noticed, or will soon realize, that the world of hospitality and tourism is full of acronyms, abbreviations, or what many call "alphabet soup." The jargon, or language, of hospitality and tourism is often abbreviated to save time, and industry associations, professional certification, and industry rating services are no exception. An example of this would be a hotel general manager (or GM) who is a certified hotel administrator (CHA) from the American Hotel & Lodging Association (AH&LA) and whose property holds a 4-diamond rating from the American Automobile Association (AAA).

A career in the dynamic and fast-paced hospitality and tourism industry requires a personal and professional commitment to excellence. Industry associations and rating services assist professionals and our guests in seeking excellence in a rapidly changing industry. This premise is supported by many in the industry, including John Bell, Chief Executive Officer of the Caribbean Hotel Association, who said, *"Any hotel or group of hotels that does not recognize the dynamic nature of this industry, and the phenomenal changes taking place within it, will have little chance of being competitive."* Participation in industry associations, engaging in professional development that leads to an industry recognized certification, and holding your business to the quality standards of an industry rating service will be key factors of success in hospitality and tourism careers.

Over the next few pages, you will find the key to many of the acronyms found in hospitality and tourism. A look at the role and benefits of industry associations includes a resource list of many hospitality- and tourism-related professional associations. The role of lifelong learning and how educational resources and professional certification provided by associations can add to your professional success will be reviewed. Finally, the rating services that review and help inform the public on the level and quality of our service product will be explored.

Industry Associations

There are a variety of industry-related associations that reflect the diversity and scope of hospitality and tourism. While there are many organizations that represent broad segments of hospitality and tourism, like the American Hotel & Lodging Association (AH&LA), some represent smaller segments, or special interests, like the Asian American Hotel Owners Association (AAHOA). What all associations have in common are the promotion and developmental interests of the industry segment it represents. The term *represents* is central to discussing associations. Associations are made up of individual, organizational, and allied or affiliated members who are drawn together to promote and develop their industry through a variety of services or benefits to the membership.

According to a 1998 study by the American Association of Retired Persons (AARP), 90 percent of all adults in America belong to an association. In the United States alone, there are more than 147,000 associations, according to the *Encyclopedia of Associations* for industry, professional, and special interest groups. In hospitality and tourism, there are hundreds of associations worldwide, and associations exist at local, state, regional, national, and international levels. The largest association in the United States is the American Automobile Association (AAA), with 43,000,000 members, according to the American Society of Association Executives (ASAE). Ironically, AAA serves hospitality and tourism through a variety of member services, including travel agencies, travel planners, custom trip mapping, and a hospitality rating service that will be discussed later in this chapter.

So what is it that associations do? The American Society of Association Executives (ASAE) cites the following member services typical of member associations:

- Government Affairs—Most industry and trade-related associations have governmental affairs staffs that promote member and industry interests at the state and national level.
- Joint Purchasing Power—Associations offer members a variety of purchasing services including insurances. Association rank is a major segment of the health insurance market, with $6 billion in health premiums annually that cover more than eight million people. Associations collect $65.7 billion annually from insurance casualty and property insurance premiums and $61.9 billion on personal lines.
- Promotion of the Industry via Printed Materials—Virtually all associations (95 percent) publish a periodical and 39 percent publish books.
- Educational Opportunities—95 percent of associations offer educational programs to their members. Seventy-nine percent offer public information and education opportunities.

- Industry Standards and Practices—Many associations develop codes of ethics and professional and safety standards for their industry.
- Industry Research—71 percent of all associations conduct industry research or develop statistical information. Businesses and government depend heavily on associations for their statistical information, which is often not available elsewhere.
- Service Projects—More than 173 million volunteer hours in community service are documented annually by associations, often using members' skills for the greater common good.

So why should you join a hospitality and tourism association now as a student, or as an industry professional in the future? The reason for joining an industry association can be answered in two words: *career success.* Your ability to remain current in your field, develop professionally, meet prospective employers, colleagues, and employees can be greatly enhanced through your membership and participation in any number of hospitality and tourism related associations.

Although there are almost as many associations as there are careers in hospitality and tourism, an example of the benefits of membership in the National Restaurant Association (NRA) follow:

- Professional Affiliation—Membership network of over 52,000 restaurant organizations with more than 254,000 restaurant outlets.
- Government Representation—Ranked by *Fortune* magazine as the 10th most effective lobbying organization in the country. The NRA works to make Congress understand the challenges of being a restaurateur.
- Education—The NRA provides training through their Educational Foundation, publications, management tools, and benchmarking data for the restaurant industry.
- Promotion—The NRA promotes dining out, encourages restaurant careers, demonstrates the industry's commitment to food safety, and provides information about the economic impact of restaurants.
- Two-for-One Membership—NRA membership automatically includes membership in a state restaurant association.
- Information—Subscription to the association's monthly magazine, *Restaurants USA,* and the newsletter *Washington Weekly* to keep up-to-

date on what's happening on Capitol Hill and in the association.
- Networking—The NRA hosts the nation's largest trade show, *The National Restaurant Associations' Restaurant, Hotel-Motel Show* in Chicago each year, with 2,000 exhibitors and 75,000 attendees.

Specific student membership benefits with the National Restaurant Association include:

- *Restaurants USA* magazine subscription
- Complimentary NRA show badge
- Information about educational programs
- Discounts on NRA publications and seminars
- Access to information services and the library
- NRA scholarship opportunities

According to student member Sherra Meyers at the University of Memphis, "The resources in the NRA library and the statistical data provided by the NRA research department are extremely helpful. With the 50 percent off member discount, I can afford to order all the publications that I need." This is just one example of an industry association and how membership can benefit you now, as a student. Other immediate benefits include networking, industry involvement, resume building, and scholarship opportunities.

Your association membership gives you a great opportunity to meet people with the same professional interests as you. The process of meeting and getting to know other members of an association is called networking. As a student member, you will find that industry professionals enjoy sharing their knowledge and expertise. Active networking may lead to a mentoring relationship, a part-time job, internship experience, or a career opportunity.

Being a member of an association gives you access to meetings, conferences, and trade shows that help build a greater understanding of the industry and shows your commitment and involvement with your chosen profession. Your membership and participation in association activities, particularly leadership roles, are excellent resume builders. Many industry recruiters seek students who show a high level of commitment to their career goals, and active membership in an association is an easy way to convey that.

An important benefit of many professional and trade associations is their support of both higher education and lifelong learning. As a student member, many associations offer scholarships to assist with financial need and reward academic achievement. Although seeking a scholarship shouldn't be your primary motivation for joining an industry association, you may find it to be a valuable secondary benefit. In addition to supporting scholarships for students, the central educational focus of hospitality and tourism industry associations is on the professional development of their members throughout their careers.

Hospitality and Tourism Associations

A listing of hospitality and tourism associations can be found in the chart that follows and includes the respective home page Internet addresses. This is just a partial list, so I encourage you to surf these Web sites and learn about the many industry associations in the world of hospitality and tourism.

Association Acronym	Hospitality and Tourism Association Name	Association Home Page Web Address
AAHOA	Asian American Hotel Owners Association	http://www.aahoa.org/
ABA	American Bakers Association	http://www.americanbakers.org/
ACF	American Culinary Federation	http://www.acfchefs.org/
ACTE	Association of Corporate Travel Executives	http://www.acte.org/
ADA	American Dietetic Association	http://www.eatright.org/
AGA	American Gaming Association	http://www.americangaming.org/
AH&LA	American Hotel & Lodging Association	http://www.ahla.com/
AIWF	American Institute of Wine and Food	http://www.aiwf.org/
ARDA	American Resort & Development Association	http://www.arda.org/
ASBE	American Society of Baking	http://www.asbe.org/
ASTA	American Society of Travel Agents	http://www.astanet.com/
ATA	Air Transport Association	http://www.air-transport.org/
CDR	Chaine des Rotisseurs—USA	http://www.chaineus.org/
CMA	Casino Management Association	http://www.cmaweb.org/
CMAA	Club Managers Association of America	http://www.cmaa.org/
CIC	Convention Industry Council	http://www.clc-online.org/
CHRIE	Council on Hotel, Restaurant & Institutional Education	http://www.chrie.org/
CLIA	Cruise Lines International Association	http://www.cruising.org/
FCG	Food Consultants Group	http://www.foodconsultants.com/
HFTP	Hospitality Financial and Technology Professionals	http://www.hftp.org/
HSMAI	Hospitality Sales & Marketing Association Int.	http://www.hsmai.org/
HFM	Society of Healthcare Foodservice Management	http://www.hfm.org/
HITA	Hospitality Information Technology Association	http://www.hita.co.uk/
IAAPA	International Association of Amusement Parks & Attractions	http://www.iaapa.org/
IAACC	International Association of Conference Centers	http://www.iacconline.org/
IACP	International Association of Culinary Professionals	http://www.iacp.com/
IACVB	International Association of Convention & Visitor Bureau	http://www.iacvb.org/
IAEM	International Association for Exposition Management	http://www.iaem.org/
ICTA	Institute of Certified Travel Agents	http://www.icta.com/
IEHA	International Executive Housekeepers Association	http://www.ieha.org/
IFEA	International Festival & Events Association	http://www.ifea.com/
IH&RA	International Hotel & Restaurant Association	http://www.ih-ra.com/
ISES	International Special Events Society	http://www.ises.com/
ISG	International Sommelier Guild	http://www.internationalsommelier.com/

Association Acronym	Hospitality and Tourism Association Name	Association Home Page Web Address
ISHC	International Society of Hospitality Consultants	http://www.ishc.com/
LCDO	Les Clefs d'Or—USA	http://www.lesclefsdorusa.com/
MPI	Meeting Professionals International	http://www.mpiweb.org/
NACE	National Association of Catering Executives	http://www.ienace.org/
NCBMP	National Coalition of Black Meeting Planners	http://www.ncbmp.com/
NCA	National Concierge Association	http://www.conciergeassoc.org/
NRPA	National Recreation & Park Association	http://www.nrpa.org/
NRA	National Restaurant Association	http://www.restaurant.org/
NTA	National Tour Association	http://www.ntaonline.com/
PAII	Professional Association of Innkeepers International	http://www.paii.org/
PCA	Professional Chef's Association	http://www.professionalchef.com/
PGA	Professional Golf Association	http://www.pga.com/
PCMA	Professional Convention Management Association	http://www.pcma.org/
RBA	Retail Bakers Association	http://www.rbanet.com/
RWF	Roundtable for Women in Foodservice	http://www.rwf.org/
SATW	Society of American Travel Writers	http://www.satw.org/
SCMP	Society of Corporate Meeting Professionals	http://www.scmp.org/
SFM	Society for Foodservice Management	http://www.sfm-online.org/
SITE	Society of Incentive Travel Executives	http://www.site-intl.org/
TIA	Travel Industry Association of America	http://www.tia.org/
TJG	Travel Journalists Guild	http://www.tjgonline.com/
WCR	Women Chefs & Restaurateurs	http://www.chefnet.com/wcr
WSEA	Wedding and Special Events Association	http://www.wsea.com/
WTO	World Tourism Association	http://www.world-tourism.org/
WTTC	World Travel & Tourism Council	http://www.wttc.org/

Professional Certification

The nature of hospitality and tourism is one of constant change. In the International Hotel & Restaurant Association's (IH&RA) paper on the global hospitality industry, "Into the New Millennium," is the following quote on our industry: "Few executives care to admit they are unable to keep pace with change. But the forces affecting the business environment are becoming so complex and change with such speed, that it is increasingly difficult to monitor or predict the impact this will have on hospitality organizations." The need to understand the changing nature of hospitality and tourism businesses can be met by active association membership and through lifelong learning opportunities and professional certification.

Noted management author John P. Kotter writes about the relationship of lifelong learning, leadership skills and the capacity to succeed in the future (Kotter, 1996, p. 179). Kotter discusses the need for managers to have a willingness to seek new challenges and improve skills and abilities to be competitive. A professional certification program offered by industry associations provides the opportunity to validate your knowledge of a specific area of your field, and demonstrates to employers and peers alike, your commitment to lifelong learning and your industry. Professional certification is a key to future career success. This can best be summarized by Kotter who said, "People who are making an effort to embrace the future are a lot happier than those who are clinging to the past . . . people who are attempting to grow, to become more comfortable with change, to develop leadership skills—these men and women are typically driven by a sense that they are doing what is right for themselves, their families, and their organizations" (Kotter, 1996, p. 186).

A listing of hospitality and tourism professional certifications can be found in the table that follows and includes the hospitality and tourism association that grants the certification.

Certification Acronym	Hospitality and Tourism Certification Name	Granting Hospitality and Tourism Association
CBM	Certified Bar Manager	International Foodservice Executives Association
CC	Certified Culinarian	American Culinary Federation
CCC	Certified Chef de Cuisine	American Culinary Federation
CCE	Certified Chef Educator	American Culinary Federation
CCM	Certified Club Manager	Club Managers Association of America
CEC	Certified Executive Chef	American Culinary Federation
CEH	Certified Executive Housekeeper	International Executive Housekeeper Association
CEOE	Certified Engineering Operations Executive	American Hotel & Lodging Association
CEPC	Certified Executive Pastry Chef	American Culinary Federation
CFBE	Certified Food and Beverage Executive	American Hotel & Lodging Association
CFE	Certified Festival Executive	International Festivals & Events Association
CFE	Certified Food Executive	International Foodservice Executives Association
CFM	Certified Food Manager	International Foodservice Executives Association
CGS	Certified Gaming Supervisor	American Hotel & Lodging Association
CHA	Certified Hotel Administrator	American Hotel & Lodging Association
CHDT	Certified Hospitality Department Trainer	American Hotel & Lodging Association
CHE	Certified Hospitality Educator	American Hotel & Lodging Association
CHHE	Certified Hospitality Housekeeping Executive	American Hotel & Lodging Association
CHME	Certified Hospitality Marketing Executive	H.S. M.A. I.
CHO	Certified Hotel Owner	Asian American Hotel Owners Association
CHRE	Certified Human Resources Executive	American Hotel & Lodging Association
CHS	Certified Hospitality Supervisor	American Hotel & Lodging Association
CHSP	Certified Hospitality Sales Professional	American Hotel & Lodging Association
CHT	Certified Hospitality Trainer	American Hotel & Lodging Association
CHTP	Certified Hospitality Technology Professional	American Hotel & Lodging Association
CITE	Certified Incentive Travel Executive	Society of Incentive Travel Executives
CLM	Certified Lodging Manager	American Hotel & Lodging Association
CLSM	Certified Lodging Security Director	American Hotel & Lodging Association
CLSO	Certified Lodging Security Officer	American Hotel & Lodging Association
CLSS	Certified Lodging Security Supervisor	American Hotel & Lodging Association
CMB	Certified Master Baker	Retail Bakers Association
CMC	Certified Master Chef	American Culinary Federation
CMM	Certified Meeting Manager	Meeting Planners International
CMP	Certified Meeting Professional	Convention Industry Council
CMPC	Certified Master Pastry Chef	American Culinary Federation
CPRP	Certified Parks & Recreation Professional	National Recreation & Park Association
CRDE	Certified Rooms Division Executive	American Hotel & Lodging Association
CPC	Certified Pastry Culinarian	American Culinary Federation
CS	Certified Sommelier	International Sommelier Guild
CSC	Certified Sous Chef	American Culinary Federation
CSCE	Certified Secondary Culinary Educator	American Culinary Federation
CSEP	Certified Special Events Professional	International Special Events Society
CTA	Certified Travel Associate	Institute of Certified Travel Agents

Certification Acronym	Hospitality and Tourism Certification Name	Granting Hospitality and Tourism Association
CTC	Certified Travel Consultant	Institute of Certified Travel Agents
CWPC	Certified Working Pastry Chef	American Culinary Federation
FMP	Foodservice Management Professional	National Restaurant Association
MCM	Master Club Manager	Club Managers Association of America
MCC	Master Cruise Counselor	Cruise Lines International Association
MHS	Master Hotel Supplier	American Hotel & Lodging Association
PCC	Personal Certified Chef	American Culinary Federation
PCEC	Personal Certified Executive Chef	American Culinary Federation
REH	Registered Executive Housekeeper	International Executive Housekeeper Association

Industry Rating Services

There are two primary types of rating services for hotels and restaurants, government tourist offices and private guides. I will reserve my comments to North America, where the primary rating services are the Automobile Association (AAA and CAA) Tour Books and Mobil Travel Guide. The AAA/CAA Tour Books rate over 22,000 lodging properties, 13,000 attractions, and restaurants and special events at destinations throughout the United States and Canada. Mobil Travel Guide rates over 22,000 lodging and restaurant properties across the United States and Canada in eight regional guidebooks. Mobil's guides cover more than 3,000 cities and towns and include destination information on 11,000 historical sites, sightseeing, sports, recreation, cultural events, and attractions.

AAA/CAA offer traditional regional destination guidebooks, as well as an online, searchable guide available to members. Local attractions, lodging, restaurants, and special events are included in this database. All guidebook entries have been reviewed for AAA/CAA standards set by field inspectors. Lodging and restaurant establishments are rated annually and given one to five diamonds, with five being the highest. There are no paid listings, as all attractions, lodging, restaurants, and special events are listed on their merit. Attractions of exceptional merit, interest and quality are designated by AAA/CAA as a "GEM"—and the guide states that these gems offer "a great experience for members."

Mobil Travel Guide has been serving the hospitality and tourism industry for over 40 years. Similar to AAA/CAA, the Mobil Travel Guide rates

establishments based on information gathered, using a set of criteria determined by their respective inspection teams. Mobil awards one to five star ratings, with five being the highest, and prides itself on the level of the criteria at each star level. Lodging and restaurant properties must offer a service, product, and level of experience appropriate to the cost. Stars are awarded based on the quality of the physical product, including decor, comfort, amenities, food, and beverage, as well as appropriate levels of guest service.

Recognized by most industry professionals as being the most thorough and well respected, the Mobil Travel Guide is the "Academy Awards" for the lodging and restaurant business. In their evaluation for 2000, only 30 lodging properties received the coveted five-star award, and 14 restaurants were awarded five stars in all of the United States!

In evaluating hotels, inns, and resorts, Mobil Travel Guide seeks excellence in cleanliness, service, and guest safety. Physical product characteristics considered are the quality and condition of guest rooms, public spaces, and furnishings. The service product characteristics considered includes the professionalism and helpfulness of the staff. Mobil inspectors use a six-point evaluation tool that details the entire guest experience. Components of the Mobil lodging inspection and evaluation include: the guest arrival phase, the guest room and bath, public spaces of the property, specific products/services, food and beverage offerings, and the departure phase.

The evaluation of restaurants, bistros, and lounges by Mobil Travel Guide is similar to that for lodging properties. The inspection/evaluation looks for excellence in cleanliness and service in all

Mobil Travel Guide—2003 Five-Star Winners

Lodging Recipients

The Beverly Hills Hotel
Beverly Hills, California

Chateau du Sureau
Oakhurst, California

Four Seasons Hotel
San Francisco, California

Mandarin Oriental
San Francisco, California

The Peninsula, Beverly Hills
Beverly Hills, California

Raffles L'Ermitage Beverly Hills
Beverly Hills, California

The Ritz-Carlton, San Francisco
San Francisco, California

The Little Nell
Aspen, Colorado

The Broadmoor
Colorado Springs, Colorado

Tall Timber
Durango, Colorado

The Mayflower Inn
Washington, Connecticut

Four Seasons Resort
Palm Beach, Florida

The Ritz-Carlton, Palm Beach
Palm Beach, Florida

The Ritz-Carlton, Naples
Naples, Florida

Four Seasons Hotel
Atlanta, Georgia

The Lodge at Sea Island Golf Club
Sea Island, Georgia

Four Seasons Hotel
Chicago, Illinois

**The Ritz-Carlton, Chicago—
A Four Seasons Hotel**
Chicago, Illinois

The Peninsula Chicago
Chicago, Illinois

Four Seasons Hotel
Boston, Massachusetts

Blantyre
Lenox, Massachusetts

The Point
Saranac Lake, New York

Four Seasons Hotel
Manhattan, New York

The St. Regis
Manhattan, New York

Trump International Hotel and Tower
Manhattan, New York

The Fearrington House
Pittsboro, North Carolina

The Mansion at Turtle Creek
Dallas, Texas

Twin Farms
Woodstock, Vermont

The Inn at Little Washington
Washington, Virginia

The Jefferson
Richmond, Virginia

Restaurant Recipients

Mary Elaine's
Scottsdale, Arizona

Ginza Sushiko
Beverly Hills, California

Gary Danko's
San Francisco, California

The French Laundry
Yountville, California

Seeger's
Atlanta, Georgia

The Dining Room
Atlanta, Georgia

Charlie Trotter's
Chicago, Illinois

Alain Ducasse
Manhattan, New York

Daniel
Manhattan, New York

Jean Georges
Manhattan, New York

Lespinasse
Manhattan, New York

Maisonette
Cincinnati, Ohio

Le Bec-Fin
Philadelphia, Pennsylvania

The Inn at Little Washington
Washington, Virginia

areas, including the bar and restrooms. Physical product characteristics considered are the quality and condition of furnishings, tabletop (settings), room layout (for comfort), menus, and food quality. The service product characteristics considered include the professionalism and attentiveness of the staff, in addition to service pace and timing. Mobil inspectors use a six-point evaluation tool that details the entire guest experience. Components of the Mobil restaurant inspection and evaluation include: the guest arrival, the physical property, service, culinary arts, beverages, and guest departure.

Conclusion

The world of hospitality and tourism certainly offers industry associations, professional certification, and rating services that focus on excellence. Associations excel in providing quality professional development, lifelong learning, and networking opportunities. A wide range of professional certification programs recognizes individual areas of expertise and offer external validation of knowledge and skills. Finally, industry rating services strive for standards of excellence that assist hospitality and tourism professionals in meeting and exceeding guest expectations, while providing a valuable service to the traveling public.

The world of hospitality and tourism may utilize a language full of acronyms, abbreviations, or "alphabet soup," but the focus on excellence in career development and on guest expectations is universal. Your career potential in hospitality and tourism is vast and can benefit greatly from active membership in industry associations, earning appropriate professional certifications, and by learning from the standards of excellence set by rating services like AAA/CAA and Mobil Travel Guide. A great way to start is to join an on-campus chapter of an industry association or become a member of Eta Sigma Delta (ESD), the honor society for hospitality and tourism students. Ask your professor or faculty advisor about opportunities on your campus.

References

American Automobile Association. *Tour Book Guides.* http://www.aaanne.com/travel/default.asp
American Society of Association Executives. *Association Meeting Trends.* Washington, DC, 1999.
Gale Research. *Encyclopedia of Associations.* Farmington Hills, MI, 2002.
International Hotel & Restaurant Association's White Paper on the global hospitality industry, *Into the New Millennium,* 1996.
Kotter, John P. *Leading Change.* Boston: Harvard Business School Press, 1996.
Mobil Travel Guides. *Travel Guides Criteria.*
http://www.exxonmobiltravel.com/mtg_rating_criteria_star.jsp
Mobil Travel Guides. *Year 2003 Five-star Winners.*
http://www.exxonmobiltravel.com/index.jsp?menu=rating_criteria&module=fivestar
National Restaurant Association. *Benefits of Membership.* http://www.restaurant.org/aboutus/
Travel Industry Association of America. *Industry Links.* http://www.tia.org/JoinTIA/member_links.asp

5 | Name_____ Date_____

Chapter Five Review Questions

1. What service does a hospitality rating company provide for the guests? To the industry?

2. What key factors were discussed by the author that impacts the professional success of the hospitality manager?

3. What key factors were discussed by the author that impacts the professional success of the hospitality business?

4. What is a professional association?

5. What are the seven primary services that associations offer their members?

6. List four benefits of networking with industry professionals?

7. Why should a hospitality manager seek out a professional certification in his/her chosen field?

8. How many five star properties are in the U.S.?

9. List 3 five star properties that are the closest to you geographically.

10. Would you like an internship or entry-level job at one of these five star properties? Why or why not?

Chapter **6** *Career Realities and Opportunities*

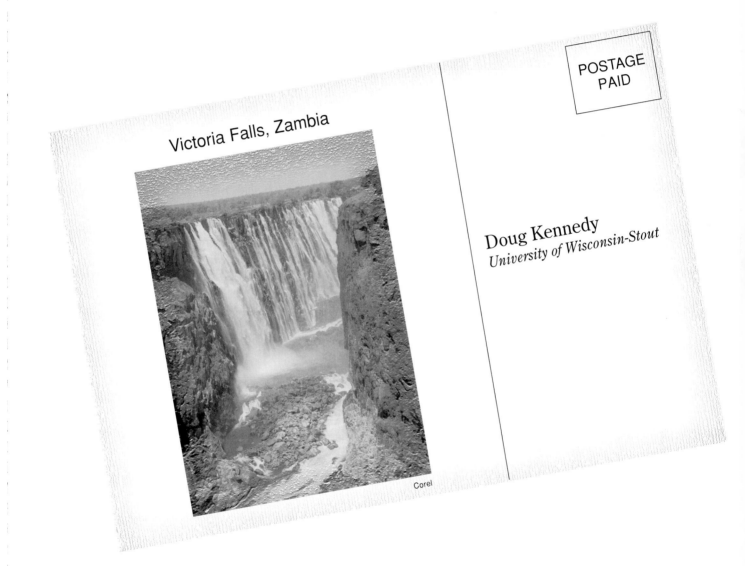

Victoria Falls, Zambia

Corel

POSTAGE PAID

Doug Kennedy
University of Wisconsin-Stout

What Is It I Am Getting Into?

Why do you want to work in the hospitality industry? This is a question you will no doubt be asking yourself as you are taking this course, throughout your college career, and even once you are out working in the industry. You will find out soon if you like this business or not. Perhaps by now you are doing some work in the industry, and there was something about the work that struck you and caused you to select hospitality as your major or at least take an introductory course on the subject matter to learn more about it. Or maybe you have just been fascinated by this broad-based industry as a consumer of its services that you want to further explore a career in it.

If you have done any work in the industry, you already know it is all about people and providing a service to them. We have seen our economy change from a manufacturing economy to a service economy during the latter part of the 20th century. So by working in this industry, you will be in the thick of things in the American economy. You may even find some great global opportunities as you develop your hospitality career path.

In today's fast paced society with all of its demands and stresses, people are demanding the services the hospitality industry has to offer. The hospitality industry offers people a reprieve from the time crunch and high stress in their daily lives. People are willing to spend money to experience the wide variety of leisure experiences our industry has to offer.

An Industry of Tradeoffs

Back in the 1970s, a leader of a growing restaurant organization described the job of a restaurant manager to his people by telling them they would "work long and work hard." Has this image of the industry changed in 30 years? In many organizations, the answer is yes! With the growth of opportunities not only in the hospitality industry, but in competing service fields, the competition to attract qualified candidates has increased ferociously in the hospitality arena. As a graduate of a hospitality program with a resume of practical and related work experience, you will be sought after by hospitality employers. You will be in a position to decide how many hours you want to work each

week, depending on the segment of the industry and the reputation of the employer. In many cases, the financial rewards will increase as the work week increases, but that is the reality in many professions, especially for those starting out in entry-level positions.

What you do in the early stages of your career will impact the rest of your life, both personally and professionally. Generally, when people start out in their career, they have fewer commitments in their personal life. This makes it easier to meet the demands of the job. If you can advance early in your career, you can attain greater personal stability in your work life as your personal commitments grow. Also, as you research organizations to work for, you will want to determine the depth of their management strength to insure it is adequate so you can lead a balanced life instead of always being a phone call away from bailing out the ship. Nevertheless, there will be times when duty calls, and that is the nature of our industry. One way to think about it is "we work, so others can play."

Are you comfortable working nights and weekends? Chances are, you are doing it now as a student. How about after you graduate? Personal chores, errands, and the like can be more easily accomplished when the majority of the people are at work. It will be easier to get a tee time at the golf course or schedule personal appointments. So there are advantages to those hours!

You need to be a "people person" to succeed in this industry. You will be surrounded by people, employees, and customers. Your job will have everything to do with how well you can deal with the demands and pressures they place upon you in their respective roles of subordinate and guest. You can be taught the technical skills of the business, and, over time, you will not only learn them, but you will master them through on-the-job experience and repetition. People relations skills are not as easily learned. You will be trained in human relations skill areas and have many opportunities to practice. But the bottom line is that you have to like people and all the challenges and problems they bring your way. There will be days you will want to be left alone just to do your job, but the times that is possible are rare in the hospitality business, a people business.

Finally, for anyone working in this industry, it is important that, to a degree, they enjoy physical labor. You should enjoy it, because at times you will be called upon to do it! It will keep you on your toes and force you to "think on your feet." It will also help you to set a good example for your employees, who will watch how you perform your tasks with keen interest.

How Do I Best Prepare for a Career in This Industry While in School?

Your job now is to be a student. Never thought of it that way? Well, there is no better time than the present. We are all endowed with a certain level of academic skills. As with any skill set, we can only build intellectual skills through hard work. Hard work in school and on the job does pay off, but not overnight. As the saying goes, "by the inch it's a cinch; by the yard it is hard." If you can apply yourself in school on a consistent basis, you will see a payoff in the long run.

One of the dilemmas many students face is having to work while in school. For some, there is

A conservative and well-manicured look will give you a great deal of added confidence in the job search process.

no choice; it is a matter of economic survival. Studies over time have shown that students who work some versus not at all or too much, do better academically. It all comes down to budgeting and planning one's time, something you will be forced to do throughout your career in the hospitality industry. There is no better time than the present to procure some type of time management tool to help you in this regard. There are many, from the simple to the complex, from technical (palm pilot, laptop) to non-technical (weekly planner, daily planner).

Balancing work and school throughout your academic career is good preparation for the "real world." But moreover, you are getting the best of both worlds. If you work in the hospitality industry while in school, and you should, you will be able to take some of the learnings from the classroom environment and see their workplace application. You will also take your experiences from work and bring them into the classroom. Get used to this working and learning. Your employer in the hospitality industry will continuously send you for training and development to improve your performance on the job. Learning is life-long, as is applying the learning to your day-to-day responsibilities. So while preparing for your career, you are also building up your resume to be more inviting to prospective employers when you finish your coursework.

One critical area to focus on while in school is to, as much as possible, fully develop your computer capabilities. Sign up for courses that will give you practical hands-on experience in this area. The more computer savvy you are once you get into the industry, the more it will help you to advance your career. In addition, if this is a strong point for you, it will give you the opportunity to focus on other areas of your personal development. Moreover, new technology will continuously be added to the workplace, and the ability to adapt quickly will be a boost to you, your employees, and your operation.

Why get a four-year degree in a hospitality related field, when you could be working full time in the industry now and making more money than you can with only part-time work? The answer is that a four-year degree will take you further. Studies have shown that a person on the average earns one million dollars in a lifetime with a high school degree versus two million with a college degree. The path you are on will be well worth the time and money in the long run.

What Type of Work Experience Should I Get During My College Years and How Do I Find It?

The sooner in your college career you become familiar with the services of your placement office, the better. After all, this is the first point of contact for employers, and, secondly, you are paying for these services with your tuition, so use them. The key to getting an interview, and eventually a job, is a resume. Most people who apply for the type of work you are seeking during your college years will not have a resume. So when you show up with one, you will have a distinct advantage over them. The unspoken message you will be sending the employer is that you are very serious about getting a job. Even better, when they see that you are studying in the field they are working in, you will gain further ground over the competition.

Your placement office is in the business of helping you put together a resume. They are measured in their job performance by the percent of the school's graduates who get employed. The more related experience they can help you obtain while you are in school, the better your chances of successful job placement upon graduation. You will need a resume throughout your career. It is an ongoing, evolving document that portrays your skills, experiences, training, and occupational desires. In today's electronic document environment, it is easy to keep a resume in your computer files and update it as your career evolves. So start now, while there is less to input. You may be thinking there is little to put on paper at this stage of your work life. No matter, what ever there is, start it now and take it to the experts in your placement office for their help in refining it. There are numerous examples of resume development that can be obtained from your library, bookstores, and online. Many placement offices even have an electronic format that will guide you in the development of a resume.

Your options for work during the school year may be limited by the size of the town where your school is located and how much time you can devote to a job while in school. Your summer employment will be the best experience you can find, as your availability will then best match the needs of many employers in the hospitality industry. You need to start this process early in the school year. The best jobs will fill up first.

Your placement office will have job postings online and host a career fair. Find out how receptive your placement office feels employers who attend your school's career fair are to students seeking summer or part-time employment while in school. Send out cover letters and resumes to employers in your hometown prior to going home on break, and then use that break time to "pound the pavement" and conduct a follow-up visit to those employers you contacted through the mail or email.

You may want to give some thought to working in a part of the country other than your hometown during the summer. Many great employment experiences can be found in remote resort areas where the population base does not have an adequate supply of employees for the seasonal needs of the business. This is also a great opportunity for you to find out your comfort level with working away from the area you grew up and also to find out what it is like working in different parts of the United States. Once you are out in the industry, one of the major career decisions you will need to make is your willingness to relocate. Many employers in the hospitality industry are desirous of management candidates who are willing to move to different properties. This can open greater opportunities, not only in the organization, but in the industry as well.

What Other Activities Should I Be Involved in During School to Enhance My Career Choices?

There are a variety of activities that would be profitable for a hospitality student to engage in throughout college to help in their career choice. Take advantage of the opportunity to read the various trade publications that your school receives. There are many excellent publications that are targeted to key segments of the industry. Throughout your time in school, periodically read certain publications as a way of tracking important trends and key players in the various segments of the industry that interest you.

As a consumer, talk to various operators whom you patronize. Tell them you are planning a career in the industry and ask them for a tour of their facility and any advice, such as elective classes they would recommend for someone going into their area. Be sure to attend any trade shows that are offered during the year in your area when vendors and operators meet to learn the latest trends in their industry.

Your school will have clubs that are active in various segments of the industry. Get active and involved in one of your choosing. Attend meetings, listen to guest speakers, and go on field trips.

One of the foremost activities in your curriculum would be to become involved in a co-op or intern experience. These are more structured than, say, a summer job and will require you to analyze your experience for classroom credit. Many employers will list these types of opportunities with your placement office. It would be a good practice to periodically check your placement office's Web site for current listings. Even better, alert one of the counselors to an area or employer you have a keen interest in, so they can notify you in the event something comes up. Also, many employers will make special visits to campus outside of career conferences on dates that fit their needs and schedule. Your attendance at these sessions, especially early in your time at school, can be invaluable learning experiences and help you eliminate or consider more seriously certain career opportunities.

As you can see, all these suggested activities take time, which is a precious commodity as you will be busy with classes, studying, and probably a job. But it is up to you to take charge of your career; no one is going to do it for you. The earlier you focus on some of these outside-the-classroom learning experiences, the better able you will be to fine tune your vocational areas of interest.

What Will It Be Like When I Start Pursuing My First Career Job?

Everything you do during your college career will somehow prepare you for the moment when you have to decide whether or not you're going to accept a certain job offer. You need to first ask yourself if the grass is really greener on the other side of the fence. Were there any of your prior work experiences with organizations you would want to consider working for after school? Did anybody ever approach you about staying there after graduation? What would this employer have to offer? Do not automatically dismiss this possibility. For one,

Recruiters use the first interview to determine if you are a possible management candidate.

you already know a lot about the company and the business and could literally "jump start" your career. You should definitely explore other opportunities as a way of making a comparison with one that could be staring you in the face.

As much as you can arrange your course of study, try to get many of the more demanding and time consuming courses behind you, prior to your last semester in school. This way, you can also focus your energies during your last semester on a job search.

Attend any seminars your school puts on for students embarking on a career search. Read up on the do's and don'ts of interviewing from all the literature that is available. Practice answers to questions you think may be asked in an interview. Does your placement office offer mock interviewing sessions on video as a way for you to get feedback on your interviewing skills?

The biggest thing to remember about an interview is that it is a two-way street. It is a tool (though not perfect) for both you and the employer to see if you want to and are capable of doing a particular job and if you would "fit" into that company's culture. "Fit" is a very important factor, not just for the job, but more importantly for the organization. Besides knowing whether or not you can successfully perform the job, the employer wants to know how you line up with what they look for in a person who operates successfully in their environment. You also want to know after some assimilation time how you will fit in. Do your values line up with the organizations'? How can you ascertain that? It will take more than reading a company's mission statement to make that determination.

What has your own research led you to conclude about this company? Have you been able to get enough information to make a quality decision about where you are going to invest your energies for at least the next several years? You need to have questions prepared to ask your interviewer at the appropriate time (when they ask you) about any areas you would like greater detail on than was offered in the interview. Can you describe the company? Where has it been and where is it going? Do you understand the true nature of the job? For what are you going to be held accountable? What will you do in a typical day, if there is such a thing? What is the training like: on-the-job, classroom, self-paced, scheduled? How well does the company keep to its timetable for its training and development programs? What are the advancement opportunities? What does it take to get promoted in their company? What are the promotional timeframes? How will you be compensated? How much pay is base vs. incentive? How achievable are the incentive payment criteria? What are the benefits like? When do you become eligible for certain benefits? Of course, always ask questions about pay and benefits last. These are just some of the questions you need good answers to so you will be able to make a quality decision that is in your best career interests.

If you are not offered a field day or preview day in the interview, ask if one is available or if you can at least get some exposure to some of the managers in the organization. This will give you a chance to re-pose some of the same questions you asked in the first interview to see how the answers compare, and possibly you will get more detail. Look at the job description that you have hopefully been given. As you talk to the people actually doing the job, ask them what they do in a typical day.

Be certain to ask what the next step is in the process and when it will happen, so you know as much as possible about where you stand as you pursue other possible employment situations. This can be a nerve-racking time as you wait for people to get back to you. But it is also an excellent time to evaluate a company on how well they keep their commitments, for example, when they get back to you and how well organized they seem to be in their hiring and recruitment processes. This will be an excellent clue as to how they operate their business overall and should not be taken lightly as you evaluate them as a prospective employer.

While you need to make your own decision about whom you want to work for, do not hesitate to solicit opinions from family and friends about the reputation of the various companies you are considering. At the end of the day, you need to have pride in the organization you are going to cast your lot with in order to be able to give them your best effort.

How to Handle the Job Offer

As a rule of thumb, don't take the first job you are offered. There are exceptions, however. There are some things you need to consider. What was the chemistry like between you and the people who interviewed you? Did you like them? If you didn't, you won't like working there, as they are probably good representative examples of what the organization has to offer in the way of their employee make-up. Is this a job you can see yourself doing for at least 2–3 years? It is important to establish a solid track record, and this starts with your first professional position. Are the hours, location, and pay feasible for you? Are you comfortable? Are you up to meeting this employer's expectations?

You will need to understand what timeframe you have to respond to the offer. It is a good practice to let the employer know as soon as you have decided to turn down a particular offer, instead of waiting out the string and hoping something better will turn up. Pay will rarely be negotiable for entry-level positions, but if you feel the pay is a stumbling block, you need to tell the employer it is preventing you from accepting their offer.

Now That I Am on Board, What's in Store for Me?

Most positions in the hospitality industry will have you starting out in what is called "operations." What this means is the day-to-day managing and running of the business. It is the largest department typically in a hospitality company and is where the employees come into contact with the guest. As a manager in the operations division, one of your most important tasks will be directing and overseeing the organization's employees in their servicing of the guests.

Starting out in operations, on the firing line so to speak, is the best way to learn the business. This experience will be invaluable to you, as experience is sometimes the best teacher. This will build for you a solid foundation in the business, especially if you desire to advance into staff or support positions down the road. These positions exist to "support" those employees who serve the customer in the hospitality organization. Without "operations," these positions would not exist.

Operations also offers a great career opportunity for those who get fired up by the day-to-day contact with customers and the myriad of challenges and surprises that arise in the business. Even if one decides to leave the industry someday, which happens in all industries, the exposure to the many aspects of running a hospitality business will prepare one well for their next career move. This is an industry where one is less likely to be pigeon-holed and not be able to see the "big picture."

One of the major tasks you will have as an entry-level manager will be hiring, training, and supervising employees. Another criterion you should take into account as you decide on your place of employment is how the organization treats its hourly staff. To a large degree, what their policies and practices are with their employees can go a long way to making your job easier or more difficult. The hospitality industry has a core of dedicated, hardworking, long-term employees who are essential to the success of the business. On the other hand, there are many people who work in our industry who are there temporarily until they are able to secure employment more suited to their eventual career field. Nonetheless, the industry is a major training ground for many other segments of commerce. Regardless of someone's length of tenure in the industry, they are going to gravitate toward those employers that provide a positive work experience.

In the 1990s when our economy was booming and unemployment was at a record low, many hospitality employers had trouble attracting an adequate number of skilled workers to staff their businesses. One major source of employees for the industry came from non-English speaking immigrants who were willing to perform some of the more menial tasks that are part of the hospitality industry. One area that continues to be a challenge for managers in the hospitality industry is the area of oral and written communication with its non-English speaking and reading work force. While taking courses in Spanish will help hospitality managers with this issue, it cannot be seen as a cure all, as many other nationalities who do not speak English are prevalent in the workforce. It should be noted that other industries are not immune from this challenge either.

What Will My Training Be Like?

Training will be an important part of the first several months in your first career position in the industry. How well you conduct yourself in completing the company's training programs will be a key factor in how you are evaluated and looked upon by not only your supervisors, but by the employees in your charge. It is important you try to lead as balanced a life as possible when you first start out on a new job. Starting any new job is a major stressor in one's life, and you should anticipate that some days you will feel overwhelmed by what you are up against. Remember, not all days are going to be like this. You control how you respond to them by having a positive mental attitude, eating three healthy meals a day, and getting a good night's rest. Try to get some form of exercise other than on the job. After work, try to associate with people who are outside of our industry. It is always good to have an outsider's perspective.

Try to volunteer for assignments and special projects as a way of getting known in your organization. Also, if your company has a mentor program, by all means, participate. If they do not, but you meet a manager who you admire, see if that person would be willing to be your mentor, someone you can talk with now and then for advice and counsel, for what you are experiencing on the job. Particularly if you are a woman or a person of color, someone in a similar circumstance who has progressed in the organization would be an extremely valuable resource for you.

Being open to feedback as you get started in your new career is critical to your success. The worst position to be in is "when you don't know what it is that you don't know." This is called a blind spot and has been known to handicap people in their careers. Look at feedback as a learning opportunity; don't get defensive. You cannot solve a problem unless you know it is there. Asking for feedback is healthy and looked upon positively by your superiors. It is even more critical if you work for a boss who is reluctant to give feedback.

Summing It All Up

Whether you realize it or not, this is an exciting time for you. You ask how can that be when I am not sure what I want to do and where I want to go? Well, this course of study you are taking about the hospitality industry is going to expose you to its many facets and opportunities. As you venture through each chapter, think about who you are, what you like to do, and what you are good at. Ask yourself if you can see yourself in any of these industry portraits that are going to be laid out for you in the following chapters. This is the time for you to be a dreamer and a visionary. After all, this is what many of the people who have become famous in this industry did and still are doing. More importantly, the same goes for those people who look to this industry for their livelihood and meaning in their day-to-day work life.

Name _____ Date _____

Chapter Six Review Questions

1. Describe the workweek of a hospitality manager.

2. What is a common motto about the time of day/workweek of a hospitality manager?

3. How will computer application skills help your career options in the hospitality industry?

4. How can a college placement office assist you in your career development?

5. What is the role of a resume?

6. What does the author suggest about the appropriate time to find a summer job?

7. Describe at least three successful strategies for finding a summer job.

8. What are some of the activities you can partake in to broaden your hospitality career knowledge base?

9. What are four ways you can practice your interviewing skills?

10. What are three questions you could ask a potential employer to determine if you would "fit in" well with their organization?

11. When is it appropriate to ask about job options and follow up after the interview?

12. Where will you likely start out in your first entry-level management job?

13. Give four examples of entry-level type positions in the hospitality industry.

14. The hiring, training, and supervising of employees will likely be one of your primary jobs as an entry-level manager. Write out five "do's" and five "don'ts" you intend to uphold.

Do's   *Don'ts*

a.   a.

b.   b.

c.   c.

d.   d.

e.   e.

15. What skills are you likely to need as a manager related to languages?

16. What are some things you can do to minimize stress in your life?

17. Discuss the concept of getting feedback from your employees. Why is it important?

18. In your opinion, how should a manager best respond to positive feedback?

19. In your opinion, how should a manager best respond to negative feedback?

20. As a manager, once you gain feedback information, what should you do with this information?

Part II
Hospitality and
Tourism Companies

7

E-Hospitality: The Future of E-Business

8

Independent and Entrepreneurial Operations

9

Chain Operations

10

Franchising and Referral Associations

11

Contract Management

E-Hospitality: The Future of E-Business

Mayan Ruins
Tikal, Guatemala

POSTAGE
PAID

Radesh Palakurthi
San Jose State University

Corel

How Is the Internet Transforming the Travel and Hospitality Business?

The promise of the Internet has perhaps had more effect on the hospitality and travel industry than any other industry. Every aspect of the hospitality and travel industry is being transformed by the ubiquitous nature of the Web. Travel companies are leveraging Internet technologies to perform myriads of tasks from streamlining operations to supporting customers. By integrating Web technologies in all aspects of the business, hospitality and travel companies are becoming integrated e-businesses. *See Web Effects in Travel and Hospitality*. This chapter will discuss the essence of conducting e-business, and its ramifications in the hospitality and travel industry.

What Is an E-Business?

The Internet is evolving from a confusing "network of networks" into a life force that is enriching our lifestyles. There is hardly any aspect of our life that is not influenced by the Internet today. Starting right from birth where hospitals now offer free domain name registration in the child's name along with ample disk space to post pictures of the new arrival for the whole world to see, people can use the Internet to make every critical decision in their lives—choosing schools or courses to take; choosing partners for dating and marriage; choosing jobs and careers to pursue; choosing a place to live or a house to buy; or choosing mature service options such as retirement planning and funeral services. Clearly, the Internet has not only touched our lives, but promises to be *the* medium for communication and collaboration in the future. E-businesses are companies that expand the use of such technologies to include all major stakeholders in their businesses: customers, employees, management, government, business partners, bankers, suppliers/vendors, and stockholders. This is obviously more elaborate than e-commerce, where the focus is only the customers or the suppliers and the transactions that transpire with them online. In other words, e-commerce is just a small part of the e-business model. This distinction is illustrated in Figure 7.1.

It should also be noted that the term e-business has a strategic connotation and, therefore, takes a more holistic approach to business. In an e-business, the focus is on synergy, integration,

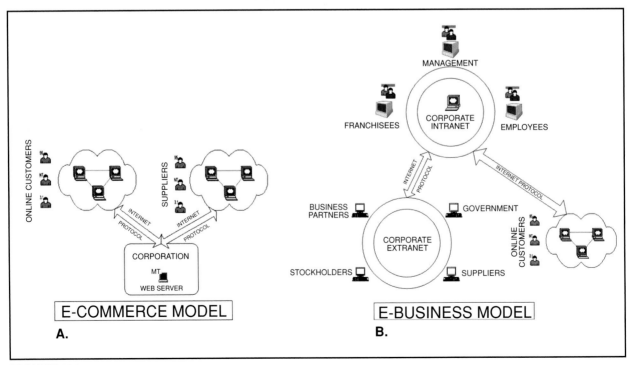

FIGURE 7.1

Web Effects in Travel and Hospitality

Companies in the travel and hospitality business are taking to the Internet like a fish takes to water. At a time when "profitable e-business" seems like an oxymoron, Internet travel companies are bucking the trend and setting a shining example of how to creatively use the Internet to be profitable. In a recent report published by *Business Week* magazine, the travel industry was declared the valedictorian and was the only industry to be given an "A" grade among the eight major industries studied for their effective use of the Internet. The eight major industries studied were travel, finance, media and advertising, retail, exchanges, software, access/infrastructure, and consulting. Travel and hospitality companies are using the Internet to drive demand and cut costs at all levels. In addition, all major segments of the travel and hospitality industry are finding ways to use the Internet to help their operations become more efficient.

The perception of getting better deals on the Internet is pushing consumers to use travel Web sites to buy travel services. Many such Web sites now exist, and they accounted for about 20 percent ($21 billion) of all travel sales in 2001. Travel and hospitality companies in turn are more than willing to satisfy the consumer needs because it helps them reduce costs by directly selling to the consumers and by decreasing the need for booking and customer service agents. For example, fees for GDSs and travel agents cost Alaska Airlines 6 percent to 8 percent the cost of each ticket. However, since it started selling tickets online, Alaska Airlines has saved $15 million per year since 2000. Similarly, Delta Airlines not only conducted $1 billion in sales on its Web site in 2001, but it also saved $40 million in costs providing customer services online.

The cost savings apply to hotels, rental car companies, and cruise lines, too. By not paying commissions and using proprietary booking systems, companies are saving 15–20 percent on the price of each booking. The online avenue is adding an additional interactive sales channel to the industry by allowing the companies to not only unload "distressed inventory" (unsold rooms, seats, etc.) through online auctions and last-minute deals, but to also offer targeted and personal marketing/sales messages and alerts through emails to potential customers who opt for such services. Such interactivity is allowing hospitality companies to even out fluctuating demand and to increase operational yields.

Some other ways in which the travel and hospitality companies are trying to reduce costs is by migrating parts of their entire operation to their Web site and reducing intervention by employees. For example, by offering detailed information about how far a particular hotel is from a convention center or an airport, hotel companies are reducing the amount of time guests spend on the phone asking operators for such information. By providing online frequent flyer miles program management tools such as automatic upgrades, or redeeming miles for free tickets, airlines are saving substantial amounts of money by not manning large offices to manage such programs. Corporate travel pioneers such American Express now process about 75 percent of their transactions over the Web without involving staff. Some of the company's corporate customers are using the Web 90 percent of the time. This reduces phone calls to the card service center by 30 percent, cuts mail volume by 80 percent, and saves 70 percent of the time customers spend managing card usage.

Case Questions

How are the airlines using the Internet to reduce costs?

What consumer perceptions about the Internet are increasing the popularity of online booking of travel and hospitality related services?

How are the stakeholders of a company being included in the e-business models?

and collaboration. The goal is to establish systems that will reduce overall costs, increase efficiencies, and, consequently, improve customer satisfaction. E-commerce, on the other hand, is more concerned with enabling and successfully completing sales transactions online in the most efficient way possible.

E-Business Benefits

The foundation of commerce in hospitality is customers and companies seek each other out to assess the value of the products and services and exchange money. E-commerce does not change this, but allows hospitality companies to realize the huge potential of Internet solutions for increased sales, stronger customer relationships, more focused marketing programs, streamlined internal systems, and better supply chain integration. The difference is that e-business, by providing access to more information and better communications, empowers all the entities involved in the transaction to make the markets more dynamic and precise, and, consequently, enhances efficiency. Specifically, e-business provides the following benefits:

- *Streamlines Operations and Reduces Costs*— Many large hospitality companies have already used networks and information technology to connect their operations directly to their core constituencies such as employees, suppliers, contractors, and distributors. The result is a more streamlined operation and reduced costs. Using Internet technologies, e-business models now allow even the smallest hospitality company to reap the same benefits without the expensive cost of hosting a network. For example, a chef in a small restaurant can place food and beverage purchase orders electronically (no paperwork or phone calls required) using a company such as Instill (http://www.instill.com), and check his or her account status or track all deliveries made online. Additionally, the chef can generate detailed reports of his or her buying patterns and payment history. Such efficiencies will allow the chef to not only manage the operation better in less time, but may also allow him or her to reduce the money tied up in inventory.
- *Enhances Market Efficiencies*—E-business models allow hospitality companies to benefit

from the synergies that develop from using Internet technologies with market intelligence. For example, many airlines now use the Internet to electronically issue special last minute fares at very low cost to fill open seats on selected flights. The low fares are publicized via email to travel agents, pre-registered company Web site visitors, frequent flyer program members, or are simply posted as a newsflash on the company Web site. The reduced prices enable airlines to fill their planes to capacity, thereby maximizing revenue and enabling consumers to fly at a fraction of the usual cost.

- *Increases Competition and Reduces Prices*—It is said that e-commerce and e-business are great levelers in hospitality. They allow hospitality companies of all sizes and characteristics to compete on the same playing field. Since the Internet conveniently makes all companies' online information available to all customers, the result is more competition, better quality products and services, as well as reduced prices. For example, many restaurants post their menu and nutritional information on the Web, encouraging consumers to learn more about their products and how much better they are than their competition. Other hospitality companies, such as hotel chains, offer online customer service centers that field customer queries 24 hours a day. These changes not only signal a shift in the market, but also a shift in the way consumers will redefine the value they receive for their money.
- *Facilitates Global Reach*—Every hospitality operation is bounded by the customers it can reach effectively. The hackneyed phrase, "location is everything" is gaining a new meaning in the industry as more and more companies set up shop on the Web. E-business models are helping erase geographic boundaries, so even the smallest operation (say a motel or a corner deli) can market their products and services to customers around the globe, if they so wish. Similarly, customers could also shop at a hospitality company's Web site as easily as they could at a store next to their house. So, the new mantra seems to be "location is everywhere!"
- *Increases Customer Convenience and Choice*—Customers can make more informed buying

decisions by consulting numerous electronic hospitality references and catalogs, comparison shopping, and even virtually experiencing the products (such as guest and meeting rooms) without ever leaving the comfort of their homes or offices. Because e-business technology enables electronic filing of volumes of online travel product information, consumers can specify preferences, leaving sellers to respond only to the particular criteria selected by potential customers. In addition, e-business allows hospitality companies to increase customer convenience by allowing them to locate and purchase travel-related goods and services 24-hours a day, seven days a week.

Although the benefits are phenomenal for implementing e-business models, the challenges are equally daunting. Implementing e-business solutions requires companies to take a macro view of their competitive environment. No longer can a company focus within itself to come up with solutions. This poses an extraordinary challenge to companies in hospitality since many of them think in terms of competing in their immediate geographic vicinity. There are many other challenges to implementing e-business solutions including: the need to rethink and reengineer operations; the need to understand the large scope of the e-business projects; and the need to involve and convince everybody in the company about the required changes that e-businesses would entail.

In spite of the above challenges, e-business ventures are receiving extraordinary support from top executives in the hospitality business. In a 2001 *InternetWeek 100* survey of companies, the travel and hospitality industry performed better than the average among eight other industries in terms of e-business performance. The results of the survey are summarized in Figure 7.2.

The research shows that the "conversion rate," i.e., the percentage of Web visitors that actually buy a product online is still in the low single digits (three to four percent) for all e-business companies. While these percentages might seem very low, they are better than the response rates for

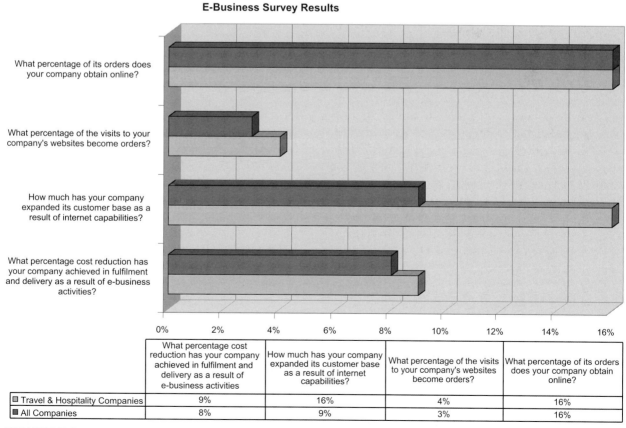

E-Business Survey Results

	What percentage cost reduction has your company achieved in fulfilment and delivery as a result of e-business activities	How much has your company expanded its customer base as a result of internet capabilities?	What percentage of the visits to your company's websites become orders?	What percentage of its orders does your company obtain online?
Travel & Hospitality Companies	9%	16%	4%	16%
All Companies	8%	9%	3%	16%

FIGURE 7.2

mass marketing (think junk mail!) where the percentages can be as low as one to two percent. The executives in the survey reported that on average their customer base increased by 16 percent because of their Internet capabilities compared to an across-industries average of only nine percent. The soft (digital) products that travel and hospitality companies sell on the Internet, such as electronic booking of tickets, lends itself well to online distribution channels compared to hard products, such as chemicals, and apparel that other industries sell online. Travel and hospitality companies reported slightly greater reduction in costs due to their e-business efforts than the rest of the industries (eight percent vs. nine percent). The percentage reduction is close to the average commission that travel and hospitality companies pay for electronic booking through other media (GDSes, Travel Agents, etc.). Fully, about 16 percent of the orders are obtained online in the travel and hospitality business.

The results show that the travel and hospitality industry is gradually making considerable strides in the digital marketplace. Companies are slowly realizing that many synergies can be derived by migrating their businesses online.

E-Business Functions

E-business activities cover the entire spectrum of functions an enterprise undertakes in its daily course of operations. AMR Research[1] categorizes these activities into three distinct areas: Supply Chain Management (SCM); Enterprise Resource Management (ERM); and Customer Relationship Management (CRM). Figure 7.3 illustrates the typical activities involved in any e-business, including hospitality and travel operations.

Supply Chain Management deals with the management of information related to the flow of material along the entire production cycle. This cycle begins with procurement of raw material (such as food and paper products), then moves into production for finished goods (such as in the kitchen), and finally ends with the delivery of the finished goods (such as menu items at guests tables). The demand cycle, on the other hand, is front-facing. It deals with the front part of the process chain where the consumers are the ones who

_____

[1] http://www.amrresearch.com

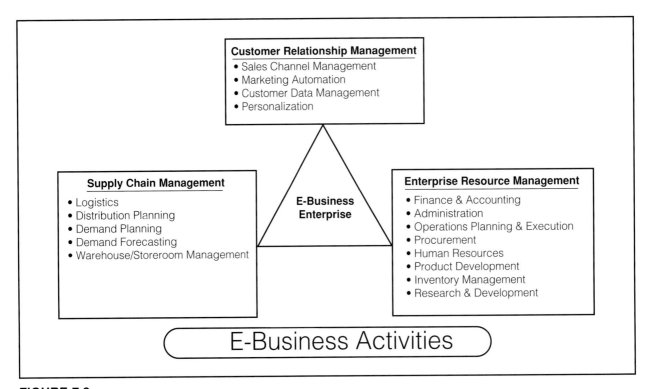

FIGURE 7.3

actually drive the demand for the products. In a restaurant, the supply chain is the vendors and food distributors that are suppliers of all raw material needed for food production. On the other hand, the consumers and syndicated data companies that provide market information can be seen as a part of the demand cycle. Typical activities in SCM include: logistics, distribution planning, demand planning, forecasting, and warehouse/inventory management.

Enterprise Resource Management originated from inventory management systems in the manufacturing industry. The logic was very simple. Each independent department in a company maintained its own applications and "silos" of information about all aspects of the business. Often this information was not available to other departments and was many times in conflict with information maintained in other departments. This created many problems, as an integrated view of the customer and the business was impossible under the circumstances. Some pioneering software companies then expanded the scope of inventory management software to also manage information across the enterprise so that the same information was available to everybody. This trend led to the development of a new generation of computer applications called Enterprise Resource Management or Enterprise

Resource Planning (ERP). The typical activities undertaken by such applications include managing data from finance and accounting, administration, operations planning and execution, procurement, human resources, product development, inventory management, and research and development.

Customer Relationship Management software is designed to increase customer intimacy and loyalty. The software enables a company to stay "close to the customer" in order to keep them satisfied and, hence, loyal to the brand. Many factors, such as increasing competition and globalization, are making such tools essential in the hospitality business. Companies are realizing that competing in customer service is more prudent than competing on price alone. The enhanced experience created by knowing more about the customer's preferences of room or food and beverage. Any special needs of the customers are also logged in for referral on the next visit. Multiple avenues are provided for feedback from the customers, including phone, fax, email, and Web-forms. All such information is stored in a central repository that can easily be accessed by everybody in the company using simple Web applications. Typical functions performed in this area include: sales channel management, marketing automation, customer data management, and service personalization.

Name_____ Date_____

Chapter Seven Review Questions

1. Describe how hospitality companies can save money by allowing consumers to book services online.

2. Who are the stakeholders/constituents of e-business?

3. Discuss the challenges for businesses that are trying to increase the availability of online services for their customers.

4. What are three of the benefits provided by e-business?

5. What impact does e-business have on consumer pricing?

6. What are three major challenges associated with managing e-business?

7. How do hospitality companies compare to other companies related to the amount of e-business generated?

8. Describe the three categories of e-business activities and how they interrelate.

9. What are the three major activities involved in e-business?

10. What are some of the functions performed in CRM?

11. What are some of the functions performed in ERM?

12. What are some of the functions performed in SCM?

13. What is the demand cycle?

Chapter **8**

Independent and Entrepreneurial Operations

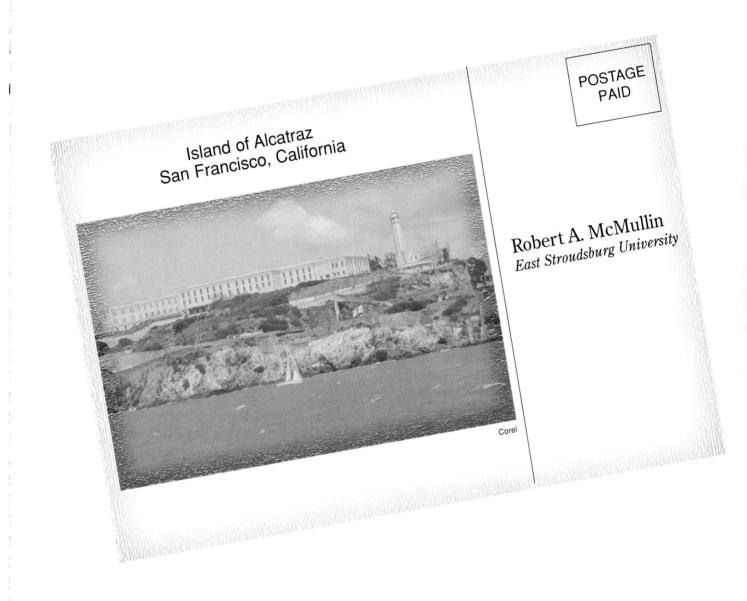

Island of Alcatraz
San Francisco, California

POSTAGE
PAID

Robert A. McMullin
East Stroudsburg University

Corel

If you like a challenge, if you are driven to succeed, and if you want to be rewarded for your accomplishments, you should consider becoming an entrepreneur or an independent operator in the hospitality and tourism industry.

Becoming your own boss is the American Dream and has become a reality for many in the United States in all types of businesses. This phenomenon began as immigrants relocated from Asia, Europe, and other parts of the world, during the industrial revolution in America. Throughout American history, nearly 40 percent of the top one percent of the wealthiest Americans were once small business owners (Messinson, 1997). Small business currently accounts for nine million self-employed Americans, and by the year 2005, this number is estimated to exceed 11.5 million persons (*Wall Street Journal,* 1995). During the last decade, small business created more than 63 percent of all new jobs in the United States and is responsible for 43 percent of the Gross National Product (Moore 1993).

A record number of new businesses were created in the 1990s: approximately 700,000 each year (Hiam and Olander, p. VII). New business development attracts and enriches a diverse cross section of Americans, offering more opportunity for women and minorities than corporate business does. Analysis of data from the U.S. Bureau of Census reveals that the number of women-owned, eating-and-drinking establishments climbed 41.4 percent between 1987 and 1992. Currently, women own more than 128,000 restaurant-oriented businesses, more than one-third of all such U.S. operations. Minority and female-owned food and beverage operations contribute to the estimated $399 billion in industry sales.

Predicted restaurant industry growth is 30 percent in the next two years (Bureau of Labor Statistics). Fifty-seven percent of those employees in restaurant occupations are women. This segment is eight percent of total United States employment (National Restaurant Association).

"Success in this industry is determined by hard work, not by gender," says Thomas Kershaw, Chairman of the Board of the National Restaurant Association, and president of the Hampshire House Corporation and Bull & Finch Enterprises, both based in Boston. "Whether they have climbed their way up the corporate career ladder, run the family-owned restaurant, or financed and built a business of their own, the unceasing number of women restaurant professionals prove that career opportunities abound in the restaurant and hospitality industry" (www.restaurant.org).

Opportunities for hard-working, innovative people to start a new company or work on their own are practically limitless in the hospitality and tourism industry. There are more than 30,000 bed and breakfast inns in North America, and the majority of them are independently owned. According to the National Restaurant Association, 45 percent of eating and drinking establishments are sole proprietorships (owned by one person) or partnerships (owned by two or more people).

The Terms "Entrepreneur" and "Independent Operator" Defined

An entrepreneur is defined as someone who starts, manages, and assumes the risks and rewards of a new business enterprise (Hiam and Olander, p. 1). Generally, an entrepreneur is not content with simply starting a new business; he/she also strives to achieve business growth. Thus, expansion into different geographic locations or into a variety of customer markets is included in the business plan of an entrepreneur.

On the other hand, an independent is a person who maintains a limit to the size and scope of the business operation. An independent operation means the owner or general manager directs a business that has no affiliation with any other facilities or operations. This is not to say that independents do not want growth, because they do. Growth is a desired element for the volume of business transacted by the independent business. However, expansion in terms of various locations is not a deliberate goal. Sometimes individuals successfully make the transition from independent to entrepreneur not by design, but by luck. For a fortunate few, the change means "financial rewards far beyond expectations." For example, Anne Beiler turned a mistake made by one of her suppliers into a nationwide specialty food chain.

In 1987, Beiler sold soft pretzels, pizza, stromboli, and ice cream at a farmer's market booth in Downingtown, Pennsylvania. Sales were not good from the start, so she was about to remove pretzels from the menu. Since time was of

Twenty-one million Americans made travel bookings online in 2000.

the essence, Anne experimented with various ingredients, while adding a few of her own ideas, and Auntie Anne's hand-rolled pretzels were born.

In 1995, sales for the entire company reached $81 million, and by 1996, sales topped $100 million. Her small, independent business grew from a farmer's market stall into 16 company-owned stores and 332 franchises because of an exceptionally novel idea: flavored soft pretzels. Anne Beiler did not actively pursue franchise growth, yet she continues to receive 20 and 30 calls each day from persons interested in opening an Auntie Anne's pretzel franchise (Fish 1996). As of 2002, her company supports over 700 Auntie Anne's soft pretzels stores worldwide (Auntie Anne: My Story 2002).

During 2002, Anne Beiler wrote and published an autobiography entitled *Auntie Anne: My Story.* The story is not a traditional autobiography, but a colorful children's book embracing strong work ethics and family.

Others who started with a good idea and saw it prosper into worldwide success were Tom Monaghan, founder of Domino's Pizza, Harlen Sanders who originated KFC (formerly the fast food chain called Kentucky Fried Chicken), and R. David Thomas, founder of Wendy's International, Inc.

Pros and Cons of Being an Entrepreneur/Independent Operator

Tom and Sue Carroll are the owners and independent operators of the Mainstay Inn, a Victorian-style bed-and-breakfast establishment located in Cape May, New Jersey. The inn was originally built in 1872 as an elaborate entertainment facility for wealthy businessmen of the era. By the time the Carrolls purchased the property in 1971, however, what remained of the grand villa with its 14-foot ceilings, elaborate chandeliers, and a sweeping veranda in the front was not much. But it did have potential, so the couple immediately started the task of restoring the building and its contents to its former architectural grandeur and historical significance. As a guest room or suite was reconditioned, it would be made available for guests who could recognize and appreciate the preservation efforts of the couple.

The innkeepers continue to add items or do a little wallpapering to the guest rooms and suites from time to time, but most of their effort now is taken up with hosting the year-round guests who want to relive (as much as they can) the opulence and splendor of the Victorian age. Having spent a quarter of a century revitalizing the inn, the couple now gets great satisfaction both from the structure that has been saved and from the guests who have come to expect the best in service and attention.

"One of the major advantages of being an independent operator of this kind of property is that we were able to use our own ideas, our own creativity, to produce a unique place of hospitality," said Tom Carroll. "And we certainly look at the guest coming to our inn much the same way we would if company was coming to our home. Guests who come here purposefully want to be in this type of atmosphere, and that is one of the most rewarding feelings you can get in this industry."

The Carrolls spend a great deal of time with their guests, particularly at breakfast and afternoon tea. Many conversations during these meals center around the efforts and the research involved in restoring the property to its current status. Other conversations are about the activities available in the seaside town or what it is like to be an innkeeper.

"There is incredible job variety in owning your own hospitality business," Mr. Carroll explained. "On a beautiful day I can always find work that has to be done in the garden. On a rainy day I can catch up on the bookkeeping. And at other times, I have had to learn about marketing, accounting, the ADA (Americans with Disabilities Act) requirements, fire codes, building restoration, furniture purchasing, decorating, and every type of maintenance skill needed to keep a lodging facility operating."

Being so involved in the property has its drawbacks, too. "One of the biggest disadvantages is that you are TOTALLY tied to your enterprise," Mr. Carroll emphasized. "When you develop your business around your own interests and personality, you have a great deal of trouble turning the entire operation over to someone else and escaping for a bit."

The couple has found a few employees who have the same intensity and understanding of its workings as they do, so they have been able to get away on occasion. But when they return, Mr. Carroll reports they resume their seven-day-a-week job with the intention of personally keeping the guests as happy and as comfortable as possible.

Knowledge, Skills, and Characteristics Needed to Open and Operate a Successful Enterprise

Being a successful entrepreneur or independent operator involves more than having expert management skills. An understanding of basic business procedures is essential, and knowledge about operating procedures in the specific field (i.e., hotels, travel agencies, fast food franchises) is also necessary. However, an individual must also possess a variety of personal characteristics to prosper as a business owner in the hospitality and tourism industry.

Hiam and Olander describe two categories of characteristics that researchers have found to be important in determining the success or failure of an entrepreneur. Leading the category of core characteristics is creativity.

Creativity, important at the outset, will also be necessary all along the way, from start-up through stages of growth and into maturity. Innovative ideas will enable you to set yourself apart from the crowd. Staying on top of technological changes is important, but is only part of successful business innovation. New approaches to customer service or quality, new distribution methods or packaging concepts, and many other options also exist for the innovator (p. xxiv).

Someone thinking about opening his/her own business should also consider the risk involved in undertaking such a venture. According to Hiam and Olander, the rate of business failures has doubled in the United States in the last decade (p. viii). Among the reasons for the surge in disappointing results: a more volatile marketplace, more frequent technological breakthroughs and commercialization, and global competition (p. viii). For the person who is uncomfortable with uncertainty, starting a new business is not recommended.

Being able to work alone is also a core characteristic entrepreneurs or independent operators must have to be successful. To get the work done, you must be self-disciplined; no one else will be setting your schedule. And, as the chief decision maker, you must trust your own judgment.

Most people understand that long hours are involved in establishing your own business, especially in the start-up phase. But the significance is not in the number of hours, but rather in their productivity. An individual must be determined to achieve success and must focus all activities on accomplishing the overall goal.

Above are all the major characteristics discovered to be common among successful business owners. Additional personality traits indicated as requirements by Hiam and Olander (1996) are good health, a realistic attitude, self-reliance, superior conceptual ability, self-confidence, a need to control or direct, an attraction to challenges, emotional stability, and self-control.

Clark L. Shuster, Director of the Lower Bucks County Chamber of Commerce, works closely with small businesses near a suburban Philadelphia region of Pennsylvania. Prior to his successful career in the Chamber of Commerce, Clark was a sales director for a prominent hotel chain in lower Bucks County. Because of his employment in the hospitality industry, coupled with involvement in Chamber of Commerce Committees, he was selected to become "The Director." The mission of the Chamber of Commerce is to aid and enhance small business development. This includes bed and breakfasts, inns, taverns, pubs, tour planners, and restaurants, as well as other independent and entrepreneurial operations.

Shuster credits his success to his hospitality coursework at Bucks County Community College and his bachelor's degree at Bloomsburg University of Pennsylvania (formerly Bloomsburg State College). As a Hotel Sales Director, he formed many business contacts, which ultimately endorsed his application to the Chamber of Commerce. Clark's advice to undergraduate students is to complete your education, get related hospitality experience, develop a strong work ethic, and network your contacts.

References

Megginson, W.L., et al. *Small Business Management/An Entrepreneur's Guide to Success.* 2nd ed. Boston: Irwin, 1997, p.4.

"Small Talk." *Wall Street Journal.* 6 July 1995, B2.

Moore, R. "Mr. Clinton, Please Check the Label." *Wall Street Journal.* 22 Mar. 1993, A14.

Hiam, A.W. and K.W. Olander. *The Entrepreneur's Complete Sourcebook.* Upper Saddle River, NJ: Prentice Hall, 1996, p. viii, 1, 24.

Fisk, H.C. "Twists of Fate." *Entrepreneur* (July 1996), p. 207.

Bieler, A., *Auntie Annes, My Story,* PA: Acorn Press, 2002.

Chapter Eight Review Questions

1. How many small businesses are in the U.S. now?

2. What are the projections for future growth of small businesses?

3. How do opportunities for women and minorities in small business compare to their opportunities in the corporate world?

4. What is the financial impact of small businesses on the economy?

5. Who owns the majority of Bed and Breakfast properties?

6. Do entrepreneurs typically stay in one location, or like to expand and develop other opportunities?

7. What are some of the advantages and disadvantages of being an independent operator?

8. Why would creativity be important at the beginning, growth, and mature stages of a business venture?

   Beginning

   Growth

   Mature

9. How does the characteristic of "working alone" impact the success of an independent operator?

Chain Operations

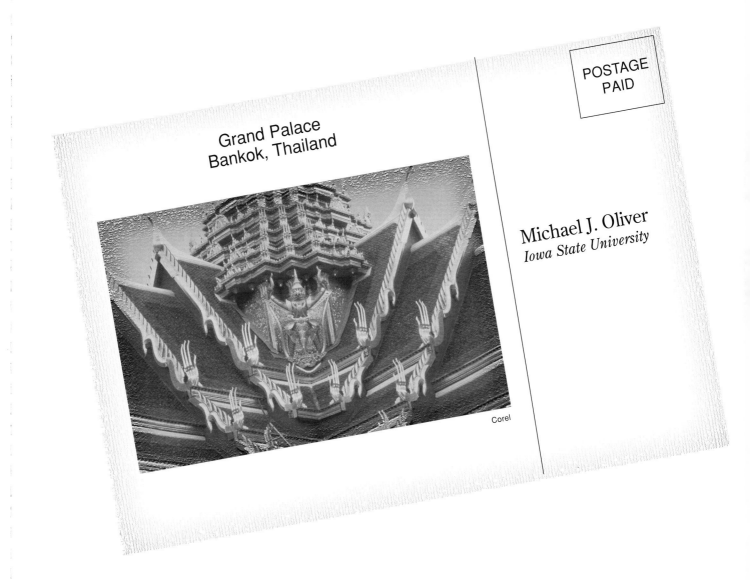

Grand Palace
Bankok, Thailand

Corel

Michael J. Oliver
Iowa State University

POSTAGE
PAID

Introduction

For many students, deciding to study the hospitality industry is based on a desire or goal to one day own and operate a restaurant. This may be a supper club, bistro, fine dining, or a quick service operation. Whatever the vision, with a successful restaurant concept, the next step may be to seek opportunities for growth of the business. This growth can come via expansion of existing operations or developing another restaurant with the same operating systems that brought success in the first facility. Soon, there may be a desire for a third and fourth restaurant. Now, the decision is whether to continue as a company-owned multi-unit chain or perhaps franchise your successful restaurant concept.

The scenario described above is not unlike that of any well known company-owned operations anywhere in the world. In fact, this was the goal of Mr. Kuni Toyoda, President of the Seed Restaurant Group, Inc., parent company of Fazoli's. As a Japanese student at a mid-western university, Mr. Toyoda's goal while attending college was to own his own restaurant by the age of forty (Toyoda, 1998). He and many successful hospitality industry leaders before him, Ray Croc, Colonel Sanders, and Dave Thomas, all started with a vision and built some of the best known chains in the world.

The chapter will discuss the common characteristics of company owned (chain) operations and the advantages they bring. For the most part, this discussion will pay particular attention to company-owned foodservice operations.

Defining Chain Operations

The first part of any discussion regarding chains or, for the purpose of this chapter, multi-unit operations, is to distinguish them from franchises. For many people, seeing a hotel or restaurant with the same name, identical layout, and serving methods represents a chain, and they are probably correct. Walk into any McDonald's Restaurant or Holiday Inn Hotel and you will recognize that each has the common characteristics of any of its namesake operations. However, what is not so obvious to the guests is the ownership of the operation. Yes, that typical McDonald's restaurant may, in fact, be part of a chain, but is most likely a franchised operation.

For example, today, nearly 70 percent of the over 30,000 McDonald's restaurants around the world are owned and operated by franchisees (McDonald's, 2002). In contrast, Darden Restaurants owns and operates each of the more than 1,200 Red Lobster, Olive Garden, Bahama Breeze, and Smokey Bones restaurants, and does not offer franchises domestically (Darden, 2002). Each of these name-brand companies are considered chains; however, each differs in the ownership of each operation.

Therefore, a chain can be defined as a business with three or more separate outlets baring the same name, concept style of service, and systems of operation (AAA, 2000). Many successful, independent restaurant operators will grow and open multiple operations throughout a city, state, or region under the same name. In addition, the *Dictionary of Hospitality, Travel, and Tourism* defines a chain as, "A Company that owns or has a financial interest in more than one unit/property. The underlying financial arrangement does not need to be advertised to the customers but in most cases the numerous units are promoted as such to stress availability and popularity" (Metelka, 1990).

Therefore, by definition, the above scenario of restaurants growth and development is considered a chain and again, quite typical of how chains are started. The problem here is that one really never knows who the owner is. As a consumer, we look for familiar symbols that give us a sense of security in how we spend our money. Therefore, we tend to purchase from operations with a recognizable name, which is a benefit that multi-unit operators have over an independent.

The alternatives to multi-unit operations would be a franchise, independent, and independent group. Although a franchise may be a part of a larger group or chain, it is owned by an individual, the franchisee, who pays for the rights to operate under the larger groups name, the franchisor, and its operating systems. The franchisee benefits from the success of the larger group, but must continually pay a fee, often a percentage of sales or profits, to the franchisor (Powers & Clayton, 2003, p. 1).

Independent operations and independent groups are similar in their ownership. Both may be owned and operated by an individual or group of individual investors. The independent owns one or two operations and enjoys greater business decision-making freedoms than that of the franchisee. The independent groups grow from successful independents by opening additional operations. While not quite a chain, they benefit because they have similar advantages while maintaining the "hands-on" control of an independent.

Planning for Growth

Successful restaurants all have an important and valuable common characteristic: consistency. In order to guarantee a guest's return patronage, the guest must know that their dining expectations will be met each time they visit. For example, people know that the Big Mac at McDonald's will be the same whether the restaurant is in Wisconsin or Pennsylvania. It is the consistency in product and service that have enabled chains to grow. Planning for growth requires planning for consistency.

There are many restaurants that have been operating for years by handing down the systems and procedures from one employee to another by the owner or long-time employees. Although this method may generate success for one facility, many of these systems and procedures may be lost or forgotten over time. Furthermore, some systems and procedures are often unique to one specific restaurant due to layout, size, and available equipment and, therefore, are not appropriate in a second facility. It is important, therefore, to plan, organize, and develop systems and procedures that have been perfected over time at one facility to insure consistency at the second, third, and fourth.

Many may recall their first job at the local quick service restaurant. Often, the first day on the job called for one to sit and read a procedure manual, view a training video, and possibly take a test on how to perform the duties in each position. These training methods are designed with one goal in mind, to ensure consistency in every restaurant. Each and every task had been planned and thought out to ensure the desired level of service, desired product quality, and cleanliness of environment for every patron.

These same systems of operation and procedures are the standard for which chain organizations evaluate their facilities in order to determine if each is maintaining the required level of performance. McDonald's, for example, evaluates their restaurants on the basis of how well each operation maintains their individual QSC, which stands for quality, service, and cleanliness. Each procedure for each position, if performed correctly, will produce the level of performance demanded by the organization. Some chains and franchise operations impose strict guidelines for non-compliance in maintaining certain minimum performance standards.

By consistently maintaining these performance standards, whether restaurants or hotels, chain operations have instilled an ideal or level of expectation in the traveling and dining public. The name of a chain and its reputation convey a message to guests. Whether it is Wendy's or Holiday Inn, people know what to expect. In contrast, the XYZ restaurant or hotel means nothing to the unfamiliar guest and their level of expectations.

Multi-unit Strengths

Whether hotels or restaurants, multi-unit operations possess several strengths over other types of ownership. Tom Powers and Clayton Barrows, arguably, identify seven strengths of chain operations. These are (1) brand identification, (2) site selection expertise, (3) access to capital, (4) purchasing economics, (5) central control and information systems, (6) centralized personnel administration, and (7) marketing strength (Powers & Barrows, 1999, pp. 118–121). However, with current sophisticated information technology, a service economy, and business specialization, four of these strengths—brand identification, marketing strength, purchasing economics, and access to capital—will virtually always remain direct strengths of multi-unit operations.

Brand Identification

There are many well known corporations that are recognized by a symbol or trademark. For example, the swoosh of Nike; the red, white, and blue wave of Pepsi; the orange roof of Howard Johnson's; the green Holiday Inn sign; and the golden arches of McDonald's. Each of these corporate trademarks represents distinct images to the consumer. Consumers use brand recognition as a primary reference point when spending discretionary money. The consistency discussed earlier is the key factor in developing the reputation and image for each of any name-brand company. Establishing a reputation for providing consistent value, quality, and service to the guest is paramount for multi-unit operations.

Marketing

You may ask yourself, what's in a name? A well known name can mean a lot to both the customer and the company. It is often said that word-of-mouth advertisement is the best form of advertisement. The truth is, *positive* word-of-mouth advertisement is the best form of advertisement. With multi-unit operations, the opportunity to demonstrate this positive experience is increased by the number of operational units. Brand recognition is, therefore, increased throughout the marketing area. Moreover, marketing and advertising costs can be spread out and divided among the units.

Purchasing Economics

Purchasing economics is perhaps the most valuable strength to any multi-unit operation. Because the multi-unit operators are purchasing products and services for several operations, substantial discounts can be negotiated with suppliers. Centralized purchasing practices allow chains to purchase products in larger volume and then redistribute the products among the many units of operation. This presents a significant challenge to the independent operator, who often pays more for the same products, to remain competitive with multi-unit operators.

Access to Capital

For those who have the goal of one day owning and operating their own business, it is somewhat reassuring that money is available from all types of lending institutions and for all types of small business ventures. However, multi-unit operators have greater access to capital because of their original operational success and greater assets for collateral. Naturally, with existing profitable operations, the multi-unit company is a lower investment risk to the lending institution. In contrast, the unproven independent operator is a greater risk, especially during the early years of operation. The United States Small Business Administration reports that over 55 percent of the small business eating and drinking establishments failed between 1992 and 1996 (Boden, Cited in SBA, 2000). Furthermore, of the small business failures, 85 percent did so in the first five years of operation (Saito, 1995).

Food Service

Of the nation's 870,000 restaurants with over $407.8 billion in sales, company-owned restaurants are among the top when it comes to pleasing the customer (National Restaurant Association, 2003). Each year, *Nations Restaurant News* ranks leading food service companies based on their system-wide sales. Accordingly, thirteen company-owned restaurant chains were ranked in the top 100 operations. Boston Market, with 707 units and owned by McDonald's, ranked 44th and was the highest ranking, company-owned chain. Cracker Barrel Old Country Stores (437 units); White Castle (359 units); Lone Star Steakhouse and Saloon (251 units); Luby's Cafeterias (213 units); Piccadilly Cafeteria (211 units); Romano's Macaroni Grill (177 units); O'Charley's (161 units); Longhorn Steakhouse (154 units); and perhaps most interestingly, ranked number 99 was The Cheesecake Factory with only 40 restaurants. This shows that a company does not need hundreds of outlets to produce high volume sales.

For company-owned food service operations, sales volume is not the only measure of a good company. *Restaurant and Institutions Magazine* (2002) surveyed customers to rank chain restaurants by the experience of food, service, value, cleanliness, and convenience. Once again, several of the above restaurant companies ranked at the

Segment	Restaurant Chain
Italian	Romano's Macaroni Grill*
Burgers	In-N-Out Burger*
Dinner House	The Cheesecake Factory*
Pizza	CiCi's Pizza
Chicken	Chick-fil-A
Family Dining	Cracker Barrel Old Country Store*
Sandwiches/Bread	Panera Bread*
Seafood	Red Lobster*
Steakhouse	Steak and Ale
Doughnuts/Cookies/ Coffee	Krispy Kreme Doughnuts
Mexican	Chevy's Fresh Mex
Ice Cream/Frozen Yogurt	Baskin-Robbins
Cafeteria/Buffet	Old Country Buffet

* denotes company-owned chain operations

top of their respective food service segment. Moreover, six of the thirteen chains are company owned.

In the *non-commercial* or *on-site* segment of the food service industry, there are three major leaders and company-owned operators. The Compass Groups PLC is perhaps the largest and is the parent company of Canteen Service, which ranked number one for system-wide sales for 2001 by *Nations Restaurant News,* Chartwells, Eurest Dining Services, and Morrison Management Specialties. There is also Sodexho Marriott with multiple ranking food service operations in education, healthcare, school, and corporate services. There is also ARAMARK, which ranked number 16 for food service sales.

Lodging

In 2001, the lodging industry generated sales of $103.6 billion with 41,393 properties and 4.2 million rooms (http://www.ahma.com/infocenter/lip.asp).

A 2001 study by J.D. Power and Associates ranked the top U.S. hotel chains based on guest satisfaction. The study identifies the top ranking hotels from 52 hotel chains in six market segments (Business/Travel Editors, 2001).

Market Segment	Chain
Luxury Hotel Chains	Four Seasons
Upscale Hotel Chains	Embassy Suites
Extended Stay Hotel Chains	Homewood Suites
Mid-Price Hotel Chains w/ Full Food Service	Courtyard by Marriott
Mid-Price Hotel Chains w/ Limited Food Service	Hampton Inn
Economy/Budget Hotel Chains	Fairfield Inn by Marriott

The American Hotel & Lodging Association, Information Center lists the top 50 hotel companies and their brand-name holdings. The top five companies are Cendant Corporation, Six Continents Hotels, Marriott International, Choice Hotels International, and Hilton Hotels International (http://www.ahma.com/infocenter/top50.asp). However, of these top 50 hotel chains, only Homestead Village, Inc., ranked 45, owns all of its properties. Two other U.S. hotel companies, Extended Stay America and Drury Inns, own all of their hotel properties according to their respective company Web sites.

References

Toyoda, Kuni (1998) Keynote Address, Upper Midwest Hospitality, Restaurant, and Lodging Show, (Toyoda, 1998) Presentation at UP SHOW.

MacDonald's Corporation, (2002). http://www.mcdonalds.com

Darden Corporation, (2002). http://dardenrestaurants.com/darden.asp

AAA Web Site, Retrieved January 13, 2003 from http://www.aaa.com/scripts/WebObjects.dll/AAAOnline.woa/1014/wc

Metelka, Charles J., (1990), *The Dictionary of Hospitality, Travel and Tourism* (3rd ed.). Delmar Publishing, Inc.

Boden, Richard J., (2000). *Analysis of Business Dissolution by Demographic Category of Business Ownership.* Retrieved January 14, 2003, http://www.sba.gov/advo/research/rs204tot.pdf

Powers, T., & Barrows, C.W., (2003). *Introduction to Management in the Hospitality Industry,* (7th ed.), New York: John Wiley & Sons, Inc.

National Restaurant Association, Industry Research. Retrieved January 13, 2003 from http://www.restaurant.org/research/

Allison Perlik, (2002). *The Strongest Links: Customers have their say, rating America's restaurant chains* [Electronic version] Restaurant and Institutions Magazine, March 1, 2002, http://www.findarticles.com/cf_ntrstnws/m3191/5_112/83586231/print.jhtml

Top 100, Nations Restaurant News, June 24, 2002. Retrieved January 13, 2003 from http://www.findarticles.com/cf_ntrstnws/m3190/25_36/87917850/print.jhtml

(Business/Travel Editors, 2001) J.D. Power and Associates: Top U.S. Hotel Chains Ranked on Guest Satisfaction; Nothing Shy of an "Outstanding" Experience is Key to Guest Loyalty.

Top 50 Hotel Companies, Retrieved January 13, 2003 from http://www.ahma.com/infocenter/top50.asp

Extended Stay America, Inc. (2002). http://www.extendedstay.com/investor.html

Homestead Village, Inc. (2002). http://www.homesteadhotels.com

Drury Inns, Inc. (2002). http://www.druryhotels.com

Chapter Nine Review Questions

1. Describe the differences between a chain restaurant and a franchise restaurant.

2. How can a guest walking into a restaurant operation tell who owns the property?

3. As a consumer, what do the familiar symbols and characteristics of a chain restaurant or hotel mean to you?

4. How does a potential franchisee acquire rights to open an operation?

5. What are the typical franchise fees?

6. Why is "consistency" important for growth to independent operators?

7. Why is "consistency" important for growth to the franchisee?

8. What is the ultimate goal of training?

9. What are performance standards?

10. How are performance standards measured in McDonald's restaurants?

11. If a franchisee of a restaurant or hotel property chose to not follow the performance standards of the brand, what would likely occur?

12. How do performance standards impact the brand's reputation?

13. What are the strengths of chain operations?

14. What are the strengths of independent operations?

15. How do the strengths of independent operations compare to the strengths of chain operations?

16. What are the advantages to "purchasing economics?"

17. Discuss the research provided on company-owned restaurants and sales. What apparent relationship(s) do you see?

18. Who are the three major leaders in the non-commercial food service industry?

19. Compare the restaurant industry to the lodging industry. Who has the highest sales volume per year? Why?

20. Compare the restaurant industry to the lodging industry. Which segment has more businesses that own all of their units? Why?

Chapter 10

Franchising and Referral Associations

Mayan Temple, Belize

Corel

POSTAGE
PAID

Richard J. Mills, Jr.
Seton Hill University

Both franchising and referral associations have played a major role in the development of numerous segments in the hospitality and travel industry. Over the past decade, hotel companies have used both franchising and referral techniques as the primary growth and development strategy to distinguish themselves from their competitors. Highlighting their brand names and levels of services has provided both owners and operators ways to strengthen their market position and generate additional revenue while using limited resources. Not all hotels that have the same name belong to a proprietary chain. Franchise chains and referral associations are comprised of properties that have the same name and design but are owned and operated by different parties. There is an important technical difference between a *franchise system* (in which the franchise company grants a right) and a *referral system* (in which a property and its ownership become members). However, operationally, there is not a great deal of difference; the significant difference is that the referral group is often characterized by greater owner autonomy.

Ice cream is what fueled the fastest growth in hospitality franchising.

Definition of Franchising

Franchising can be described as a method of distributing goods and services that allows the franchisee the right to establish and operate a unit, or units, of a hotel, restaurant, travel agency, or rental car company using the franchisor's name and business system. In addition, through contractual agreement and payment, the franchisee must agree to abide by all the standards and operational rules established by the franchisor. Simply put, a franchise is a license given by a company, or franchisor, and allows the franchisee to use the company's ideas, methods, and trademarks in a business. By paying a fee, a private investor, or franchisee, can obtain a trademark license, architectural plans, blueprints, designs, training, and operating methods.

Definition of Referral Associations

Referral associations provide the benefits of an international lodging affiliation while maintaining the independence of an individual hotel. Compared to a franchising system, a referral system promotes services to prospective customers in an efficient

manner with fewer stipulations than are required by a franchise system. By combining their resources, independent hotels can maximize their marketing potential through a central reservation system (CRS) and national and international marketing program in order to make their brand names more recognizable. This makes it possible for a company to compete with chain and franchise systems. Some travelers confuse chains, such as Holiday Inn or Hilton, with referral organizations, such as Best Western. A Best Western property is neither a chain hotel nor a franchise, but rather an independent member property of a cooperative association that is owned and run by its membership. The main function of the association is to conduct advertising and generate customer referrals for the member properties.

Like a national chain or franchise system, a referral organization promises travelers that they will encounter certain standards of service and sanitation at its members' facilities. By meeting these standards and paying annual dues to the organization, the property owners benefit from brand name recognition, national and international advertising, and customer referrals from the association's central reservation system. Best Western is the largest U.S. referral organization. The Golden Tulip network, headquartered in the Netherlands, provides similar referral services for properties throughout Europe and the Caribbean.

Definition of Hotel Representative

Like referral organizations, hotel representatives also operate reservation services on behalf of independent properties. A representative is a company that provides advertising services and books reservations for independent hotels. The representative receives a fee or commission for each reservation that it books. Unlike a referral organization, representatives do not impose quality standards on participating properties. Utell, which represents over 2,000 properties worldwide, is an example of a major hotel representative.

A Franchising and Referral Association Historical Design

Franchise Systems

The word *franchise* comes from the language of political science and refers to a right bestowed by some authority. When Kemmons Wilson developed a successful format for a motor hotel, he began to "*enfranchise*" others with the right to use Holiday Inn's name. To do this, he adopted a practice similar to "*referral groups*" already in existence and operated notably by Quality Courts and Best Western Motels (now Quality Inns and Best Western). At the time, as now, the franchiser provided the name and some managerial and technical know-how. In the motor hotel field, however, the role of the franchising company was crucial.

A National Identity and Brand Name

In a market of national travelers, the identity of individual property has limited meaning beyond local

Hotel and Motel Management's 2002 Limited-Service-Hotel-Chain Survey

2002 Rank	2001 Rank	Chain	Parent Company	Franchise, Ownership	Guestrooms	Properties
1	1	Days Inn Worldwide	Cendant Corp.	Franchise	163,725	1,938
2	2	Comfort Inn	Choice Hotels International	Franchise	131,354	1,706
3	3	Super 8 Motels	Cendant Corp.	Franchise	124,193	2,039
4	4	Hampton Inn/Inn Suites	Hilton Hotels Corp.	Franchise Own	117,056	1,136
5	5	Motel 6	Accor Economy Lodging	Franchise Own	85,424	815
6	7	Travel Lodge Hotels	Cendant Corp.	Franchise	46,148	574
7	9	Fairfield Inns	Marriott International	Franchise Own	44,900	471
8	8	Econolodge	Choice Hotels International	Franchise	44,592	725
9	10	Red Roof Inns	Accor Economy Lodging	Franchise Own	39,621	360
10	11	La Quinta Inns	The La Quinta Cos.	Franchise Own	39,307	301

Source: Hotel & Motel Management's 2002 Limited-Service-Hotel-Chain Survey, February 4, 2002.

townspeople and its frequent visitors. On the other hand, "Hilton Inn," or "Holiday Inn," conveys meaning to travelers from any part of the nation. To these travelers, the mere mention of these names suggests the kind, degree, and probable cost of services available.

National franchising companies spend portions of their own budgets on advertising in appropriate regional markets, national markets, and international markets. Even more significantly, most franchise systems levy an advertising fee on each franchise and pool these funds. Thus, the collective advertising fund makes it possible to purchase expensive ads beyond the capabilities of an individual property. These include such media efforts as commercials on national radio and television and layouts in national magazines.

Franchise hotel-motel, restaurant chains, and rental car companies also print national directories showing the location of each system's properties. Perhaps the most important services franchisers provide the guest are referral systems and quality assurance programs.

Referral Systems

When a guest wants to make a reservation, he or she can call a single number and either have a reservation at a distant point confirmed immediately or obtain help locating alternative accommodations. Once the guest begins a trip, accommodations for subsequent nights' stops are only as far away as the room telephone. Thus, once a hotel system has a guest patronage for a single night, it is in position to sell the guest all subsequent accommodations. Moreover, most referral or reservation systems are either computer-based or use a WATS (Wide area Telephone System) line. WATS systems permit leasing of telephone lines, which drastically reduce the cost per call for high-volume use.

The first successful computerized reservation system was Holiday Inn's Holidex. Each inn has a terminal connected to a central computer by telephone wires. For each day of the year, the local innkeeper "deposits" a certain number of rooms for each available type. The computer acts as a kind of "bank" or clearinghouse for Holiday Inns. The computer sells all rooms "on deposit" for the day in question without consulting the inn in which the

reservation is made. As each room is sold, the inn is notified of the guest's name, the type of room wanted, and other information (arrival time, etc.). This information is used to make up a reservation card for the arriving guest.

If the local innkeeper must increase or decrease the number of rooms available for a given day, or stop taking reservations entirely for that day, he or she sends a simple message through the inn's terminal to the central computer, which alters the number of rooms available as instructed. At the end of each month, the innkeeper receives a report of sales refused and can use this as a basis for planning sales strategies and front desk procedures, or for constructing additional rooms, if the demand is present.

Some chains rely solely on a WATS reservation system. Callers call an 800 number (at no charge to them) that reaches a central reservation office. Using leased WATS lines to reach the receiving property allows that office to call the property and secure a reservation, if possible, and then confirms it for the guest. (Some WATS systems also make use of computers and "deposit" rooms similar to the way the Holidex system operates, except that terminals are not present in all properties.) With either a WATS line or a computer-based system, an effort is made to accommodate the guest in a nearby property in the system if the guest's first preference is not available.

Inspection Systems: Quality Assurance

Almost all franchise and referral groups specify a minimum level of physical plant and service requirements before admitting a new operation to the system. These requirements generally include a restaurant, a swimming pool, certain types of furniture and fixtures, and such operating services as room service and 24-hour front desk.

In addition, to specify operating standards, a system usually enforces the maintenance of these standards through regular inspections made by either the system's inspection department or an established member of the system. The detail and care devoted to quality assurance by the modern hotel/restaurant chain system is based on chain or referral group inspection systems.

Marketing and Referral Organization

Organization	Date Est.	# of Properties	# of Rooms	# of Countries	Head Office	Web site
Utell	1930	7,700	1,500,000	180	Omaha, NE	Utell.com
Best Western	1946	4,082	309,371	83	Phoenix, AZ	Bestwestern.com
Golden Tulip Worldwide	1962	407	48,000	51	Hilversum, Netherlands	Goldentulip.com
SRS Worldhotels	1978	378	66,347	65	Frankfurt, Germany	Srsworldhotels.com
Leading Hotels of the World	1928	366	75,000	75	New York, NY	Lhw.com
Relais & Chateaux	1954	301	9,300	43	Paris, France	Relaischateaux.com
Small Luxury Hotels	1991	252	14,545	44	Surrey, UK	Shw.com
Small Luxury Hotels	1976	180	7,300	2	Arlington, TX	Budgethost.com

Source: Brymer R., *Hospitality and Tourism: An Introduction to the Industry,* Tenth Edition.

Modern Perspectives and Advantages of Franchising & Referral Associations

Advantages to Franchising

Companies who choose to pursue franchising do so for many reasons. From a franchisor perspective, it provides a relatively inexpensive way to build a business in a quick and efficient manner. The franchisor is able to enter the market without dealing with capital cost, time, and risk of having to finance and establish a business location.

The franchisor also benefits from additional income that is provided through fees paid by the franchisees. Start up fees, continuing regular fees such as royalties, advertising and promotional fees, as well as other fees are paid by the franchisees. These fees provide the franchiser with a large pool of funds for marketing efforts, as well as contributing to the bottom line of the business.

In addition, the franchisor will benefit from the ideas and innovations of the franchises. For example, many of Taco Bell's most popular menu items were created by franchisees. Franchising is truly an attractive way for business operators to enter the hospitality industry with a greatly reduced chance of failure. Traditional business studies have proven that somewhere between 25 to 30 percent of new businesses fail in the first year, and up to 70 percent fail within their first five years. However, the failure rate for franchised businesses is less than 5 percent. By purchasing a franchise, the franchised business buys the years of experience, tried and proven methods, and, most important, a well-known brand name. In essence, the franchisor is selling all the distinguishing characteristics of an already established business. This includes trade names, trademarks, architectural plans and specifications, procedures of service, marketing plans, and often proprietary computer systems.

Another benefit to franchising lies in the concepts provided through training and a variety of management support in the areas of accounting, data processing, legal services, real estate design, equipment, and marketing. In addition, the franchise has access to the purchasing system and power of the franchiser. These services become important to most business developers who buy franchises instead of creating their own concept.

Advantages of Referral Associations

Referral associations offer some of the same benefits as franchises, but at a much lower cost. A referral association may provide the independent hotel with increased visibility, marketing, and buying power, without the necessity of giving up control or ownership. Hotels and motels within a referral association generally share some sort of centralized reservation system and common image such as a logo or advertising slogan. The referral association publishes a membership directory, usually given away free or for a small fee to interested guests. In addition, the referral association may offer group buying discounts to members, as well as management training and continuing education.

Hotels and motels pay an initial fee to join the referral association and an annual membership fee. Generally, this fee is much less than that paid to become a member of a hotel franchise system. Size and appearance standards for member establishments within the referral association are less stringent than those found in the franchise agreement, so guests may find more variation between facilities than with franchise members.

In the United States, one of the largest referral associations is Best Western, with more than 4,000 properties in over 80 countries. Budget Host International and Best Value Inn are also large associations. Some referral associations appeal to particular specialty hotel properties, such as the 150-member Historic Hotels of America Association. The association lists hotels that are at least 50 years old, are recognized as having a historical significance, and have maintained their historic architecture.

Differences in Franchise Systems and Referral Associations Today

In most cases, it is hard to clearly define the differences between referral organizations and chain or franchise systems. Although a lot of the concepts are similar to franchise systems, there are some modern perspectives that set the two apart.

The typical referral association is a nonprofit affiliation owned by members of independently owned and managed lodging operations. Referral associations do not have shareholders or investors. Typically, administrative expenses are covered by fees paid by its members, rules, regulations, policies, and governance of the referral organization are determined by the voting members as a whole body. A typical franchise does not have as much voice because the franchise head office sets the majority of rules and regulations.

Membership and License Agreements

Referral systems are made up of member affiliates comprised of a group of businesses, which share similar ideas and interests. Franchising, on the other hand, is a license agreement between franchiser and franchisee. Franchisees are allowed to use franchisers intellectual property during the contract period in exchange for fees. Referral associations have fewer stipulations regarding architectural design, layout, and operating procedures, allowing more business freedom for owners and managers in the referral association.

Contract Arrangements

The contract period may clearly define the differences between the two types of systems by emphasizing length of time of the contractual agreements. Referral organizations have no long-term locked in contract period. Referral systems usually offer an annual fee or a renewal agreement. With proper notice, the referral organization is permitted to exit the system without penalties. In a typical franchise agreement, the contract period ranges from 5 to 20 years, and the franchise must pay a termination fee if the franchise decides to leave before the contract expires.

Payment and Fee Structures

For many hotel operators, the decision to join a referral association or franchise is dependent upon the fee and payment structure. In both the franchise system and the referral association, fees and payment structures are determined in most cases by the size of the property. Referral associations are based on the number of rooms in relationship to the fees and payment structure. Franchise systems, on the other hand, charge an initial fee, ongoing royalties, advertising fees, and other costs associated with assisting franchisees.

Financial Obligations for Referral Associations

Most referral organizations have three major financial obligations: *entrance fees, annual dues,* and *reservation fees.* Entrance fees are usually a one-time fee paid to the association at the time of application and are composed of two types: an affiliation fee and an evaluation fee. The evaluation fees are non-refundable, but the affiliation fees are returned if the prospective hotel does not meet the requirements. The entrance fee is similar to that of the initial franchise fee in which the franchise organization pays a one-time fee at the beginning of the purchase of the franchise itself. Both new and existing members are expected to pay annual dues. In most cases, annual dues are nonrefundable and are charged for each fiscal year, payable prior to the beginning of the fiscal. For partial membership, annual dues are prorated from the date the applicant signs the contract.

Reservation fees are based on the number of nights booked through the referral system's central reservation system. Association members are advised about detailed information concerning the number of room nights produced by the system, along with information about denials and regrets. Members of the referral association use these statistics to determine what percent of the hotel's occupied room nights come from the central reservation system.

Financial Obligations for Franchise Systems

Franchisors commonly require monetary contributions by the franchisees that encompass some or all of the following initial financial obligations: an initial franchise or license fee, training cost, on-site start-up assistant, and periodic royalty fees related to marketing. In addition, there may also be necessary initial payments to cover such things as equipment, supplies, and opening inventory.

The initial franchise or license fee is paid for the right to establish a franchise for specific length of time, with 15 years being the most common length. The typical franchise fee for hotels is between $25,000–$50,000, but can also range from $3,000 for an economy operation all the way up to $100,000 for an upscale hotel operation. For restaurants and food chain outlets, the fees will also vary from $10,000–$60,000. The average fee for fast food companies starts around $20,000 and can go as high as $200,000, depending upon location and franchise choice. The initial fees usually include items like site selection assistance, standard blueprints, training, operating manuals, and, in most cases, each franchise agreement stipulates clearly what is involved.

Once the operation is up and running, the franchisee pays additional fees to the franchiser. Total annual costs for hotel franchise range anywhere from 4 to almost 10 percent of room revenues. For most restaurants, the range is based upon gross sales. In both cases, the royalty fee is based on percentage revenues. The royalties are paid for the use of the trade name and for services performed by franchisors instead of franchisees creating their own concept.

Referral Profile

Best Western International

For more than 55 years, Best Western International has been a cornerstone in the lodging industry, offering its members a strong brand affiliation and global recognition without sacrificing individuality. With more than 4,000 properties in over 80 countries, Best Western International is recognized world-wide for its quality, service and value. Global reservation systems, marketing and advertising support, training, and quality standards put Best Western at the top of the leading referral organizations. Best Western, like many brands in the industry, has it all. But what makes Best Western International unique and a better choice is company structure.

Members Only

Best Western International is a non-profit corporation owned by its members who, in essence, are the final decision makers on everything that happens within the company structure. Seven Best Western members are elected to oversee the company, with assistance of more than 150 governors who represent smaller regions of the United States, Canada, and the Caribbean. Because the focus is on helping its members make money, Best Western offers a member friendly fee structure for membership, and reservations help to increase a member's total return on investment. Members work on a year-to-year commitment instead of long-term contracts of five or more years, which many franchisors require. The key to the ongoing success is the 99 percent membership renewal rate.

Looking Ahead

As the industry continues to grow, Best Western plans to increase its market share by targeting specific markets, where the brand is under-represented. In addition to expanding its new markets, Best Western also wants to expand its scope of membership to include larger players in the market.

As you can see, Best Western is not your ordinary hotel chain. Members can retain their individuality and still enjoy the benefits of a powerful global brand with multiple resources close at hand.

Franchise Profile

Baymont Inns & Suites

Never has a hotel brand been more prepared for the challenges of varied difficult markets than Baymont Inns & Suites. Baymont shares with its franchises the challenges faced in property operations that are not a concern for nearly all other hotel franchise companies. As owners and operators, as well as a franchisor, Baymont plays a unique role in an industry that thrives when the relationship between franchisor and franchisee is as close as possible. Baymont Inns & Suites is a division of Milwaukee-based Marcus Corporation. Marcus currently operates or franchises 190 Baymont Inns & Suites in 31 states.

Baymont Inns & Suites Advisory Council and Reservation Services

The Baymont Inns Franchisee advisory council works closely with Baymont management on the Brand's strategic direction and by offering advice in all areas that are important to Baymont Inns & Suites. The advisory council works with franchisees to help eliminate the roadblocks to development and to ensure their success.

Looking Ahead

In October of 2001, Baymont launched its association with InnLink Central Reservations Services, which offers reservation services on par with the big brands.

Conclusion

In a business environment characterized by increasing competition and globalization, both franchising and referral associations will continue to be powerful marketing strategies for the hospitality industry. Both franchising and referral systems will be faced with developing new and innovative marketing services. In the past, the primary role of franchising and referral systems dealt with processing reservations on behalf of individual members and franchise outlets. However, recent advances in electronic forms of communications and its related technologies have led to a revolution in information distribution. As a result, households have the ability to access a personal computer, and conventional methods of telephone reservations are preferred less by a growing number of consumers.

In this chapter, we have discussed the evolution and effectiveness of both franchising and referral systems. The description has emphasized the guest's needs and wishes and overall company variation. These needs include the purpose of travel and the needs of the community. In general, new marketing strategies and innovations have continued to evolve and emphasize an upgrade in amenities in both the franchising and referral associations today.

References

Allen, R.L. (1996, October 14). "Franchising relations: Is it a more level playing field?" *Nation's Restaurant News,* 30(40), pp. 94–115.

Bond, H. (1998, May 18). "Building a Brand." *Hotel & Motel Management,* 213(9), pp. 32–33.

Brymer, Robert A. Hospitality and Tourism: An Introduction to the Industry, Ninth Edition. Dubuque, Iowa: Kendall/Hunt Publishing Company, 2000.

"Hotel & Motel Management's 2001 Franchising-Fees Guide." (2001, March 4) *Hotel & Motel Management. Franchising Market Place* (2001. February 18) Company Franchise Profiles.

Morrison, M. (1989). Hospitality and Travel Marketing, Albany, New York: Delmar Publishing Company.

Powers, F. (1989). *Introduction To Management In The Hospitality Industry.* New York: John Wiley and Sons.

Name_____ Date_____

Chapter Ten Review Questions

1. Compare and contrast a franchise system to a referral system.

2. Describe briefly the history of referral systems.

3. What is the role of a national franchising company?

4. What services does the national franchising company offer to the franchisee?

5. How does a centralized reservation system work?

6. What are the typical quality assurance amenities offered by a hotel?

7. What are the different types of referral systems?

8. What is the typical time commitment with a referral system?

9. What is the typical time commitment with a franchise?

10. Identify and define the three major financial obligations a member has who is associated with a referral system.

11. Identify and define the financial obligations associated with franchise systems.

12. What is a royalty fee?

13. How much money, and to whom is a royalty fee paid?

11 *Contract Management*

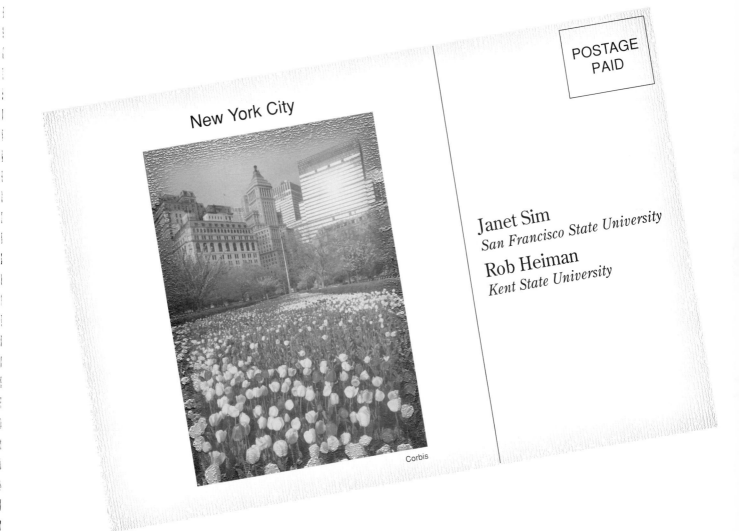

New York City

POSTAGE PAID

Janet Sim
San Francisco State University

Rob Heiman
Kent State University

Corbis

Contract management encompasses the management of services in a very broad range of settings. In the hospitality industry, it means that a contract, a mutually binding legal relationship, has been negotiated between the operator who furnishes management services to manage the foodservice and/ or lodging operation and the owner who pays for these services. Often one organization specializes in providing food, refreshment, facility, and other support systems that the "parent" or "host" organization is not an expert in the management of. The parent may operate a primary business with a mission, and expertise is in other areas. Parent organizations may include businesses in the non-commercial segment of the foodservice industry, such as healthcare systems, school districts, college campuses, conference and convention centers, national parks, sports and entertainment venues, correctional institutions, business and industry, and vending operations. Usually, the owner lacks either the expertise or the desire to manage the foodservice or lodging operation, and must, therefore, buy the service from a management company.

Foodservice Contracts

Before a discussion of foodservice management contracts can occur, several "new" or different concepts or terms needs to be examined. The following words are often used in the discussion of food service management contracts:

- Onsite—The opposite of the "commercial" segment of the food service industry, this term refers to the segment of food service which entails the operation of food services and other integrated services within the physical structure of the host organization whose primary mission is NOT that of food and beverage operation or service.
- Institutional Food Service—Once used quite often to describe this segment of food service, it refers to a segment of food service that we now define as the "contract food service" segment. The term "institutional food service" has be misconstrued and stigmatized negatively in the past.
- Independent Food Service Operation—Within the parent or host organization, the company operates their own food service, employing administrators and employees of the food op-

eration, maintaining total fiscal and operational responsibility within the parent organization.
- Self-op —"Self Operating"—Similar to the "Independent Food Service Operation," this term refers to the parent company choosing to take the full responsibility to operate the food service (or other integrated services) themselves.
- Management Contract—This refers to the actual agreement by the parent organization and the "food service management service" company, whereas responsibility for the operation and supplying of services becomes that of the food service management company.
- Captive Food Service—This is the segment of the food service industry where the customer has little or no choice in his or her decision to pay for and consume the food on a regular (or semi-regular) basis. In effect, the customers are a 'captive audience' for the food service operator. Examples would be a student within an elementary school lunch program, fans attending a professional sports contest, or a patient staying any length in a health care facility.
- Non-Captive Food Service—Similar to what is referred as the 'commercial' segment of the food service industry, this refers to all other operations other than the 'captive' food service operations, whereas the customer has definitive choices in his or her decision to pay for and consume the food he or she chooses.

Depending on the segment of food service, those companies opting for contracting versus self-op will vary. For example in the hospital segment, 30 percent are contracted and 70 percent are self-op. The opposite is true in the business and industry segment. (B & I) 80 percent are contracted out and 20 percent are self-op. Trends indicate more parent organizations are seeking management service companies to operate their food services. U.S. organizations now spend $300 billion to contract out their "non-core" functions to management contract organizations. The companies listed below are the 2002 leading food service contract-management companies with their total of U.S. food service contracts (each contract will vary as to their generated level of sales dollars):

ARAMARK, Philadelphia, PA	5,875
Compass Group North America, Charlotte, NC	26,626
Delaware North Companies, Buffalo, NY	225

Sodexho USA, Gaithersburg, MD   6,000
HMSHost Corp., Bethesda, MD   82
Volume Services America, Spartanburg, SC 128
Bon Appetit Management Co.,
    Palo Alto, CA   150

To illustrate the scope of the "service management contract" segment of the food service industry, a quick profile of the ARAMARK organization is presented below:

- $8.77 billion world leader in providing managed services. 7,000 corporate locations, 300 healthcare facilities, 350 school districts, 400 colleges and universities, 70 stadiums, 27 convention centers, 14 conference centers, 15 national parks, resorts, and tourist attractions in 2002.
- Contracted to operate food service at several past summer and winter U.S. hosted Olympic games.
- Privately owned, principally by its employee managers (93 percent).
- 160,000 employees.
- Founded in 1936 as a food service and vending operation.
- Operates in over 25 countries.
- Reported 13 percent increase in sales over year 2001.
- Recently (2002) enhanced their long-term contract with Ford Motor Company, resulting in over $1 billion dollars in sales.
- Ranked by *Fortune Magazine* as one of the top 50 "Most Admired Companies in America."

Hotel Contract Management

The hotel industry has undergone a constantly changing situation in the last two decades. In the 1970s and 1980s, the hotel industry experienced prosperity, and the number of hotels expanded rapidly. Much of this development was undertaken by people who were not experienced in hotel operations. The hotel owners invited management companies to operate the food service and/or lodging operations for a given monetary consideration.

The number of hotel management companies multiplied rapidly until the recession and the Persian Gulf War. The hotel industry was faced with financial difficulties and distressed properties. While the 1980s were characterized by contracts weighed toward operators, the early 1990s revealed a resurgence of owner rights. The economic prosperity in the 1990s contributed to growth in contract management for lodging needs.[1] While the industry is currently optimistically waiting for its rebound, there has been a turnaround in the way management companies think and operate.

Length of Contract Terms

Management companies used to run hotels under long-term management contracts. Some of them have kept their contracts for as long as three decades. In the 1990s, lengths of initial contract terms and number of renewals decreased for both chain and independent operators. Shorter terms and fewer renewal periods have created flexibility for owners, but increased the operator's sense of urgency to perform well.

Length of term correlates with whether the operator represents a brand name. A survey conducted by the Hotel Asset Managers Association (HAMA) in 1999 showed a bimodal distribution that two distinct groups have emerged. One set of contracts for independent operators favors an initial term of less than six years. The other set of operators representing brand operators provides for an initial term of 20 or more years (Johnson, 1999).

Management Fees

Management companies typically receive a base fee and often an incentive fee. *Base Fee* is a percentage of total revenue, averaging between two to three percent of gross revenue. Management contracts, which provide automatic base fees, are a thing of the past. There is a continuing downward trend in base fees. *Incentive fees,* which began in the late 1980s, are generally based on performance improvement after at least a year. Incentive fees are typically calculated as a percentage of the amount over a specific goal, a percentage improvement in gross operating profit, or a percentage of net operating income (Sangree & Hathaway, 1996). The most common method of structuring incentive fees is to set those fees as a percentage of a given net-income line. There is a reverse correlation between the level of the base fee and the levels of incentive fees. Thus, the lower the base-fee percentage, the higher the incentive-fee levels (Johnson, 1999). While contracts continue to have low base fees, in-

---

[1] Trends and Stats (2002, March). *Hotel and Motel Management,* 217 (4): 24.

A school lunch program is considered a captive food service operation.

centive fees continue to be more important, particularly for full-service hotels. With the management fee weighed toward net income rather than total revenue, it is in the management company's interest to operate as profitably as possible. Competition among operators for more contracts has also intensified, setting off a fee war among operators who find they have to bid lower and lower on fees to obtain additional contracts.

Loan and Equity Contributors

Another aspect of changing hotel management is that management companies have become owners. Loan and equity contributions from the management companies have been a source of negotiation for a long time. With increased competition in the industry, management companies contribute more equity or loans to the hotels before they get major contracts that are longer terms with higher incentive fees. Many management companies would rather not make any equity contributions to the properties. On the other hand, equity participation inspires them to perform better, since their own money is at risk. Therefore, they become owners and risk-takers, not just fee-takers. Johnson (1999) reported a reverse correlation between contract

length and whether the operator contributed equity. Independent operators who generally sign short-term contracts have a greater propensity to contribute equity.

Performance Clause

To protect against poor management, the owner may also require the management company to agree on a performance clause. Such a clause may specify that if management does not achieve a pre-agreed level of financial results for a specified number of consecutive years, the owner then has the right to terminate the contract (Hotels, 1995). There are a number of criteria utilized to structure a management company's performance clause. However, they typically contain four components: criteria standard, such as revenue per available room (RevPAR); implementation period, which is usually one to three years to achieve the specified standard after taking over the operation of the property; ability for the operator to cure the default in the event they missed meeting the standard; and a list of exceptions that allows an operator to perform below a standard in the event there are circumstances beyond the operator's control (Hotels, November 2002).

Management Companies in the Lodging Industry

There are two types of hotel management companies. First, most chain organizations, such as Marriott International or Sheraton Corporation, serve as management companies for hotels under their franchises. The others are independent management companies that are also able to operate properties under several franchises. In the August, 2002 issue of *Lodging Hospitality,* the top hotel management contract companies were ranked, based on the total rooms in their portfolios. Starwood Hotels and Resorts was ranked at the top with 124,698 rooms managed. Interstate Hotels and Resorts was ranked second with 86,256 rooms managed.

Some of the companies have taken on new roles, such as forming financial programs with brokerage houses and offering loans to owners who wish to seek financial support. These giants also make equity investments in participating properties. Some of them offer special services to handle a wide range of management services.

Choosing a management company can be overwhelming for an owner because of the large number of companies that exist. However, it also can be rewarding when an owner can successfully find the best management company to operate the property.

Current Trends

Hotel owners are now taking a much more active role in overseeing functions of their management companies. Perhaps the greatest change in the 1990s' hotel management contracts involves owners' increased ability to review and approve key management positions, budgets, and marketing plans (Johnson, 1999). With the recent influx of litigation between hotel owners and their management companies over suspected contract violation, fraudulent dealings, and management, owners now want more control over their assets. Owners want more say in decision making, budgets, and capital improvements. They may approve budgets, change executive committee members, and renegotiate contractual rights on policies and procedures (Hotels, October 2002).

The recent trends of management companies have been toward higher and more structured performance standards. Owners are also demanding lower management fees, shorter contracts, special services and greater returns on investments. Balance of power is shifting, as owners vie for more control over their hotels as they become more knowledgeable and an increased voice in decision-making about how their hotels are run.

Career Opportunities

The career opportunities and career paths within "contract management" companies are often the least known by students in academic programs of hospitality management.

Some of the Positive Aspects of a Career in Contract Management

1. Diverse operations. Often the contract calls for quick-service, cafeteria service, fine-dining, off-premise catering, and other industry components all within one operation.
2. Relatively "normal" hours of operation. As opposed to other facets of the hospitality industry, "institutions" operate closer to a "regular" work schedule.
3. Corporate and large organizational support. Corporate training, fiscal, and operational support pieces are often in place for the contract food service manager.

Some of the Challenging Aspects of a Career in Contract Management

1. With many components of the operation, organizational skills are critical. The ability to coordinate and manage different types of operations is an everyday occurrence in contract management.
2. Marketing challenges due to competition both from the "self-op" initiatives, as well as external food service operations in competition with the consumer dollar.

Conclusion

Based on survey studies, onsite (contract management) food service as a career choice is portrayed as a desirable, personal-life-friendly, career path with greater challenges and opportunities than it is often given credit. Quality of life, working with people, good benefits and salary, and opportunity for career advancement are the most frequently cited reasons for satisfaction of people in management within this segment of the food service industry. Although not receiving the glamour and excitement of the commercial segment of the food service industry, the management contract business is an exciting and dynamic opportunity for students of hospitality management. Recently, contract management companies have been acquiring a diverse set of new contracts, therefore expanding numerous present and future opportunities.

Studies indicate that when a student experiences contract food service management before he or she makes a first "real" commitment to full-time management, they are much more likely to stay with contract management as a firm career choice, as the great quality of life benefits and advantages over commercial food service become evident.

References

1. "Global Update: In the Owner's Court." (2002, October) *Hotels*, 36 (10):12.
2. Johnson, K. (1999, April). "Hotel Management Contract Terms: Still in Flux." *The Cornell Hotel and Restaurant Administration Quarterly*, 40(2): 34–39.
3. Rushmore, S. (2002, November). "Performance Clauses Essential in Contract." *Hotels*, 36 (11A): 36.
4. Sangree, D. J. and P. P. Hathaway. (1996, October). "Trends in Hotel Management Contracts." *Cornell Hotel and Restaurant Administration Quarterly*, 37(5): 29.
5. "Tips on Selecting a Management Company." (1995, September). *Hotels*, 29 (9): 40.
6. "Top Management Companies." (2002, August). *Lodging Hospitality*, 58(11):56.
7. "Is onsite hiding its light?" (1998, October) *Food Management*, 34–43.
8. ARAMARK.com (2002, December).
9. Restaurant Voice (2002, December) "Career paths in Contract Management."
10. Restaurants and Institutions (September 15, 2002).

Name _____ Date _____

Chapter 11 Review Questions

1. List seven types of businesses where you would likely find a contract management food service company.

2. List three types of businesses where you would likely find a contract management lodging company.

3. What is "self-op?" Why might a business not care to engage in it?

4. Within the hospital industry, how do the numbers compare between self-op and contract management?

5. Within the business and industry (B&I) segment, how do the numbers compare between self-op and contract management?

6. In your opinion, why is there a difference in number of contract management food service operations between hospitals and business and industry (B&I)?

7. Describe the trends seen in hotel management from 1970–2000.

8. What is a base fee?

9. How much is a base fee, typically?

10. What is an incentive fee?

11. How is an incentive fee typically calculated?

12. List the major components of a management company's performance clause.

13. Give two examples of who would be "owners" and two examples of "management companies."

14. What are three of the benefits of working in the "contract management" segment of the hospitality industry?

Part III
Hospitality and
Tourism Operations

12
Human Resource Management

13
Principles of Marketing

14
Principles of Management

15
Physical Plant Management and Security

16
Revenue and Cost Management

17
Law and Ethics

Chapter **12**

Human Resource Management

Twelve Apostles
Port Campbell National Park, Australia

Corel

John M. Wolper
Paula Wolper
University of Findlay

What is human resource management? It is the department within the organization that handles the paperwork regarding selection, termination, legal mandates, benefits, training, and compensation. In the past, this department handled these responsibilities following policies formulated by top management. Today, human resource (HR) managers no longer just follow policy. They are also responsible for formulating policy and assisting with strategic planning related to department functions. Although the HR department performs these functions, there is more to human resource management than paperwork. These departmental functions will be discussed; however, the reader must understand that HR goes beyond the functions of any department and is the responsibility of all supervisors/managers and every worker within the organization. Human resource management is concerned with the management of and caring for the hospitality businesses' most important asset—the people who work for the organization.

J. W. Marriott, founder of the Marriott Corporation, is noted for saying that if a company takes care of the people who work for it, then the people will take care of the company. This translates into a well-balanced 360° company/employee/customer relationship that can be evaluated at any of the three levels. To play a productive role in the organization, HR must be involved in activities to enhance the ability of the company to meet the needs of the guest, while satisfying the needs of the worker. As in every department, customer satisfaction is the bottom line. Simply stated, *human resource management is the process of how organizations treat their people in order to accomplish the goals and objectives of the firm.*

How Human Resources Is Involved in Every Supervisory/Management Position

The HR department works in concert with all management at every level. HR plays a critical role in keeping all managers and supervisors appraised of changing legislative and court judgments that affect management functions. The HR department may be responsible for recruiting prospective employees, performing initial interviews, completing reference checks, and completing the appropriate paperwork. However, the manager or supervisor of the department where this employee will work makes the outright decision regarding the hiring of an individual. This is not the only area that must employ a combined effort, and from this you can see that the HR department and all managers must work closely together to achieve the employment goals of the organization, which should be to hire the very best you can and keep them for a long as possible. Economies of scale are critical to the cost effectiveness of the HR tasks no matter who is responsible, yielding appropriate cost control management. Retention is vital to reducing hiring costs.

In a small organization, there is no formal HR department. Those responsibilities are relegated to the operational management or owners. Here the organization's management staff is responsible for all of the HR functions, along with all of the other management functions relegated to their duties. Managers in a unit of a multi-unit chain find themselves responsible for the day-to-day functions; however, an HR department at corporate headquarters backs them up. In the latter instance, the management staff must play a more active role in HR activities due to the distance from the corporate HR staff. Looking at this example more closely, we observe that the selection procedure, in this multi-unit situation, finds the management responsible for all selection functions, such as recruiting, interviewing, completing reference checks, making the final decision, and completing the paperwork. The HR department at the corporate office plays more of an advisory role and is responsible for the upkeep of the appropriate files and keeping unit managers aware of current accepted hiring practices, as well as legal issues. As you can see from this example, it is critical that all management personnel have a thorough understanding of the functions involved in the management of human resources.

This is a shift from what we were accustomed to in years past. Corporate offices were attempting to control too many of these critical functions, and they often failed. Today, the cost of making mistakes does not afford organizations the luxury of simply hiring someone else to do the job. While there are still attitudes that exist in the hospitality industry that good employees are easily replaceable, they are becoming passé thoughts, as they are very outdated and costly to the company.

Human Resource Department Functions

Planning

As a management function, planning is one of the most important activities. This certainly is the case in the HR area. The HR department must not only attempt to predict future employment needs, they must also look at future trends to prepare the staff and assist the company with growth. Therefore, the HR department cannot work in a vacuum. They must work with all departments to assess employment needs. Additionally, they must be kept updated regarding industry shifts to enable them to assist the workforce in handling the ongoing changes. Moreover, they must remain competitive with wages in order to attract the best and the brightest to our industry.

Before an organization can determine how many people are needed to meet the demands of the business, planning functions are necessary to determine what work must be accomplished, how the work should be completed, and the skills necessary to complete the job. There are tools available to the HR professional to fulfill these tasks. The first is *job analysis*. This is a process to determine the tasks and skills necessary to complete a job. This analysis allows us to write job descriptions and job specifications. *Job descriptions* identify the purpose, duties, and conditions under which jobs are performed. *Job specifications* are the qualifications, knowledge, and skills necessary to perform the position. Job descriptions and specifications are the basis for advertising positions, selecting, training, and evaluating.

Determining how the job should be performed is the function of *job design.* This looks at how the job is organized and how it can be planned to provide both productivity to the organization and the most job satisfaction to the employee. Once essential qualifications needed for the job are identified, you can then determine the type of position in the organization and how many people are necessary to fill the vacancy. Additionally, these tools assist in determining where and how to recruit, the criteria to select employees, and the training methods necessary.

Staffing

Once the organization determines the number and type of employment positions available, the task of staffing for these positions begins. This includes recruiting candidates for the positions and selecting the best person for the position, while working within the guidelines set forth in both federal and state laws.

A thorough job of recruiting must be performed to afford the organization the best choice of available candidates. Selection is not as easy as putting an ad in the paper and choosing a new employee from the stack of applications. The key element is finding the right employee for the job. The labor market demonstrates fluctuations dependent on the economy at any given time. When the economy is tight, there are more applications; however, when the economy is booming, it is often difficult to find qualified personnel to fill the vacancies. Not only does the economy impact the number and quality of the potential applicants, the sometimes-negative perception concerning employment in the hospitality industry can also affect the pool of qualified applicants. We employ many entry-level employees in minimum wage jobs; this makes the challenge significantly greater for finding the right employee for every position. Given these variables, the current labor market conditions and shifting dynamics inherent in the labor force, a company today must go well beyond the traditional want ad and look for innovative ways to attract good employees. The scope of this introductory article prohibits describing the vast pool of creative methods for finding and keeping good employees; however, it is safe to say, several hospitality firms have had much success with a variety of programs designed to attract and retain competent workers and managers.

One increasingly popular tool is the Internet, with many Web sites available for the job seeker to research companies and pursue lists of jobs available. There are also services available to showcase the talents of the job seeker to any interested employer.

Once the company receives the individual's application, the task of interviewing begins. Many interviewing styles may be used; however, the overriding concern is to ensure fairness to the applicants and achieve the best match for the job. The interviewer must be sure they do not ask any questions that could be considered illegal or discriminatory in nature. Courses in human resource management will reveal key areas for design of the interview in depth. Often, one of the functions of the HR department is training the interviewing managers in the proper methodology to conduct the interviews. One must also try to structure the interview in such a way that you can compare the candidates' qualifications without bias. Increasingly, behavioral or situational interviewing methods are used. These methods show greater validity (via statistical accumulation) in choosing the right person for the job. Other tools being used to help in the decision-making process are checking references and administering a number of pre-employment tests. Many organizations today are employing outside firms to administer appropriate personality and honesty tests in order to obtain unbiased information suitable to a particular job and/or company. The goal of this process is to find employees that will enjoy their work and fit well into the organizational structure.

Turnover and Employee Loyalty

Failure to adequately perform the recruiting and selection processes will often lead to unnecessary turnover. Turnover is the term used to describe the situation when an employee leaves and must be replaced. Turnover is an expensive occurrence, as the company must not only go through the entire recruitment and selection process once again, but it must also retrain a person for the position. Frequently, this ongoing training may produce negative effects of inefficiency until the new employee can achieve the expected level of productivity that the departed employee demonstrated.

Another expense to the organization is the time a manager needs to oversee this process. The replacement also takes a manager away from other responsibilities in situations where a manager performs all of the recruiting and selection duties. Previously, turnover was an accepted occurrence in the hospitality industry because there were always new bodies to fill the shoes of the departing employee. However, this is not always the case. Therefore, more companies are emphasizing the need to select new hires wisely and to put programs in place to retain the existing employees.

Retention programs can focus around activities such as softball leagues and opportunities for socialization. Still, it is widely believed that the best method to enhance employee retention is an atmosphere of fair treatment, where employees enjoy working, where they feel they make a difference, and are rewarded based on their own individual needs. Because employee satisfaction is an ongoing process, managers will need to continually monitor the climate as new generations come into the labor market. The tangible and intangible assets of the job are becoming increasingly important to successful retention programs coupled with creative packaging that either entices and/or satisfies the employee. A *value-added relationship* is the term of the day, not only from a consumer perspective, but an employee perspective, as well.

Legislation

Organizations, in managing their employees, must comply with many laws, regulations, court decision, and mandates arising from the social legislation, most of which were developed after 1960. Personnel departments had to become much more professional and more concerned about the legal ramifications of policies and practices enacted by their organizations. All management and supervisory personnel must continuously be updated and coached with regard to the legalities of the ever-changing fabric of our work environment.

Sweeping federal legislation that forever changed the standards for employment in the United States was passed under the Johnson administration. The impetus for this change was the Civil Rights Act of 1964. This act prohibits discrimination on the basis of race, color, religion, sex, or national origin and has become the cornerstone piece of legislation protecting workers and their rights.

Key governmental agencies generally impact many HR activities. The HR professional must be familiar with many of these agencies and their functions. Among the more important ones to be familiar with are the Equal Employment Opportunity Commission, Occupational Safety and Health Administration, Immigration and Naturalization Services, the Department of Labor, and the various state and city equal employment commissions and human or civil rights commissions. If the individual entrusted with the legalities of employment fails to maintain an awareness of current laws and regulations either through an HR department or individual actions, organizations may find themselves faced with costly lawsuits and significant fines. Much of this can be avoided by constantly monitoring the legal environment, by complying with changes, and by careful management of employees. It is important to note here that even today many of the individuals who work in the hospitality business are not formally trained. Our industry is still plagued with individuals who, more than likely, out of a lack of education, fail to uphold both professional and legal standards as set forth via legislation.

Evaluation

Employee evaluations take place after an employee has been selected, trained, and on the job for a period of time. Today, most jobs have a 30–90 day evaluation period. It is during this period that certain benefits may be withheld and the promise of offering continued employment non-binding. This means that termination may occur for stipulated reasons anytime during that evaluation period. Evaluations have many organizational purposes. They can be used to determine if the employee may require more training, is in the best job for him/her, or is ready for a promotion, incentive pay, or any situation based on job performance. The best reason to evaluate an employee's performance is for official feedback; however, this should be the official documentation. The employee should be receiving feedback concerning performance on a regular basis. A significant reason for discontent on the job results from an employee not being aware of how they are doing on the job, and this feedback must be completed in a timely fashion. This is just like a student's desire to know where they stand regarding a grade in any given class. Evaluations play a significant motivational role by encouraging employees to improve on their performance based on the outcomes of the evaluation. The HR department's role in this process is one of providing the form and filing the evaluations for future reference, as well as training managers how best to complete the process. Evaluations are usually completed and administered by the employees' supervisor. There are a variety of evaluation types used for different reasons, but for the purpose of discussion, we will use the 360° evaluation as the most optimal method of total performance evaluation. A 360° evaluation is where the supervisor evaluates the employee performance as do the employees they supervise, peers, and customer evaluations. However, most organizations would not undergo such an exhaustive review of every employee due to the expense and time involved.

Employee evaluations also are used as backup documentation necessary if an employee is terminated based on performance. Although there are provisions for "employment at will" that allow an employer to terminate employment at the employer's discretion, most employers prefer to have a policy in place where an employee's performance is scrutinized, warnings are given, and an opportunity for retraining is provided before that termination takes place. This is also known as a progressive discipline policy. In this scenario, the evaluations serve as documentation if the former employee brings forward discrimination charges.

In many organizations, employee evaluations are the link between performance and pay raises. This makes it critical that the evaluations are performed in an impartial manner to ensure consistency regarding compensation across all areas of the organization. This approach of identifying employees who are performing at or above expected levels and providing them with increased wages is referred to as merit pay. You must make every effort to evaluate the employee on the promised anniversary date, as it is one of the most contentious complaints employees levy against their supervisors. Failing to evaluate and process the appropriate paperwork is essential to maintaining a professional posture and image.

Compensation and Benefits

Employees receive compensation for the work that they do in three ways—direct compensation (often referred to as base pay), merit pay (previously discussed), and benefits. The motivational effect of wages is often debated, but within the scope of this discussion, employers continually look for better methods of materially rewarding people for the work they do. Each form of compensation was introduced as a motivational tool. Benefits are introduced in this fashion and used to motivate or entice persons to work for their company; however, today benefits are often taken for granted and act more as a deterrent, if absent, than as a motivational tool. The predominant focus on wages today is that of merit pay, where only expected and above-expected performance is rewarded above a base level.

One of the greatest challenges for the HR department today is finding and devising benefit packages that employees find attractive and that are affordable to the company. One of the most expensive components of any benefits package is the health insurance. As the cost of health care continues to rise rapidly, it becomes increasingly more difficult for companies to find insurance carriers with reasonable premiums. Companies are looking for innovative methods to solve this dilemma and must be sensitive to both the needs of the employees and the profitability of the company. As in other HR areas, some companies have found the way to balance both needs. Some organizations are outsourcing some portion of the HR functions. Each company must weigh the advantages and disadvantages of this move and proceed with the path that is best for that organization. HR professionals also look for a range of benefits that help employees meet personal goals and concerns. It should be duly noted, as in other HR areas, the overriding principle in compensation is one of fairness and equity and is the law!

Health and Safety

Organizations are obligated to provide employees with a safe and healthy work environment. Requiring them to work with unsafe equipment or in areas where hazards are not controlled is a highly questionable and often costly practice. It is also the responsibility of managers to ensure that employees are safety conscious and maintain good health. Preventative safety is often one of the best ways to avert an unsafe environment for the employee and the customer. Both the manager and the HR specialist are involved in health and safety practices in an organization. HR specialists coordinate programs, develop safety-reporting systems, and provide expertise on investigation, technical, research, and prevention methods. Managers coach, monitor, investigate, and observe employees practicing safety in the functional areas of the operation. Communication and good record keeping is vital in this area, as it is with any area of the business. A newer piece of legislation is the **Americans with Disabilities Act** or **ADA**, put into law by the Clinton administration. It calls for "reasonable" accommodations for both employees and customers who are functionally challenged. The term functionally challenged covers a wide array of physical and spatial challenges.

Conclusion

Much of what has been discussed in this brief overview of HR essentials is procedural in nature. Nonetheless, truly taking care of employees involves much more than a daily routine can provide. Hospitality organizations are dynamic entities. So are the individuals we seek to hire and have represent our organizations. Companies must be positioned to meet the needs of their employees every day. There can be no exception to this imperative. If your company does not provide and care for the employee, and consequently meeting the customer's expectations, then failure is eminent. Longitudinal studies indicate a direct relationship between a hospitality business's failure and poor management. The numbers of annual failures are staggering, with a clear majority of these failures pointing to poor management practices. There is always someone else out there who is able, willing, and ready to meet the challenges presented through the human resource functions.

The source of strength for successful companies is their ability to assess their surroundings and to adapt and change. In fact, a proactive posture generally accompanies these successful organizations. They are the industry leaders who remain in the forefront, representing the most successful hospitality businesses in the world today. The future is very dynamic, and you have a wonderful opportunity to be a part of all the excitement and promise that is yet to come. Don't forget, we are a people business, and we must take care of all the people who work for and utilize our places of business.

In conclusion, we should never forget that people have to eat and sleep, and that is our business. We will always have work, but choose wisely and act professionally. Remember, we are lifelong learners, and this process never stops. Keep yourself current and involved with your most important asset—your employees! It has been said many times before, "take care of your employees and they will take care of your customers!"

Chapter 12 Review Questions

1. Describe the duties of the human resource office.

2. Who typically does the actual hiring of employees?

3. Which operational department(s) does the human resources department work with?

4. In a single unit or small chain, who conducts the human resources functions?

5. In a multiunit chain, who conducts the human resources functions?

6. What business related items would the human resources professional need to consider in his/her planning?

7. Define the following:

   a. Job analysis

   b. Job descriptions

   c. Job specifications

   d. Job design

8. Describe the differences between job analysis, job descriptions, job specifications, and job design.

9. Describe three effective recruiting tools you have seen used in the hospitality industry.

10. What are the challenges of staffing?

11. Write two behavioral interview questions for an entry-level restaurant job.

12. Write two behavioral interview questions for an entry-level hotel job.

13. Write two behavioral interview questions for an entry-level tourism/travel job.

14. Create a list of at least six items that attribute to turnover costs.

15. List three of the acts or laws, which impact human resource practices in the hospitality industry.

16. What is the Americans with Disabilities Act?

17. How has the Americans with Disabilities Act affected the hospitality industry?

18. What is the purpose(s) of an evaluation after 30–90 days of employment?

19. Describe a 360-degree evaluation.

20. What are the pros and cons of a 360-degree evaluation?

21. Discuss the issue of employer/employee feedback. What is it? Why is it important?

22. Why is it important to an employee to be evaluated on a timely basis?

23. What are three different forms of compensation?

24. Describe several items one might find in a benefits package.

25. Give three examples of management's "taking care of employees."

26. Give three examples of employees' "taking care of the customer."

Chapter **13**

Principles of Marketing

Covered Bridge
Lucerne, Switzerland

Corel

POSTAGE
PAID

John C. Crotts
Stephen W. Litvin
College of Charleston

Richard G. McNeill, Jr.
Northern Arizona University

Introduction

Consider for a moment: The family who vacations at a resort for a week then returns home and raves about the experience to their friends; the association meeting planner who has just finished a successful convention; and the restaurant manager of a fine Italian bistro who has just opened a new account with a food wholesaler. At one time, all three of these satisfied customers were no more than a lead or prospect. In each case, someone in the marketing and sales department for the resort, the convention hotel, and the food wholesaler did something right in gaining these buyers' attention and winning their business.

Make no mistake, the hospitality and tourism industry is competitive, and customers have a tremendous amount of choice regarding with whom they do business. It takes more for a firm to be successful than to simply put an *open for business* sign in the window. It takes effective marketing and sales efforts to create the level of awareness, interest, desire, and ultimately action (AIDA for short) on the part of consumers in order to make a profitable and viable business.

The goal of all organizations is to create and retain satisfied, profitable customers. This is true whether or not the organization is a tourism destination, a national hotel property, a restaurant, or for that matter an owner-operated hospitality or tourism enterprise. For example, a hotel (which has supply) wants to sell rooms and other services to guests (who provide demand) at rates that both satisfy the guest and produce a fair profit. Bringing supply and demand together to make a profit is essential for any organization. Doing it in such a way that creates satisfied loyal customers is the key to long-term profitability. This chapter follows a framework that presents *marketing* and *sales* as an active *relationship development process* that links hospitality *supply* and *demand* in such a way that it creates *repeat patronage* and *positive word-of-mouth* (customer referrals).

The Marketing Mix

In today's marketplace, enterprises not in-step with changing consumer demands are quickly replaced by companies that understand their customers. Consumer's needs, tastes, and preferences are constantly evolving, and it is ultimately consumers who determine which hospitality and tourism products succeed. Only those businesses and destinations that can identify consumer needs and fulfill them more effectively than others in the marketplace will flourish. Success is accomplished, in part, through a mix of marketing inducements designed by the marketing and sales department to create and keep customers.

Operators of hospitality enterprises must develop a marketing strategy that will influence consumers to buy their products and services. In a single competitive environment, it is not surprising to find several unique approaches to the task. Some managers believe that the only condition needed to make a sale is to deliver a quality product or service. An example of this product-approach to marketing is the restaurant owner whose primary concern is the quality of the guest experience (e.g., food, presentation, service, and ambiance). By maintaining and improving the guest's experience in terms of the owner's own taste and preferences, the product becomes positioned in the marketplace. The approach can be successful if what the restaurant offers fits consumers' tastes. However, when these tastes change or increased competition occurs, a product-approach may become a blueprint for failure.

Another owner focuses his/her marketing efforts on advertising and promoting the restaurant in the marketplace. Since the restaurant's key measure of success is return on investment, investing in advertising and promotional campaigns designed to reach and influence potential customers appears logical. Over the past decade, numerous studies have reported the sources of information consumers are using in their decision making. In virtually every case, previous experience and word-of-mouth (recommendations from friends and relatives) have far and away dominated the response. Assuming that guest satisfaction contributes to both repeat patronage and positive word-of-mouth, perhaps the owner should find equilibrium between promoting the restaurant and ensuring a quality guest experience to best serve the restaurant's organizational goals.

It is not that either a product or promotional approach is wrong, but that each are only partly right. It is necessary that the product or service offered be of value. Only when customers begin to recognize the value of a product or service and begin buying it will you be in business. It is also necessary that the product or service is promoted effectively. Without information, the consumer cannot act; without promotions, the marketer cannot sell. However, even a combined product and promotional approach is considered insufficient in today's competitive environment. One must recognize that a successful marketing mix, like a recipe, is a blending of several ingredients to reach and satisfy customers at a profit.

The key to understanding the concept of the marketing mix is that it is a carefully developed reasoning process that is built solely around the consumer. By reasoning from the consumers' perspective, a marketing and sales manager can prepare a recipe for success (a mix of inducements to buy) that fits the needs and preferences of the target market more so than the competition does. The elements of this mix are traditionally referred to as the 4 Ps: product, place, price, and promotion.

1. Design or offer a **product** (good or service) that consumers want;
2. Offer the product in a **place** (both location and channel of distribution) that is both convenient and available to the consumer;
3. **Price** the product in relation to its value to the consumer and the prices charged by competitors;
4. **Promote** the offering to potential customers through appropriate and cost-effective activities (advertising, sales, and other forms of communication channels).

Leading hospitality and tourism enterprises have added additional "Ps" to the marketing mix. Some of these are:

1. A focus on the satisfaction of one's **personnel**, sometimes referred to as an organization's internal customers. As J. W. Marriott once said, "You can't make happy guests with unhappy employees." Likewise, Hal Rosenbluth advocates a philosophy that the "customer comes second," suggesting that satisfied frontline travel agents ultimately translate into satisfied Rosenbluth Travel clients. Both quotes illustrate the connection between employee satisfaction, customer satisfaction, and corporate profits.
2. Providing *physical* **cues** that provide an inviting atmosphere to guests and an indication of the quality and experience they can expect to receive.

3. **Packaging** that increases customer value through the bundling of multiple products and services (e.g., get-away packages that combine lodging, food and beverage, spa packages).
4. **Partnerships** and strategic alliances with other firms designed to creatively find ways to produce more value by effectively working with one another (e.g., airline/lodging joint frequent traveler programs).

It is important to remind ourselves that the 4 Ps (or expanded marketing mix variables for that matter) are, by themselves, insufficient in ensuring a firm's long-term profitability. Profitability hinges more on the ability to *retain* profitable customers than to *create* new ones. Influencing a customer to make a first-time purchase through price and promotions is an expensive process. The most important customer contacts, from a marketing success point of view, are the ones outside the realm of the 4 Ps and the marketing specialists. The concept of relationship marketing, adopted by many of today's leading hospitality and tourism firms, has expanded the marketing concept to a wider context where everyone in the organization has a marketing role in fulfilling promises that have been made to the visitor or guest. As such, some employees take on full-time marketing roles (e.g., marketing and sales staff), while those in operations assume a part-time, but always present, marketing role.

The key concepts that we can take away from this discussion are that marketing is: (1) a carefully designed strategy composed of inducements intended to create and retain profitable customers, (2) a customer relationship development process that is influenced by everyone in the organization, and (3) a process that must be actively managed, often by those assigned full-time marketing and sales responsibilities.

Let us now look at how these ingredients of the marketing mix are used in the hospitality and tourism industry by marketing and sales professionals.

The Hospitality Marketing System

Marketing managers have several alternative ways in which to deliver their message to consumers.

1. Their direct sales force can reach potential customers *directly* through personal interactions and increasingly through technologies, such as the Internet.

2. Their sales force can reach potential customers *indirectly* by marketing through wholesale intermediaries (such as tour operators or independent meeting planners) who might, in turn, sell to retail travel agencies, who then sell to the final customer.

3. They can reach potential customers *impersonally* through marketing promotional tools, such as advertising and public relations.

Let's more closely examine the lodging sector since, arguably, it has the most developed marketing system in the hospitality industry. First, we will examine the nature of *demand* since demand is the determining factor of *supply*. Second, we will examine the nature of *supply*.

Lodging Facility Market Demand and Segments

Different types of hotels are designed and created to be responsive to different travelers' preferences and needs. For example, people traveling for the purposes of pleasure and driving across the United States on the interstate system, need a clean, easily accessible place to spend the night. Services such as meeting rooms are not needed; so limited-service hotels are usually found along these highways. On the other hand, organizations that have groups of people who need to hold meetings require other types of properties. They, for example, may prefer a large downtown convention hotel that offers many meeting rooms and specialized services for group meetings.

Demand for a lodging product is commonly *segmented* according to the purpose of travel: for pleasure or for business. Additionally, business or pleasure travel takes place in groups or through individual travel. This creates four segments: (1) business groups, (2) business individuals, (3) pleasure groups, and (4) pleasure individuals. As a general rule, when marketing to *groups*, a sales force is the primary source of leads. When marketing to *individuals*, advertising and other non-personal promotional media are used to attract the segment.

Business/Organizational Segment

This segment is composed of demand from businesses and organizations of all types. Group demand comes from corporations, associations, social groups, educational groups, government groups,

religious groups, and so on. Individual demand comes from individual members of these businesses and organizations who are traveling for business purposes.

Groups. Groups attending meetings and conventions are a large source of business for the lodging industry. Group sizes may range from ten attendees (typically the minimum party size to be considered a group) to groups of thousands. On average, groups occupy hotel rooms for an average of three nights. Groups in the business/organization segment meet for a variety of reasons, including training, management development, executive and board of director retreats, national and regional sales conferences, as well as international, national, regional, and state association conventions. They select meeting sites based upon the facilities' ability to satisfy the purposes of these meetings.

Individual attendees do not select the lodging facility where these meetings will be held; thus, the lodging facility's sales forces must identify and work through group decision makers. These include organizational executives or intermediaries, such as independent meeting planners and sometimes travel agencies.

Individuals. Individuals traveling for business purposes make up a large portion of lodging industry revenues. In addition to having the potential for frequent repeat business, they are easier to identify and reach than pleasure travelers. Thus, lodging facility sales forces are able to contact the organizations from which these travelers depart and/or the local organizations within the destination they will visit in order to offer accommodations and services. Most lodging facilities have at least one salesperson specializing in obtaining this type of business. Additionally, advertising may be heavily used to attract this group.

Pleasure/Recreational/Personal Segment

The pleasure/recreational/personal traveler is motivated to travel by four primary factors: physical, cultural, interpersonal, and status and prestige. They choose to reach their objectives by traveling in groups or essentially alone.

Groups. These pleasure/recreation/personal travelers purchase what is known as group tours or tour packages. Group tours became an important

Groups attending meetings and conventions are a large source of business for the lodging industry.

travel segment following World War II and have expanded rapidly since 1960. These tour packages are put together by knowledgeable tour wholesalers and offer the traveler the advantage of security and greater affordability. These wholesalers generally offer vacation packages to the traveling public at prices lower than individual travelers would be able to arrange by themselves. Wholesalers buy travel services, such as transportation, hotel rooms, sight-seeing services, airport transfers (ground transportation), and meals in large quantities at discounted prices. They then package the components, add a markup, and resell this package to a group of individual travelers. All retail travel agencies offer packages for sale ranging from traditional trips through the United States and Europe to exotic packaged tours to the rain forests of the Amazon.

Individuals. Individual pleasure travelers choose to travel alone or with close companions. They do not usually require the services of a group tour operator. They are willing to contact directly (today commonly using Internet) or through their travel agent, the specific travel suppliers needed.

As mentioned earlier, supply in the lodging industry is determined by the nature of demand. For example, group business travelers may require a convention hotel, while an individual pleasure traveler may require a limited-service lodging facility. A variety of hotel segments have been created to specifically match customer (demand) needs. Marketing and sales organizations in each of these various types of facilities will also vary.

Organizing for Marketing and Sales

Hotel chains at the national level maintain a centralized marketing office and a national sales force. Depending on the individual hotel property size and mix of market segments they want to attract, the marketing and sales department will vary greatly. For example, in a large property (250 or more rooms) that obtains its revenue primarily from groups (50 percent to 75 percent of the revenue), you might expect to see a well-staffed and well-developed marketing and sales department. On the other hand, a limited service property may have one or no sales person on staff with the General Manager also serving as a marketing manager with the support of a regional or national marketing office.

For a convention hotel obtaining 70 percent of its revenue from group business, marketing serves

Tour wholesalers offer vacation packages to the traveling public at lower prices.

as a support for sales, providing needed marketing positioning and awareness to assist the salespeople in making sales. The 30 percent of individual travelers coming to this hotel would primarily be attracted by marketing activities as opposed to sales activities. While modern marketing attempts to create relationships between the organization and all customers, the sales staff focuses on creating relationships on a one-to-one basis with the organizational buyer (groups).

A sales force is the most expensive marketing and sales channel and, therefore, should not be used to indiscriminately "chase" all potential business. Instead, marketing managers need to be selective in their use of salespeople, utilizing them solely for those customer accounts (a) large enough to justify the salesperson's costs and (b) sufficiently complex (a large group meeting is complex) that the customer cannot be handled by lower cost alternatives.

Examples of lower cost promotional alternatives include:

- Advertising—Paid, on-going, non-personal communications designed to inform the consumer of the product or service in such media as newspapers, magazines, television, Internet, and direct mail;

- Promotions—Short-term inducements such as discount coupons or drawings for free prizes designed to influence non-users to purchase the product or service in hopes that they will make repeated purchases in the future;
- Publicity—Unpaid communication about the firm or its products in the mass media. Favorable publicity is attained by gaining the attention of news editors of newspapers, magazines, television, and radio who are always looking for stories that provide value to their audience.

The lesson to be learned from this discussion is that the marketing and sales manager has available a number of promotional tools. Each should be used where they can produce awareness, interest, desire, and ultimately action on the part of the target market. However, costs and return on investment will influence the promotional mix to be employed.

Conclusion

The marketing and sales manager is a kind of a cook who is continually experimenting with new blends and new kinds of ingredients to yield the highest return on investment from their inventory.

The manager ultimately hopes to produce the highest amount of revenue by filling the hotel, airline, etc., with the best mix of customers based upon the customer's willingness to pay.

Hospitality and tourism marketing and sales is a rewarding and challenging field. The marketing career ladder often begins in sales, and graduates will find sales positions are more abundant than marketing positions. Often, students in their part-time jobs as wait staff, front desk attendants, or any other customer contact position find their work helps to develop sales skills (e.g., order taking, up-selling) that will prepare them well for a professional sales and marketing career. What is needed is training that can take them to the next level of demand creators.

Marketing and sales professionals as demand creators must master their skills in market research, segmentation, targeting, and positioning. We also know that to be successful, one must possess strong people skills. Research has shown us that what buyers want in a marketing and sales professional is someone who:

- is polite, efficient, and respectful of the buyer's time,
- as an in-depth knowledge of their own products and its capabilities,
- has an in-depth knowledge of the customer's industry,
- represents a product or service that is consistent in quality; and
- is honest and keeps promises.

References

Grönroos, C. (1989). "Defining Marketing: A Market-oriented Approach," *European Journal of Marketing,* Vol. 23 No. 1, pp. 52–60.

McNeil, R. and Crotts, J. (2004). *Selling Hospitality: A Situational Approach.* New York: Delmar/Thompson Learning.

Chapter 13 Review Questions

1. What is typically needed within marketing and sales for a business to become successful?

2. Who are the participants in the supply and demand model in hospitality?

3. What are the marketing characteristics of a successful business?

4. Discuss the dilemma as to where a restaurateur or hotelier should invest their marketing dollars—in advertising or customer service? Support your answer with an example.

5. What would be a successful marketing mix for Disney?

6. What are the 4-P's of marketing?

7. Consider a major chain such as McDonald's or Best Western. What are the 4-P's in their marketing mix?
   Chain:

   a.

   b.

   c.

   d.

8. Explain how service giants such as Disney and Ritz Carlton have implemented the marketing concept "everyone in the organization fulfills promises."

9. Give an example for each company (Disney and Ritz Carlton) as to how an employee can fulfill a promise.

10. Write a profile of the "group traveler."

11. What are the reasons a group might come together at a hotel?

12. What motivates the "personal traveler" to travel?

13. Explain how a local travel agent makes money off of selling tour packages.

14. How does the marketing and sales department vary with the type of facility?

15. What skills does a person in marketing and sales need to possess?

16. Describe the personal profile of a successful marketing and sales person.

Chapter **14**

Principles of Management

Brandenburg Gate
Berlin, Germany

POSTAGE
PAID

Albert J. Moranville
East Stroudsburg University
Michael J. McCorkle
Richard Stockton College

Management in Hospitality and Tourism

Students of hospitality management frequently raise questions concerning the art and science of management. The questions generally fall into three broad, but very important, categories. They are: *What is management? What do managers in the hospitality industry do? How can I become a successful manager?* Although complete answers to these questions are complex and require considerable study and experience, one fact is certain: To be successful in the hospitality industry, it is imperative that a manager has an understanding of the principles of management, the skills required of a manager, and the personal qualities necessary to be effective.

Management and Managers

There have been many definitions applied to the term *management,* but the one that seems to get directly to the point is: *Management is the process of getting tasks accomplished through people.* The hospitality industry, particularly restaurants and lodging establishments, is relatively labor intensive. That is, establishments in our industry must employ large numbers of people to provide customers with a product or service. Additionally, many of our employees interact directly with guests on a frequent basis and are the most critical element in providing our services. For success at any level in the hospitality industry, the key is to develop, direct, and maintain an effective and efficient workforce that accomplishes the tasks necessary to satisfy customers. A manager, then, is a person who is responsible for the work of others, deciding what employees need to accomplish and how they should do it. Managers accomplish their goals by acquiring skills, knowledge, and personal qualities and applying these skills in their interactions with employees at the workplace.

Levels of Management

Managers in any organization usually are considered to belong to one of three different groups or levels: *top management, middle management, or supervisory management.* Managers are determined to be a member of one of these groups based primarily on the nature of their work and responsibilities. It is important to understand that there is not necessarily a clear distinction between the different levels of management. The tasks and responsibilities of managers at different levels may overlap, and sometimes the size of a hotel or restaurant company may determine the level of a specific manager. As an example, in a large corporation such as Marriott or Hyatt, the general manager of an individual property would probably be considered a member of middle management. However, in a small company consisting of only one or two properties, a general manager might be considered a member of the top management team.

Top Management

Members of top management usually have titles such as Chairman of the Board, Chief Executive Officer, Chief Operating Officer, President, or Executive Vice-President. Top managers determine the direction of the company by identifying its basic mission and objectives and developing goals and plans to reach the company's objectives.

Middle Management

Regional Director, General Manager, Rooms Division Manager, and Food and Beverage Director are common titles for middle managers in our industry. Middle managers communicate the goals and plans developed by top management to managers and workers at the lower levels of the company. In addition, they coordinate the activities of supervisory managers.

Supervisory Management

Typical titles of supervisory managers are Front Office Manager, Executive Housekeeper, or Restaurant Manager. Supervisory managers implement the goals and plans of the organization by directing work of the line-level employees, who provide our guests with products and services.

Management Functions

A discussion of management in the hospitality industry, or any other industry, usually centers around five basic management activities or functions: *planning, organizing, staffing, leading, and control.* These functions were identified in the early part of this century by French scholar and industrialist Henri Fayole and are sometimes referred to as the universal principles of management. Although usually explained individually, it is important to understand that in practice they are interrelated, as one function is dependent on another for success. For example, it would be difficult to staff a hotel without having a plan in place that determines employment needs. Employees in a restaurant, even if carefully selected and well trained, are not likely to be productive in a disorganized work environment.

Planning

Planning is the establishment of goals and objectives and deciding how to accomplish these goals. Because of its importance, planning is often referred to as the primary management function. The result of inadequate planning is chaos. Successful companies engage in some type of planning at all management levels.

Organizing

Organizing refers to the efforts involved with determining what activities are to be done and how employees are grouped together to accomplish specific tasks. Dividing the employees and their tasks into departments such as reservations, housekeeping, or maintenance would be an example of organizing. At a higher level, many large hotel companies are divided into several divisions, according to the geographic location of their properties or the product or service they provide.

Staffing

Staffing involves supplying the human requirements necessary to service guests at a lodging, food and beverage, or tourism establishment. Managers involved with staffing have several responsibilities. They determine the number and type of employees needed, recruit and select employees, and develop and implement training programs. Determining compensation and benefits received by employees is also a part of the staffing function.

Leading and Directing

Leadership is influencing others to channel their activities toward assisting the hotel or restaurant to reach its goals. Leadership can be viewed as having two separate components or elements—success and effectiveness. A successful leader can get people to follow; an effective leader gets people to follow in the right direction.

An obvious omission in the traditional discussion of leadership and management is the role and

Through leadership, the manager empowers staff members so that guests' needs are met or exceeded.

importance of the customer or guest. Leadership activities in a service business are not performed in a vacuum but usually in the presence of the customer. In fact, many of the service delivery systems managers put in place create a role for the customer that actually makes him or her a part of the delivery process.

Contemporary leadership and management practices have directed a new focus on the guest and her or his wants and needs. Many of the premier hospitality organizations, such as the Ritz-Carlton, are changing the manner in which management activities are undertaken to include the guest, first and foremost. The new measure of high quality in the hospitality business is *consistently meeting or exceeding the customer's expectations.* In order to accomplish this formidable task, managers must become leaders. Through leadership, the manager is able to enable, empower, and support staff members so that in each service encounter the staff member is able to take whatever action is necessary to ensure that the guest's needs are consistently met or exceeded.

Empowering staff members requires managers to move away from the traditional command and control organizational structure. The contemporary leader must create, instead, an organizational environment in which staff members are trained in necessary skills, enabling them to handle most customer service encounters. Management then must support the decisions that staff members make. Good managers are not always good leaders, and good leaders are not always good managers. For a hospitality organization to be successful in the highly competitive service environment of the twenty-first century, managers must become good leaders by creating a culture in which high-level quality and customer satisfaction is the primary mission of the organization.

Control

Control is comparing the performance of employees in a workforce against the objectives and goals that have been set by the company. The purpose of any control system is to be sure that the company is headed in the right direction and can make corrections when necessary. Control can be viewed as being of three distinct types: **preliminary, concurrent,** and **postactional**. Preliminary controls take place before an event occurs, such as a restaurant manager developing a seating chart before

banquet guests arrive. Concurrent controls take place during an actual event, as when a housekeeping supervisor directs the daily operations in the department. Postactional controls take place after an event, as when a general manager reviews a monthly profit and loss statement for a hotel. All managers are responsible for control at some level.

Another way of attempting to understand what managers do is to consider the amount of time managers spend involved with the various functions of planning, organizing, staffing, leading, and control. Top-level managers spend most of their time engaged in the functions of planning and organizing and very little time in direct supervision of employees. Top-level managers, as previously mentioned, plan at the highest level and prepare the basic strategy for the company. Top-level or strategic planning is long term in nature, usually looking into the future five or more years. This type of planning is broad in nature and affects the entire company. Examples of this type of planning in the hospitality industry are Marriott's decision to develop Fairfield Inns and Courtyard as new brands or Starwood Lodging's decision to acquire ITT Sheraton.

Middle managers also spend a great deal of time planning and organizing, but of a slightly different nature. Middle managers spend their time developing tactics to implement top management plans throughout the organization. Tactical plans tend to be slightly shorter term and focus on the actions necessary to put long-term plans into effect. As an example, a middle manager might spend time developing a plan to market a hotel to a specific clientele or reorganize a kitchen to accommodate the demands of a new menu.

Supervisors typically spend most of their time involved with staffing and the leading and directing of employees and little time planning and organizing. Supervisors are usually responsible for making the final decision on selecting and training employees and monitoring their daily performance. Planning and organizing are important to supervisory managers, but they are generally short term in scope and operational in nature. For example, a restaurant manager might organize the dining room for a banquet, then schedule and coordinate the service staff for the event. A front office manager might develop a staffing plan for the next several weeks that depends on the occupancy levels of the hotel.

Management Skills

Technical Skills

Technical skills involve having the knowledge of and the ability to perform a particular job or task. Supervisory managers, and often middle managers, are directly involved with the operation of a department, such as the front office or housekeeping. Because supervisory managers train and direct employees on a daily basis, a high level of technical skill and knowledge is necessary. It would be difficult or impossible for an executive chef to supervise workers in a kitchen without knowledge of culinary arts and kitchen procedures. Similarly, a front office manager in a hotel needs to know the operation of the computer system at the front desk and the procedures for registering a guest. Although top level managers do not often have the opportunity to display technical skills, most have been promoted from lower management positions, have extensive experience at all levels of the organization, and have excellent technical skills.

Conceptual Skills

Conceptual skills involve the ability to see the company or department as a whole and understand how the different parts work together. Problem solving, decision making, planning, and organizing are tasks that require technical skills. Managers with conceptual skills are able to look at problems from a broad perspective and from different points of view. Conceptual skills are important at all levels of management, but they are essential for top managers who make decisions that can dramatically affect the future of the hotel or restaurant company.

Interpersonal Skills

Interpersonal or human skills involve the ability to understand people and work well with them on an individual basis and in groups. Interpersonal skills include a manager's ability to lead, motivate, and communicate with those around them. Because all managers must deal with other people, and at certain times guests, interpersonal skills are equally important at all levels of management.

Personal Qualities

In order to become an effective manager, one must not only understand the basic management functions and acquire management skills, but also develop some basic personal qualities. Many personal characteristics have been identified with success as a manager, but not all managers share the same personal qualities, although there are several that seem to be cited most frequently as being critical.

A Passion for the Industry

It has been said by many managers and workers in our industry that the business is "in their blood." What they are really saying is that they have developed a passion or a love for the hospitality industry. The most successful managers in our industry enjoy their jobs and are excited by the challenges and rewards that come from the interaction with the guests and employees. They are enthusiastic and excited about working and display a positive attitude. Their enthusiasm is infectious and motivates workers around them. If you don't love the hospitality industry and are not excited by interacting with guests and employees, you probably should investigate another career.

Hands-On, Value Driven

Related to the idea of having a passion for the hospitality industry is the idea of hands-on management. Tom Peters, in his book *In Search of Excellence* uses the term *hands-on, value driven* to describe managers who like to be involved with the basic daily operations of a business. The better managers in our industry spend a significant amount of time out of their offices interacting with employees and guests; they get involved with the industry and the people they work with. Because of their involvement, hands-on managers are able to identify problems or potential problems more easily and can recommend appropriate action more quickly. Also, because hands-on managers are typically respected, admired, and well liked by their staff, there is a tendency for the staff to be more dedicated to reaching the goals of the company.

A Sense of Ethics

Ethics, in a business sense, is a set of principles that managers apply when interacting with people in their organizations. Ethics should govern the general behavior of managers and guide them in making business decisions. Managers are responsible for the ethical treatment of five different groups of people: customers, employees, suppliers, ownership, and the community at large. Basically, ethical behavior means fair and consistent treatment towards members of each of these groups. It is important for a manager to develop a personal code of ethics that ensures truth, a lack of bias, consistency, and respect when interacting with others. A hotel manager, for example, should be certain that the property provides guests with services that are advertised. A supplier has the right to expect timely payment for goods provided to the hotel.

Self-Confidence

Successful managers are confident in their abilities, decisive in their actions, and are able to gain trust and support from workers. If a manager is not sure of what direction to take or displays uncertainty, then followers are not as likely to trust the manager and be committed to the goals. Managers who display self-confidence, especially when problems exist, are a steadying force in a hotel or restaurant because others feel they can rely on them for assistance and direction. Self-confidence is gained, in part, through the process of developing managerial and technical skills. Experience, the knowledge gained from being in a situation before, is critical in developing self-confidence.

References

Rue, L., and L. Bears. *Management Skills and Application.* 8th ed. Burr Ridge, IL: Irwin, 1997, pp. 6–7, 372.

Robbins, S., and M. Coulter. *Management.* 6th ed. Upper Saddle River, NJ: Prentice Hall, 1999, p. 11.

Holt D. *Management Principles and Practices.* 3rd ed. Upper Saddle River, NJ: Prentice Hall, 1993, pp. 18–19.

Durbin, A. *Essentials of Management.* 2nd ed. Cincinnati, OH: South-Western, 1990, pp. 7–8.

Hall, Stephen S. J. *Ethics in Hospitality Management.* East Lansing, Mich.: Educational Institute of the American Hotel & Motel Association, 1992.

Marriott, J. W., Jr., and K. A. Brown. *The Spirit to Serve.* New York: Harper Collins, 1997, pp. 3–7.

Peters, T., and R. Waterman. *In Search of Excellence.* New York: Harper & Row, 1982, pp. 279–281.

Chapter 14 Review Questions

1. What are the primary factors needed by an individual for success in the hospitality industry?

2. What is the author's definition of management?

3. What is meant by the concept that the hospitality business is labor intensive? How might this change in the future?

4. What are the three traditional levels of management?

5. What are the primary duties of top management?

6. What are the primary duties of middle management?

7. What are the primary duties of supervisory management?

8. What are the five universal principles of management?

9. Which of these universal principles is considered to be the primary management function?

10. Define planning as a management function.

11. Define staffing as a management function.

12. What are management's daily/weekly duties related to staffing?

13. Define organizing as a management function.

14. Define leading and directing as a management function.

15. Where does the guest "fit in" to the traditional leadership role?

16. Where does the guest "fit in" to the current or contemporary leadership role?

17. What are the defining characteristics of a "successful leader?"

18. What are the defining characteristics of an "effective leader?"

19. What managerial traits are important for success in a high-quality minded hospitality business?

20. What is meant by "empowering" employees?

21. How does a hospitality manager effectively empower his/her staff? Give an example.

22. Define control as a management function.

23. What are the three types of control? Define each.

a.

b.

c.

24. Where do top-level managers spend most of their time? Give an example.

25. What is strategic planning?

26. Where do middle level managers spend most of their time? Give an example.

27. Where do supervisory level managers spend most of their time? Give an example.

28. Define technical skills. To which level of management are these skills most needed?

29. Define conceptual skills. To which level of management are these skills most needed?

30. Define interpersonal skills. To which level of management are these skills most needed?

31. What are the four personal qualities described by the author?

32. Why are these four important in the hospitality industry? Give an example of each.

33. How can you tell if a person is passionate about his/her job?

34. Who coined the term "hands-on, value driven" and why is that appropriate to the hospitality industry?

35. Why are "hands-on" managers often perceived as the "better" managers?

36. How does an entry-level manager develop self-confidence?

37. Of the managers you have worked for, or had the opportunity to meet, what is an outstanding characteristic they emulated?

Chapter

15

Physical Plant Management and Security

Skylon Tower
Niagara Falls, Ontario

POSTAGE
PAID

Ronald A. Usiewicz
*International College of
Hospitality Management
"Cesar Ritz"*

Corbis

Introduction

The physical plant of a hospitality operation is the manufacturing facility in which the products and services guests purchase are created, delivered, and generally consumed. It is comprised of both visible elements, such as the grounds, exterior building structure, interior finishes, building systems, and the FF&E (furniture, fixtures, and equipment), and elements seldom seen by the guests or most of the employees, such as the structural materials, plumbing, environmental control systems, and much of the HVAC (heating, ventilating, and air conditioning) system. The equipment and elements of the facility are the production tools of the hospitality industry.

The maintenance and/or engineering department (the two terms are used interchangeably) is responsible for insuring that the facility and its equipment and systems operate in a manner that allows the staff to perform their tasks efficiently and provide a memorable experience for guests. In addition, protection of the physical plant investment and controlling and minimizing energy and maintenance costs are of primary concern. Both technical and managerial functions must be performed to become an efficient department within the operation.

Management of the Physical Plant

The maintenance and engineering manager is responsible for budgeting, management systems, energy control systems, accounting and financial statements, capital projects, and personnel. A budget can help the engineering manager communicate departmental needs to upper management and other departments and monitor and control departmental expenditures. The manager must explain clearly how the department's budgeted needs relate to the property's goals. The basic components of the departmental budget are the energy and POM (property operation and maintenance) accounts. Energy is budgeted through analysis of the effects of business levels, climatic factors, and energy conservation measures. The POM budget is derived by estimating the costs of labor, materials, and contracted services for various anticipated tasks.

Records, management systems, and standards are necessary for a cost- and time-efficient engineering department. Records include work orders, building plans, equipment data cards, equipment history records, building plans, and instruction and/or repair manuals. Maintenance schedules and inventories of parts and supplies must also be maintained. Standards are used to measure both employee performance and departmental performance; they should be flexible enough to change, as property needs also change.

To control energy expenditures effectively, management must monitor both consumption and cost, as well as occupancy rates and climatic conditions. An individual property's energy can be compared with standards, which may be derived from external sources, and historical consumption information from previous years. The best way to determine the success or failure of an energy management program is to monitor performance over time. Often, analysis of the utility bill will also reveal savings opportunities. Another factor to consider in effective energy management is that employees should be trained to use systems and equipment in an energy-efficient manner. Engineering expenses are reported as undistributed operating expenses. Engineering is charged for energy and maintenance throughout the facility, even though the department has no control over activities in other departments.

Capital projects usually require special approval and are not charged to a specific account of a uniform system of accounts. All capital projects affect the engineering department, which must maintain whatever is purchased and sometimes must connect it to existing systems and include it in the energy budget. Capital projects are performed for financial reasons (which may relate to income at the property or to goals of a parent company), to maintain and/or improve the market position of the property, to expand the size or facilities of the property, to improve the efficiency of the facility operation, to obtain tax advantages, and physical reasons (which may include appearance, internal deterioration, and safety). The project analysis technique called life cycle costing considers and quantifies cost and benefit elements, which include:

- Initial Costs—For example, costs of the item itself including costs of installation, interconnection, and modification of supporting systems or equipment.

- Operating Costs—For example, costs of energy or water to operate the equipment and supporting systems of those systems affected by the equipment; maintenance labor and supplies or contract maintenance services.

- Fixed Costs—For example, insurance and property tax changes resulting from the equipment or system.
- Tax Implications—For example, income taxes and tax credits such as investment tax credits and depreciation deductions.

The three most important factors in keeping engineering turnover low are quality of supervision, management support, and employee selection and training. Working conditions, job status, and compensation seem to be less important. Particular approaches include a supervisory style that encourages autonomy, recognition by top management, and consideration of guest interaction in recruiting. Appropriate personnel policies should improve the morale and performance of the engineering staff.

Engineering Systems

An understanding of engineering systems and their design and operation will help the hospitality manager meet the needs of guests and employees. Most major systems can be divided into sources, distribution systems, delivery of utilization devices, and control and safety equipment.

The quality and quantity of the water supply can affect the guest and several departments. Wastewater (sewage) systems that remove and sometimes treat wastewater are also necessary. Sources are utilities, internal storage devices, and equipment that produce water of special characteristics; distribution systems are pipes and pumps; delivery devices include water-using appliances; and control and safety devices such as valves, temperature controllers, and pressure regulators help keep water safe and usable. Concerns include potability, treatment, and availability.

A refrigeration system maintains the temperature of a space by removing any heat that enters the space. When the temperature is too high, the system turns on until the temperature falls below a preset limit, then turns off and awaits the next signal. Heat is transferred to the outside in a continuous cycle: it is absorbed, transported by a refrigerant, and dissipated into a cooling medium. Units can be self-contained or remote, and air-cooled or water-cooled. Concerns include energy efficiency, reliability, and proper usage of the systems.

The heating, ventilating, and air conditioning (HVAC) system delivers heating or cooling on demand, while maintaining the proper humidity and air quality. Sources convert utilities into either heat or cold; distribution systems include pipes, ducts, pumps, and fans; delivery systems such as radiators and air-conditioning units transfer heat or cold to room air; and control and safety devices include thermostats, valves, and pressure sensors. Systems can be decentralized or centralized with water, air, or a combination of the two as the distribution medium. The major concern is energy-efficiency improvement. It can be achieved by improving the physical plant to minimize cooling or heating losses, as well as utilization of modern energy-efficient equipment designed for the specific task. Other concerns include fuel selection and system aesthetics.

The electrical system chiefly serves other building systems. The source is usually the local electric utility; the distribution system consists of wires; delivery devices include appliances and building systems that use the electricity; and control and safety devices range from light switches to circuit breakers. The major hospitality establishments also have a backup electrical source system (on-site electrical generators) to provide electrical supply when there is no outside electricity (electrical failure) due to the unforeseen circumstances. Other major concerns involve appropriate and reliable supply, computer and emergency systems, safety, and cost. Lighting may be installed for marketing purposes, a safety/security purpose, to create a mood, or to provide for the guests' needs. The most common interior artificial sources are incandescent and fluorescent lamps; exterior lighting is typically incandescent—mercury vapor, metal halide, or sodium. Lamp fixtures can significantly affect lighting system efficiency. Of particular concerns are lighting near computer screens, lighting for security, and systems efficiency.

Fire protection involves both equipment and training, according to local codes and property standards; fire protection systems include detection, notification, suppression, and smoke control systems of various types. Security systems and equipment vary with the property, its risks, and choices it makes; security equipment includes locks, closed-circuit television, occupancy sensors, elevator key controls, exit alarms, and door chains. Telephone lines are either switched (for ordinary call) or dedicated (for constant connection); equipment and procedures for monitoring guest calls to allow charging guests for calls. Choice of vertical transport (escalator, elevator, or dumbwaiter) depends on travel height, traffic volume, and whether or not people will ride.

Systems design requires the services of many specialists, each with different interests; resolving their conflicts is necessary to a successful facility. Quantitative steps include load analysis, preliminary system and equipment selection, annual energy usage estimation, life cycle costing, considerations of equipment interconnections and interactions, and final design; the final design is incorporated into specifications and building plans. Choices are influenced by both objective criteria (such as cost, capacity, size, and consumption) and subjective criteria (such as appearance, reliability, public relations features, and noise). All buildings are subject to local and property specification and performance codes. Systems interact when one system produces a load for or requires the output of another. Systems are integrally connected to make one larger system, the physical plant itself.

Types of Maintenance

Buildings and systems require basic maintenance, repair, and attention. If management ignores these needs, employee performance, safety, profitability, and guest perceptions can be affected. The following maintenance programs are necessary for a hospitality operation to be managed efficiently.

Routine maintenance pertains to the general upkeep of the property, recurs regularly, and requires little training or skill. It is outside of formal records or work orders. The engineering department benefits from working with the housekeeping department on routine maintenance. Preventive maintenance is specific, recurs over longer periods, and requires more advanced skills and training. It is directed at prolonging equipment life and minimizing breakdown, based on guidelines from equipment suppliers and the facilities engineer. It consists of three parts: inspection (generally by checklist), minor corrections (at the time of inspection), and work order initiation (to bring problems and needs to the attention of management).

Scheduled maintenance is initiated by a formal work order and attempts to meet a known need in an orderly and timely manner. The timing, plan-

A quality maintenance staff is crucial for a hospitality operation to be managed efficiently.

ning, and coordination of scheduled maintenance are important, as its scope is large and it may remove an item from service.

Emergency maintenance and breakdown maintenance are expensive and unpredictable. A guest-initiated request for emergency maintenance relates directly to their perception of the property and calls for a prompt and courteous response; an employee-initiated request also denotes problems likely to affect guest satisfaction. When equipment or a structural component completely fails, it requires immediate breakdown maintenance or the operation will be shut down, although some initial action may shift the problem to either emergency or scheduled maintenance. These forms of maintenance are particularly costly for the facility because:

- They are usually solved only with the application of premium pay (overtime),
- They often bypass the traditional parts or supplies purchasing system, leading to premium costs,
- They often have other costs associated with their solution (for example, a leaking pipe may also damage walls and ceilings), and
- They often affect the guests and thus, potentially lead to the loss of revenue.

Guest room maintenance refers to preventive and/or scheduled maintenance. The condition and proper operation of furniture, fixtures, and equipment, the appearance of ceilings and walls (whether painted, plastered, or wallpapered), the condition of carpets and floor coverings, and the cleanliness of the exteriors of windows are all included in the maintenance and repair of guest rooms. Window cleaning, refuse disposal, kitchen duct cleaning, elevator maintenance, pest control, landscaping, water treatment, and HVAC calibration are common contract maintenance services. Contract maintenance is a combination of in-house and contract activities that may be taken for a variety of reasons, including (but not limited to):

- A desire to minimize the commitment of staff on the payroll to handle these needs,
- A recognition that special tools or licenses are required to perform the required work effectively,
- A temporary staffing shortage,
- A need to deal with emergencies,

- A recognition that the complexity of the task is beyond the skills of the existing maintenance staff,
- Reduction of total labor costs,
- Use of the latest techniques and methods,
- Reduction of the cost of supplies and equipment
- Savings in administrative time,
- Removal of the need to negotiate with labor unions.

Potential disadvantages of contract maintenance services include:

- False labor cost savings unless staffing levels are actually reduced,
- Gradual escalation in total costs without property level monitoring or control,
- Managerial laziness resulting in a failure to negotiate the best price for the service or a lack of competitive bidding,
- Unavailability of employees for other tasks,
- Loss of control over employees (security, attitude, identity with the property), and
- Loss of contact with the need of the facility and staff.

Security in Hospitality Facilities

Providing security in a hospitality operation is the task of protecting both people—guests, employees, and others—and assets. Crimes involving the theft of assets usually result in greater losses to lodging properties than crimes against persons, but crimes against persons have a greater effect on public relations and may cause unforeseen legal expenses. Lodging property security efforts may involve such areas of concern as guest room security, access control, alarm systems, key control, perimeter control, locks, lighting, safe deposit boxes, communication systems, closed-circuit television, inventory control, credit and billing procedures, staffing, emergency procedures, pre-employment screening, employee training, safety procedures, the responsible service of alcoholic beverages, and record keeping.

The hospitality industry's concern with security has increased considerably in recent years as a result of the rising crime rate against both assets and people and the rapidly growing number of lawsuits filed against management and employees for failure to provide adequate security. In most states, management has a legal duty to provide "reasonable care" for the protection of guests and guests' business invitees, including the duty to inspect the property and correct dangerous conditions. Management may be held liable for injuries to guests caused by their employees in the course of their employment and/or for injuries caused by negligence on premises.

Management must ensure the routine inspections of furniture, windows, bathroom appliances, elevators, hallways, and stairways to provide safe accommodation to guests. Plumbing systems and electrical and heating devices must be also checked on a regular basis. Maintaining premises in good condition may protect the establishment from liability. It is important to keep in mind that all properties are different, and security programs must be adjusted to each particular property, not to hospitality establishment in general. It should be also taken into consideration that a property's layout and design will greatly influence the security program. However, all security programs should have one common detail: they should be focused on prevention of security-related problems. Security should be recognized and used as a management tool. Whether the size of the property requires a large security staff or allows for the security function to be assigned to one or several on-premises supervisory personnel, the security role must be clearly defined and implemented. The protection of guests, employees, and assets requires management to be constantly alert to security breaches.

Safety considerations are a critical aspect of the security function within the hospitality property. Employee training plays an essential role in establishing the security program. All employees must receive adequate safety and security training to be able to identify security issues. After the training is complete, employees have a greater awareness of potential issues at their work place and will be more likely to react in a proper way. A safety program can protect employees, the public, guests, and their assets from accidents that may result in needless injury and pain to people and damage to property and equipment. It is essential that management be involved with the safety program and provide full support for its implementation. There must be a consistent program to provide a safe property and a safe working environment. The Occupational Safety and Health Act of 1970

(OSHA) mandates safety regulations and practices at the federal level that apply to businesses throughout the United States, including hospitality properties.

Physical Plant Management and the Americans with Disabilities Act (ADA)

Congress signed the Americans with Disabilities Act into law on July 26, 1990. It was a dramatically new and revolutionary civil rights legislation that mandated changes in the way that hospitality operations, and indeed many American businesses, conduct their employment practices and in the way that they provide services and products to the public. The law is designed to protect the civil rights of people who have physical and/or mental disabilities. This law requires, in some cases, modification in the facilities and the way products and services are provided.

The ADA provides individuals with disabilities the right to participate in and enjoy the goods, ser-

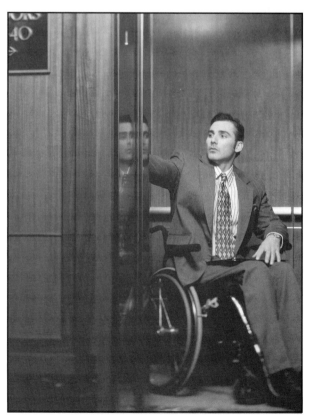

Facilities must be made accessible to individuals with disabilities.

vices, privileges, benefits, and accommodations offered to the general public. It is the first federal law that requires privately financed businesses to provide physical accessibility to existing buildings. Hospitality facilities are faced with the cost of trying to build accessibility into an existing building. Although the ADA only requires "readily achievable" modifications, the costs and maintenance can still be significant. Management may need to allocate funds for equipment purchases and readily achievable architectural modifications. In order for management to determine if their facility is in compliance, barriers must be identified that would make it difficult or impossible for:

- Anyone to get from the property line, drop-off, or parking facility into the building,
- Anyone to get into the building through entrances and doors,
- Anyone to get around to all important public areas within the property,
- Anyone to be able to eat a meal with privacy and dignity,
- Anyone to enter and use meeting rooms as a presenter or attendee,
- Any guest to find and enter a guest room; wheelchair-accessible guest rooms must be available and identified, and proper signage especially important for guests with visual impairments,
- Any guest who is mobility-impaired to enter and use the bathroom,
- Any guest to use the storage, furniture, and equipment in the wheelchair-accessible guest rooms,
- Any hearing-impaired guest to use the communication system in an equipped guest room,
- Any guest to enter and use any toilet facility within the building,
- Any guest to get to and use any recreation or retail facilities that are available to guests of the property, and
- Anyone to use controls that are available for the public (including electrical, mechanical, and self-service controls).

In conclusion, managers who want to control costs, create value for owners and stockholders, have high departmental efficiency and productivity, well-satisfied guests, and a secure and safe operation must take physical plant management seriously. The services provided by a properly funded and well-run maintenance and engineering department are of significant value to the property. When it comes to facilities maintenance, you can pay now or pay more later.

References

Borsenik, F. D., and A. T. Stutts. *The Management of Maintenance and Engineering Systems in the Hospitality Industry.* 4th ed. New York: John Wiley & Sons, 1997.

Cournoyer, G. N., and A. G. Marshall, et al. *Hotel, Restaurant, and Travel Law: A Preventive Approach.* 5th ed. Albany: Delmar, Thomson Learning, 1999.

Ellis, R. C., and D. M. Stipanuk. *Security and Loss Prevention Management.* 2nd ed. Educational Institute of the American Hotel and Motel Association, 1999.

Palmer, J. D. *Principles of Hospitality Engineering.* New York: Van Nostrand Reinhold, 1990.

Redlin, M. H., and D. M. Stipanuk. *Managing Hospitality Engineering Systems.* East Lansing, MI: Educational Institute of the American Hotel and Motel Association, 1987.

Salmen, John P. S. *Accommodating All Guests.* Washington, DC: The American Hotel and Lodging Association, 1992.

Stipanuk, D. M., and H. Roffmann. *Hospitality Facilities Management and Design.* 2nd ed. Lansing, MI: Educational Institute of the American Hotel and Motel Association, 2002.

Stutts, A. T., and F. D. Borsenik. *Maintenance Handbook for Hotels, Motels and Resorts.* New York: Van Nostrand Reinhold, 1990.

Name _____ Date _____

Chapter 15 Review Questions

1. What are the main functions of the maintenance/engineering department?

2. What is the purpose of a budget for the maintenance or engineering manager?

3. What are the basic components of the budget? How are the budget projections determined?

4. What types of processes characterize a cost-and-time efficient engineering department?

5. What is involved in effectively controlling energy expenditures?

6. How are engineering expenses reported on property financial statements? For what is the engineering department charged?

7. How are capital projects typically handled regarding the budgetary process?

8. What are six types of reasons for performing capital projects?

9. What are the four categories of cost and benefit elements considered in the project analysis technique of life cycle costing?

10. What are the three most important factors in minimizing engineering employee turnover?

11. What are the four main components of most major engineering systems?

12. Describe the four components as related to the water supply system.

13. Describe the basic operation of a refrigeration system, as related to the four main components.

14. Describe the four main components of an HVAC system and of an electrical system.

15. List the four general elements involved in fire protection and the four components of fire protection systems.

16. What is involved in systems design including quantitative steps, objective criteria, and subjective criteria?

17. Identify and describe the seven types of maintenance programs.

18. Delineate typical areas of concern in providing security for lodging properties.

19. Describe the impact of the Americans with Disabilities Act in relation to removing potential barriers in hospitality facilities.

16

Revenue and Cost Management

Perce Rock
Quebec, Canada

Corel

POSTAGE
PAID

Denver E. Severt
Eastern Michigan University

Introduction

Cost control knowledge is essential for a successful hospitality and tourism management career. An understanding of the concepts discussed in this chapter will aid the future hospitality manager regardless of career choice. This chapter introduces the primary responsibilities for the hospitality business manager by (1) explaining some of the practical responsibilities for controlling costs and revenue and, (2) presenting the two primary statements of business performance that are used by hospitality businesses. The chapter concludes with some comments from hospitality alums regarding cost control.

Controlling Costs for the Hospitality Business

Managers can control the costs (outflow of money) from the business by being observant. This may involve purchasing wisely, minimizing employees wages by making sure that everyone "on the clock" or "on the payroll" is needed, and finding lower insurance premiums or ensuring that all possible discounts are received. As managers gain experience, the control of costs becomes more instinctive. However, the lack of fiscal (financial) control by the manager can result in the loss of employment. The proper management of costs (outflow of money) means the difference between staying in business and not staying in business.

Controlling the costs for a business does not require that you be a mathematician. It requires the manager to be highly observant for wastes and to train and empower employees to be observant for company wastes. Some simple but realistic examples of cost control in the hospitality industry follow.

1. Bob is a new assistant director for housekeeping at the Hotel California. Bob notices that many towels out of the weekly delivery are going unused. Bob checks the invoice from the towel company and discovers that Hotel California is billed according to number of towels delivered. Next week when the linen delivery arrives, Bob sees the driver take all the clean and dirty towels away and bring in 500 clean towels. After asking housekeeping about towel usage, Bob cuts the linen order to 350 towels.

For 500 towels, the Hotel California paid $60 per week or $3120 ($60 × 52 weeks) yearly. After Bob reduced the order to 350 towels, the charge decreased to $40 per week or $2080 ($40 × 52 weeks) annually. Bob saved $1040 for the company by simply ordering the amount of towels needed. If, however, the manager were not endeavoring to control costs, the wastes would have continued. If Bob gets a 10% bonus on what he saves Hotel California, he made $104 for being observant.

2. One evening, Sherry, the new assistant manager at the Neptune Café, notices many employees doing nothing. This results in unnecessary labor costs. In turn, Sherry found that the 6 restaurant employees are paid $6 per hour, she knows the rest of the evening will be slow, she knows the cleaning is done, and she knows employees have nothing to do. Sherry determines that only two employees are needed for the remaining 3 hours. Six are "on the clock" and only 2 are needed. Sherry sends 4 home instead of having them "on the clock" for 3 more hours. Sherry saved the cafe $72 in one evening (4 employees × 3 hours × $6 per hour wage). An unobservant manager may have kept all the employees, let them eat because it was slow, and potentially wasted $72 plus food. This does not count other costs that the company will pay on employees: for example, social security tax on a percentage of the employee earnings. Remember, the $72 is only labor wasted for one evening. Failing to observe and send employees home for 6 nights would result in $432 (6 days × $72 per day excess labor) wasted in a week and in $1728 (4 weeks × $432) wasted in a month. This business would possibly not be open the next year due to mismanagement of labor costs.

The above examples illustrate what can easily happen if managers and employees are not trained to observe the flow of money in the daily behaviors of employees and to observe what is happening with products, known as cost control. The keen-eyed manager is the one promoted because he or she is always controlling costs for the company by being observant. Just as Sherry did above, the keen manager will observe employee behaviors, consider their hourly pay rate, compute how much money the company is wasting by having idle employees, and make the decision to send the unneeded employees home early. The manager that is not observant simply becomes a cost to the business and allows costs to be out of control. This is why many new businesses close their doors within the first few years.

Controlling Revenue for the Hospitality Business

Aside from cutting costs, the hospitality business manager is also responsible for helping to control the sales (dollars flowing into) of the business. The sales dollars are what the company gets for selling its primary products. For example, a busy hotel sells room nights, food, beverage, and phone services. A restaurant sells food, beverages, and products related to the restaurant such as a Neptune Café t-shirt or a Neptune Café coffee mug. Not only is the hospitality manager responsible for maintaining or increasing the sales of the business, but for managing that money once the business has collected it.

Money flowing into the business is known as sales or revenue. For example, in a hotel, the primary revenue is generated from room charges. Therefore, the higher the occupancy rate, the higher the revenue. Hotels can generate additional revenue (dollars flowing into) by providing additional services and amenities. Some properties refer to this as revenue enhancement. This requires the hospitality student to be comfortable with learning to manage cash transactions and credit transactions, which are the primary methods that hospitality businesses get paid their revenue.

Cash Transactions

Hospitality students must have an understanding of and comfort with counting, handling, and safeguarding money. When it comes to money matters, no assumptions can be made.

Counting money and giving change to a guest will occur hundreds of thousands of times in most hospitality businesses. Cash handling activities for managers can be in the form of deposits, counting money back to customers, paying vendors on- and off-site, going to buy or sending an employee to buy product that is 86ed (you are out of that product), and payroll, to name a few. The hospitality manager is accountable to ensure that his or her employees are trained properly in all cash han-

dling procedures. The best way to insure employee's competence with cash transactions is to have and help employees practice the skill during on-going training meetings and to constantly audit the employees to ensure that accurate cash handling is occurring. The following are examples of how cash transactions can become costs that are out of control.

1. Sarah was checking guests out, and their bill was $53.89. The guests hand Sarah $100. Sarah should have given the guests back $46.11; instead she gave back $76.11. The business just lost $30, which is more than the average return they would have made on a $53.89 guest check. In this example, the company lost money by selling food. Of course, mistakes and practices like Sarah's cannot persist. This should become second nature to employees who handle money. All employees should be audited when it comes to cash handling procedures because accountability is a key component to any successful operation.

2. David finds that he needs to send an employee to buy certain products that he can only obtain at the local store. David decides to pay for this out of the petty cash fund that has $600. Each week that David sends Bob to the store to buy the groceries, he tells Bob to take $10 out of petty cash for gas, but no one writes this down or accounts for the $10. At the end of one month or 4 trips ($10 × 4), the petty cash fund is $40 short and no one knows why because no record was kept. Most managers have many more areas of accountability, and this is just one. Can you imagine what the cash situation would look like if it was managed like David was doing? Eventually, corporate offices would think that David or some employee is embezzling money from the company.

Credit Card Transactions

Another way money flows into a business involves credit. Generally, employees will be crediting credit cards, occasionally debiting credit cards, and always settling the account at the end of the period. Continuous training and auditing of these procedures is critical in managing a hospitality business. Usually, credit card sales are very similar to cash sales because the company gets the money rapidly. However, the company must pay fees to the credit card companies, so the actual sales on credit are lower by anywhere from 1.5 to 4.5 percent, the percentage range that is charged by most credit card companies for providing credit card services.

Other Credit Transactions

The other credit is the credit that is not paid when services are rendered. In this case, the hospitality manager must follow up to make sure that the business paid for the service it has already performed. An example of this type of transaction is a wedding at a private country club. Typically, the country club requires a deposit on the wedding and full payment later. Terms usually vary according to business. Once the event has passed, the sales event manager must make sure that he or she collects the remainder of the wedding payment. Credit transactions can be difficult because once the $20,000 wedding has finished, the club has already spent money on food, labor, rentals, valet, etc. If the $20,000 party only paid a $4,000 deposit and then were unhappy with their product, then they could refuse to pay the remainder. This could force the business into serious cash flow problems and enough events like this could easily force the club out of business. This highlights the importance of collecting credit sales quickly, or else sales revenues becomes losses. Later on in your hospitality cost control class, you will read about this referred to as accounts receivable management.

The elementary part of money has been included because (1) this knowledge is essential because all employees deal with product or money, (2) if dollars are not controlled as they flow into the business then the dollars will never reside at the bottom of the profit and loss (P & L) or income statement in the net income column.

In closing, this section on the flow of money in and out of a business, the student must be watchful at the business they are managing. They must maximize the sales (inflow of dollars) while minimizing the costs (outflow of dollars). Every manager should keep in mind if he or she cannot measure something, then they cannot fix the problem. This relates to many areas. For example, if a person wants to weigh 162 pounds, the person cannot achieve that if they have no way of determining their current weight. In business, many people want to make a fortune, but if the measurement systems are not in place and they do not know where they stand, it is impossible to move forward.

For example, if the manager does not know the sales amount, there is no concrete basis to compare to, making it difficult for the manager to know if sales are rising or falling. This is why measuring revenue and costs is at the heart of a hospitality business manager's job.

Gain Experience Controlling Costs and Revenues

Hospitality students can improve their business cost control knowledge and experience while in school and enhance their job preparation through the following activities:

1. Get experience in a business and begin to observe the flow of products and the employee behaviors within the business. The student can then relate those products and behaviors to money (revenues, costs, and expenses), regardless of job position.

2. Interview management professionals regarding their cost control duties. Ask them what the most difficult part of their job related to cost controls has been, ask them what they have learned since becoming responsible for the cost controls. Great people to interview include supervisors, assistant managers, general managers, controllers, area directors, vice presidents and presidents. Each will be able to offer valuable input from a slightly different angle. The successful hospitality business manager will want to learn all of those different angles. Still, other interviews that would prove helpful would be to interview accountants about what they think every business owner needs to know, or what the most likely revenue and cost traps are for the new business owner or manager.

3. Get a better grasp on your personal finances by learning to save money and finding out the exact amount that something costs. Learn that saving money is equivalent to making money.

4. Work problems in the cost controls, finance, and accounting classes that are offered in most hospitality curricula. The repetition is essential in order to be able to understand the value of revenue and cost controls for the business.

5. Basic mathematical skills are essential to practice and keep up-to-date. For example, if one has difficulty with percentages, it is not likely

that, as a manager, he will accurately solve problems regarding the profit percentage of certain items or how to price those items so they are profitable for the business.

Measurement Statements

While many statements are used to measure performance of the business, only the two essential statements will be introduced here. Other statements will be covered in your cost control, accounting, or finance classes. Two statements measure the business performance for the firm: (1) the income statement, and (2) the balance sheet statement. All hospitality students will want to understand these statements since they are the gauges that inform the business, whether it is profitable or not and whether the net worth of the business is increasing or decreasing. All hospitality business managers want to have a basic understanding of statements that help to measure the flow of funds.

The Income Statement

The net income for the business can be compared to the net income figure that is at the bottom of an employee's paycheck. That is, the money that you get from the employer, minus the taxes that you owe and any other deductions you may have, then yields the employees net pay (or income from that job) for that pay period. For the business, all of the inflows of dollars, minus the outflows of dollars, equals net income. Reward systems for managers are often based on the amount of profitability that can be achieved. Typically, there is a percentage range of profitability that the company expects the manager to achieve and the manager's bonus or raise is based on whether she meets or does not meet that percentage range. Successful hospitality managers understand cash and credit systems in a business and are always looking for ways to improve.

The income statement is also known as the profit and loss statement. The basic formula for the income statement is:

Total Revenue (Inflows) − Total Costs (Outflows)
= Net Income

It is simply the money that came into the business minus the money it cost to run the business plus the "costs that are out of control" equals net income. Let's repeat the last statement regarding total costs. The total costs for the business includes the costs of doing business plus the cost wasted trying to do business. This statement allows the business to diagnose their performance across a period of time. The format for income statements may vary from business to business. However, there are several accounts on all income statements, regardless of the type of business. These accounts include: total sales, cost of goods sold, gross profit, expenses, taxes, and net income.

Revenue (inflows) includes what the primary business is. For example, a hotdog stand's revenue is from selling hotdogs and other products that people buy when at the hotdog stand. A Dairy Queen's revenue is from ice cream sales plus ice cream cakes, sandwiches, burgers, etc. Costs (outflows or expenses) would be operating expenses, cost of sales, occupancy costs, property taxes, insurance, utility costs, and, salaries and benefits for employees. For an example of an income statement refer to Figure 16-1.

The Balance Sheet Statement

One of the main financial statements that a business uses to measure money flow is the balance sheet. This sheet is important to any business because a business can determine net worth from the balance sheet. The balance sheet contains all the information about what the company has possession of (total assets), what the company owes on what it has possession of or has used (total liabilities) and the portion of those assets that the company owns (owner's equity). Simply put, the balance sheet equation is:

Total Assets = Total Liabilities + Owner's Equity

A further division that is important for any business manager to understand is the division of the total assets into short-term (current or temporary) assets and long-term (non-current or fixed) assets. The same division happens with total liabilities. Total liabilities equals short-term (current or temporary) liabilities plus long-term (non-current or fixed) liabilities. Therefore, an extended equation for the balance sheet is:

Short-term + Long-term Assets = Short-term + Long-term Liabilities + Owner's Equity

By looking at the balance sheet and either viewing owner's equity or subtracting total liabilities

FIGURE 16.1	The ABC Restaurant Statement of Income Year Ended December 31, 20xx	

In Dollars

Sales		
Food	$1,250,000	
Beverage	300,000	
Total sales		$1,550,000
Cost of sales		
Food	450,000	
Beverage	105,000	
Total Cost of sales		555,000
Gross profit		995,000
Expenses:		
Salaries and Wages	387,500	
Employee Benefits	62,000	
Other Expenses	232,500	
Interest Expense	31,000	
Depreciation	77,500	
Occupancy Costs	108,500	
Total Expenses		899,000
Net Income before Taxes		96,000
Taxes (28%)		26,880
Net Income		$ 69,120

Summary—The statement indicates the business performance over a period of time. It tells the business the amount of costs (outflows) and the amount of sales (inflows). The difference between the inflows and outflows determines net income.

from total assets, you can derive the net worth of a business.

Managing the short-term assets and the short-term liabilities is the main responsibility of unit managers. This is referred to as the management of working capital for a business. Management of working capital involves balancing the timing of what the company currently has (short-term assets) and what the company currently owes (short-term liabilities). The word "working" in front of capital implies short term. Thus, working capital management refers to the short-term management of what the company owns (inflows) and what the company owes (outflows). It is the management and the safeguarding or controlling of the current assets that have been brought in and the safe-

guarding or controlling of the current liabilities that must be paid out. Simply put, once sales are made, the hospitality receives those sales in the form of current assets (cash transactions, account receivables, credit transactions), and inventory (sales to be made); and then there are obligations to keep the sales flowing, and that involves short-term liabilities (accounts payable, rent payable, wages payable, etc.).

Each time an individual goes into a bank to apply for a loan, the bank will request the individual to complete a personal balance sheet and reveal to the bank the total assets (what an individual has), the total liabilities (what portion of what the individual has is owed on) and the individual's owner's equity (net worth of the individual). The bank is simply asking for the individual's net worth by asking for a personal balance sheet. When the bank asks for the W-2 forms of the person, the bank is asking for the income statement. Some businesses check a potential job candidate's credit references prior to hiring the applicant. The credit reference tells the company how good the individual is at managing his or her own working capital. For an example of a balance sheet, refer to Figure 16-2.

As you can see from the former explanations, the control of costs and revenue as measured by the income statement and the balance sheet will be important to the future success of any business manager. Below are some recent hospitality graduates' comments regarding the knowledge of cost controls. Good luck as you reach for your success by understanding the numbers.

Statements of Recent Hospitality Alum Regarding Cost Controls

I had just graduated from Eastern Michigan University and moved to Texas. I immediately began interviewing for hospitality management positions. Because I had taken a minor, I had avoided the Cost Controls class because I was weak in mathematics and any course that concerned numbers. The minute I started interviewing for jobs, I found that most companies were very concerned with the knowledge of cost controls. If I had to rethink my position, I would certainly take the cost controls

	20X1	20X2
Total Assets		
Current Assets		
Cash	15,000	28,000
Accounts Receivable	15,000	20,000
Marketable Securities	80,000	60,000
Inventory	12,000	22,000
Prepaid Expenses	10,000	5,000
Total Current Assets	132,000	135,000
Non-Current Assets		
Property	300,000	300,000
Plant	1,000,000	1,000,000
Equipment	100,000	170,000
Less: Depreciation	(500,000)	(550,000)
Total Non-Current Assets	900,000	920,000
Total Assets	1,032,000	1,055,000
Total Liabilities		
Current Liabilities		
Accounts Payables	19,000	29,000
Current Maturities of Debts	25,000	25,000
Wages Payable	10,000	8,000
Total Non-Current Assets	54,000	62,000
Non-current Liabilities		
Long-term Debt	600,000	575,000
Total Liabilities	654,000	637,000
Owner's Equity	378,000	418,000
Total Liabilities and Owner's Equity	1,032,000	1,055,000

Statement Summary—The balance sheet indicates the performance of a business at a "snapshot" in time. It indicates the net worth of the business, which can be determined by subtracting total liabilities from total assets. Subtracting total current assets from total current liabilities allows one to determine net working capital, a key responsibility for the entry level hospitality graduate.

class, plus do many other activities to learn this area better.

Stephanie Anderson
Java Cup, Restaurant Manager
Hospitality Graduate

Knowing the formulas for average room rate and for food and beverage cost was critical. I still have my cheat sheet (it was allowed) from my Cost Controls class.

Alison Tarpley
University of Michigan, Hotel Manager
Hospitality Graduate

Most of the formulas are done for you in the computer, but you must understand how the numbers got on your profit and loss statement and what they mean to the business. Your pay is directly linked to your understanding of hospitality cost controls.

Kris Tarpley
Assistant Manager, Panera Bread Company
Hospitality Graduate

Name_____ Date_____

Chapter 16 Review Questions

1. List three ways a manager can control costs (outflow of money).

2. What is meant by the term "fiscal?"

3. Why is effective cost control important to a manager's ability to stay employed?

4. Define the term "revenue."

5. How does a manager effectively manage money after it has been generated by the business?

6. What does the term "86ed" mean? Why is this important in cost controls?

7. Why should a manager audit an employee's cash drawer?

8. In your opinion, how often should an employee's cash drawer be audited?

9. What are the two primary means of payment received within the hospitality industry?

10. Who is responsible for training employees on cash handling?

11. Who pays whom a fee when a consumer at a hospitality business uses a credit card?

12. What is the range of credit card fees?

13. Why is managing the collection of "credit" transactions important to a business?

14. List the five ways described that a hospitality student can gain experience in cost controls.

15. What are the courses offered at your school that teach students the elements of cost control?

16. Define "net income."

17. How can net income likely affect a manager's bonus or raise?

18. What is another name for the income statement?

19. What are the standard items/accounts on all income statements?

20. How does a business determine net worth?

21. What are some items that would be included as total assets?

22. What is the difference between "total liabilities" and "owners equity?" Give an example of each.

23. Define "short term assets" and "long term assets." How do they differ?

24. Define "short term liabilities" and "long term liabilities." How do they differ?

25. What is meant by the term "working capital?"

26. Which level of management deals most closely with working capital?

27. Why would a company conduct a credit report/credit check on a potential candidate applying for a management level position?

28. Why is the balance sheet considered a snapshot of finances?

Chapter **17**

Law and Ethics

POSTAGE
PAID

Mather Point
Grand Canyon, Arizona

Robert Alan Palmer
*California State Polytechnic
University*

Corel

No one would hire me to teach culinary arts or food production. Yet, many of my fellow faculty members outside the hospitality program seem genuinely surprised when they learn this. To them, hospitality management is synonymous with, and limited to, cooking.

"No," I have to tell them. "I'm no culinary expert. My field is law."

"Law?" is their amazed response. "What would a hospitality student need to learn about law?"

Don't get me started!

Are We in Business Yet?

A hospitality business may be structured in various ways. There is, for example, the sole proprietorship, the partnership, the corporation, the limited liability company. These business formats differ from each other in terms of who is responsible for the debts and obligations of the business, who is responsible for taxes on the income of the business, and how the business may be sold or financed. The legal formalities for setting up a business differ, depending on which of these business types you select. So, some familiarity with the law of business is necessary even before you start in business.

Many hospitality businesses today are franchises. A franchise agreement is a contractual obligation that binds the franchisee to accept a fairly high degree of control by the franchising company, to meet strict operational standards, to pay a franchise fee, and make periodic royalty payments. Certainly, no businessperson should enter into a franchise agreement without some understanding of contract law, franchise law, and the federal and state disclosure requirements imposed on companies that offer franchises.

Where Are We Located?

Hospitality businesses occupy actual physical space, and there are legal considerations in every step of acquiring that space and getting the business into operation.

Zoning

No, just because you own land does not mean that you can build a restaurant on it. Your big old family home might make a great bed and breakfast, but you cannot necessarily go right ahead and start renting rooms. Most built-up areas have zoning regulations that specify the uses to which land may be put. A commercial enterprise (even a small one) is usually prohibited in a residential area.

Leasing

You may own the building that your hospitality establishment occupies, but most hospitality operators rent space from a landlord or building owner. The lease, of course, is a legal contract, and you will need to be prepared to negotiate a number of questions.

How many years will the lease run? How much rent will be paid, and will the rental payment be a set figure per month, or will it be a percentage of the establishment's sales? Will the landlord agree to make changes in the building that might be necessary to accommodate food service equipment, extra utilities, or computer needs? Who will be responsible for building repairs? Who will maintain outside or lobby areas that may be common to several tenants? If you want to go out of business or move out of the space, will you have the right to sublease? Will you owe the landlord any "damage" payments for leaving before the expiration of the lease?

The lease agreement you negotiate will answer these questions. But once you agree to these terms, you are bound by them, even if business turns bad or other unforeseen problems arise. Legal knowledge is essential to protect your business interests and to acquire the necessary space on the most favorable terms for your business.

Who Is Working Here?

The field of employment law is big, and, is growing bigger. The United States Congress and the state legislatures have, during the last forty years or so, passed a wealth of laws regulating the employment relationship, more than we have seen in any other period of our history.

Employment Discrimination

Laws at both national and state levels prohibit employers from basing employment decisions on the race, sex, religion, national origin, disability status, or age of the applicant or employee. Some states have expanded their discrimination laws to cover such topics as sexual orientation, marital, and family status. Workplace sexual harassment is likewise prohibited by law.

A basic understanding of employment law is essential, from the hiring stage through termination and its aftermath.

Wage and Hour Law

This is the area of law that requires the employer to pay at least a minimum wage, to pay extra for overtime work, and to pay employees for all time that they work. This area also determines who can be paid on a salaried basis versus who must be paid for each hour that they work. Child labor (special restrictions applicable to those employees who are under 18 years of age) is another topic of wage and hour law. Hospitality employers are especially affected by this area of the law, since we have many employees paid at or near the minimum wage, and we hire more people in the child labor category than do most other businesses.

Workers' Compensation

These state-regulated insurance programs are meant to compensate employees for medical expenses, lost wages, and rehabilitation costs that may be incurred as a result of work-related injuries. These payments are guaranteed, regardless of who is at fault for the injury. Employers who have higher injury rates will pay higher premiums, making workers compensation a potentially expensive proposition for the less-careful employer. A manager needs some familiarity with coverage rules and claims procedures.

Labor Relations

There is an entire specialized area of the law devoted to unionized workplaces. This portion of the law spells out the rights of employees to form or be represented by labor unions, and the rights of employers to resist or campaign against union organization. The law defines so-called "unfair labor practices," actions that an employer may not take, such as firing an employee because she supports unionization or promising benefits to an employee group if they will vote against union representation. Labor law seeks to balance the rights of employers, unions, and employees and, in so doing, draws some fine lines of permissible versus impermissible behavior and speech that are very easy to

Extra precautions need to be taken to protect children.

cross. You will need to know these if you ever have to deal with a union organizing campaign.

And, when you manage a unionized workforce, labor law also influences the negotiating, or collective bargaining, process and deals with such topics as your duty to bargain with the union, strikes, boycotts, and what happens to the union contract if the business is sold or goes bankrupt.

Did Someone Fall Down?

Negligence

Every business owes its customers and others a general duty to exercise reasonable care in removing or warning about hazards on its premises that may cause accident or injury. Accidents do happen, however, and negligence is that area of law that attempts to define who is legally responsible for a particular accident and to make that person, or entity, pay for the reasonable costs of the accident victim.

Fault is not always easy to determine. Plaintiff and defendant usually have different versions of what happened and who was careless. There may be multiple plaintiffs and defendants, each bearing some responsibility. Most states today are "comparative negligence" jurisdictions, in which a jury or judge must determine the percentage of fault applicable to the parties in a negligence action in order to apportion financial liability.

There are defenses to a negligence action, the best of which is abundant evidence that you inspect, repair, maintain, and generally do everything that might constitute "reasonable care" in the hospitality business. You might also be able to point to negligent or careless acts of the plaintiff that might be the total or partial cause of his/her injury.

On the other hand, most hospitality properties entertain a great diversity of customers, some of whom may pose special problems. Small children, for example, are difficult to protect, since they lack the judgment and safety awareness of the average adult and take risks that a reasonable adult would not. The elderly, or others who may be particularly prone to injury, should cause you to be especially careful. And you may, under some circumstances, even be liable for injuries to trespassers.

Liquor Liability

The sale of alcohol is heavily regulated by the states. The state in which you operate establishes requirements you must meet to obtain and keep a liquor license, and the state controls the licensing process. Your state law also prohibits you from selling alcohol to customers who are already intoxicated, or to persons under the age of 21, and the state may fine you, or suspend or even revoke your license for violation of these laws.

But there is even greater potential liability to persons who may be injured by your sales to minors or the intoxicated. In so-called "third party liability," or "dram shop" suits, people who are injured by your drinking customer have the right to sue you, the alcohol seller, to receive compensation for their injuries caused by your service of alcohol. Since there is so much state-by-state variation in liquor liability laws, and since mistakes in service can have especially great consequences, this is another legal area with which you need to be familiar.

They Lost What?

Hotelkeepers deal with a large amount of guest property—luggage, valuables, cars, etc.—and have special legal requirements imposed on them for any loss of that property. Even restaurateurs and other types of hospitality operators may have some responsibility for customers' personal property brought onto the premises.

State laws require the innkeeper to reimburse guests for lost property, but only up to a limited dollar amount. However, in order to take advantage of this limited liability, hotel operators usually pro-

vide safes for the storage of valuables and must notify the guest in some way about the presence of that safe and the dollar limits of the hotel operator's liability.

Separate limits usually apply to luggage and contents, items which guests normally keep in their rooms, rather than in hotel safes. But many state laws specify that you may not limit your liability, and may be responsible for full reimbursement, if a loss results from your own or your employees' careless acts, rather than from any action or failure on the part of the guest.

And the law has gaps: What do you tell the customer who asks, "Where is a safe place to park in your hotel's lot?" A fully loaded van or truck may be especially vulnerable to break-in or theft, yet we would not normally require the guest to unload these vehicles and place their contents in the room or the safe. Liability limitation statutes, originally drafted in the days of rail travel when guests usually brought along no more than they could carry, often fail to address these newer legal problems. So managers need to know what to say and do regarding guest property.

Are We Done Yet?

The law is involved in many other aspects of hospitality operations as well.

Trademark law gives you the right to protect your business name, signs, and other advertising material from misappropriation by your competitors, but it can also trip you up if you copy, even inadvertently, some of these items from other hospitality companies.

Copyright law governs your right to play live or recorded music in a business establishment. Music is not free for the taking when you are using it in a commercial setting, and there are royalty and license obligations that accompany the use of most music in hospitality facilities.

Anti-trust law prohibits you from conspiring with other hospitality operators to fix prices, to boycott certain suppliers, or to avoid competing with each other.

Food safety laws and regulations subject you to regular inspections for food safety and sanitation, and also impose a high degree of responsibility on you when contaminated food, or foreign objects in food, cause injury to your customers. Also, most states require food service facilities to post detailed instructions about performing the Heimlich maneuver on choking customers, and to call in emergency medical assistance when necessary.

Anti-discrimination laws also come into play if guests or potential customers allege that you treated them differently because of their race, sex, national origin, disability, or other factors.

Specialized types of hospitality operations may have particular legal problems. A hospital food service operation, for example, may be caught up in medical malpractice if a serious mistake is made in determining the content of a patient's meals. School food service managers need to know the requirements of federal surplus food and school lunch programs.

A country club has to deal with all the usual problems of a large landowner, plus liability for flying golf or tennis balls, or even lightning strikes. A club manager may also need to know the criteria for gaining or retaining a club's tax-exempt status, and what commercial activities of the club might jeopardize that status, or result in unexpected tax obligations. Casino operators must master an entire body of law dealing with gaming.

It should be clear that a hospitality manager needs some basic familiarity with many aspects of the law. While that manager will want to seek out professional advice on most major legal problems, she/he will frequently need to be able to make smart and fast decisions in situations where professional legal advice is not immediately available. Also, a hospitality manager will need a legal knowledge base to work with insurance companies, risk management specialists, and outside legal counsel.

Major lesson here: The law is an area of management responsibility that you cannot totally delegate to others.

Even if It's Legal, It Might Not Be Ethical

Finally, business people are becoming increasingly aware of the interplay between law and ethics. Many actions or practices that may be legal may still be inappropriate ethically. Your purchasing manager may accept "skybox" tickets to the big football game from a major food service distributor. You may hire someone for a particular job without telling him that you plan to eliminate that job in the near future. Or you may quote an attractively low room rate to a guest for a popular weekend, knowing that you can probably get away with raising it once the guest arrives and finds no other rooms available.

These are primarily ethical, rather than legal, issues, though each might have a legal component under some circumstances. And, yes, such practices might have some potentially noticeable effects on the company's purchasing decisions, on employee morale, or on customers' willingness to do business with your company.

But do ethical considerations really matter? If there isn't a significant threat of a lawsuit, do we need to worry about ethics? Isn't ethics just the concern of naïve and foolish "do-gooders" who do not understand the financial and practical imperatives of running a business?

That is frequently how we view the subject of ethics. Recently, there have been many high profile examples of corporate executives' ethical mistakes causing huge financial damage to their companies. Major American corporations have been driven to bankruptcy, with their stock values wiped out and their employees stripped of their jobs and pensions, because of questionable accounting and business practices that have both legal and ethical implications. Today we have large- and small-scale examples everywhere of how ethics make a difference in the bottom line.

Certainly, no customer wants to be lied to, or wants to patronize a business that she/he perceives to be dishonest in its dealings with customers. Unethical employment practices will drive away good employees and applicants and possibly customers, as well. Investors will refuse to put money into companies perceived to "cook" their books. So, yes, ethical concerns do relate to the "bottom line."

Chapter 17 Review Questions

1. How would a strong legal knowledge assist a person considering a franchise agreement?

2. What are some specifics likely to be found in a lease agreement?

3. Describe the components of the employment discrimination law.

4. Describe the components of the wage and hour law.

5. Why does a hospitality manager need to know the child labor laws?

6. What is meant by "unfair labor practices?" In what type of setting would they apply?

7. Give three examples of potential lawsuits of negligence in the hospitality industry.

8. What is meant by the term "comparative negligence?"

9. Who are the plaintiff and the defendant in a lawsuit?

10. What is the best defense in a negligence case?

11. Describe how a hotelier may be responsible for lost items of a guest.

12. What are some unique liabilities a club manager could face?

13. What are some unique liabilities a casino manager might face?

14. Can a manager delegate to his/her employees the responsibility of upholding the law?

15. Compare/contrast the differences between ethics and law.

16. How could the unethical behavior of a hospitality manager drive away good employees?

17. How could the unethical behavior of a hospitality manager drive away good customers?

Part IV
Hospitality and
Tourism Career Menu

18
Attractions Management

19
Bar and Beverage Operations

20
Casinos

21
Club Operations

22
Cruise Ships

23
Culinary Arts

24
Distribution Services

25
Education Careers

26
Golf Management

27

Hotel and Lodging Operations

28

Interior Design

29

International Hospitality

30

Management Consulting

31

Meeting and Event Management

32

Non-Commercial Food Service

33

Quick Service Operations

34

Real Estate

35

Resorts

36

Restaurant Operations

37

Senior Services Management

38

Travel Agencies and Tour Operators

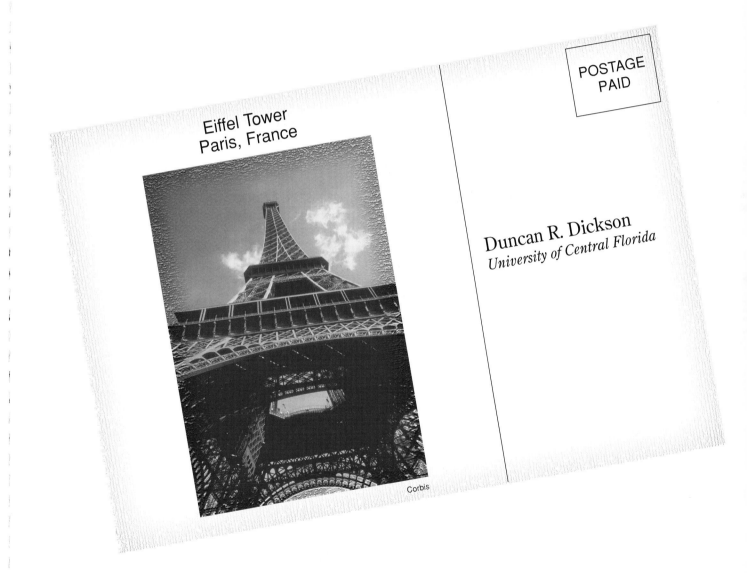

POSTAGE
PAID

Eiffel Tower
Paris, France

Corbis

Duncan R. Dickson
University of Central Florida

Typically, the study of hospitality management does an excellent job in covering hotels and restaurants. When it comes to covering leisure activities, most curricula will include cruise and casino management; however, most ignore the exciting and rewarding career opportunities available in attractions management.

As the twentieth century drew to a close, more and more leisure time was available to individuals in the developed world. Some European nations were even instituting 35-hour workweeks. With this expanded leisure time available, people, particularly as family units, are looking for more and more things to do and attractions provide that for them. The fight for the discretionary dollar will continue to get more and more brutal as the baby-boomers begin to retire en mass in 2010. That date sparks the largest, wealthiest group of retirees that the world has ever seen.

The Leisure Industry

How the leisure industry adapts to guests' expectations could mean phenomenal success to those who do it correctly. Traditionally, we talk about entertainment, attractions, recreation, cruises, gaming, and even shopping as leisure activities. From these we single out attractions for this chapter.

For academic purposes we will categorize attractions as:

- Cultural attractions
- Natural attractions
- Amusement and theme parks

The first two are typically organized and controlled by public (governmental) or voluntary (not for profit) groups, the last by private (for profit) groups. We will concentrate on the latter.

Cultural Attractions

Sites set up to preserve or further the culture of the community are included in this group. These can be historical in nature or be considered a refinement of society, such as a theater. Virtually anything made by humans that draw people to it can be considered a cultural attraction.

Natural Attractions

Our natural attractions are being claimed and re-claimed by organizations throughout the world in

The Eiffel Tower has been a popular attraction for over 100 years.

an effort to protect these gifts. We have realized that what nature has given through the millennia, man can ruin in a very short period of time. Consequently, the growth of volunteer organizations such as Green Peace, Save the Rainforest, and any other number of Save the, actively work to protect the world's natural attractions. We are lucky to have groups like this. While they are quite often a thorn in the side of governments, those seeking economic development, and industrialists, they do make society aware of those things that are irreplaceable and need protecting.

Amusement and Theme Parks

The history of the amusement park can be traced back to the festivals of the Middle Ages when people gathered to trade and barter or celebrate a harvest. As these gatherings grew around the medieval cathedrals, it was natural for entertainment to become a part of the celebration. From this came the early amusement parks; the oldest still in business dates from 1655 in Bakken, Denmark.

Most of these revolved around simple rides, gardens, and entertainment such as Tivoli Gardens in Copenhagen. But, three hundred years ago, the parks typically operated on a limited schedule. In St. Petersburg, Russia the ice slides were popular, but only in winter. The Paris Frascati Gardens became popular because of its Chemin de Centrifuge. Yet most of the leisure parks gave way to the political unrest of the 19th century in Europe.

On the American side of the Atlantic, the popularity of amusement parks started to rise with the increased concentration of people in the cities due to the industrialization of the U.S. The need for ridership on weekends of the new electric railways brought a new phenomenon—the "American Pleasure Garden." These new-age amusement parks were built at the terminal points of these electric railways; the most famous of these was Coney Island built in 1884 with its wonderfully named "Switchback Gravity Pleasure Railway."

The popularity of these "Pleasure Gardens" rose until there were nearly 1,400 of them in 1920. A combination of several economic events and the introduction of radio and talking motion pictures caused the drastic decline of amusement parks to less than 400. Other reasons for the decline were a world-wide depression, followed by a world war.

The Birth of the Modern Theme Park

As the urban legend goes, one day in the early 1950s, Walt Disney was in a little amusement park with his daughters, Diane and Sharon, watching them as they played on the kiddie rides. Walt became more and more irritated as he just sat on a bench and watched. Walt went back to his studio and vowed to create a place where families could go and all be entertained together.

Thus, 17 July 1955 became the watershed date for the modern theme park. That is the day that Disneyland (the Happiest Place in the World) opened to the world. But if you were in the U.S., your appetite was whetted for two years prior by watching "The Wonderful World of Disney" on Sunday evenings at 7 p.m. Walt cleverly wedged a few minutes of the Disneyland plans into each show and, thus, on the advertising of others, he

created a pent up demand for his new (or recreated) brand of family entertainment.

Investors were difficult to find for the project. Walt had to mortgage everything he owned, including his life insurance and movie studio. Through the financial acumen of his brother Roy, he was able to make his opening date. Those who watched the opening on TV with hosts Art Linkletter and Ronald Reagan (long before he thought of becoming Governor of California or President of the United States) were amazed at what there was to do. Disneyland quickly became the most popular attraction in the world.

Suddenly, terms like *audioanimatronic, Tomorrowland, cast member* and *Jungle Cruise* had meaning to the general population. Kids everywhere were begging their parents to visit Anaheim, then a center of orange groves southwest of Los Angeles.

Walt's theme park concept has now spread worldwide, and many refinements have been made since that wild opening in July of 1955. One of the first things Walt did after Disneyland became established was to buy back all the leases for restaurants and merchandise locations that he was forced to sell just to get it open. The first lesson Walt learned was that if you are to have a successful "theme park,' you have to have full control over the environment.

Amusement versus Theme Park—What's the Difference?

Typically, an amusement park is a collection of rides and food stands located in one central area with no congruence. Most of the time, each ride requires its own admission, or ticket.

Theme Parks strive to create a fantasy atmosphere that transports the visitor to another place and time. Normally, they are in closed geographical boundaries with an admission price at the gate. Theme parks concentrate on one dominant theme with possible sub-themes. The theming is reflected in architecture, landscaping, costumed personnel, rides, shows, food services, merchandising, and any other guest experiences.

In a theme park environment, the theme is mainly communicated through visual and vocal statements, but, in reality, attempts to incorporate all the senses. Authenticity is not the key to good

Based on 2002 attendance statistics the top five theme parks are: (Amusement Business)

Magic Kingdom, WDW	14.0 million admissions
Tokyo Disneyland	13.0 million admissions
Disneyland, CA	12.7 million admissions
Tokyo Disneysea	12.0 million admissions
Disneyland, Paris	10.3 million admissions

The top corporate entities involved in theme parks are:*

Six Flags Theme Parks	35 parks
Cedar Fairs Ltd.	12 parks
Walt Disney Attractions (The Walt Disney Company)	10 parks
Anheuser-Busch Theme Parks	9 parks
Universal Studios Inc. (Vivendi Int'l.)	6 parks
Paramount Parks (Viacom Company)	5 parks

theming; believability is. But, it all starts with a story.

Since 1955, the theme park business has become big business. The playing field changed significantly when Disney decided to get into the business. Now you had corporate ownership of theme parks, which has legitimized the business. Disneyland quickly became a destination, showing potential investors and marketing gurus that a theme park had a broad customer base. Then in 1961, competition entered the theme park industry as Six Flags Over Texas opened in Dallas.

Major corporations dominate today's theme park industry. The Walt Disney Company is not the largest in terms of number of parks, but it dominates in attendance figures with all of their parks (eight included—two parks were too new to have attendance rankings at the end of 2002) ranking in the top 15 with the top five being Disney Parks. Six Flags Corporation has the most theme parks with a total of 35. Many of them do not operate on a year around schedule. Quite often, the more regional parks will operate daily during the summer season, on weekends in shoulder season, and close for several months in the winter season. There are some parks, like "Spooky World" in Foxboro, Massachusetts that operate less than 30 days per year.

In the theme park business, the primary reason to visit is the rides, but spending on admission, parking, food and beverage, merchandise, souvenirs, and other purchases generates revenue. Most theme park operators, however, will tell you what they sell are "memories."

Successful parks provide a safe, clean, and happy environment for their visitors. Most give their guests an unforgettable family-oriented experience that combines fantasy and thrills with outstanding services.

A theme park takes a great deal of initial capital investment to install its complex operating sys-

tems. There is also a need to reinvest to maintain a competitive position. To operate on a year around schedule, you also need sensible weather.

Communities generally like theme parks because they generate a high number of jobs. They also work to boost tourism to the area and, in some instances, are the destination in and of themselves. Parks generate a lot of tax revenue, easing the tax burden on local residents. Some economic forecasters estimate that for every job created in a theme park, 4–7 jobs are created in the local community.[1]

The Future of Theme Parks

IAAPA (International Association of Amusement Parks & Attractions—founded in 1918 is the largest amusement industry association with more than 4,000 members in 72 countries) predicts continued growth in their market segment. Annual attendance in 2001 at IAAPA member parks was in excess of 703 million (14 percent captured by Disney). This is projected to increase by 4.2 percent by 2006. Worldwide spending in 2001 was estimated at $18.4 billion and is projected to climb to $22.6 billion in 2006.

The U.S. theme parks accounted for 45 percent of the world's total attendance (319 million—this is more than the entire population of the U.S.), and were more than all of the people attending sporting events in the year. On a percentage basis, Asian theme parks will grow faster than the U.S. followed by Europe and the Middle East. Disney opens in Hong Kong in 2005, followed by Shanghai Universal in 2006.

---

[1] * Alain Baldacci—President of IAAPA speech to AMFORHT; Marne la Vallee, France, November, 2002.

Careers in Theme Parks

As major corporations have acquired and expanded the theme park business along with increased in revenue and attendance, career opportunities have grown to meet the staffing demands of complex operations. In Orlando, Florida, home to ten theme parks and four water parks, over eighty thousand people are employed directly by theme park companies. This does not begin to include the thousands of others who work in hotels and restaurants providing travel related services for the theme parks' guests. As with most hospitality companies, careers with theme park companies tend to fall into *operating* and *support* positions.

Operations

Since the bulk of the revenue falls into three distinct areas, these are also the three largest areas of operating employment—attractions, food and beverage, and merchandise. Other operating areas include entertainment, security, parking, and custodial. Like the housekeeping department of a hotel, the custodial department of a theme park is of tremendous importance. At Disney, one of the areas most often commented on by guests is the cleanliness.

All operating segments have a management hierarchy that allows for either entry-level additions or promotion from within, which is very typical in the attractions group. An individual who de-

sires a fantastic career with upward mobility, yet is not interested in the angst of relocating for promotion that hotels and restaurants have, could do well in a theme park environment.

The management issues and challenges in a theme park career are not dissimilar to other management positions in the hospitality industry. The one common difference with theme park management is that all of your guests came to have fun—thus, exceeding their expectations is equally enjoyable. One major difference would be the number of schedule changes that theme parks endure annually. With the parks' operating schedules changing so often and by season, there is a high reliance on part-time and casual labor.

Support

As with all corporations, there are a myriad of support areas in which individuals can find extremely rewarding careers. Many times, these can come after a beginning in operations or those with the appropriate education and experience may enter into those departments directly.

Just think of the range of talents needed to complete the finance division. Aside from the typical accounting functions of accounts receivable and accounts payable, heavy cash operations require a teller or cash control to distribute the funds and then a deposit operations team to send it to the bank and recirculate as appropriate. Add to that internal audit, financial planning and analysis, and

Many attractions, such as the Vietnam Memorial, are visited because of a personal connection.

a research and statistics group and you have a very diverse finance function.

The marketing and sales team can be just as diverse, challenging, and rewarding. Imagine the promotions, advertising schemes, or public relations events you must conjure up to lure new guests to your theme park. Add to that all the deals you would need to broker to feature various products in your park with participant companies.

Human resources requires a complex set of skills, as well. From recruiting for thousands of different jobs and schedules to orienting the new hires to the company, training them for the knowledge, skills, and abilities to do their jobs and developing them for their next job, HR has a full plate. Throw in all the retention programs that must be developed to keep your staff and the consultation with line management to assure that the policies and procedures are applied equitably, and there are great opportunities in HR, especially for a line manager with an HR interest.

Line managers may make a career shift at times from attractions management to ride design and installation. What the theme park companies have found is that the engineering and design whizzes sometimes lack the grounded operational knowledge necessary for the design and installation of an attraction. The need for someone who truly understands what works on a 95° day with 98 percent humidity and a forty-five minute wait cannot be understated.

Beyond these there are the professional departments concerned with such things as:

- Law
- Construction
- Waste Control

- Safety
- Loss Control
- Purchasing
- Traffic
- Crafts/Maintenance
- Horticulture
- Landscaping
- Wardrobe

This is certainly not a comprehensive list, nor do all theme parks have these departments. They are, however, representative of what a major theme park company would have to support their parks. It also gives you an idea of the great diversity of talent necessary to run a theme park. Career opportunities abound for all types of individuals with all types of backgrounds. The most important thing in theme parks is not worrying about where you start, because there are numerous opportunities for promotion from within.

Conclusion

If the leisure side of the hospitality industry is attractive to you, there are many opportunities. Whether you want to have a position with less pressure in the public sector managing natural or cultural attractions or you are ready to hit the highly charged private sector of amusement and theme parks, there is a career for you. With the changing demographics we are seeing in the next twenty years coupled with the globalization of companies, we predict the opportunities will become greater.

With great thanks and appreciation to Dr. Paul Rompf of the Rosen School of Hospitality Management for his support and editorial virtuosity.

References

Milman, Ady (2000). "The Future of the Theme Park and Attraction Industry." *Funworld,* November, 180–185.

Milman, Ady (1992). *Theme Parks and Attractions.* In Kahn, A. K., Olsen, M. D., & Var, T. (eds.), VNR'S Encyclopedia of Hospitality Management (pp 934–944). New York: Van Nostrand Reinhold.

Milman, Ady (1991). "The Role of Theme Parks as a Leisure Activity for Local Communities." *Journal of Travel Research* 29(3): 11–16.

Rubin, Judith (2001). "Theming by Any Other Name." *Funworld,* April 42–47.

Swarbrooke, John (2002). *The Development and Management of Visitor Attractions.* Boston. Butterworth-Hienneman.

Name _____ Date _____

Chapter 18 Review Questions

1. What is projected to happen in the attractions industry as the baby boomer generation retires?

2. List several types of "not for profit" attractions.

3. List several types of "for profit" attractions.

4. What is the history behind amusement parks?

5. What was the connection between the early "American Pleasure Garden" and the railway?

6. When and how did Disneyland get started?

7. Compare and contrast theme parks and amusement parks.

8. Describe a theme park experience you had with your family. What are key points you remember?

9. What economic impact does a theme park have on its local community?

10. What economic impact does a theme park have on its state?

11. What are the future business projections for theme parks?

12. How do theme parks compare to sporting events for the numbers of people they attract?

13. What are the three major areas of revenues in theme parks?

14. Create a list of at least six positions in attraction operations.

15. Create a list of at least three positions in attraction support services.

16. What are the different positions/departments where a hospitality graduate may become employed in attractions management?

17. Discuss the role of communication within the hierarchy of management.

Chapter 19

Bar and Beverage Operations

The Coliseum
Rome, Italy

POSTAGE
PAID

T. C. Girard
Southern Illinois University

Corel

187

The beverage business is an extensive business, employing millions of people. Farmers, grape producers, brewery workers, distillers, and bartenders are all in the economic structure of the beverage business. Alcoholic beverages may contribute 30 percent to 40 percent of a full-service operation's sales and generate up to 70 percent of its profit, whereas supply costs are but a quarter of beverage generated revenues. Profit margins of 20 percent are typical, while margins of up to 50 percent have been obtained. Wine consumption, mixed and specialty drinks, and increased beer consumption bolstered by new product lines are bringing more consumption per capita than the previous half-decade. In all, alcoholic beverages have contributed to our economic growth and pleasure throughout history.

Purpose

While we cannot propose to cover the entire perspective of the beverage industry in this chapter, it can be an introduction to the prospective student about the bar and beverage business. Thus, we will begin with a mini-historical view, succinct discussion on legal aspects, proceed to careers and responsibilities, and finish with critical operational points.

History

Today we still hear of Dionysus, the Greek god of wine and Bacchus the Roman god of wine and indulgence. These civilizations left us images of those celebrations of drunkenness and debauchery in art, tapestry, and the written word. The Babylonians, Assyrians, and Egyptians produced mead, wine, and liqueurs. Vineyards from the Middle Ages are still productive today in Germany and central Europe. The Church became the prime producer and distributor of beverages during the Renaissance. The sixteenth century brought gin from Holland, whiskey from Scotland and Ireland, brandy from France, and rum from England. It seems that humanity has attempted to produce alcoholic drink since the beginning of time.

From Europe to the Americas, the old inns, taverns, and ordinaries were the center of social congregations. Historically, these were the gathering places of our pre-revolutionary fathers of America to plan the American Revolution. As Americans traveled west, saloons were ever present and provided the local community with a place to enjoy their leisure hours and even hold trials. Today, modern bars, cocktail lounges, and beverage service in many restaurants are the norm. What characterizes the beverage business today, as well as in the past, is the social, celebratory atmosphere that brings people together.

Legal Aspects

To engage in alcohol service, obtaining a license on-premises or off-premises or both are necessary. To do this, you must meet these two legal considerations: the license holder must be of legal age and not have any felony convictions. If you pass those requirements, the next step is to retain a lawyer. They can furnish advice on all local, state, and federal laws and provide assistance in filling out and filing forms, since the local community or the state controls all liquor licenses. Beyond the license, there are state Alcohol Beverage Commission (ABCs) restrictions for hours of sale, approval for expansion or equipment, records, and methods of operation. Local regulations may include zoning, fire codes, building codes, and the type of establishment (food sales) or types of beverages sold.

Dram shop laws are the largest legal concern for those who own or operate bars. These laws impose penalties on the establishment if guests leave intoxicated and are involved in an accident. This imposes third-party liability on all who sell or serve alcohol when these circumstances exist: the individual served was intoxicated, a clear danger to themselves and others, and intoxication was the cause of the incident. This encumbrance is a great insurance liability that sometimes prohibits some prospective owners from operating.

Every owner should provide training for every employee to help reduce the risk of this liability. Training programs are available from the following sources:

- American Hotel and Motel Association—Controlling Alcohol Risks Effectively (CARE)
- National Restaurant Association BARCODE
- National Institute on Alcohol Abuse and Alcoholism—Training for Intervention Procedures by Servers of Alcohol (TIPS)
- In addition, check your state ABC board for programs.

The comfortable and relaxing atmosphere of a bar can be used to unwind.

Other activities regulated are refilling liquor bottles or transferring liquor to other bottles, absence of federal tax stamps, watering down liquor, display of license, and gambling on premises. All of these and other regulations can cause loss of license for violation. Local, state, and federal laws are extensive, and thorough knowledge is essential to the license holder to operate legally.

Careers and Responsibilities

Although not considered as the lead career choice for hospitality graduates, bartending is a viable vocation. *Cocktail* and *Coyote Ugly* are two movies that have given this occupation glamour. Perhaps many students reading today will work at this position while attending school or perhaps chose it as an internship. Either will provide a "real world" look at the beverage industry and provide valuable experience.

Bartenders directly serve and interact with patrons. Patrons frequent drinking establishments for the social atmosphere; thus, bartenders must be amiable with patrons. Beyond this, knowledge of hundreds of drink recipes and the skill to quickly and accurately mix drinks without waste is necessary. Bartenders also check identification for age requirements, collect sales, operate cash registers, maintain an impeccable service area, and may or-

der and maintain inventory for their establishment. Bartending schools have been established to polish skills for those interested in this career choice and may soon be required by many establishments as an entry-level requirement.

In larger hotels, full service operations, and clubs, one would find the beverage steward position. This position comes with many responsibilities. Among them are purchasing, receiving, storage, requisitioning, and inventory control. The beverage steward must know operation, cost and sales control methods, and be able to perceive their local market and act accordingly. As well, extensive knowledge of wines may be necessary to occupy this position. Overall, this position is a natural transition from bartender in the career ladder.

Bar manager or assistant food and beverage manager are two positions that many graduates strive for after college for their entry-level career path. Most hospitality programs provide the management background for these positions. Some offer specific concentrations in beverage management. It is important to note here that applicants with a bachelor's degree have the best opportunities for these positions. These positions have one major responsibility—the entire operation.

Because managers direct the activities of the business that provides a service to customers, most employers emphasize personal qualities when hiring managers. Self-discipline, initiative, and leadership abilities are essential. Managers must be able to solve problems and concentrate on details. They need good communication skills to interact with customers, suppliers, and staff. Because of the many demands, good health and stamina are important. Lastly, a willingness to relocate often may be essential for advancement.

The daily responsibilities can often be complicated. In addition to the traditional duties of beverage management, administrative and human resource tasks are also part of the position obligation. On a daily basis, managers estimate consumption, place orders, schedule deliveries, receive and document shipments, ensure good service, meet with sales representatives, and suppliers, purchase equipment, and arrange for equipment maintenance and repair. Overseeing the bar staff, observing the quality and quantity of beverages served, investigating and resolving customer complaints, maintaining sanitation, and monitoring employee actions to ensure that health, safety, and local liquor regulations are obeyed are also fundamental responsibilities.

Administrative duties may include contracts, managing insurance, records of hours and wages, payroll, and paperwork in compliance with licensing laws and reporting requirements of tax, wage and hour, unemployment compensation, and Social Security laws. Human Resource tasks are also part of the job. Finding and evaluating ways to recruit and legally select employees in a tight job market is important. Creating ways to retain experienced workers is a high priority. Employment relationships in the areas of discrimination, sexual harassment, termination, and possible court appearances are critical.

Critical Operational Points

- Know the cost of your operation at all times. To do this, develop a management control system. Make it inexpensive, timely, have documented responsibility and accountability for everything, analyze the information, take appropriate action, and do it continuously.
- Remember what you are selling: atmosphere, courtesy, comfort, a social gathering place, and the hospitality experience—not booze.
- Hire, develop, and retain excellence in service. Your service staff is a reflection of what you sell. Hold onto the character and values that reflect what you sell.
- Provide structure and consistency in policies, procedures, guidance, discipline, and rewards.
- Know thoroughly and sell only the highest quality wines, spirits, liqueur aperitifs, beer, and non-alcoholic beverages. Do not surprise your customers.
- Own and use the best equipment available.
- Surround yourself with professionals. Realize what you do not know, then seek guidance from those with expertise before you make decisions.

Conclusions

To face the daily challenges of the beverage business, you must keep your customers excited, motivate workers, and exploit change before it is necessary, be it in technology, product, market, or regulation. Those of you reading this today are tomorrow's potential managers, so be ever diligent, work hard, and take advantage of every opportunity to achieve your individual goals.

Chapter 19 Review Questions

1. Describe the history of wine related to the Greek and Roman empires.

2. What are the characteristics of the bar/beverage industry?

3. What are the general restrictions one must pass before obtaining a liquor license?

4. What are "dram shop" laws?

5. When does third-party liability exist?

6. Why do patrons typically visit beverage businesses?

7. Describe the duties of a beverage steward.

8. How many drink recipes does a typical bartender know in his/her head?

9. List five of the personal qualities often sought after in hiring beverage managers.

10. Describe the daily duties of a bar manager.

11. Describe the administrative duties of a bar manager.

Casinos

Expo 86 Center
Vancouver, British Columbia

Corel

POSTAGE
PAID

Kathryn Hashimoto
University of New Orleans

Why learn about casinos? Don't all hospitality operations run pretty much the same way? Well, not exactly. Certainly, a good manager can function in many environments. However, this industry has some differences that are important to understand. We'll begin externally by examining the impact of casinos on the surrounding communities. Think you might want to work in one? We'll discuss the differences between casino operations with hotels/F&B and traditional hospitality operations.

Casinos are a unique industry because their reputation has been less than socially acceptable. However, despite this perception, the American casino business has grown by leaps and bounds. When politicians see the amount of money generated by the gaming industry, everyone wants a piece of the action. As a result, legislators push to have gambling legalized. In the year 2001, more than 425 commercial casinos were operating in 11 states. In addition, some form of casino gaming was approved in 30 states across the country. These casinos hired over 370,000 employees who earned more than $10.9 billion in wages. From the states' point of view, tax revenues were a little less than $3.5 billion, and these figures did not include additional revenues from property taxes, corporate income taxes, local use taxes, or payroll taxes paid by individual casino employees.[1] As you can see, the state budgets are greatly improved by the gaming industry.

Gaming can be an economic goldmine in other ways, as well. Typically, gambling establishments begin by developing an infrastructure to bring in outsiders to the area. This creates jobs for the locals and generates many different tax bases for the government. Then, to meet the needs of the visitors, the new tax revenues are used to improve the infrastructures that support the traffic. As the commercial base expands, new businesses open to support the growing number of tourists and locals. As a result, gaming is a very strong, economic development tool. Casino development creates an upward spiral that increases jobs, adds more taxes from businesses and tourists, and decreases taxes for the townspeople. When residents see the projected economic impact, the positive aspects of gaming are impressive.

However, as with any growth in tourism, this expansion comes with costs. The main problem is rooted in the business itself. Casinos generate millions of dollars a day in hard currency. For example, to convert the customers' paper money to chips and back again, the casinos have many areas called "cages." They act as mini-banks. However, one cage may have five million dollars in cash. That does not even include all the money that is on the tables, in the slot machines, or on the patrons!

Think about being around that kind of money! Does it make you contemplate some different ideas? Everyone does. This brings about the negative aspects of the industry. It is perfectly normal to watch millions of dollars changing hands and think what it would be like to have some of it for your very own. Politicians, employees, customers, or local people are not exempt from this fantasy. Because of the enormous amount of money all in one place, organized crime has always been reputed to be a part of gambling. This resulted in bribery and graft in politicians and criminal activity like money laundering and illegal criminal operations, creating a negative image for gambling. However, as more respectable business people like Howard Hughes and Baron Hilton invested their money in these properties, casinos gained respectability. While the criminal background will always be part of the excitement of a casino, strict regulations on employees and owners, as well as the large business conglomerates, have helped to alter the reality.

There are two main problems for employees and players: wanting the casino's money and spending too much of your own. Some people want the cash they see in the casinos. If they cannot win it, stealing is another option. This is one of the perceived problems that many anti-gaming advocates use to deter people from voting for gaming. They assume that crime increases in the areas where casinos operate. This is simple logic. With any increase in population density, problems are going to arise. On the other hand, with some more thought, this becomes counterintuitive. Casino owners understand that this open display of cash is a temptation. Therefore, security and surveillance are a major part of any casino operation to deter people from thinking along these lines for too long. The casinos do not want big winners to get robbed because it is bad for business. People who do not feel

[1] American Gaming Association, *State of the States: the AGA Survey of Casino Entertainment*. Washington, D.C.: American Gaming Association (2001).

secure are not going to come back. Reinforcing this premise are newer longitudinal studies that show crime increases during the introductory phases of casino development, but then the rates actually decrease over the long term.

The second aspect of the money problem revolves around the fact that some people get caught up in trying to win the jackpot and stay too long. A select few will become pathological gamblers. Problem gamblers tend to follow a similar pattern. Usually, they win big early in their careers, and then they chase their losses. This means that if you lose, you double the bet to get the money back. This is a bad strategy and rapidly increases gambling debts. However, less than 2 percent of the population is at risk of becoming addicted. Some researchers have stretched this percentage to 40–50 percent of the population. However, the key point to remember is that it all depends on how you define problem. Is it when you spend $10 more than you budgeted or is it when you steal to get money to gamble? Keep in mind, this is a very small percent of the population. On the whole, over 98 percent of the people who come to a casino will not suffer any ill effects from the experience. Because of the large amounts of money generated, gaming has inherent bonuses and risks. Understanding both sides of the issues is important for each person so that they can decide how they stand on each issue.

Differences between Casino Operations and Traditional Hospitality Enterprises

Controlling the Money

With all these people spending their cash, the primary focus of casino management is to track the money. With $100 bills and $10,000 chips floating around the floor, controlling and securing the flow of cash is the name of the game. Computers, accounting departments, security, and surveillance are very important in this process. With all this money, there is a serious temptation to walk away with cash that is not yours. Therefore, the organizational structure is set up to accommodate the primary directive: track the money.

Accountants use computers to access credit information and verify customer accounts. Casino floor people can quickly determine credit lines for

Craps is one of the most prevalent table games found in a casino.

vouchers by searching the computer online or calling the credit department. Because money watching is the most important activity in the casino, accounting terminology is important. When casinos talk about profits, they describe them in terms of the process. For example, the "drop" is the total amount of cash plus the value of the markers (credit slips) the casino takes in. This is similar to gross revenues. However, the "handle" is the total amount of money that has continuously changed hands before it is actually won or lost. For example, a person can start with $5, then win $45, and lose $50. The casino counts it as a "handle" of $100. However, the casino "win" for this person would be "0." "Win" is comparable to net revenues.

Why is this important? This is part of tracking the money. The money has to be accounted for each time it changes hands. If a casino cannot follow the money trail, they may be losing cash without knowing it. To begin the process, patrons can play with dollars or they can exchange the dollars for chips. Chips are easier to use. For example, $10,000 converts instantly into a single chip. It's definitely less bulky to carry around the casino. Also, the casinos would like you to carry around the chips. It makes it easier for them to keep track of their money. Psychologically, the chips make sense for the casinos. When a person throws a chip onto the table, the gambler does not perceive it as "money." Spending chips operates on the same psychological principles as credit cards. Signing a piece of paper does not "feel" like spending money. On the other hand, handing over $100 bills to a clerk empties your wallet and you know you have spent your paycheck. The last step in tracking the money is when the customer leaves the casino. Gamblers must cash in their remaining chips because you cannot play in one casino with chips from another "house" (casino). This allows the casino to track the cash flow from the time it enters the casino to the final moment when the gambler leaves.

Following the money trail also means a big job for security and surveillance. The temptation to cheat the casino is particularly strong, and stealing is not just limited to the clients. Think of it. You are a dealer. In front of you could be stacks of chips worth $250,000 in different denominations. One chip, the size of a half dollar, is worth $5,000. Ok. You are an honest person and you have a code of ethics that says you do not steal from other people. Then you get in a car accident and need a car, but you haven't saved enough money to buy one. If you took just one chip . . . a small one . . . $5,000 . . . that's small money for a casino, and it would help you get back on your feet again. Would you be tempted? The assumption is that anyone would.

Therefore, the casino has two departments to watch everyone. This is the security and surveillance or "eye in the sky" department. The security people walk the casino floor and make sure everything is above board. Their surveillance counterparts are in an office above the gaming floor. They watch hundreds of cameras embedded in the ceiling of the casino. Every square inch of the casino can be watched, photographed, and recorded on videotape. Surveillance can zoom in to a table and read the face of a coin at that table. A call to security can have cheaters picked up on the floor. Anytime there is trouble, surveillance can rewind and view what happened on the casino floor. Also, there are customer safety people, who help protect the customers. As we said before, it is very tempting to palm a $50,000 chip, so security and surveillance design procedures to minimize the risk.

Organizational Structure

In addition, because everyone is watching everyone else, the hierarchy of power in the casino comprises several layers to act as additional security. All levels of management are responsible for making sure no one under him is taking money that does not belong to him. Typically, there are two main divisions with many layers of management: table games and slots.

Table games They define table games as any game played on a table. This encompasses the most prevalent games like blackjack, baccarat (*bah-ka-ra*), roulette, and craps that are played against the house (casino). The front line personnel for the table games are the dealers, who are responsible for keeping the games moving and for making sure the games are played according to the rules. They also watch the games for players who cheat. For each two to four tables, there is a floor person, who looks for irregularities and handles most customer conflicts. Several floor people and their respective dealers work in an area called the "pit." The pit boss is the most senior gaming supervisor in the pit. This person is responsible for maintaining the record of customer activity and handling the financial accounting like fills, credits, and closing inventory. A fill is when a table needs more chips. Overlooking all the different pits is the shift manager. He/she does the scheduling, oversees the operations for a specific time and supervises the floor and dealers. Finally, there is the casino manager. Status reports, radical changes in operations, suspicions of misconduct, personnel, and long term planning are the domains of the casino manager. Because of these layers, the games are well protected.

Slots Traditionally, the table games were where the "real" gamblers played, usually men. However, casino operators realized that wives and girlfriends needed something to do while the men gambled. Otherwise, the women would insist that the men leave the games before they were ready to go. Slot machines were the perfect decoys. The women

Gaming can be an economic gold mine.

could sit, chat, and "pretend" to gamble in a lady-like fashion. These are games that include slots, video poker, and other computerized games. Because computers have revolutionized the industry, all the table games in the casino usually have a video equivalent. Instead of playing around a table with a dealer, the computer chip is the competition. This is less threatening for novices and it gives them a chance to practice the games. Some machines allow a person to play any table game at a single machine. The screens are user friendly and touch sensitized for game selection. The quarter slots are the most popular denomination. If you think that's not much. . . imagine four spins per minute . . . 240/hour . . . more than 1,000 in less than five hours . . . with three coins in a 25-cent machine, that's 75 cents per spin . . . in less than five hours, a person could wager $750 on a quarter slot machine. In the high stakes groupings, there are slots for $5, $25, $100 or $500. As it turns out, slots have become a bigger profit center than anyone could have imagined. In many casinos, slot machines account for 60–70 percent of the win. (Remember win? It does NOT refer to how much the gambler wins.) As casino managers realize this is a gold mine, more slots are added to the casino floor.

Slot departments have several layers of managers. On the floor, the slot attendants supervise an assigned area to cater to customer needs like change, payouts, and problems with the machines. Slot shift managers are in charge for a specific period and oversee slot personnel, verify major slot payoffs, and sign major jackpot slips. Finally, the slot manager handles slot operations, verifies authenticity of major payouts, looks for unusual variations in operations and works on promotional programs. Each manager has the responsibility of making sure the patrons have gambling change and ensuring the safety and honesty of each machine.

The primary goal of casino management is to follow the money. With cash being the primary product of a casino, it is imperative that many layers of management be employed in order to ensure the honesty of everyone involved. More management positions are available as a result.

Power Structures

In any organization, the department that directly brings in revenues is considered a profit center. This means that they have more control in the ev-eryday operations than other departments. In the hotel, the rooms division directly generates the money, and, therefore, they are the most influential. What happens when a rooms division manager moves to a casino/hotel? Many casino operations use rooms and F&B as marketing tools or "comps." "Comps" are free items that players can receive as bonuses for playing at the casino. Therefore, in casino/hotels, the rooms division manager does not always have control over how many rooms are in inventory or what price the clients will pay. There must always be a block of rooms for "comping"; therefore, 100 percent occupancy is *NOT* optimal planning. The casinos like to have a certain percentage, say 10 percent of the room inventory available at all times. As a result, the power positions, types of responsibilities, and goals will change when a person moves from a traditional hotel to a casino/hotel.

Levels of Service

Comps Depending on how much money you wager, the casino has different levels of service and rewards. Like other hospitality operations, casinos treat each patron according to their level of involvement. However, casinos offer a much wider variety of services for free ("comps"), and the level of service can be radically different. "Comps" are based on a special formula that each casino generates. To create the information, they have to track a player's "action" or amount of play. When a casino "tracks" a player, they watch and record information like length of time at the casino, amount of money wagered, how often they come, and credit line. Because this is a time consuming, labor intensive process, historically high rollers (people who bet large sums of money) were the only ones who received ratings and, therefore, "comps." However, with the age of computers, the casino generates player information quickly and easily. Therefore, they can track any individual for "comps." Although they rate each person individually, casinos can categorize levels of "comps" to three major groups of people.

Low rollers "Low rollers" are people who play the nickel, dime, and quarter slots. They only gamble small amounts of money. For example, bus programs were created to accommodate low rollers and can include round-trip bus fare, $20 in tokens for the slot machines, and a complimentary lunch at the buffet. While this might seem like an extravagance for the casinos, it pays off. On average, each person on the bus will leave approximately $40–$50 of their own money at the casino. This is the McDonald's principle. Price low, but sell volumes.

Middle rollers This relatively new category of player was added with the arrival of computers. Previously, casinos ignored these players because there were too many of them, and it was hard to find a way for the casino people to keep track of them all. Now, players can request that they be "tracked" at the casino's Players' Club. The casino immediately puts personal information into the computer and hands back a Player's Club Card. All a gambler has to do is insert the card into each slot machine he/she plays. Once inserted, the gambler's personal information file keeps track of play. It also keeps track of playing time, machines used, amount bet, etc. So no matter where the customer goes in the casino, management can follow their "action."

High rollers "High rollers" are people who gamble large amounts of money at the tables. At one casino in Las Vegas, there is a penthouse suite with 10,000 square feet of floor space, a butler, a swimming pool, jacuzzi, and an optional chef. To expedite the "high roller's" request, there is a special casino person called a "host." The sole purpose of the host is to be available for a particular high roller while he/she is in town and make sure that everything is in order. "Instant gratification" is the name of the game. They will obtain anything for this guest on demand, no questions asked. Every-

thing is "comped." In addition to free room and board, casinos invite "high rollers" on "junkets." These are special event parties where the casinos obtain top seats to heavyweight title fights, Super Bowl games, or professional golf tournaments. The casino will invite these "high rollers" to join them, free, provided that they spend a certain number of hours playing at the casino. So as you can see, they treat "high rollers" with a great deal of respect and lots of service. The levels of service can be met because they carefully track the money. Each patron is followed around the casino, and the casino notes and documents each monetary action with employees and computers. The number of different managers and marketing people guarantee that each person will be treated to the level of their spending habits.

Conclusion

To evaluate this business effectively, one must understand two relationships: (1) the pros and cons of gaming as an industry and (2) the differences between the traditional hospitality operations and a casino driven one. Of course, this chapter has only dealt with the casino positions that are different from the traditional hospitality operations. There are still all the regular positions in marketing, accounting, human resources, etc. Because of the multiple layers of managers, there are many opportunities for people who want to be a part of this industry. The main thing to keep in mind when evaluating a career in gaming: money is the product. As a result, this makes it different from other hospitality operations. Knowledge about the industry is the first step to making good career choices.

Chapter 20 Review Questions

1. Describe your opinion of casinos and their impact on society.

2. Why are legislators interested in gaming?

3. List at least five ways gaming can bring revenue to an area/state.

4. What is the history associated with crime and casinos? How is it different today?

5. What does the research show about crime in casino areas? How does this differ from perception?

6. What is the main problem for both employees and players in a casino?

7. What is meant by "chase your losses?" Is it an effective strategy?

8. What tools are used in casinos to control the money?

9. Define the following casino terms:

   a. Action

   b. Pit

   c. Fill

d. House

e. Handle

f. Cage

g. Drop

10. How do chips compare to credit cards?

11. How does a surveillance system work in the casino?

12. Who does the surveillance team watch?

13. Sketch the hierarchy of positions in the table games segment of a casino.

14. Compare and contrast the rooms division in a hotel with the rooms division in a casino.

15. What are the differences in people who are classified as:

a. "Low rollers"

b. "Middle rollers"

c. "High rollers"

16. When, why, and to whom is a casino manager likely to comp room nights?

17. What is the role of the "host" assigned to a high roller?

18. What is a "junket?"

19. How has the casino industry perfected the relationship between level of service given and the level of money spent by the consumer?

20. Could other hospitality segments benefit from this service to money-spent ratio? If so, which segment(s)? Give an example.

Chapter

21

Club Operations

Los Angeles, California

Corel

Denis P. Rudd
Robert Morris University

Alina Zapalska
Marshall University

POSTAGE
PAID

Introduction

A **club** is defined as a group of persons organized for social, literary, athletic, political or other purposes. People join clubs to engage in social discourses and to surround themselves with others who have similar interests. Growing steadily each year are the increasing markets for private clubs. Catering to a large number of clientele, clubs have existed for many years and included various interest groups, recreational activities, and organizations. With over 14,000 private clubs in the United States, they have created an atmosphere favorable to friendliness and comfort. A recent survey compiled by the Club Managers Association of America (CMAA) indicated that the annual gross revenue for these clubs is over 11.322 billion in dollars per year. Club dues account for 4.5 billion dollars, food and beverage revenue equals 3.795 billion dollars, and the average club income is approximately 4.9 million dollars and generates 320 million in sales tax revenue. The club industry employs over 302,000 people and has a payroll of approximately 4.4 billion dollars; clubs in America provide over 165 million in charitable contributions and in excess of 8.3 million dollars in scholarships to students each year according to CMAA.

Private Clubs

Although there are a variety of clubs throughout the world, all clubs share a common bond: the member. The member is considered a guest and, as such, must pay some type of fee or due. Listed and described below are some of the most common clubs in existence today.

Country Clubs

Around 50 percent of all private clubs are country clubs. They often provide elaborate social services along with outdoor recreational facilities. Activities in a typical country club usually center around the golf course; yet, many country clubs provide members with outdoor facilities for swimming, tennis, horseback riding, and other interests. Members are inclined to hold weddings, reunions, or other social events there. Recently, many upscale housing projects have encouraged the building and growth of country clubs to attract neighboring communities and new residents. There are two types of memberships at country clubs; full mem-

Most yacht clubs operate a marina for their members.

berships, which entitle the club member to the full use of the facilities the club offers; and social membership, which permits the member to use specific facilities, such as the restaurant, lounge, bar, tennis courts, etc. Social memberships may require that club members use the club's facilities at certain times or days. In the past, country clubs were seen as the last fortress of the upper class elite. In some cases, this is still true; however, in most instances, the stuffy cigar smoke and the Mayflower context are no longer used to determine whether an individual should qualify for membership.

Yacht Clubs

These clubs are designated for establishments near or on the water, and generally promote and regulate boating and yachting. The Montauk and Rochester yacht clubs are examples of this type of organization. Most yacht clubs own and operate a marina for their members, which may include the operation of a clubhouse with dining and recreation facilities.

Military Clubs

Military clubs cater to the enlisted man, the non-commissioned officer, and the officer. Military bases in the United States and overseas provide these clubs for the welfare and the benefit of the soldiers. They provide extended amenities for their club members, such as guest quarters, recreational activities, food and beverage operations, and entertainment. In the past, the clubs have been run by military personnel, but recent changes in resource

Profile

The Edgeworth Club was formed in 1893. Under their bylaws, its purpose was to promote interaction and friendship among its members, as well as furnish facilities for athletics and other sports, plus the construction and maintenance of a building or buildings thereafter. Sports that were emphasized at the club were tennis, bowling, and golf. The architectural style of the Edgeworth Club is decidedly Elizabethan, which lends itself particularly to the ground upon which it was built and the uses for which it was designed. The Edgeworth Club hosted the Wightman Tennis Cup match, a prestigious international tennis event. Since then, its emphasis has been on tennis and paddle tennis. The club is the principal location for charity events to raise funds for health associations and other organizations.

allocation have required the military to contract civilian firms to provide services. These facilities are located around the world and include the Bamberg Officer's Club in Bamberg, Germany and the Fort Benning Officer's Club in Fort Benning, Georgia. An example is the 911th Airlift Wing of the United States Air Force in Pittsburgh, Pennsylvania. Before 1974, they had two Military Clubs on base. The Non-Commissioned Officer (NCO) Club was for the enlisted members of the base and the Officer's Club was designated for the Officers of the base. Due to the downsizing in the military and the costs of running two clubs, the 911th NCO and Officer's Club became a Consolidated Open Mess (Club) in February 1974. Today's club is open to Officers and enlisted members of all branches of the Armed Forces—Air Force, Army, Navy, Marines, and Coast Guard and is currently 1,133 members strong. Being a member of the Club is a tradition at the 911th Airlift Wing. Members join the Club for several reasons, but the biggest include camaraderie and a place to share military experiences with other armed services members. It is also a gathering place for the numerous retirees in the area. The 911th Club hosts several events each month for its members, ranging from official functions to holiday celebrations, as well as membership nights, sports parties, meet-and-greets, birthday parties, wedding receptions, and other functions. The Club offers excellent dining opportunities and does promotions with giveaways.

Professional clubs Are for people in the same profession for social and business interaction. The Engineer's Club of St. Louis is a professional club that appeals to engineers from the St. Louis area.

Social clubs Similar to the Everglades Club in Palm Beach, Florida, concentrate on serving the social needs of members who are normally from similar social-economic backgrounds.

City clubs As the name implies, are usually located in urban communities and range from luncheon-only clubs that serve segments of the business population to fully integrated dining and athletic clubs. Unlike most private clubs, city clubs may rent out guest rooms, organize themselves around a specialized profession, or associate with a particular college or university. City clubs fall into the following categories: professional, social, athletic, dining, fraternal, and university. The Duquesne Club has achieved the number one ranking among America's ten thousand private clubs, according to a national survey conducted by the Club Managers Association of America.

Athletic clubs Such as the Palm Beach Bath and Tennis Club and the Toronto Cricket and Skating Club, provide an outlet for working out, athletic activities, dining and meeting.

Dining clubs Are usually located in large office buildings, offering their members top-quality food service in urban surroundings. Examples include the Toronto Hunt Club and the Union Club of British Columbia.

Fraternal clubs Like the Elks Club and the Veterans of Foreign Wars, provide fraternal organizations with a central location for meetings, dining, and social activities.

University clubs Are reserved for the activities of faculty, alumni, and guests. The Harvard, Yale, Princeton and Pittsburgh University clubs are perfect examples of this.

Profile

The Duquesne Club was founded as a "voluntary association" in 1873 and incorporated as "a club for social enjoyment" in 1881. Membership was limited to 300, and annual dues were $50. Only two years later, many of Pittsburgh's most well-known citizens had been admitted, including Andrew Carnegie, Henry Clay Frick, B. B. Jones, Frank B. Laughlin, Andrew W. Mellon, Henry Oliver, Jr., and George Westinghouse. Many of their portraits can be seen hanging in the Founders Room. By 1902, membership limits were increased to 1,100, and in 1980, members voted to elect women to membership. Today, the Club has 1,457 active resident members, 465 senior resident members and 448 non-resident members.

First situated on Penn Avenue between 8th and 9th Street, in 1879 the Club leased a brick house on its present site. Membership flourished, and shortly thereafter, the club commissioned architects Longefellow, Alden, and Harlow (who later designed the Carnegie Institute), to plan the new club-house. The firm submitted an elegant plan in the Richardson Romanesque style, reflecting the success of H. H. Richardson's Allegheny County Courthouse and Jail.

The Club occupied its new quarters in 1889. In 1902, LA&H designed a matching addition, which broadened the facade and expanded the Club's space. Upon completion, it was reported that the Duquesne Club was the best-appointed club in America.

In 1994, the Club opened a 22,000 square foot state-of-the-art health and fitness center located in the adjacent Gimbels building. This facility has been an outstanding success and offers members one of the most extensive fitness facilities in the area. With 325 employees, excellent facilities, central location, and a persistent membership waiting list, the Duquesne Club remains one of America's greatest and most respected private clubs and is considered a Pittsburgh treasure by its members.

Melvin Rex explains that obtaining good managers can be difficult, but at the same time it can be threatening to some upper level managers, "I think the best way to run an establishment is to surround yourself with the finest people that you can possibly attain. Some managers are intimidated by hiring someone who might be more educated than them. You have to be confident in yourself."

Melvin Rex witnesses the turnover rate in general managers on a daily basis and commented by saying, "General managers have an employment expectancy rate in private clubs of about two and a half to three and a half years. Half of these managers leave for various reasons such as money or better positions at more accredited establishments and the other half of the managers are termi-nated. Being a club manager is highly stressful. These members own the club. If you have 2,600 members, then you have 2,600 opinions to satisfy."

I asked Melvin Rex how he has kept his managers well informed. He answered, "I use a program that I call accountability management. I use this plan to set annual goals for my executive staff. For instance, the goal for the executive chef is to reduce turnover." Mr. Rex acknowledged it is not just from an economical standpoint. "You will have a more consistent product when you obtain an experienced staff."

Club Employment

As club types, country clubs are the largest employers, followed by golf clubs and city clubs. Taken together, the total employment in country clubs is four times the number employed in golf clubs, and almost 10 times the number of those employed by city clubs. The ratio of full-time and part-time non-seasonal employees is almost exactly the same for both golf clubs and country clubs. Approximately 43 percent of all employees in these clubs are full-time and non-seasonal. This contrasts sharply with city clubs, where 74 percent of the employees are full-time non-seasonal employees. Similar ratios were found among full-time and part-time seasonal employees in both golf and country clubs. However, among city clubs, only one-third of the seasonal employees are part-time.

The Duquesne Club
Facility Description

7th–11th Floors: Bedrooms and private suites
6th Floor: Business offices, human resources, linen room, tailor shop, sewing room, and locker rooms

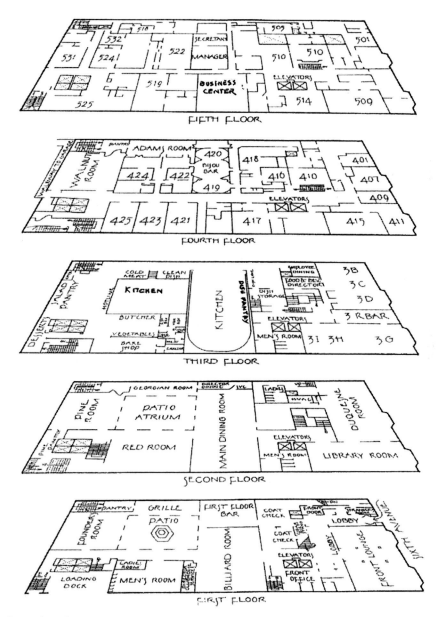

Basement: Laundry, print shop, carpenter shop, paint shop, engineering department, and locker rooms.

Club Ownership

Club ownership includes two categories: equity clubs and proprietary clubs. **Equity clubs** are non-profit clubs and are the oldest form of club management; yet, they are still the most common form of ownership today. These clubs are owned and organized by the members for their own enjoyment. The board of directors then establishes the policies, budget, and does the hiring and firing of executives, such as the club manager. Any profits that are generated from the dues or club operations must be reinvested in the clubs' services and facilities and cannot be returned to the members.

Proprietary clubs are operated for profit and are owned by a corporation, company, business, or individual. These clubs became popular in the 1970s and 80s and provided an expansion of club membership with stringent admission requirements. Club members purchase a membership from the club's owner(s) and have limited input and control over the activities or management of the daily operations of the club. In some cases, contract organizations run the facility for the owner. The club manager reports to this organization or the owner of the facility.

Club Management

As a student, one of the most challenging experiences in life will be to choose a career. If you're looking for a career that is creative and combines business skills, human resource management, marketing, and public relations, welcome to the world of club management. It is one of the fastest-growing industries and hospitality fields and will provide you with outstanding career opportunities in the future. Club management is similar to that of hospitality management because it offers similar facilities. The largest difference is that the club, unlike a hotel or restaurant, is actually looked at as being owned by the members. The member pays a fee each year, which can vary drastically depending on the nature of the club. In turn, the members feel that they are the owners of the facility. Having one boss may be difficult, but imagine having thousands! This sometimes can put the manager in a difficult situation.

The manager of a club is actually governed by a constitution and the by-laws of the club. The board of directors and club president are elected by their peers to insure the goals and mission of the club are carried out effectively, and they create the constitution and by-laws that govern members' policies and standards. Club management structure is similar to that of company structure. There is a president, vice president, treasurer, secretary, and different committees. The manager of a club, usually referred to as the Chief Operating Officer or the General Manager, has to answer to and abide by the rules set forth by the governing body, and is responsible for all areas of club operation. While the board of directors and president may be responsible for the policy setting and implementation, it is the club manager's job to hire personnel to run the day-to-day operations of the club.

Club Managers Association of America (CMAA)

Many club managers belong to the Club Managers Association of America (CMAA). This organization is the oldest and most widely respected association representing the club management professionals, and is comprised of more than 5,000 professional managers from the most prestigious private, country, city, yacht, and military clubs in the United States and around the world. In the early 1920s, professional club managers recognized the impact clubs had on the American way of life and the need for a professional association of these clubs. In February of 1927, the first annual meeting of the CMAA took place.

CMAA actively promotes and advances cooperation among individuals directly engaged in the club management profession, as well as other associations in the hospitality industry. In addition, CMAA encourages the education and professional advancement of it members and assists club officers and managers through their management to secure the most efficient and successful operations. The organization recognizes its responsibility to assist students in gaining a better understanding of the private club management profession and in selecting a career in this sector of the hospitality industry.

A student chapter of CMAA can be offered at any higher institutions that offer an undergraduate or graduate program in hospitality. As chapter members, students participate in professional development programs, site-visitation at local clubs, hands-on club operations and demonstrations, and leadership development programs. The CMAA pro-

A Club Manager's Perspective—Dan Brennan, Edgeworth Club

Entering into the year 2000 and beyond has been quite difficult for many of the private clubs nationwide. Member expectations have changed dramatically. The private club members of today have the same high expectations for service and food as they had thirty years ago, but they want it faster and more casual. Private club members of today are searching for the value in their investment and have put aside family tradition and legacy as reasons for joining a given club. The age of technology has played a large part in that. Club members are constantly on the go. They want to eat fast and be able to use their laptops or cell phones while they dine. The older established clubs across the country have been fighting that change. Many have figured out how to permit it without giving up their status.

Members want to make reservations online, they want to use e-mail for committee reports. The Edgeworth Club has found that managing a club that encourages their senior staff to be progressive with technology is quite challenging. Members in this computer age want to check their statements online and have the club at their fingertips 24 hours a day. Purchasing the right hardware and software and keeping in line with updates is a challenge. Purchases made today may be obsolete in 3 to 5 years. Long-term employees of 20 years are asked to change their habits and become "high tech." Emphasizing education has never been more important in the club industry. The Club Managers Association of America has done a wonderful job in preparing managers for the present, as well as the future.

As clubs move along trying to figure out what is right for them, we also must maintain our private club status. "High tech" can open a whole new set of problems, such as understanding the privacy laws and tax implications. It is so important to keep up with education and to hire the right person to lead your club. Hiring intelligent, well-educated, and well-rounded individuals to manage the various departments in and around the club is of the utmost importance. They are the leaders who determine club success. No one person has ever successfully run a private club, been successful financially, and kept their job longer than three years, doing it all by themselves.

vides its student chapters with an internship directory, which provides more than two hundred internships at private clubs around the world.

National Club Association (NCA)

The mission of the **National Club Association** is to serve the club community by protecting, preserving, and enhancing the interests and well-being of private social and recreational clubs.

Specifically, NCA strives to

- Provide support and information to assist club leaders in addressing legal, governance and business concerns, helping clubs strengthen their financial health and protect their assets;
- Ensure recognition and advancement of club interests through lobbying and other government relation activities, seeking to preserve the independence of clubs to operate; and

- Assist clubs in complying with laws and regulations.

Student memberships are available in most club organizations, and many clubs offer internships and summer jobs.

Conclusion

Clubs provide a unique managing experience that combines many elements of the hospitality and tourism industries. Club managers must be adaptable and open to the changing needs of the club members and the world around them. The most important job of a club manager is to provide club members with a positive experience every time they attend a function at the club. If managers fail to do this, attendance and membership will drop and the club will cease to exist. Service is the key to a club manager's success. Managers must realize that **SERVICE** is our business, and we serve the world.

References

Barnhart, C. L., ed. *The American College Dictionary*. New York: Random House, 1990.

Brown, Mark M., Lu Donnelly, and David G. Wilkins. *The History of the Duquesne Club*. Pittsburgh: Art and Library Committee, 1989.

"Club Management Forum" Virginia: Club Managers Association of America, 2000. http://www.cmaa.org/conf/conf2000/time.htm (Jan. 2, 2001).

Crossley, John C. and Lynn M. Jamieson. *Introduction to Commercial and Entrepreneurial Recreation*. Illinois: Sagamore Publishing, 1997.

Perdue, Joe., ed. *Contemporary Club Management*. Virginia: Club Managers Association of America, 1997.

Singerling, James, Robert Wood, Jack Nimemeier, and Joe Purdue. "Success Factors in Private Clubs." *Cornell Hotel and Restaurant Administration Quarterly* 38.5 (Oct. 1997).

"The CMAA Student Advantage: A Commitment to Your Future." Virginia: Club Managers Association of America, 1999. http://www.cmaa.org/ student /adv_bro/ index.htm (Jan. 4, 2001).

Walker, John R. *Introduction to Hospitality* 3rd ed. New Jersey: Prentice-Hall, 2001.

Chapter 21 Review Questions

1. What types of facilities are likely to be found at a country club?

2. What types of services are likely to be offered at a city club?

3. Describe the types of military clubs and the purposes they serve.

4. What is the mix of full time to part time staff at country clubs?

5. What is the mix of full time to part time staff at city clubs?

6. What is the mix of year round to seasonal staff in country clubs?

7. What is the mix of year round to seasonal staff in city clubs?

8. Define an equity club.

9. Define a proprietary club.

10. Sketch an organization chart that shows which positions report to whom.

11. What is CMAA? Visit their website at www.cmaa.org.

12. What is NCA?

13. What are the goals of NCA?

Chapter
22

Cruise Ships

Royal Princess Cruise Ship

POSTAGE
PAID

Marcia H. Taylor
Georgia State University
Lincoln H. Marshall
George Washington University

Corel

Introduction

The cruise industry, the fastest growing segment of the leisure travel market, has experienced tremendous growth since 1970, at more than one thousand percent, according to Cruise Line International Association (CLIA)—a non-profit association representing 24 cruise lines. This growth is expected to continue at an average rate of 7.9 percent over the next three years. The year 2002 was an exceptional year for the cruise line industry as cruise passengers reached the 7 million mark. As the number of passengers increases, the industry is responding by adding more ships to their fleet. In 2002, 12 new ships were introduced with accommodations for more than 20,000 additional passengers. In 2003, 14 more ships are expected to enter the worldwide fleet, with berths for another 30,000 passengers, and by 2004, another 10 ships with over 25,000 berths are expected. It is estimated, based on the number of ships on order, that by 2006 the number of passengers that can be accommodated will exceed 260,000.

The cruise industry is both international and multinational. Cruise passengers come from all over the world. However, North American cruise passengers represent 75 percent of the total world passengers. There are 179 cruise ships in the North American fleet, representing 193,846 berths. According to a study conducted by Business Research and Economic Advisors, the cruise companies contributed $20 billion to the U.S. economy in 2001 and directly employ over 101,000 in the companies' U.S. headquarters offices in field sales positions and in support and administrative positions worldwide and onboard the ships. Wages, salaries, benefits, and taxes paid in 2001 in the U.S. totaled $9.7 billion. The direct spending on purchases in the U.S. by cruise lines totaled $11 billion in 2001 and supported an estimated 166,000 jobs in industries throughout the economy.

The cruise industry also contributes indirectly to the ports of call and ports of embarkation and provides an added boost to tourism through money spent for pre- and post-cruise stays, sightseeing, restaurants, retail shops, and other purchases made by cruise passengers. It is estimated that the typical cruise passenger spends almost $104 at each visit. Cruise lines employ over 100,000 shipboard crew and they also contribute to the ports of call economies.

Brief History

Albert Ballin of the Hamburg-Amerika Line is regarded as one of the pioneers in the industry. He coordinated the first recorded cruise, on the *Augusta* with 241 passengers in 1891. After this time, sailing on ships became more refined. The cruise industry developed for many reasons. Originally, the sailing vessels were used primarily to transport travelers from one place to another. As economic conditions changed, wealthy individuals began to take cruises—round trip sailing—returning passengers to their point of origin.

In 1906, the Cunard Company entered the cruise industry on a large scale. Their flagship was the *Mauretina*, which was regarded as "the gem of the sea." Another notable event within the cruise industry was the sinking of the *Titanic* in 1912. Two years after the sinking of the Titanic, World War I started, which caused a decline in the cruise industry. After World War I, business improved when American Express chartered the *Laconia* for the first cruise around the world. When World War II started, once again the cruise industry declined. Immediately after World War II ended, however, cruise ships started sailing between Europe and the United States of America. The industry flourished until 1958 when the first jet crossed the Atlantic in six hours, which had an adverse impact on the number of passengers using the cruise ship as a primary means of traveling across the Atlantic.

In the early eighties, the cruise industry catapulted due mainly to the notoriety of the television series "Love Boat," which first aired in 1977. The "Love Boat" is responsible for publicizing modern-day cruising and creating awareness of cruise ship vacations to the world.

Cruise Line International Association—CLIA

The Cruise Line International Association (CLIA) was founded in 1975. Currently, it represents approximately 97 percent of the world's deluxe cruise operators, accounting for at least 24 cruise lines serving North America. Its primary purpose is to develop marketing strategies and assist with the training of professionals involved in the cruise industry. It does not have regulatory powers, but serves as a powerful lobbying group because of the research data it gathers. The CLIA has an informative website, www.clia.org, which provides current information about the cruise line industry and its members. CLIA also provides its members with two manuals, *Cruise Manual, Agent's Reference Manual* and *Cruise Night Planning Guide.* Both of these manuals are invaluable tools for cruise professionals.

Anatomy of a Cruise Ship

It is important to be familiar with the anatomy of a cruise ship whether you are a passenger or crewmember. There are at least six essential terms vital to understanding the anatomy of a ship, namely: the bow, stern, aft, port, starboard, and the mid-ship. These terms refer to the front, extreme rear of the ship, rear, left side, right side, and towards the middle of the ship, respectively. Most ships have a "lido deck," which denotes a deck that offers informal activities such as indoor and outdoor buffets.

A ship is classified by its "gross registered tonnage" (GRT). This is a formula that gauges the volume of public spaces on a ship. The larger the GRT, the greater the number of passengers a ship can carry. In thinking of a ship's size, the space ratio is an important concept to consider. The larger the space ratio, the greater the space a passenger has to roam while on the ship without interacting with other passengers. Unlike a resort that refers to the different levels as floors, a ship has decks with specific names: bridge, boat, sun, promenade, and sports decks. On each deck, in addition to the staterooms, there are different facilities, such as dining rooms, lounges, bars, theatre, meeting rooms, shops, and a variety of recreational areas.

Registration

Registering a cruise ship is a lengthy process that involves many people. This process is necessary to ensure the safety of all passengers, crew, and inhabitants of countries where the ships are registered. Although the registering process may be different in some countries, all of the major registration venues adhere to the same standards and guidelines mandated by the International Maritime Organization.

All ships, cruise, or cargo, must be registered within a country. The registration of a ship is similar to licensing an automobile. Just as the cost and requirements vary from state to state or country to country, the same principle applies with a ship's registration. Each cruise ship is required to pay both a registration and an annual fee, which are assessed by its tonnage weight. The annual fee is usually a percentage of the registration fee. During the initial registration, the ships are fully inspected and must obtain a registration every subsequent year. Regardless of the country of registration, ships must adhere to the laws of the country in which they make their port of call.

Companies register their ships in another country to benefit from the sometimes-relaxed laws in that country, such as the registration fees and the ease of conducting business. Cruise ships fly the flag of the country of registration and not necessarily the country of the owner. This registration process is also known as "flag of convenience."

The creation of a shipping registry creates jobs both within and outside the country for its residents. The Bahamas, Cyprus, Liberia, and Panama have built reputations for registering cruise ships. The Bahamas, in particular, prides itself with the absence of income tax, corporation tax, and value added tax. Panama promotes itself as being "the largest registry in the world."

Cruise Ships' Profile

There are over 35 cruise line companies operating in the world today. Several of them have only one ship in their fleet, while some have as many as 18. Cruise ships can fit into one of eight classifications: traditional, small luxury, masted sailing (tall ships), adventure/expedition, river ship, barges, steamboats, and passenger freighters. Cruise lines serve four distinct markets:

- The luxury/upscale cruise lines segment, with yacht-like upscale cruises, accounts for approximately 10 percent of the total industry fleet, and carries less than 10 percent of the passengers.
- The mass-market cruise lines segment, the most dominant segment of the industry, operates medium to large ships and carries approximately 75 percent of the industry's overall passengers.
- Niche/specialty—market cruise lines concentrate on specialized, exotic and adventurous itineraries.

- Bargain basement cruise lines use older ships and are, therefore, able to offer cruises at a lower price.

Carnival Cruise Line, Cunard, P&O Princess, and the Delta Queen Steamboat are considered the leaders in the mass market, luxury/upscale and niche and boutique, respectively.

Marketing plays a very important role in the success of the cruise industry today. According to CLIA, the cruise industry spends an estimated $500 million annually to generate awareness and create demand. Although the cruise line industry represents only 2.5 percent of the worldwide tourism product, it competes with resorts and destinations worldwide. The industry is now more diversified, offering cruises to suit every taste. In a recent research, study conducted by CLIA, nine out of 10 persons in the U.S. say they are interested in cruising. With ninety percent of U.S. adults having never cruised, there remains an enormous untapped market for cruises. Major cruise line companies are using "mega-ships" to lure more people onboard. These new breeds of cruise ships are often referred to as "floating resorts" or "hotels at sea." They provide the same amenities resorts offer, such as accommodations, restaurants, bars and lounges, entertainment, personalized services, and a wide variety of activities, and look more like hotels than ships.

The top five major cruise lines are listed in the table below.

Name of Cruise Line	Number of Ships	Characteristics
Carnival Cruise Line	18	The fun ships—relaxed and casual atmosphere—world's largest brand
Royal Caribbean International	12	Serves the volume contemporary and premium segment market—cruises to every area of the world
Holland America Line	11	Pampering service—worldwide itineraries
Princess	10	One of the fourth largest in the industry— one of the widest varieties of destinations and itineraries
Radisson Seven Seas	7	Fifth largest luxury cruise line—exotic ports

Organizational Structure

The organizational structure of a cruise ship varies according to the size of the ship. There are three main operation departments on a ship. The hotel department functions as a typical resort and is responsible for the passengers' activities, rooms, food, beverage, entertainment, and all other personal services offered. The fleet department is responsible for the maintenance of the ship and includes the ship's officers, radio operators, and engine and deck crews. The sanitation department includes the health and sanitation officers who are responsible for the health and safety of the passengers and crew.

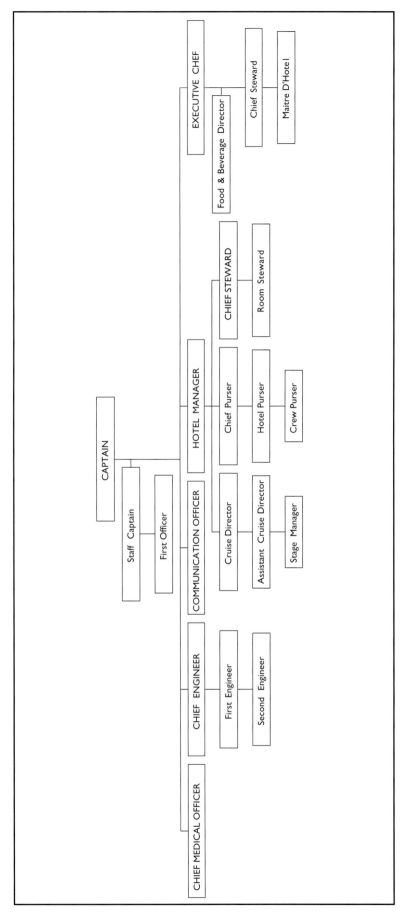

Typical Cruise Ship Organizational Chart

Safety and Security

The North American cruise industry is governed by the rules and regulations of many jurisdictions. Cruise lines are required to meet international regulations that protect the environment. They have adopted aggressive programs of waste minimization, waste reuse, and recycling. A majority of the cruise lines currently have policies that meet or exceed the standards set forth in international treaties and applicable U.S. laws.

The cruise industry's highest priority is the security and safety of its passengers and crewmembers. Cruising is considered the safest way to travel. Studies have shown that major cruise ship operators maintain safety practices and standards that are above and beyond the international SOLAS requirements. Cruise lines employ highly trained security personnel on each ship and use metal detectors and photo identification for all passengers and crewmembers when they go through security check at board or re-boarding at ports of call. Screenings of luggage are similar to procedures at airports. There are trained fire teams on each ship and over 4,000 smoke detectors strategically placed onboard.

Destinations

The Caribbean and Alaska are the most popular destinations, but cruises call on over 1,800 ports worldwide. These destinations vary from well-known ports to unusual ports, depending on the type of cruise.

Career Opportunities

The cruise line industry is labor intensive with many specialty and skilled workers. It is anticipated that during the next decade mega ships (102,000 tons and more, carrying more than 3,000 passengers) will dominate the industry. The implication from a career perspective is that there will be a plethora of job opportunities within the cruise line industry. There will be a need for individuals who are service-oriented and enjoy being away from home for long periods of time at different intervals. Emphasis is also placed on team work and communications. Traditionally, the cruise lines employed foreign labor and use the principle of one—nationality officers and crews. However, companies are now recruiting U.S. nationals to work in different areas on the ships.

Cruise Ship Destinations

Alaska
Antarctica
Africa
Australia and New Zealand
Bermuda
The Far East and the Orient
The Bahamas and the Caribbean
Canada, New England and the U.S. Coast
Central America and the Panama Canal
Hawaii, Polynesia, Tahiti, and the South Pacific
Northern Europe and the Mediterranean
Mexico
South America
Transatlantic

The career opportunities with a cruise line company are similar to those within a land-based resort. Mid-management career opportunities will become available for both the land-based and the sea-based operations. Within the sea-based operations, the majority of positions will be available in the food and beverage services, housekeeping, and kitchen (chef, specialty cooks, and bakers). Most of the cruise lines promote from within; therefore, a limited number of positions will be available in the guests' areas (pursers). There is a continuous need for qualified persons to work in the bridge (ship officers, engine and deck crew, and radio operators). The ultimate responsibility of the ship belongs to the captain. This individual is assisted by a staff captain who is responsible for the administrative and human side of the management of the ship. The staff captain is assisted by the first, second, third, and junior officer. The top position in the hotel department is the hotel manager, who is assisted by three direct reports. The three direct reports are the chief purser, who is responsible for accounting, personnel services and the concessions; the cruise director who plays a vital role in securing and procuring continuous entertainment for the ship; and the chief steward who is responsible for the dining room and the food services.

All too often, many hospitality students forget about the land-based operation of the cruise industry. The career positions within the land-based offices can be very specific, or they may require a generalist. Positions are always available in marketing and sales, reservations, and finance/accounting.

Trends

One of the major trends in cruise ships is the World of ResidenSea, the first resort community at sea. "The World" is the newest concept in cruising. It is a 44,000-ton ship, which carries 285 passengers and a crew of 252. This floating resort contains 110 private apartments, ranging in size from 1,100 to 3,200 square feet on six different floors. The price of purchasing an exclusive floating residence ranges from $2 million to $7 million. These units are sold by invitation only. This mammoth sailing vessel also has 88 guest suites, which are rented for between $5,000 and $35,000 per person, depending on the itinerary or the location of the suite. The wave of the future for the sophisticated cruiser will be these floating resorts with three-year fixed itineraries. Passengers may embark and disembark at their own convenience, and also sell their units like their land-based condominium counterparts. Additional information about this futuristic trend can be obtained at www.residensea.com.

Other cruise ships trends are:

- Secret discounts—These are unpublished prices sold though cruise brokers and travel agents who specialize in cruises.
- A growing variety of ships—Mega ships, carrying over 3,000 passengers are being built by the major companies, along with a new wave of small ships known as "exploration cruise ships" with a capacity between 100 and 250 passengers.
- Growth of the "drive-market"—Ports within driving distance of major cities are opening up in places such as New York, Boston, Baltimore, San Francisco, and Charleston.
- The rebirth of the passenger-carrying freighter.
- The expansion of itineraries—Cruise ships are now going to more destinations than ever before. Destinations such as Southeast Asia, the coastlines of Africa and India, the Antarctic and South America, and the South Seas are now added to cruise ship itineraries.
- Theme cruises—Cruise ships are moving toward special themes such as style of music, food specialties, murder mysteries, lectures, chefs, poets, and cultural enrichment.
- Longer cruises—There is a move toward ten-day and fifteen-day cruises, versus the traditional 4, 5, and 7-day cruise.
- All-inclusive cruises—Although publicized as all-inclusive, not everything is included in a cruise package. Now cruise lines are adding all-inclusive packages, similar to the all-inclusive resorts.
- "Freestyle cruising"—This is designed to meet the changing needs of today's cruise passengers rather than the conventional model of cruising. Freestyle offers passengers a more relaxed, resort-style cruise product with a range of flexible services—the freedom of choice in dining, attire, activities, gratuities, and disembarkation.

References

Business Research & Economic Advisors: The Contribution of the North American Cruise Industry to the U.S. Economy in 2001 (2002). Prepared for International Council of Cruise Lines. <http://iccl.org>

Cruise Industry FAQ's. Inside Cruising: A Guide for Travel Professionals. <http://iccl.org/faq/crusing.htm>

Cruise News (2003). Cruise Industry Brings in 2003 With New Ships, Innovations, Close to Home and Worldwide Ports. January 3, 2003. <http://www.cruising.org/CruiseNews/news.cfm>

Cruise News (2002). Over 2 Million Cruisers Sail in Third Quarter: Industry on Pace for Record-Breaking Year. December 6, <http://www.cruising.org/CruiseNews/news.cfm>

Cudahy, Brian (2001). *The Cruise Ship Phenomenon in North America*. Centreville, MD: Cornell Maritime Press.

Dickinson, Bob, & Vladimir, Andy (1997). *Selling the Sea*. New York, NY: John Wiley & Sons, 1997.

Vlaun, Richard, Kirkbride, Gregory, Pfister, Jeffrey (2001). Large Passenger Vessel Safety Study: Report on the Analysis of Safety Influences. Prepared for International Council of Cruise Lines. http://iccl.org

Zvoncheck, Juls (1993). *Cruises: Selecting, Selling, and Booking*. Englewood Cliffs, NJ: Regents/ Prentice Hall.

RCI Endless Vacation—Smoothing Sailing (January/February 2003). www.rci.com

Name_____ Date_____

Chapter 22 Review Questions

1. What event is responsible for the success of cruising today?

2. What are the major departments of a ship?

3. Where are the major cruise areas of the world?

4. What organization assists with the education of cruise line employees?

5. What are the different career opportunities in the cruise industry?

6. What are the current trends affecting the cruise line industry today?

7. What are the future trends for the cruise line industry?

8. What is the economic impact of the cruise industry in the U.S.?

9. What is the purpose of a ship's registry?

10. What are the classification categories of cruise ships?

11. Where are the major ports located in the U.S.?

Culinary Arts

Casa Loma
Toronto, Ontario

Corel

POSTAGE
PAID

John C. Hartley
New Mexico State University

The Culinary Industry

The modern culinary industry is a dynamic, energetic field full of new innovations and competition. Our modern cuisine has its roots in the ethnic dishes of virtually every society in the world. The history of the culinary expert, or chef, begins with service to royalty, which is perhaps the source of its glamorous and prestigious reputation. This is compounded with the fact that the industry deals exclusively with food, one of the binding ties of societies.

Today, no special event or occasion is complete without good food to accompany it, and that is where the food service professional steps in. People wishing to travel, relax, celebrate, or even seek comfort turn to food to fulfill their experience. The modern chef has to deliver on those expectations, and when that chef is successful, he is often celebrated as an integral part of the experience. Often in today's industry, the chef becomes a focal point for the restaurant, hotel, or other business.

Becoming a Chef

There are several ways in which one may become a chef. Perhaps the oldest is to simply work one's way up through ongoing industry experience. Although possible, today this is a very long and difficult road for most who attempt it. Today's competitive workplace demands more than just experience. Although it is crucial for success, experience alone may not be enough to land successively higher positions.

The European training model is through apprenticeship. One must gain employment in a large hotel or resort property and through the tutelage of the chefs on premises, hone one's skills, and progress through the ranks of a single kitchen. This not only provides both the education and experience needed for success, but also provides the structured format and documentation necessary to advertise those skills.

The most modern training method is through formal education. Culinary schools provide the needed education and expose the student to a greater number of chefs and professionals. This is probably the most widely available method today. There are a wide variety of programs available from simple one or two week courses on specific subjects to a four-year bachelor's degree.

No matter the educational model that is chosen, most career chefs choose to pursue certification as a means of establishing a formal benchmark for their level of expertise and experience. The only nationally recognized method of certification is currently through the American Culinary Federation (ACF). Through organization membership, continuing education, experience, and service achievements, a chef can secure such titles as Certified Executive Chef, Master Chef, Chef de Cuisine, and even Certified Culinary Educator for those who choose to teach the culinary arts to others. These certifications are obtained by building up the necessary education and experience levels and then taking a competency exam given by the ACF.

The Duties of the Chef

The daily duties of chefs can vary greatly depending upon the type of establishment in which they work. According to the U.S. Department of Labor,

Chefs are required to have an internship along with formal education to complete their training.

Arranging food to create a pleasing combination of shapes, textures, and aromas is a goal of the culinary arts.

the duties of a chef are as follows: "Coordinates activities of and directs indoctrination and training of CHEFS (hotel and restaurant); COOKS (hotel and restaurant); and other kitchen workers engaged in preparing and cooking foods in hotels or restaurants to ensure an efficient and profitable food service: Plans or participates in planning menus and utilization of food surpluses and leftovers, taking into account probable number of guests, marketing conditions, popularity of various dishes, and recency of menu. Estimates food consumption, and purchases or requisitions foodstuffs and kitchen supplies. Reviews menus, analyzes recipes, determines food, labor, and overhead costs, and assigns prices to menu items. Directs food apportionment policy to control costs. Supervises cooking and other kitchen personnel and coordinates their assignments to ensure economical and timely food production. Observes methods of food preparation and cooking, sizes of portions, and garnishing of foods to ensure food is prepared in prescribed manner. Tests cooked foods by tasting and smelling them. Devises special dishes and develops recipes. Hires and discharges employees. Familiarizes newly hired CHEFS (hotel and restaurant) and COOKS (hotel and restaurant) with practices of restaurant kitchen and oversees training of COOK APPRENTICES (hotel and restaurant). Maintains time and payroll records. Establishes and enforces nutrition and sanitation standards for restaurant. May supervise or cooperate with STEWARD/STEWARDESS (hotel and restaurant) in matters pertaining to kitchen, pantry, and storeroom." As you can see, the duties of an executive chef are tremendous, although particular job descriptions can vary greatly from one organization to the next.

Chefs in very large organizations may have very narrow job scopes, specializing in only a few functions of the establishment such as menu planning and food ordering. Those who work in smaller establishments, such as independent restaurants, will probably have a greater variety of tasks to which they must attend. Much of this is due to the wide variety of business types that hire trained chefs. Some of these include restaurants, hotels, resorts, catering companies, cruise ships, and contract food service management companies (which encompasses hospitals, retirement facilities, universities, elementary through high schools, and corporate dining).

Food Quality

Although individual job descriptions may not seem similar, there are some areas that concern any chef. Probably the first of these is food quality. It is the utmost expectation of a chef. Quality food is not simply food that tastes good; that is only a small part of the goal. Food must also be appealing to the eye and appeal to the specific customers of the business. People's tastes vary greatly with their culture, age, and many other characteristics which must be accounted for. Businesspeople often do not want to wait for a leisurely lunch, so menu selections must be chosen that can be prepared quickly. People looking for a fine dining dinner experience do not want to be rushed, so foods with longer preparation times may be appropriate. College students, hospital patients, and resort vacationers all have very different demands when it comes to food. The experienced chef should be able to design and implement a menu that will please just about any audience.

Not only is meeting customer expectations a challenge, but the food must be profitable to make and sell. Creating elegant food is relatively easy for the professional. Making money through food sales is another story. A great part of the job of a chef is related to accounting skills, which will be discussed in more detail later in the chapter.

Creativity is an important part of quality food. Unique menus make a business more attractive and easier to market to the customer. Besides taste and appearance, the creativity of a well-written menu gives the *perception* of quality, which leads to customer satisfaction. That is, if the customer goes into the meal thinking it will be a good meal, it is easier to convince them that they did indeed get their money's worth. Creativity is also important to the artistic element of the culinary profession. Besides food garnishing, chefs may also be called upon for such things as ice sculptures and tallow carvings. Even the arrangement of a buffet can be the difference between an uneventful meal and the "wow" that a skilled culinary professional can solicit from the guest.

Customer Service

Despite being considered a *back of the house* position, a chef must be concerned with customer service. Oftentimes, especially in catering or banquet applications, the chef must deal directly with the customer in designing a menu that will fit with the theme of an event and the expectations of the guests. Being able to deal effectively in a one-on-one situation with the guest is an important skill not often taught in culinary schools. Besides the occasions where the chef deals directly with the client, a chef's presence in the dining room can sometimes be a powerful marketing tool. Just as the servers and maitre d' make a powerful impression with their tuxedos or uniforms, the chef in a starched white jacket wearing a tall hat (or *toque*) can create a memorable event for the guest by simply making the rounds of the dining room and talking to the customers.

Profitability

As mentioned earlier, creating a desirable menu and delivering high quality food is not enough. Being profitable is the goal of most establishments. Ensuring the profitability of a business requires knowledge of the business process and even accounting skills. Profitability in its simplest definition is a matter of two goals, maximizing sales and minimizing costs. All of the previously discussed skills relate directly to maximization of sales, that is, to sell as much as possible. Controlling costs involves other skills such as inventory control, food cost control, labor cost control, pricing, and budgeting.

Food and beverage inventory in any food service establishment is a sizable part of the worth of the business. Care must be taken to avoid overstocking of unnecessary items or under-ordering that can cause run-outs of menu items. Either can be devastatingly expensive to the business. Theft deterrence is another major part of inventory control. Food and beverage items such as meat and alcoholic beverages are highly desirable and easily hidden, making theft an ever-present danger in the industry. Being able to minimize the cost of the food being sold (*food cost*) and the cost of the labor incurred preparing and serving the food (*labor cost*) are also highly necessary skills. Food preparation is a labor-intensive task. Care must be taken to ensure that the appropriate number of employees is on staff at any given time and that they are productive during their shifts. Being able to set prices that are both profitable for the business and attractive to the customer can also be a daunting task, but it is one often left up to the chef. Lastly, *budgeting* is a very important skill necessary for chefs. Budgeting is simply being able to accurately calculate how much you plan to spend on food, labor, and other costs of doing business before actually incurring those costs. This provides benchmarks for expenses that help to minimize excessive spending.

Human Resource Management

Quite probably the most important skill of today's chef involves their ability to effectively manage their subordinate employees. One person is not enough to run a successful food service operation. The chef must be able to assemble, train, and motivate a competent staff of dishwashers, prep cooks, cooks, and sous chefs in order to make the business run smoothly. Being able to create a functional team is crucial to the success of the organization.

Part of team building is training. Employees must be taught how to effectively do their jobs in order for everything to run smoothly. Besides the obvious cooking details, food service workers must be aware of safety and sanitation issues. Kitchens are simply hazardous environments. Slips, falls, cuts, and burns are among the list of ever-present dangers. Employees must know how to prevent such things, as well as how to deal with accidents should they happen.

Sanitation is another key training element. Employees must be trained to safely handle and serve food to prevent food poisoning and meet health code requirements. The chef must ensure that the food is always wholesome and safe to eat. There is simply no way to oversee every single task performed in a business, therefore, policies and procedures must be accurately conveyed to employees to ensure that the food is handled in a safe manner. Controls should be implemented to ensure that those prescribed procedures are followed, as well. Regular visits from state health agencies not only provide the required licensing, but also act as checks to ensure that the operation is running in a safe and sanitary manner. Some states even mandate that food service workers obtain a food handling permit to ensure that they have been trained in the appropriate methods of preventing food borne illness. The importance of food safety cannot be underestimated. Even a small outbreak of food borne illness can be financially devastating to a business due to bad publicity, to say nothing of the compensation of those affected.

Working with Outside Agencies

Just some of the governmental agencies that the chef will deal with at some time include the health department, state alcohol licensing agencies, local labor departments, unions, and city fire inspectors. Many of the legal codes that the chef is required to follow will vary slightly from state to state, or even from city to city. It is a good idea for any chef to familiarize him- or herself with local ordinances and state laws regarding food safety, fire safety, sanitation, labor law, and alcohol service. Doing so will help ensure that the chef will run the business in the appropriate manner, as well as establish valuable connections in the community.

Conclusion

Today's executive chef is far more than just a cook. Due to our modern business environment, the executive chef must be an educated, highly efficient manager. The executive chef must be knowledgeable in such areas as marketing, labor management, sanitation and safety, and business. A successful chef must be able to lead a team in a coordinated effort to satisfy the guest. He or she must be able to manage the business aspects of the sale to produce a profit, develop marketing strategies, and manage safety and sanitation, all while creating a special atmosphere for the customer to enjoy. Combining these skills with the ability to create outstanding food is a recipe for an exciting career that is definitely not the typical nine-to-five fare. A career in the culinary industry will provide daily challenges, the opportunity to work with people, and the opportunity for travel. The rewards of the career are immediate. Compliments given by the guest when they have been treated to an outstanding meal are the most immediate rewards and are a large part of what makes this a worthwhile career.

Name _____ Date _____

Chapter 23 Review Questions

1. Describe the different avenues one can take to become a chef.

2. What is meant by an apprenticeship?

3. What is the American Culinary Federation (ACF)?

4. Summarize the duties of a chef.

5. List the different types of chefs likely to be employed by a large operation.

6. Why is there often an inverse relationship between size of operation and scope of a chef's job duties?

7. Describe three variables that affect food quality.

8. Why is it important for a chef to be able to occasionally converse with the guests?

9. Describe the food demands of three different types/profile of people:
   a. College students

   b. Businessmen and women

   c. Elderly

10. Why is a chef often considered an artist?

11. How can a chef affect profitability?

12. Discuss the issues of waste through the eyes of a chef.

13. Where does food waste often occur?

14. Discuss the issues of theft through the eyes of a chef.

15. What makes food an easy and attractive item(s) to steal?

16. Why is inventory control important to a chef?

17. Discuss the dangers associated with working in a kitchen.

18. What can help minimize the risk of injury in a kitchen operation?

24

Distribution Services

Jefferson Memorial, Washington, D.C.

POSTAGE
PAID

Clark Hu
David B. West
Temple University

Corbis

Introduction

Most students in hospitality and tourism management programs consider career opportunities such as managing hotels, operating restaurants, and running travel agencies. However, they often overlook tremendous career potential and advancement in distribution services. Distribution services work behind the scene to make and distribute essential products/services and to ensure continuing operations of more visible hospitality and tourism companies. "Distribution" services are based on the concept of "networking" in which operational products along with their supportive services are produced by manufacturers and then delivered by manufacturers themselves or intermediaries to hospitality and tourism operators in a collaborative manner. The operational products are those product items that hospitality and tourism operators need to purchase in order to serve their customers. For example, SYSCO (a leading distribution services company) provides food products and services to more than 415,000 food service operations (e.g., restaurants, hotels, and many catering businesses) and helps them succeed in satisfying customers' appetites (SYSCO Corporation, 2002b). Most students have not realized the size and variety of this distribution

services network. Imagining the huge volume of materials/services hospitality and tourism companies need to purchase in order to support all their daily operations and serve their hosted guests, one may start to appreciate the importance and dynamics of the distribution industry in today's service environment. Again, using SYSCO as an example, the (distribution services) industry it serves is estimated at approximately $200 billion and covers restaurants, hotels, schools, hospitals, retirement homes, and other institutions (SYSCO Corporation, 2002a). As the demands of hospitality and tourism services continue growing, the growth of the distribution services industry remains strong. Opportunities to work in this exciting industry warrant serious consideration as a career option.

Network of Distribution Services

There are thousands of companies that make up the distribution service network (that services hospitality and tourism industries). Hospitality and tourism providers, such as hotels or restaurants, will purchase supplies and services from intermediaries or directly from the manufacturer.

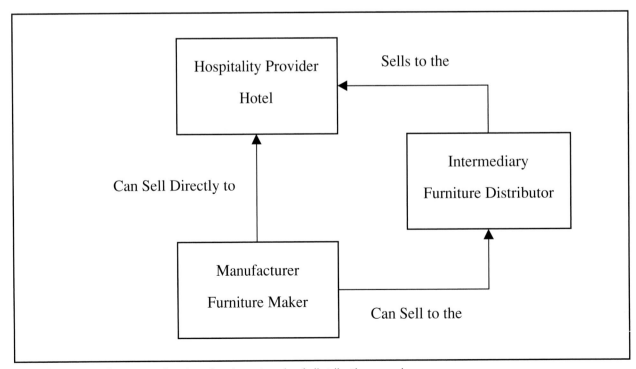

FIGURE 24.1 An example of a simple network of distribution service.

Likewise, a manufacturer can sell directly to the hospitality or tourism provider or to an intermediary. Intermediaries are distributors, wholesalers, suppliers, dealers, purveyors, and vendors, which buy products from manufacturers and sell them to the hospitality and tourism providers. Figure 24.1 is an illustration of a simple distribution service network. The hospitality provider can purchase furniture directly from the manufacturer or go through an intermediary (a distributor in this case) to purchase the furniture.

Working for Manufacturers

Manufacturers are sources of product supply. They buy or grow raw food and/or other raw materials and process them further. For example, a furniture manufacturer can take wood materials and create hotel beds, conference tables, and office desks for use in many lodging facilities. In terms of food service supply, "manufacturers" are sometimes referred as "growers" (farmers and ranchers), who provide raw food products such as fruits, vegetables, and animal products to food service outlets. Another category of manufacturers is called "fabricators or processors." These companies take one or more manufactured products and "assemble" them into a new end product. Fabricators add more "value" into the new product during the assembling process. For instance, a fabricator may take pre-made food items and process them to a specific semi-cooked condition to be frozen for later use in quick service restaurants. Quick service restaurants value these pre-cooked food items for their time-saving feature in the food preparation.

Manufacturers rely heavily on sales and marketing staff led by sales managers who are responsible for assigned geographic territories. Usually national account managers (or directors) negotiate large-volume sales directly with hospitality/tourism companies (mostly chain operators) or their designated distributors. A national account manager's work includes selling/promoting products to chain management, market testing of developed products, developing purchasing (ordering, shipping, and handling) procedures for buyers, and supervising regional sales operations. Regional sales managers supervise the field sales force and report to the national sales manager. Regional managers are responsible for training the field sales persons, maintaining contacts with important buy-

ers, and meeting any sales and service requests from buyers. The manufacturer's field sales force carries on daily sales and service activities (e.g., introducing new products, conducting product demonstrations, and calling prospective buyers, attending trade shows) and has closest contacts with distributors and buyers. These salespeople are paid by salaries plus bonuses often based on their individual sales performance. In addition to the in-house sales force, the manufacturer sometimes out-sources sales duties to contracted personnel (manufacturer agents or brokers) whenever necessary. These outsourced sales agents are paid on a commission basis to represent the manufacturer and sell/promote its products (as manufacturer agents) or put buyers in contact with the manufacturer (as brokers) in a designated geographic region. The commission rates of manufacturer agents or brokers vary depending on the negotiation and agreement.

Working for Intermediaries (Distributors)

Intermediaries (or commonly called middlemen) are distributors between the manufacturers and the hospitality/tourism operators in the service distribution network. A distributor (a generic term for wholesaler, supplier, dealer, purveyor, or vendor) purchases and warehouses products directly from manufacturers, then resells and delivers the products with some marginal profits to hospitality/tourism companies. In terms of service level and variety of distributed products, distributors can be categorized into five main types: (1) full-service or broadline distributors, (2) specialty distributors, (3) warehouse clubs, (4) buying clubs or contract houses, and (5) system distributors.

Full-service distributors distribute a wide range of products (from frozen foods to office supplies) from the manufacturers to hospitality/tourism operators. These full-service distributors deliver the one-stop shopping convenience to serve a variety of hospitality/tourism operations. Because of the large financial requirement to maintain a constant volume of full-line inventories, these distributors tend to be very large national or international distribution companies. Examples of such distributors include Kraft Foodservice, Inc., U.S. Foodservice, Inc., SYSCO Corporation, Van Eerden Distribution Company, etc. Specialty dis-

Small operators use wholesale clubs to purchase perishable items.

tributors, on the other hand, specialize in distributing limited product lines/categories, such as produce, dairy, supplies, equipment, disposables, and/or linen products. These distributors tend to be regional and smaller than their full-service counterparts. Warehouse clubs or warehouse wholesale clubs operate warehouses stocked with limited products similar to those distributed by specialty distributors. However, hospitality/tourism buyers must purchase and pick up product items by themselves. Often, these wholesale clubs cater to smaller independent hospitality/tourism buyers with local service focus. Examples of warehouse clubs in the United States include BJ's and Sam's Clubs.

Buying clubs or contract houses are made up with a group of local and regional distributors who seek a larger purchasing power and product quality assurance. Members of these buying clubs need to pay a membership fee to benefit from the club's purchasing power on national brand-name products and the marketing support of members' own generic products. Examples of this type of distributor include Premier Distributors of America (for-

merly known as Nugget Distributors), UniPro Foodservice, Inc., etc. System distributors (sometimes also called central distribution) service chain or multi-unit hospitality/tourism operations exclusively. This type of distributor includes companies who operate their own distribution network and sell to outside operators, as well as to their own operational units so that they can control their own economical services and ensure quality supply. Prime examples of system distributors include McDonald's, Wendy's, KFC, Hardee's, Domino's Pizza Distribution Corp. Services, and other large corporations who own their own warehousing facilities and deliver product to their individual units to save the costs of transportation.

Like manufacturers, intermediaries/distributors also depend on a sales force. Sales representatives of these distributors create new accounts, maintain current accounts, take orders from hospitality/tourism companies, conduct new product demonstrations, and collect money from past due accounts. These salespeople are paid by the distributors on a commission basis measured by sales performance set by the distributors.

Working with Purchasing Agents in Hospitality and Tourism Companies

Sales professionals who are employed in the distribution services industry must work with hospitality and tourism companies and satisfy their purchasing needs. This means that sales employees of both manufacturers and distributors are most likely to work closely with the purchasing agents in hospitality and tourism operators. These purchasing agents include employees who work in the purchasing, receiving, and accounting departments/divisions in the hospitality/tourism companies. In fact, this working relationship often serves as a bidirectional career path for employees on both sides. In other words, sales-related employees who work for manufacturers or distributors and learn skills/experiences in dealing with purchasing agents in hospitality/tourism companies may seek career advances in working for hospitality/tourism companies, or vise versa.

As stated earlier, most students who currently study in or already graduated from hospitality and tourism management programs have not been exposed to the diverse distribution services industry. Table 24.1 presents examples of job categories and some specific companies servicing the hospitality and tourism industry. Sales-related jobs are most likely needed by manufacturers and distributors. College graduates with some sales experience (including internship experience) can start sales jobs as a field representative with starting salaries

Table 24.1	Examples of Job Categories and Specific Companies Servicing the Hospitality and Tourism Industry

Apparel
- Companies that sell or distribute uniforms

Audio Visual
- Meeting room equipment distributors or manufacturers

Bar Equipment
- Companies that sell point of sale systems

Beds
- Manufacturers that sell beds, like Serta
- Companies that sell linens
- Companies that sell towels

Beverages
- Alcohol and spirit distributors

Carpet/Flooring manufacturers and distributors
Cleaning supplies and equipment
Computer/Software
Decorations
- Companies that sell or distribute art for the walls
- Companies that sell or distribute mirrors
- Companies that sell or distribute plants

Dishware/Flatware
Entertainment equipment
- Televisions
- Satellite service

Food
- Companies that make or distribute baked goods
- Companies that sell or distribute meat products
- Catering companies like Sky Chef or Aramark
- Suppliers of food like SYSCO

Furniture
- Chair manufacturers and distributors
- Desk manufacturers and distributors
- Cabinetry manufacturers and distributors
- Lamps/lighting manufacturers and distributors

Hardware
- Air conditioning equipment manufacturers and distributors
- Plumbing equipment (sink, faucet, and shower) manufacturers or distributors

Health club equipment manufacturers and distributors

Kitchen Equipment
- Companies that sell refrigerators
- Companies that sell cooking equipment
- Companies that sell baking equipment
- Companies that sell reservation systems
- Companies that store data

Printing equipment manufacturers and distributors

Security Equipment
- Keys and locks manufacturers and distributors

around $30,000 and a transportation allowance. After 3 to 5 years, a salesperson can make from $4,000 to $60,000 per year in commission sales, depending on job locations and/or sales skills. Sales skills may be obtained through company training and learning in the field under the supervision of a field sales manager. Established distribution services companies usually provide initial training for 6 to 18 months with the first several weeks learning the product knowledge and paperwork procedures in the sales office. As more and more distribution services are moving toward using technology to enhance service effectiveness and productivity (for example, many hospitality/tourism companies are using eProcurement system, where all manual paperwork is minimized and purchasing transactions are conducted in an electronic environment such as the Internet), students who make a career decision to enter this industry are advised to strengthen their technology background and knowledge.

Prepare Yourself for the Job

Although titles may differ, people who select careers in this area are generally sales representatives or liaisons. The success of manufacturers and distributors depends on the sales representative. Their primary responsibility is to generate sales from the hospitality and tourism provider or the distributor that services the provider. The sales representative will assist the provider on purchases, the use of the product, and product developments. Sales representatives can have very small (part of a city) to extremely large (several states or countries) territories, depending on the particular product. This may require the sales representative to travel away from home for days or weeks at a time. Although the hours may be long and often irregular, most sale representatives have the freedom to determine their own schedule. Companies usually set quotas or sales goals for the sales representative, and will usually tie the sales representative's salary or commission to that.

Many companies have formal training programs, with some lasting up to two years. Certification courses can be completed to become a Certified Professional Manufacturers' Representative (CPMR). Sales representatives stay abreast of new products and the changing needs of their customers in a variety of ways. They attend tradeshows like the International Hotel/Motel Restaurant Show in New York City, where new products and technologies are showcased. They also attend conferences and conventions to network with other sales representatives and potential clients. Also, company sales meetings are frequent where you will discuss sales performance, product development, sales goals, and profitability.

Overall, the employment outlook is good for sales representatives of manufacturers and distributors to the hospitality and tourism industries. The hospitality and tourism industry is expected to double in size by 2010 according to the World Travel and Tourism Council (World Travel & Tourism Council, 2001), which means that those servicing the industry will continue to be needed in the work force.

References

SYSCO Corporation. (2002a). *Fact book—Fiscal year end 2002*. Houston, TX: SYSCO Corporation.

SYSCO Corporation. (2002b). *The SYSCO story*. Retrieved February 2, 2003, from http://www.sysco.com/aboutus/aboutus_story.html

SYSCO West. (2002). *SYSCO Food Services West: A full line foodservice distributor*. Retrieved February 2, 2003, from http://www.serca.com/western1/html/western.cfm?id=1159&

World Travel & Tourism Council. (2001). *World Travel & Tourism Council year 2000 TSA research: World* (Research report). London, UK: World Travel & Tourism Council.

Chapter 24 Review Questions

1. What does "distribution" mean in the context of distribution services?

2. Describe a good example and explain the "distribution concept" in hospitality/tourism industries?

3. How do manufacturers differ from distributors? Please list the differences.

4. What can you expect from these professionals in their jobs for manufacturers:
   a. National account managers

   b. Regional sales managers

   c. Field salespeople

5. Explain different types of manufacturers in the context of the hospitality and tourism industry.

6. What is an intermediary?

7. Explain different types of distributors in the hospitality industry.

8. What are the systems distributors?

9. Distinguish between chain and multi-unit specialists and in-house distributors.

10. How many job categories and specific companies can you identify which can be included in the distribution services industry?

11. What is the job outlook for positions as manufacturers and wholesale sales representatives?

12. What is the typical compensation method for manufacturers and wholesale sales representatives?

Chapter

25

Education Careers

Tower of London
London, England

Corel

POSTAGE
PAID

Joan M. Janson
Niagara University

239

After a recent field trip to Toronto, students in the Introduction to Hotel/Restaurant and Recreation/Tourism Management class were talking about the professionals who took time to provide the group with tours and talk to the students about their jobs and careers. The students spoke with managers from attractions, catering, corporate sales, human resources, sports complex management, and restaurant management. Back in the classroom, I asked the students what the managers they spoke with had in common, expecting to hear things like "a customer service orientation," "a high level of professionalism," or even "excellent communication skills." But one student summed it up entirely when he said, "Passion." That's one characteristic that everyone in the hospitality and tourism industry seems to share—a passion for what they do. Hospitality educators are no less passionate about what they do.

Growth in Hospitality and Tourism Education

The hospitality and tourism industry has grown tremendously over the past four decades, and it is poised for continued growth. Vacations, time-off, or personal time, whatever you choose to call it, has moved from being a privilege to being a right in the mind of most Americans. Travel has become an integral part of the American lifestyle, and that will not be changing anytime in the foreseeable future.

The current demographic profile of the American population points to a continued need for employees in the field of hospitality and tourism. The population is aging, and the Baby Boomer generation is edging into retirement. Not only will this open jobs for younger people, but retirees are ready to spend money for out-of-home experiences—just the kinds of experiences provided by the hospitality and tourism industry. Never before, in all of history, has any segment of the population been so healthy or wealthy as it moves from age 55 to age 100 (Peterson). With advances in medicine made in the 20th century, we now have a segment of the population that will spend more years in retirement than working. All this bodes well for both the hospitality and tourism industry, and for the educators, teachers, and trainers who help people obtain jobs and launch careers in the industry.

According to the International Council on Hotel, Restaurant, and Institutional Education (CHRIE),

membership includes approximately 200 institutions that grant four-year and graduate degrees, and about the same number of schools that offer two-year degrees, certificates or diplomas. CHRIE began in 1946 with ten schools, and the organization continues to grow, just as the number of schools offering a hospitality and tourism curriculum continue to grow. The employment prospects for hospitality and tourism educators are very positive.

The Scope of Hospitality and Tourism Education

The hospitality and tourism industry needs creative, innovative, enthusiastic and hard-working team players, no matter where on the career spectrum you look—from housekeepers to CEOs. The scope of hospitality education includes in-house training for current industry employees, high school programs to prepare students for entry-level jobs, college or university management degrees to prepare managers, graduate degrees to prepare researchers, educators, and administrators, and executive development educators to prepare upper level managers for advancement. Your values, interests, and ability to communicate are likely to influence the type of educational career you choose for yourself.

Just as employees at different levels need different skills, so, too, educators must call on different skills. At the entry level, employees need mostly technical skills, and educators must focus on teaching terminology, procedures, and day-to-day operations. In order to prepare managers, the focus shifts to a managerial and human resources perspective. Students in four-year degree programs are introduced to planning, networking, statistics, research, finance, critical thinking, and the principles of team building. Professional development of executives and upper level managers may concentrate on one of these topics, in addition to helping them develop and communicate their leadership skills and vision. Graduate programs are research-oriented and give students the theoretical foundation and practical application of those principles.

High School Programs
Most high school programs provide students with training that will enable them to work entry-level positions in food service, lodging, or tourism. In

these programs, students participate in hands-on, practical, skill-building exercises.

The Academy of Travel & Tourism® and Pro-Start® are two programs designed to introduce high school students to the hospitality and tourism industry. These programs benefit high school teachers by providing a well-designed curriculum appropriate for an introduction to the industry. Students in these programs obtain knowledge, skills, and experience that enable them to become superior candidates for jobs in the industry. Students who complete a program and choose to continue with their education in hospitality and tourism are awarded college credits towards an associate's or bachelor's degree.

Post-Secondary Programs: Vocational/Technical Schools, Training Institutes

Much like high school programs, the emphasis here is on training. It's likely that the facilities will be more elaborate (commercial kitchens, front desk simulations, even small travel agencies) and allow the students to focus more narrowly on a particular area of interest. This means that the instructor, likewise, will need an appropriate background in a specific area. Students who complete a course of study, typically one year, are awarded a diploma or a certificate.

Two-Year Programs: Community Colleges, Culinary Arts Academies

Most two-year programs award the graduate an associate's degree. Typically, a four-year institution will accept transfer credits from a two-year program, thereby reducing the amount of time it will take for a student to obtain a bachelor's degree. Many two-year programs have a food service option for students. Many programs have a commercial kitchen, and students are responsible for planning, preparing, and serving meals to the public in a restaurant setting.

Four-Year Programs: Colleges, Universities

At a four-year institution, a hospitality and tourism program may be a "college," a "school," or a "center" functioning within a university (e.g., the College of Hospitality and Tourism at Niagara University). Hospitality programs can also be located within other large academic units, such as business (e.g., the Dedman School of Hospitality, College of Business, Florida State University), consumer and family services, human ecology, health and human development, food and agriculture, or applied science and technology.

Graduates of a four-year program obtain a bachelor's degree. Although the industry used to be known for promoting from within—the bellboy who ended up owning a hotel chain with 84 properties—the industry has matured considerably. A bachelor's has become the minimum credential for middle and upper management. We will always have the Rich Melmans—an entrepreneur with no college degree—but more and more, the industry demands a college degree.

Graduate Programs: Universities

Some universities provide the master's student with a choice. A student may choose a degree in applied science with the emphasis on coursework and a major project, which is most beneficial for returning to industry; or a research-oriented degree that concludes with a thesis, which is better for anyone in education or research.

Usually, doctorate programs are designed for people who wish to teach at the college or university level.

Putting Together a Curriculum Vitae

To apply for a position within the industry, you should have an excellent resume; for education, you will want an outstanding curriculum vitae. As in a resume, a vitae is added to as you acquire important job-related accomplishments. For an educator, these will fall under three major headings: teaching, research, and service. A different emphasis will be placed on each of these depending on the institution. Furthermore, different institutions define these categories each using its own specifications. Therefore, what is acceptable at one institution may not be acceptable at another.

Student evaluations are an important part of assessing a teacher's performance. High schools, post-secondary programs, and community colleges generally place the greatest emphasis on this aspect of a professional's career.

Research includes the completion of a unique project designed to add knowledge to the field, and to disseminate the results, through publication and/or conference presentation. Demonstrating mastery in this category is very important for faculty at research-oriented universities.

Service is primarily of three kinds: service to the department, service to the school/college/university, and service to the community. These activities include serving on committees, being a faculty advisor to student organizations, and donating professional expertise to charitable institutions.

Large research universities require a faculty member to have a track record of research and publication, and what is known as a "terminal degree." (The joke in graduate school is that it's called a terminal degree because it will kill you to get it.) A terminal degree means the highest degree in that field; it is the end of the line in obtaining degrees. Typically, in a university hospitality and tourism program, you'll find faculty with Ph.D.s (doctorates in philosophy), Ed.D.s (doctorates in education), or J.D.s (doctorates in law). Some universities are willing to hire a candidate who is "ABD" (all but dissertation) with the stipulation that he must complete the terminal degree within a specified time. Universities that hire an ABD candidate will probably give that teacher the academic rank of Instructor. Once the terminal degree is earned, the rank will be changed to Assistant Professor. It is customary to request promotion to Associate Professor when tenure is earned. For promotion to full Professor, an academic must be considered outstanding in the field, and to have provided outstanding contributions to the university.

Tenure and Teaching Load

Colleges and universities will place new faculty in "tenure track lines." This means that a faculty member must show development and progress in the three areas of teaching, research, and service, in order to continue in that position. A faculty member will have a periodic review, typically annually, and after the fifth year of employment, a university committee will examine that faculty member's record for a tenure decision. When tenure is granted, this means a faculty member has employment in that department on a continuing basis. Some universities have instituted periodic post-tenure reviews for faculty, to ensure that faculty who continue to develop are rewarded appropriately.

Some community colleges offer tenure, some do not. Typically, a master's degree is necessary to teach at a community college. With a decrease in the level of degree required comes an increase in the amount of experience required. Technical schools may require just a bachelor's degree, but they will probably also require years of experience in the industry. In addition, the teaching load also increases as less emphasis is placed on research and service.

High school teacher qualifications are set by each state. The minimum credential is a bachelor's degree, and some states, for instance, New York, require a teacher to earn a master's degree within a set amount of time. High school teachers are typically required to pursue a stated number of hours of professional development.

Lifestyle and Compensation

Hospitality and tourism educators tend to be like their counterparts in the industry: outgoing, enthusiastic, and very busy. For each class taught, about two to four hours of preparation are needed. But, one advantage to the profession is that, when not in the classroom or attending a meeting, a professor can arrange her schedule to suit herself. Educators must be able to work autonomously, both inside and outside the classroom. Most educators appreciate this independent aspect of their work. They also value academic freedom. This gives an educator the right to teach as she sees fit.

If your goal is to become wealthy, education is probably not the career for you. However, if your goal is to be enriched by life-long learning, you will be immensely rewarded. According to a study by Milman and Pizam (2001), salary is affected by academic rank, the average number of courses taught per year, the number of students in the institution, and whether one teaches in a graduate program. Other factors influence salary level, such as the highest degree earned, the type of institution, the extent of administrative responsibilities, geographic location (local cost of living), and gender (average salaries for men are higher than for women). That being said, Milman and Pizam report average annual salary for faculty with an associate's degree with the academic rank of Instructor employed at a two-year institution is $36,750; for faculty with a doctorate and the rank of full Professor employed at a four-year institution, it is $87,901. If you are fortunate, when alumni return to campus, you will be seated at a table with your former students who are now making far more money than you are. This is an excellent opportunity to convince them of the value of their education, and the benefits of helping other students.

The general public holds the notion that educators have three months of vacation during the summer. This is certainly a misconception. Professional development activities—research, writing, conferences, updating, and revising class material—are time-consuming, and there is scant opportunity during the academic year to pursue these. If an educator wants to remain employed, he must be making adequate progress in professional development.

Some Tips for Your Consideration

No matter in which kind of institution you want to teach, experience in the industry combined with teaching experience will be important. Not only does work experience in the industry provide credibility, but it adds immensely to a teacher's ability to bring "the real world" into the classroom. Most college or university programs require students to have at least 400 hours of field experience before graduation. Students who do well academically may be tempted to go straight through to graduate school. Don't. Working in the industry, particularly through positions of increasing responsibility, will benefit you in the long run.

If you want to attend graduate school, you will be expected to focus on one area of the industry. There will be one functional area of greatest interest to you, and that's the area you should research. That being said, whether you are looking for an honor's thesis advisor or selecting a dissertation committee, find faculty that you respect and can work with. Establishing a good relationship will be of great benefit under the stressful conditions of completing a research project.

Most universities that have graduate programs have graduate student teaching assistantships. If you plan to pursue a career in education, seek out this opportunity to teach a class. Some universities have support programs for first-time teachers or for educators who want to become more effective teachers. An assistantship, and a course in "how to be the best teacher you can be," will provide you with additional qualifications for obtaining the position you would most like to have.

To demonstrate your flexibility, adaptability, and willingness to take on new challenges, it is highly recommended that you obtain your credentials from different institutions. It begins to look as if someone who obtains a bachelor's, master's, and Ph.D. from the same place could not possibly be happy (or successful) anywhere else. Also, most institutions have a policy of "not hiring their own." So, if you are a graduate of Penn State, you will not be considered for a faculty position at Penn State until you've spent a few years somewhere else.

Beware of "mail order" graduate degrees. When applying for a faculty position, you may be removed from consideration because members of the search committee do not consider that you have earned a "real degree." It is becoming more acceptable to do a portion of your coursework as a distance learner, but you should plan to be at an institution that has a campus, and plan to spend at least a year there. Your best bet is to begin at an institution that has an accredited hospitality and tourism program. The Commission for Accreditation of Hospitality Management (CAHM) is the organization that evaluates and awards accreditation to two-year programs; and the Accreditation Commission for Programs in Hospitality Administration (ACPHA) is the group that does the same for four-year programs. From there, ask the faculty about their experiences in graduate school, and seek out the program that best suits you. Just as they may wish to "interview" you as part of the application process, so too, you should interview them to see what they have to offer to you as compared to other programs.

If you find that, when shadows lengthen and fall is in the air, you get this feeling, "Perhaps I should be back in school," then perhaps you should be. But, this time, at the front of the classroom.

References

Milman, A. and Pizam, A. (2001). Academic Characteristics & Faculty Compensation in U.S. Hospitality Management Programs: 1999–2000. *Journal of Hospitality & Tourism Education*, 13(1). pp. 4–16.

Peterson, P. G. (1999). *Gray Dawn: How the Coming Age Wave Will Transform America—and the World*. New York, Random House

Sims-Bell, B. (2002). *Career Opportunities in the Food and Beverage Industry*, 2nd edition. Facts on File, Inc. New York, NY. www.chrie.org

Chapter 25 Review Questions

1. Why is "passion" important in a career choice?

2. What impact will the aging baby boomers have on the hospitality and tourism industry?

3. What are career options (locations) for hospitality educators?

4. Explain how the teaching topic needs vary with different levels of hospitality employees.

5. What is the hospitality student exposed to in a post secondary program such as a vocational/ technical hospitality program?

6. What is the hospitality student exposed to in a two-year program such as community colleges or culinary arts hospitality program?

7. What is the hospitality student exposed to in a four-year hospitality program?

8. Describe the different places you might find a hospitality program in a university.

9. What are the components of a teacher's job if he/she works at a major university?

10. What types of service are faculty members at a university likely to engage in?

11. Explain the relationship between advanced education and/or advanced experience in order to teach.

12. What are three of the rewards that come with teaching?

13. How does the salary of educators relate to those in hospitality management?

14. What are some of the duties expected during the summer?

15. What are the advantages of attending graduate school?

16. When should a student consider attending graduate school?

17. Describe the graduate school experience.

18. Explain the advantages and disadvantages to distance learning in advanced degrees.

26

Golf Management

Corel

Stuart H. Mann
*University of Nevada,
Las Vegas*

Frank B. Guadagnolo
Pennsylvania State University

POSTAGE
PAID

Introduction and the Game

As an introduction to this chapter, we believe it is important to describe the common rituals of playing the game of golf.

With this common understanding of the culture of golf, it will be possible to introduce golf management and compare it to the more traditional hospitality professions.

Although most of us have seen some professionals play the game on TV, less than one in ten of us has actually experienced play at a golf club. We will use as our example a typical public course at which a fee for play is collected. This could be a resort course, for example, in Florida or the Carolinas or a course that is privately owned at which we can pay to play an 18-hole round of golf.

Prior to the date of play, we would have called to make a reservation, called a "tee time." Without a tee time, it is unlikely one would be able to play on many of the days at a great number of courses. The tee time would usually be made for four people, as the game is commonly played in what is known as "foursomes."

On the day of play and usually about an hour or so before the tee time, we would arrive at the golf course in our car. On arrival, we go to an area called the "bag drop." The bag drop allows outside assistants to help us unload the golf bags and clubs from our cars and put them onto golf carts or take them to a designated place if we are walking and carrying our clubs. Because so few clubs today have an option for the use of caddies to carry the clubs, we will not consider their use. On depositing the clubs and bags at the bag drop, we take our golf shoes and proceed to the "pro shop" to check in. The driver of the car must obviously take the car (unless of course the club provides valet services) to the parking area and then return to the pro shop.

At the pro shop, the assistant behind the counter checks us in and makes sure that our names match the reservation. The check-in process involves the paying of the daily fee and, if we are riding a cart, the fee for the cart as well. On payment, we are given a receipt and told that the receipt will be collected by the "starter." In the pro shop, there are all of the accoutrements necessary to outfit us for the game. So if we need apparel, new golf clubs, a golf glove, or golf balls, we can purchase them in the pro shop. If there is enough time before the tee time, usually about a half hour

In the last 15 years, there has been a 33 percent increase in the number of people golfing.

is what is needed, we may choose to practice in an area designated as the practice range and putting green.

In order to practice on the practice range, a quantity of range practice balls is needed. These balls are rented or provided without charge at the pro shop or at the practice range. If we were just practice putting, range practice balls would not be needed. We would use the balls that would be used during our upcoming game.

Prior to moving to the practice range or putting green, we might retire to a locker room to change from street shoes to golf shoes and to perhaps change clothes as well. Many clubs make lockers available to players. These lockers can be used to store street shoes and other personal belongings while on the course. Many clubs offer complimentary shoe shine service for street shoes while we are playing. Of course, a tip is expected by the person shining the shoes. There is often a locker-room attendant who sometimes serves as the shoe shine person, as well as a provider of towels for the shower and other bathroom amenities. This person expects a gratuity when we exit the locker room at the completion of the game, after perhaps showering and changing back to street shoes.

With golf shoes and proper dress, we proceed to practice at the range and on the putting green until a few minutes before tee time, when we head to the starter's area. The starter checks that the receipts indicate payment has been made for that day and proceeds to give us instructions about the golf course. These instructions normally consist of rules of golf cart use and special local rules of golf affecting the play of the game. The starter tells us when we can move to the first tee and begin play.

As we play the game of 18 holes of golf, which usually takes about four to five hours in the United States, we may encounter a couple of additional people on the golf course. We often see a food and beverage attendant driving a modified golf cart asking us if we would like to buy the products that are for sale. There is also, on most courses, a person employed as a course ranger. This person's job is to make sure that the play of the game proceeds at a pace that will allow everyone to enjoy themselves. This means that the ranger "polices" the property and "hurries up" those who are taking too long to play the game.

After playing the first nine holes, or the so-called front nine, we may choose to take a short break before starting play on the back nine. During this break, food and drink are purchased and consumed. Often there is a facility placed at the convenience of the players called a halfway house. This is a small food and beverage establishment that services only players between each nine holes.

On completion of the game, we return our carts to a designated area where there are attendants to clean the clubs and take them back to the bag drop area. These attendants expect a tip as well.

Now we may retire to the "19th hole" to rehash the game, settle our bets, have a liquid refreshment or two, and perhaps have a bite to eat. This activity takes place in a space that many clubs call the "grill room." This is an informal food service and bar area that can accept golf shoes as footwear. It is an area that usually allows smoking; card playing is often seen among the regulars. Often, there is another, more formal dining room, where such casual attire would not be allowed.

Following the enjoyment of food and drink, we would return to the locker room. Perhaps we would shower and change clothes, change to street shoes, and depart the locker room. We would then return to the car, pick up our golf bags from the bag drop area, and return home.

From this description of a normal day of golf, it is obvious that there are a number of service en-

counters. Many of these encounters are similar to those in more traditional hospitality professions like food and beverage service or lodging service. We will go into greater detail a bit later in the chapter; however, let's get a sense of the game and just how large the golf business is.

Economics

A new study commissioned by GOLF 20/20, the golf industry's initiative committed to growing interest and participation in the game, found that the golf economy in the United States accounted for over $62 billion worth of goods and services in the year 2000 (SRI International, 2002). This includes the billions of dollars associated with annual golf travel, that is, lodging, transportation, food and beverage, and entertainment. Although increased participation has been rather stagnant for the past five years, golf course construction continued at an unprecedented level through 2000. Slightly over 500 new courses were opened in 2000! For several years, the building of new golf courses has exceeded one new golf course each day; however it appears that supply is now catching up with demand. As reported in "The Golf 20/20 Industry Report for 2001," there were 352 new courses opened in 2001 and only 285 new courses projected to open in 2002. Additionally, we have seen a reduction in participation from approximately 564 rounds of golf in 1999 to an estimated 518 million rounds in both 2000 and 2001 (Beckwith, 2002). However, even with the recent economic downturn, consumers continue to demonstrate a willingness to spend a sizable portion of their discretionary dollars to join an exclusive country club, play high-end resort properties, or purchase the latest equipment.

The Consumers

The 26.4 million U.S. golfers are a population overrepresented among higher income households, college graduates, white males, homeowners, and those occupying professional, managerial, and administrative positions. According to the National Golf Foundation (2001), the average golfer is male, approximately 40 years old, has an annual household income of slightly over $68,000, and plays about 21 rounds each year. In addition, when we compare the participation rates of golfers to those engaging in other lifetime recreation activities, we find a marked difference with respect to age. Typically, as individuals age, their tendency is to constrict both the number of leisure pursuits and also the frequency of participation (Guadagnolo, 1997). Whether it's tennis, bowling, jogging, or using exercise equipment, individuals tend to give up these activities in their later years. For the most part, golfers remain with the sport well into their 60s, 70s, and 80s. Some may use larger grips on their clubs to accommodate arthritic conditions. Others may use a golf cart to address issues of mobility or use a more flexible shaft or lighter equipment to compensate for a loss of strength or, perhaps, play from the forward tees to compensate for loss of distance.

From the mid-1980s through the 1990s, an additional 6.5 million citizens have joined the golfing community; this translates into a 33 percent increase. The NGF (2001), in its *Trends in the Golf Industry—1986–1999,* notes that during the same period, women's participation only increased 11 percent, whereas juniors' growth rate increased by 43 percent to 2 million. The 1996 NGF trends report predicted significantly greater participation rates among boomers in the 30–39, 40–49, 50–59, and 60–64-year-old cohorts through the year 2010 (NGF, 1996). NGF also indicated the echo boomers will represent a significant increase among junior golfers, ages 12–17, and young adults, 18–29-year-olds. Boomers will also play more frequently and spend more money as they reach their preretirement/retirement years with greater discretionary income.

Two additional markets that continue to be untapped are women and minority participants. Although women have represented approximately 36 to 40 percent of all beginning golfers, their percentage among all golfers has dropped to approximately 19 percent. Those who stay with the game play fewer rounds than their male counterparts; however, their household income and expenditures on golf are very similar to men. Beginning in the 1980s, African American golf participation began to grow at a significant rate. For example, the 315,000 African Americans playing golf in 1980 represented only 2.4 percent of all African Americans (Warnick, 1991). A more recent study by the National Golf Foundation (2001) indicates there are currently 882,000 African American golfers. This only represents less than 3 percent of the golfing community, but it does represent a 100 percent increase since 1991.

The Venues

By the end of 2001, there were over 17,000 courses throughout the United States. Approximately 71 percent are accessible by the public. This would include daily fee facilities/resorts (approximately 9,300) and municipal courses (approximately 2,700). The remaining 29 percent, nearly 5,000, are private with nearly three-fourths of the private courses being owned by the membership (equity clubs).

The Business of Golf and Career Opportunities

When most of us think of golf, we think of it as a game, and we don't consider the supporting business organization necessary for us to enjoy the game. From the general manager or club manager to the attendant who drives the food and beverage cart around on the course, all have important service functions that are required for the golf operation to run smoothly and for the players to have an enjoyable experience.

As we discussed earlier, there are a number of different kinds of golf operations. Each type of operation would have an organizational structure necessary to meet the needs of that particular golf entity. Depending on the size of the operation, whether it is a private or public course, and the number of functions or amenities offered to the players, the organization will vary. Therefore, in order to talk meaningfully about the golfing operation, we will have to generalize a bit. The following positions represent a typical public golf resort operation. Many private clubs and municipal courses have fewer personnel.

Careers in the golf industry fall within three rather distinct tracks: the physical facility; club management and auxiliary services; and management of the game. The career track, which is more closely aligned with what we normally think of as the hospitality industry, involves the management of the club and its various services. The following organizational chart represents only one of many organizational structures that exist. This one is used for illustrative purposes only and is not meant to indicate a preferred model.

Let's discuss the roles of these employees in delivering the golf experience. That is, what do these people do in their jobs to allow the players to enjoy the game of golf? Like any business or organization, if it is to function well, that is, to make a profit or be successful, all of the employees must contribute positively by executing their jobs in the way they were intended to be executed. Each employee is critical to the success of the operation because all of the operations are interrelated. As in most organizations, it is often the lowest-paid employee or the employee way down in the organizational structure that often is the reason why customers (golfers) don't return.

The General Manager or Club Manager

This individual is assigned management responsibility for the complete golf operation. We will abbreviate this role from now on as the GM. The GM is responsible for the bottom line of the operation. People who usually would report directly to the GM are the Director of Golf and the Food and Beverage Manager. The Golf Superintendent would also report to the GM or to the Director of Golf, depending on the operation.

You can see that this person is the executive of the golf operation. It is this person's responsibility to plan so that the organizational goals are met. It is almost always the case that the GM is also responsible to a higher authority. Depending on the type of golf operation, that higher authority could be a Board of Directors, a corporate office, or a Director of Parks and Recreation.

Traditionally, the career path to the GM has been through more customary hospitality roles like Food and Beverage Manager. Recently, however, the path has become more varied. Directors of Golf and Club Professionals are now moving into GM positions with greater frequency (Gordon, 1996). (See the chapter on club management for a more detailed discussion of the club manager's position.)

The Director of Golf and Head Professional

Direct provision of golf services is an employment path leading to the position of Head Professional or Director of Golf. Among the 17,000 golf courses, approximately 58 percent are Professional Golfers' Association (PGA) affiliated courses. Those who complete the PGA's requirements for membership can, on average, expect a compensation package

Keeping a golf course well-groomed is one of the most essential jobs of the golf superintendent.

that is nearly twice that of the non-PGA member. The average 1995 compensation package for the non-PGA Head Professional was $37,929, whereas the reported compensation by PGA Head Professionals was $72,525.

In terms of preparation for a career as a golf professional, individuals should consider another option, that of completing a four-year degree program in business or closely related field, or possibly attend one of the colleges or universities offering a program in golf management. Following the four year degree, the PGA of America will require applicants to work six months under the supervision of a PGA member, pass a golfing proficiency test (Player's Ability Test), and complete the PGA's Golf Professional Training Program (GPTP). The GPTP requires the applicant to attend a number of seminars and workshops, complete a series of self-study courses, and successfully pass three levels of GPTP examinations. On average, the PGA estimates it will take an individual three years to complete the GPTP requirements. Another way of completing the GPTP would be to attend one of the PGA-endorsed Professional Golf Management programs now offered at a number of colleges and universities: Penn State University, Florida State University, Clemson University, New Mexico State, Mississippi State, Ferris State, Arizona State, Methodist College, Campbell University, and Coastal Carolina. Students attending these four-year programs will complete the PGA's GPTP while enrolled, thus reducing the time for membership by approximately three years.

Golf Superintendent

For those interested in the golf course itself as the physical facility, their focus must be in agronomy, specifically turf management. With the millions of dollars invested in today's golf courses, formal university training through two- and four-year turf management programs is essential. Individuals interested in this career track should contact the Golf Course Superintendents of America to obtain a list of recognized college and university programs. The importance of a quality agronomy program can't be overestimated. A recent reader survey of *Golf Digest* subscribers indicated that the golf course superintendent was the single most important employee.

The Food and Beverage Manager

This individual is responsible to the GM for all of the food service operations at the club. This position is a bit more varied than that of a food and beverage manager in a restaurant, but it is certainly similar to the food and beverage manager in a hotel. A hotel with its variety of outlets and functions such as room service offers the complexity similar to that of the golf operation. There are many opportunities for a food and beverage manager in golf operations as the business of golf continues to grow.

Trends

One of the most significant trends in the golf industry is that of ownership and management. Mr. Jesse Holshouser, Chief Financial Officer of the PGA of America, indicated at the April 1998 general meeting of the Philadelphia PGA Section that approximately 16 percent of all U.S. golf courses were owned and/or managed by management firms. He further indicated that some predict approximately one-half of all courses will fall under management companies within the next decade or two. Management companies such as American Golf Corporation, Club Corporation of America, Marriott Golf, Troon Golf, Golf South, Casper Golf, and others are both acquiring and managing golf courses in ever-greater numbers. How this will affect employment opportunities and public access has yet to be determined.

The second significant trend involves the information highway. Club managers and golf professionals are only now beginning to realize the significance of the Internet. Golfers are using Web sites not only to see how their favorite tour professional is doing, but also to make vacation plans, decide what courses to play, and perhaps purchase golf equipment. The challenge for those wishing to use the Internet is how they get people to their site. For example, using the Google search engine, this author in January 2003 typed in the term golf. The Google search engine identified 30,600,000 Web sites containing the term golf! An example of some of the most referenced golf Web sites would include:

Golf Course Builders Association of America—A nonprofit trade association representing all segments of the golf course construction industry.
URL: http://www.gcbaa.org/

Golf Press Association—A daily transaction golf newsletter, offered through e-mail, that keeps you abreast about equipment, events, players, etc.
URL: http://www.golftransactions.com/aboutgpa.html

Golf Web—A Web site that covers or is linked to most aspects of golf, both as a sport and a business.
URL: http://www.golfweb.com/

Ladies Professional Golf Association—As the official site of the LPGA, everything pertaining to the LPGA is provided—tour schedules, news releases, player standings, etc.
URL: http://www.lpga.com/

Multicultural Golf Association of America, Inc.—The Multicultural Golf Association of America, founded in 1991, is the first national organization to promote opportunities for minorities in golf and is recognized as a leading authority on inner-city junior golf programs with the theme "Golf Is For Everyone."
URL: http://www.mgaa.com/

National Golf Foundation—Serves as the primary research wing of the golfing industry. The foundation provides a variety of business and consulting services, houses the largest reference library, and provides an excellent series of links to many aspects of golf.
URL: http://www.ngf.org/

Off the Fringe—This newsletter offers an "unconventional perspective on the world of golf."

URL: http://www.offthefringe.com/

PGA of America—In addition to member services, pgaonline offers current headlines and stories on all of the professional tours, tour statistics, instruction, and other industry news.

URL: http://www.pgaonline.com/

United States Golf Association—Serves as the national governing body for the game of golf. The USGA writes and interprets rules, conducts national championships, provides a handicap system, maintains equipment standards, funds turfgrass and environmental research, etc.

URL: http://www.usga.org/

World Golf-Links Around the World—Eighty plus golf links ranging from a history of golf in France to the Association of Left Handed Golfers.

URL: http://www.worldgolf.com/golflinks/golfpages.html

Conclusion

We have described the game, its economic impact, and its origins. You have read about the kinds of venues at which golf is played and the people that work to make it happen. The role and impact that each employee has in the golf experience is similar to that of the hospitality employee in the more traditional food and beverage or lodging roles. Each service encounter is important to the success of the operation. It is the intent of professional golf management to make every experience a great one so that we will continue to play the game and continue to provide revenue to those for whom that is important.

References

Beckwith, R. (2002, July). *The Golf 20/20 Industry Report for 2001.* Ponte Vedre, FL, The World Golf Foundation.

Gordon, J. (1996). "Making the General Manager Jump." *PGA Magazine* 77 (9):24–31.

Guadagnolo, F. (1997). Presentation at PGA Merchandise Show, Orlando, Florida.

National Golf Foundation. (1996, May–June). "A Different Look at What's up with Golf's Growth." *Golf Market Today,* 4.

National Golf Foundation. (1997). 1977 Directory of Golf. Tempe, AZ: Peak Performance Sports, 473.

National Golf Foundation. (1997). Golf Participation in the U.S./1997 Edition. Jupiter, FL: NGF.

National Golf Foundation. (2001). [Online] http://www.ngf.org/

Professional Golfers' Association of America. (1990). PGA Teaching Manual. Florida: Greenstone Roberts, 5.

SRI International. (2002, November). U.S. Golf Economy Measures $62 Billion. [On-line] http://www.golf2020.com:80/mediacenter/fullView.cfm?aid=70

Warnick, R. (1991, November 21). "On the Green." Black Issues in Higher Education, 20.

Name _____ Date _____

Chapter 26 Review Questions

1. Explain the significance of a tee-time.

2. Describe the check-in process for playing golf at a club from the point of entering the club for a tee-time.

3. How long does it usually take to play 18 holes of golf?

4. Describe the roles of the:
   a. Starter

   b. F&B attendant

   c. Course ranger

5. What is a "grill room?"

6. What is the economic impact of golf?

7. What is the profile of the average golfer?

8. Where and when did golf begin as the game we know today?

9. What is the relationship between age and the continuation of playing golf?

10. What is the fastest growing population of golfers?

11. What are golfing trends involving females and African Americans?

12. What are three categories of golf courses?

13. What type of growth has been experienced in golf course development? In what sector of ownership/operation?

14. What are the three distinct tracks of golf industry careers?

15. Identify key responsibilities of the following positions:

    a. General Manager or Club Manager

    b. Food and Beverage Manager

    c. Director of Golf/Head Professional

    d. Golf Superintendent

16. What is the impact of PGA membership on the compensation package of a Head Professional?

17. What are the requirements for PGA membership?

18. What type of academic background is required for a Golf Superintendent?

19. Discuss two significant trends in the golf industry.

20. Cite at least five of the most referenced golf web sites.

Chapter 27

Hotel and Lodging Operations

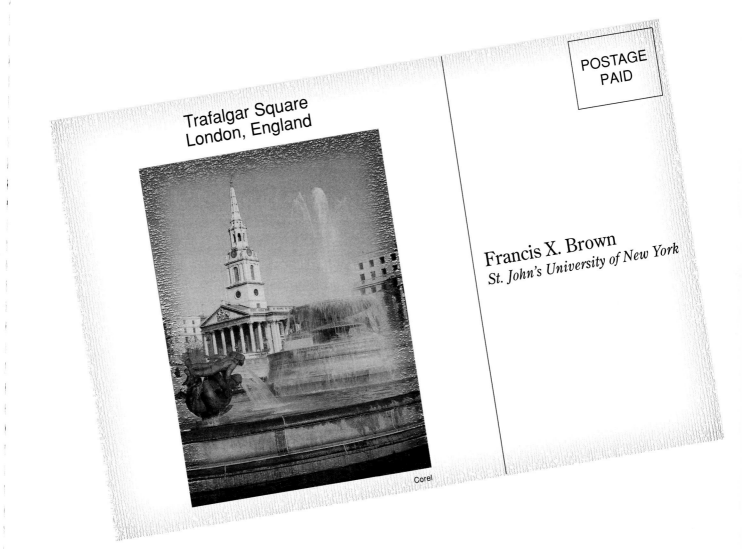

Trafalgar Square
London, England

Corel

POSTAGE
PAID

Francis X. Brown
St. John's University of New York

Overview of the Hotel and Lodging Industry

As described by Chon and Sparrowe, historians speculated that the first overnight lodging structures were erected along Mid-Eastern caravan routes about 4,000 years ago. These structures were called caravanserai and provided shelter for travelers and their beasts. Travelers supplied their own food, water, and bedding.

A major reason for travel was trade. About 3000 B.C., Summerian (from the country called Sumer in what is now south Iraq) traders traveled to sell their grain and needed shelter, food, and drink, which local people supplied willingly for a fee.

Another reason for travel was pleasure. Many Roman citizens were wealthy, and Rome had a good system of roads which gave easy access to the then known world, permitting Roman citizens to travel in relative comfort about the empire.

After the decline of the Roman Empire, from the fourth to the eleventh centuries, trade travel declined as inns closed. Monasteries helped by offering a place to eat and sleep. They did not charge a formal fee, but did expect a donation from visitors.

Religion was another reason for travel. Some traveled to religious sites to pray, and others went to distant locations to fight persons of other religions.

Finally, in 1282, Italian innkeepers incorporated and innkeeping became a business.

In 1539, in England, King Henry VIII ordered all lands owned by the church to be given away or sold. The church in England lost its role as innkeeper. Private houses, inns, and taverns were formalized as "public houses" with laws regarding guests' well being. This included the requirement that an inn receive all who presented themselves in reasonable condition and were willing to pay a reasonable price for accommodations. Similar laws exist today wherever the Common Law is applied.

In 1825, the English railroad began operations and railroad transportation began to meet the public's needs with the development of railroad lodging facilities that were usually near train stations located at the center of cities. The faster and more efficient railroads caused the death knell for the inns that had been the stops for stagecoaches permitting passengers to eat, drink, and sleep overnight.

In America the first tavern, called Coles Ordinary, commencing operations in 1634. During the Revolutionary War, the term "Ordinary" soon changed to "Inn" or "Tavern" and included service of food, drink, and occasionally lodging. By the mid-1800s, over 2,500 miles of roads were served by stagecoach lines. As in England, the introduction of railroads severely curtailed the raison d'etre of stagecoach inns.

Travel was interrupted by World War I (1914–1918). Major new hotel construction was undertaken during the 1920s. Many of these hotels entered bankruptcy during the depression of the 1930s as travel was severely curtailed. World War II (1939–1945) prohibited hotel construction as funds were spent on military operations.

With peace established in 1945, the many years of deprivation were overcome by the introduction of jet aircraft, the building of the interstate highway system, the need to travel for business purposes, and the perceived need of returning soldiers to continue to experience both international and domestic travel. Businesses were in a catch-up situation, requiring every worker they could locate to produce the items the public demanded and with advanced technology. Mass tourism was born. Hotels could not produce the number of hotel rooms to meet the demand of the 1950s.

With the introduction of the interstate highway system throughout the USA in the early 1950s, there appeared to be a motel (also known as a motor hotel) built at virtually every exit. The distinguishing feature between a motel and a hotel was the parking availability at a motel. Many motels did not have a uniformed staff of bell persons. Thus, a guest was guaranteed a room, a parking space, and no tipping.

Rural and small city hotels were at the mercy of the motel, as many travelers came by family car and saved by using the free parking provided by the motel and not having to pay for tipping as there was no uniformed bell staff.

In the mid-1950s, hotel occupancy declined and motel occupancy increased. As motels grew in size, they emulated the hotel and grew stronger. Hotels fought back.

Some hotels joined together in chains, i.e., they were able to become increasingly efficient and to obtain personnel with varying managerial skills. Other hotels formed referral organizations of independent properties that, a la Best Western, became

Many downtown hotels are large high-rise buildings offering full services and amenities.

as well known and popular as some of the chain organizations.

Chains soon realized that all guests did not want the same thing. "Market segments" were formed to serve the needs of specific groups of customers.

What Is the Hotel and Lodging Industry?

Many will answer that the hotel and lodging industry provides sleeping quarters for one night and perhaps for a longer period of time. Think about a one-night visit to Washington, D.C. to take a foreign service examination that begins at 8 AM the next morning; and then think about a ten-day vacation visit to Paris, France.

In truth, the hotel and lodging industry is much more. You must include attending industry conferences while at a convention hotel, playing golf at a summer resort hotel, skiing at a cold winter resort hotel, swimming at a warm winter resort hotel, or playing baccarat in a casino-hotel. These are all lodging properties and might be in the luxury category, or in the budget category, or in a category between them.

What Is the Marketing Concept of Hotels?

The marketing concept of the hotel is to meet the perceived needs of guests. One first must identify the needs of current and potential guests and then satisfy these needs. Hotels have become so segmented that it is not necessary to force guests into purchasing what they do not want. There are sufficient hotels to meet every need of guests. Our marketing function is to make these wonderful variables known to the potential guest so they will come to our hotel.

What Are the Segments of the United States Hotel and Lodging Industry?

Here are some of the ways of classifying segments of the U.S. lodging industry:

1. Classification by Service
   a. Luxury Hotels and Resorts—Include the finest accommodations that can be purchased. The lobby must be stunningly elegant as guests and visitors will observe its ambience and quality. Customer service is consistently superior with staff being well-trained and service-conscious. Cuisine is wide-ranging and exquisitely prepared to patrons' specific perceived needs. A full range of quality amenities is always present. Luxury resorts offer the finest recreational and entertainment facilities possible.

      These hotels maintain their exclusive image by charging the highest average rates and still enjoy high occupancy. The Four Seasons Hotels are a paradigm of the luxury hotel chain.
   b. Deluxe Hotels—Include properties that, at first, seem to be of luxury classification, but on very close examination, prove to be not quite so. They may have a stunning

Finely appointed rooms and ambiance give the sense of luxury.

lobby, well-trained staff, properly prepared cuisine and provide—but not consistently—superior customer service, a
wide-range of cuisine or a full range of
amenities. Hilton and Sheraton hotels are
at the top of the Deluxe group.

c. Midmarket Hotels and Commercial Hotels—Offer a quality of facilities and service that is below a luxury/deluxe hotel
and above a limited service hotel. They
charge rates that tend to be below the
luxury/deluxe hotel and above the limited
service hotel. They are often located in city
or suburban locations near business and
cultural sites. The hotel will have a coffee
shop, a formal dining room, room service,
and laundry/valet service. Newer properties will have a swimming pool, sauna, and
a health club. Their market is geared toward the business traveler and the middle-
income leisure traveler.

d. Full Service Hotels—Offer a full range of
guest services, particularly in-house food
and beverage operations. Full service hotels include extended stay, luxury, deluxe,
and midmarket hotels.

e. Limited Service Hotels—Budget or
economy hotels offering clean, small
rooms at low, average daily rates, usually
without in-house food and beverage ser-

vice. There may have been no lobby. They
may have vending machines and menus
from take-out restaurants at the front desk.
There may be a restaurant nearby on a
"pad." Room furnishings were kept to a
minimum.

The prime, if only, service offered was
the cleaning of the hotel rooms. In the
1960s and 1970s, the price of the lovely
motels and motor hotels had risen to a
level exceeding $100 per room per night.
The middle class traveling public rebelled
against paying such a rate just to sleep in a
room. Therefore, the economy and budget
hotels began to compete with motels by
upgrading, in the late 1970s through the
mid 1980s, by offering a coffee shop, a
lobby, a color television, and an in-room
phone. They were built using modular-type
construction and usually without banquet,
meeting, or convention rooms. Some offered a continental-style breakfast for a
minimum charge or even complimentary.

They are designed for guests who do not
spend a lot of time in their rooms and seek
low-average daily room rates. Limited service hotels generally do not have food and
beverage dining room service. They typically do have vending machines and take-
out menus from nearby restaurants avail-

able at the front desk. Amenities are usually not offered. The limited service hotel market is often families, "empty nesters" (senior citizens and couples whose adult children have left the family home) and SMERF (social, military, educational, religious and fraternal) groups.

f. All-Suite Hotels/Extended Stay Hotels—will usually feature a separate living room, bedroom, and kitchenette with refrigerator. Many suite hotels furnish the kitchenette with dishes and pots and pans. They are ideal for persons who need to stay in an area for an extended period of time (usually more than seven days), who may be relocating, for vacationing families, and for persons who are required to work and entertain at their hotel and do not want to do so in their bedroom.

2. Classification by Price
   a. Luxury and Deluxe Hotels
   b. Midmarket and Commercial Hotels
   c. Budget and Economy Hotels

3. Classification by Location
   a. City Hotels—Business took place in "City Center" hotels until about the end of World War II. Then business shifted to suburban locations, requiring the building of hotels in the suburbs. As roads, particularly the interstate highway system, were built, the Americans' love of their automobile grew. Motels were built and thrived. Many older in-city hotels did not thrive and were closed.

   Larger cities, such as New York and Chicago, had many "City Center" hotels. They were renovated or rebuilt. The modern city center hotel contains many of the features of the luxury/deluxe or midmarket hotel. The pricing is upscale, and the facilities include coffee shops and restaurants, room service, laundry and valet services, news stand, gift shops, health club, and stores. These city center hotels tend to be large, with 500 to 2,000 rooms.

   Parking, which was free at motels, is now a daily charge at most city center hotels. In New York City, the daily automobile parking fee—without in-out privileges—can be $40.00 for a 24-hour period plus 18 percent city tax.

b. Suburban Hotels—As land costs soared it became economically undesirable to build in "city center" areas, and many companies chose to move to the suburbs where land costs were more reasonable. Suburban hotels tend to be moderate in size, with an average size of 250 to 300 rooms. They are usually chain affiliated. They usually contain swimming pools, health clubs, and 24-hour food service. They often serve as the host site for local organizations' meetings. They usually offer free parking. Room rates average 50 percent to 75 percent of city center hotel prices.

c. Highway Hotels/Motels—With the interstate highway system, it is now the rule, rather than the exception, to have motels at each exit. A distinct characteristic of highway motels is abundant free parking, easy off and easy on the highway, large and easily identifiable-as-to-the-company name (Holiday Inn, etc.) sign which must be read from fast-moving vehicles. Most highway hotels offer breakfast (on premises or nearby), ice machines, vending machines, and a swimming pool. Room prices average 35 percent to 66 percent of city center hotel prices.

d. Airport Hotels—Offer the same services as city center and suburban hotels but they are aimed at the individual business traveler, the attendee at business meetings for corporate training sessions, and for airline passengers and flight crews with layovers. Prices average from 50 percent to 75 percent of city center hotel prices.

4. Other Classifications
   a. Bed and Breakfast Hotels—Provide sleeping accommodations and breakfast to guests. They are usually quite small, ranging from a few bedrooms to up to 30 bedrooms. The owner usually lives on the premises and serves the breakfast (full American or Continental) to the guests. Prices can average from 50 percent to 75 percent of city center hotel prices depending on the ambience and service at the "B&B."

   b. Casino Hotels—Are places where the wagering of money or other valuables on the outcome of a game or other event takes place. Wagering is called "gaming" by those in the business or "gambling" by some others. The place where the wagering occurs is called a "casino." A casino-hotel includes restaurants, various forms of musical entertainment, and hotel rooms. To attract people to spend money at 3 a.m. you must offer, for example, steak and eggs for $1.95 at that hour or they will not come to your casino. Food service is available 24 hours a day, seven days a week in casino-hotels. Whereas most hotels earn about 65 percent of the revenue from room revenue, 25 percent from food and beverage revenue, and 10 percent from all other revenue, the percentages at casino-hotels are more likely 65 percent from gaming, 25 percent from room revenue, and 10 percent from all other revenue. Room rates at Las Vegas, Nevada casino-hotels are about one-third the average room rate of Orlando, Florida (Disneyworld) hotel rates, which makes it attractive financially to bring children to Las Vegas if there is something to keep them occupied. Newer Las Vegas casino-hotels are being built to attract children to activities other than casino operations.

Casino operations at Atlantic City, New Jersey are dissimilar from casino operations in Las Vegas, Nevada. Although 60 percent of the U.S. population live within 300 miles of Atlantic City, it continues to attract the "day tripper" who usually arrives by bus for a day of gaming. Reasonable hotel room rates do not appear to be a market force as in Las Vegas. Additionally, the inadequacy of air transportation to Atlantic City, the competition from the midwestern riverboat casinos, and Native American gaming centers in both Connecticut and New York will not enhance Atlantic City casino-hotels room occupancy in the near future.

c. Convention Hotels—Provide extensive meeting and convention space segments of both commercial and meeting travelers. Specialized management expertise is required to operate successfully. Conventions can range in size from 100 to 100,000 persons. When the convention is extremely large, the local Convention and Visitors Bureau will handle many of the details, including assigning of housing to attendees. The enormous cost of building a full-service convention hotel limits new convention hotels and, thus, helps prevent the risk of overbuilding. The price of a convention hotel room will depend on the price negotiated by the convention meeting planner and the convention hotel.

d. Residential Hotels—Principally offer long-term accommodations, although they also accommodate short-term guests. The residential hotel offers housekeeping service, dining room, and room meal service. The food service is more for the benefit of the residents than as a source of revenue. The residential hotel may range from the luxurious, which offers full suites for families, to the moderate, offering single rooms for individuals. These hotels are being replaced by Adult Senior Homes run by major hotel companies. Prices will range about the price level of deluxe hotels.

e. Resort Hotels—Places organized to meet the needs of business meeting groups or to satisfy the various perceived pleasure or vacation needs of individual travelers. The resort hotel is usually found in an area endemic to desirable vacation sites. Seasonality is the issue today. A resort may feature basic hunting in the fall, skiing in the winter, fishing in the spring, and hiking in the summer. A resort may also feature a beach or swimming pool, a casino, and a spectacular dining room. American resorts are usually of four types: (1) summer resort, (2) year round resort; (3) cold winter resort, or (4) warm winter resort. The model statement for resorts is: "The more days you stay open, the more the chance to recoup your investment."

Resorts frequently have need of governmental sponsorship of roads from the airports or railroad stations to the resort. As many resorts are built away from developed areas, it may be necessary for the resort to be relatively self-sufficient by the addition of support areas for food and beverage storage, laundry operations, maintenance services and employee housing, food, and recreational facilities.

1. Grand/deluxe hotels
2. Four-star business hotels
3. Economy business hotels
4. Resorts (mountain, sea, lake, or spa)
5. Airport hotels
6. Country inns
7. Pensions (similar to American Bed and Breakfast operations)

Major United States Hotel Corporation Brand Names by Market Segment

Bass PLC Hotels and Resorts

Mid Price:	Holiday Inn
Deluxe:	Inter-Continental
	Crown Plaza
Luxury:	Holiday Inn Express
Extended Stay:	Staybridge Suites

Hilton Hotels Corporation

Limited Service:	Red Lion Hotels & Inns
Mid Price:	Hilton Garden Inn
	Hampton Inn
Deluxe:	Conrad International Hotels
Extended Stay:	Doubletree
	Embassy Suites
	Homewood Suites
Resorts:	Hilton Grand Vacations Club

Hyatt Corporation

Deluxe:	Grand Hyatt
Luxury:	Park Hyatt Hotels
Resorts:	Hyatt Resorts
Boutique:	Hyatt Spas

Marriott Hotels, Suites, and Resorts

Limited Services:	Fairfield Inn
Mid Price:	Courtyard
Deluxe:	Renaissance Hotels and Resorts
Extended Stay:	Residence Inn
	SpringHill Suites
	TownPlace Suites
	Marriott Executive Apartments
Resorts:	Marriott Resorts

Starwood Hotels and Resorts Worldwide

Mid Price:	Four Points
Deluxe:	Westin Hotels and Resorts
	Sheraton Hotels
Luxury:	St. Regis
	Luxury Collection
Resorts:	Westin Resort and Spa
Boutique:	W Hotels

Wyndham Hotels and Resorts

Mid Price:	Wyndham Garden Hotels
Deluxe:	Wyndham Hotels
Luxury:	Wyndham Luxury Hotels
Extended Stay:	Summerfield Inns
Resorts:	Wyndham Luxury Resorts

Mergers and acquisitions will probably continue into the twenty-first century, thus continuing to change the names of the major United States lodging companies.

Overview of the Typical United States Hotel Staff

The General Manager (GM) is the senior operating manager at a hotel, reporting to a vice president of a larger company or directly to the president or owner(s) of a smaller company. In some situations, the hotel may be operated by a management contract operator or by a franchisee. In these situations, the GM reports to his or her superior but must also need the perceived needs of hotel guests, dining room patrons, hotel owners, hotel, governments (such as building departments who periodically inspect the property), and insurance and banking companies who lend funds to the hotel and also who periodically inspect the hotel. The GM must also work prudently when a union is involved, as the National Labor Relations Act mandates that unions defend members. Unions will do so quite actively.

The GM normally distributes responsibilities to seven divisional managers. The are the rooms division manager, the food and beverage manager, the chief engineer, the director of marketing and sales, the chief accountant, the director of human resources, and the director of security.

Housekeeping keeps all guest rooms and public places clean.

These seven persons constitute the Executive Committee (EC) and meet weekly with the GM to plan and prepare for each scheduled event and to discuss what should be done about unscheduled events that have occurred or are foreseen. For example, the Beatles came to New York City in the late 1960s and checked into the Plaza Hotel. Thousands of pre-teen and teenage girls surrounded the hotel and used many tactics to get into the building to meet their idols. However, the Plaza Hotel Executive Committee had planned for this eventuality and was able to keep the hotel free of these enthusiastic underage trespassers.

Let us consider the seven divisional areas of the hotel.

1. Rooms Division includes:
    - Front Office—The hub of the hotel where every guest checks in and out. The guest agent (i.e., the room clerk) will quickly learn to solve guest problems.
    - Uniformed Service—Includes door personnel, bell staff, and valet parking attendants who are the first and last staff to meet and greet the guest. They can create and leave a positive impression on the guest depending on their attitude.
    - Telephone Department—The use of computers has improved telephone service im-

measurably. A guest can now set their own morning call time or leave messages for friends in other rooms. The computer will automatically post your local and long distance charges to your room account.
    - Housekeeping—The department that keeps hotel rooms, hallways, and public spaces clean and available for guests. The room attendant cleans the room, then notifies the housekeeper that the room is clean and available for the next guest.
    - Security has many functions, and although a separate division, frequently operates in cooperation with the room division. The security personnel will be responsible for the safety of the hotel, its guests, and staff. Surveillance of all public spaces and all means of entry and exit to and from the hotel is the responsibility of the security division, as is the responsibility of all keys and locking devices. Security personnel cooperate with the front office manager to inspect a room to determine whether it is vacant or occupied.
2. Food and Beverage Division—Usually includes five areas: food and beverage storage, food preparation (often called culinary arts), food service, beverage service, and banquet/cater-

ing. The chef, the maitre d'hotel, and the steward are the job titles of the managers of this division who report to the food and beverage manager, who in turn reports to the hotel general manager. In casino-hotels, however, the hotel general manager and the food and beverage manager usually report to the president, who is usually the casino manager.

Luxury and deluxe hotels place the greatest emphasis on food and beverage operations, including 24-hour room service, gourmet dining rooms, coffee shops, cocktail lounges, and catering/banquet facilities. Budget or economy hotels may have only a coffee shop. Airport hotels will usually have at least one 24-hour food facility.

As large city hotel food costs have skyrocketed, making it difficult to operate at both profitable levels and continue to offer quality service, it is not unusual to have hotels contract out food and beverage operations to independent restaurant contract operators.

3. Engineering and Maintenance Division—Is supervised by a chief engineer who is responsible for the proper physical condition of the property, permitting it to operate at full revenue potential. This division operates the following systems: water, electricity, refrigeration, fire protection, and HVAC (heating, ventilating, and air conditioning.)

4. Marketing and Sales Division—Is supervised by a director of marketing and sales who is responsible for the management of the "four Ps" which are: price, product, place (distribution) and promotion. This division sets budgets plans based on desired market segments and implements the plans to meet the revenue and occupancy goals.

A new unit of marketing and sales is the revenue management team, which is responsible to increase the yield management concept by maximizing revenue per occupied room (revpar) and to achieve the highest average daily rate (ADR). Web sites will be upgraded to permit anyone on the internet to review properties and to book rooms.

5. Accounting Division—Under the supervision of the "controller," this division manages property budgets, safeguards assets and cash accounts, pays accounts payable accounts, including employee payroll, and collects accounts receivable. They are actively involved in estab-

lishing controls when actual revenue is less than projected.

6. Human Resources Division—Is responsible for 1) the interviewing, hiring and training of new employees, and managing employee benefits programs; 2) reducing losses by reducing labor charges, liability costs, and excessive employee turnover; and 3) making certain that the property complies with federal and state laws governing employment.

7. Security Division—Involves the protection of the property's assets and guests, employees, owners, and personal property lawfully on the property. This could involve physical—external and internal—security, a review of employee practices, a review of guest practices, and—of prime importance—a review of the Safety Committee.

Other Areas—Resorts will have specific needs for specific units such as casinos, golf, tennis, rockclimbing. Some of their units will be described elsewhere in this text.

Careers in the Hotel and Lodging Industry

An easy question to ask and to answer is:

Q. What are the advantages of a career in the hotel and lodging industry?

A. One combines interesting work, stability of employment, and promotional opportunities while meeting and serving the traveling public.

Our work is interesting, there is no tedium as found at desk or factory jobs. We help people with needs who are grateful to us. Some folks are just plain tired and want to be assigned a room so they can go to sleep. Some folks want to locate their Embassy or Consulate. Some want to find Macy's Department Store. Whatever the need of the guest, they are usually grateful for our friendly assistance.

You can be assured of steady hotel/lodging employment as a career—meaning for many years—if you are courteous and well-groomed. Your employer wants to know that you are interested in both the hotel and the well-being of the guests. Always speak well of the hotel and its management. After all, they pay your salary. You may need to speak to a senior management person when some unusual event takes place. Do so and let the guest know you have followed through.

Promotional opportunities appear about every second year. You first have to prove yourself to management as being agreeable to both good and bad guests and even to both good and bad co-workers. Remember that "bad" may just mean someone who is tired from a long flight in economy class and is grouchy; but not a murderer. You should be able to prove to your hotel management team that you are preparing for the next step up by studying for that position. Be certain to write to: The Educational Institute of the American Hotel and Lodging Association, 1407 South Harrison Road, East Lansing, Michigan 48826, or call 1-800-344-3320 and ask about their courses and certifications.

References

Chon, Kye-Sung (Kaye), and Raymond T. Sparrowe, *Welcome to Hospitality, An Introduction,* Cincinnati, OH: South-Western Publishing Co., 1995.

Gray, William S., and Salvatore C. Liguori, *Hotel and Motel Management and Operations,* 4th edition, Upper Saddle River, NJ: Pearson Education, Inc., 2003.

Lattin, Gerald W., *Introduction to the Hospitality Industry,* 4th edition, Lansing, MI: Educational Institute of the American Hotel and Lodging Association, 1998.

Lefever, Michael M., *Hospitality in Review,* Dubuque, IA: Kendall-Hunt, 1996.

Starr, Nona, *Viewpoint, An Introduction to Travel, Tourism and Hospitality,* 3rd edition, Upper Saddle River, NJ: Prentice Hall, 2000.

Van Hoof, Hubert B., Marilyn E. McDonald, Lawrence Yu, and Gary K. Vallen, *A Host of Opportunities: An Introduction to Hospitality Management*, Richard D. Irwin, Chicago, IL: Times Mirror Higher Education Group company, 1996.

Name _____ Date _____

Chapter 27 Review Questions

1. Did the public always admire hoteliers? Why or why not?

2. When and where was it believed that the first overnight lodging structures were built for travelers?

3. What are three major reasons for travel?

4. What were English "public houses?"

5. What was a principal cause of the demise of the "stagecoach" inns?

6. What is a motel?

7. When and where were motels built in the U.S.?

8. What was the response of the hotelier to the finding that not all guests wanted the same thing in hotels?

9. What are the service characteristics of luxury hotels?

10. Midmarket hotels appeal to what classification of travelers?

11. Limited Service hotels appeal to what classification of travelers?

12. What are the three classifications of hotels by price?

13. Is parking free or not? When and where?

14. What are the differences between "City Hotels" and "Suburban Hotels?"

15. Describe a Bed and Breakfast Hotel.

16. Describe five segments of the European Hotel and Lodging Industry.

17. What is the function of the hotel General Manager?

18. What are the usual divisions in an American Hotel?

19. What are typical departments in the Rooms Division?

20. Is departmental profit an essential characteristic of the Food and Beverage Division? What is the exception, if any?

21. What are the current Food and Beverage trends in large urban hotels?

22. What are the responsibilities of the Engineering and Maintenance Division?

23. What are the "4-P's" for which a Director of Marketing is responsible?

24. What are the responsibilities of the Revenue Management Team?

25. What are the responsibilities of the Accounting Division?

26. What are the responsibilities of the Human Resources Division?

27. What are the responsibilities of the Security Division?

28. What are the advantages of a career in the hotel and lodging industry?

29. What does it take to get promoted in the hotel and lodging industry?

30. What industry organization will help you prepare for promotion?

Chapter

28

Interior Design

Garden of the Provinces
Ottawa, Ontario

Corel

POSTAGE
PAID

Ken W. Myers
Gail J. Myers
*University of Minnesota,
Crookston*

Introduction

Creating an ambience, providing for safety, buffering sound, and creating visual excitement: these are some of the goals of interior design in the hospitality industry. Interior design has come to be much more than beauty and function. It can be theatrics, special effects, or historic restoration. When you walk into a restaurant, whether it be freestanding, at the casino, or on a cruise ship, interior excitement is created by a multitude of elements. The effect can be created by the materials on the wall, ceilings, and floors, the psychological effect of color, the level and type of lighting, the flow-through of the concept into every design detail including the furniture, menu, and the centerpiece. Even the switch plate covers are preplanned to become part of a total design concept.

Hospitality facilities are known to remodel every five to seven years, and certainly new construction is an option. But no matter how old or new, the design of the inside of the building affects every aspect of the comfort and enjoyment of guests. In fact, design involves the stimulation of the five senses. How does the food smell in conjunction with the flowers on the table, the aromatherapy, and the smell of wood or leather? How does the texture of the carpet or the flooring work with the wall covering, the texture of the tablecloth and linens, and the ceiling materials? Is the room acoustically balanced so that guests can hear the music playing, and hear the conversation of the partner next to them, without hearing the conversation of the next table? Do the guests feel soothed by the colors so that they are encouraged to linger over many courses, or are the colors passionate and brash, encouraging a fast food approach? We will leave the sense of taste and the blend of exquisite flavors to the chef, but when it comes to artistic taste for the environment, the interior designer reigns. Do the styles mix: the furniture, the waiters' uniforms, the china, glass, and silver? Can a new layout increase business by adding more seats? Will a new layout train customers to stand in line, to order at a particular place, to become part of the flow of service?

These questions are answered with careful planning and a project design team that follows through from the very concept of the hospitality establishment. And, yes, whether it is a hotel, a national park, or the catering facilities of a convention center, it all starts with a very well-defined concept.

Every design aspect revolves around achieving the goals of the concept. If it is a boutique hotel with rooms spanning the decades, then the project design team will pay close attention to every detail as it applies to that decade, including the furniture styles and paintings indicated by art history. Add to that current health and safety standards required by building codes, efficiency necessary for any services that are provided, and, of course, close attention to a budget, and you can begin to understand the knowledge required by a design team.

Professionals Involved in the Design Team

Architects These professionals prepare and review plans for the overall construction. Qualified architects will have an AIA (American Institute of Architects) appellation.

Interior designers These professionals design interior spaces involving materials, finishes, colors, space planning, and layout. This person may be employed by the architects or may be freelance. The interior designer in this case should be a commercial interior designer, as residential design is very different. A qualified applicant will have an ASID appellation. See (American Society of Interior Designers) Web site.

Electrical engineers They assist the architect and interior designer with electrical planning. They may have to prepare and stamp electrical plans to obtain building permits. Usually employed by the architects.

Contractors They are the builders of the project. The general contractor will oversee specialty subcontractors needed for the project. Specialty contractors include trades people like cabinetmakers, carpet and tile installers, and painters. Contractors are hired by bid and recommendation and are licensed by the state.

Acoustical engineers They offer advice and planning for acoustical issues and suggest materials to solve noise problems. Usually employed by the architects.

Interior plantscapers They advise on the proper selection and positioning of plants and their maintenance. Usually hired by recommendation.

Commercial kitchen designers They provide planning and drawing for commercial kitchens, as well as specifying equipment. They will begin with the menu and the number of seats to make appropriate determinations of the kitchen layout and design. Often these kitchen designers are freelance or are employed by equipment sales companies. There is no professional appellation here, so check for appropriate hospitality background and equipment knowledge.

Health inspector They inspect existing facilities and review and approve plans for new or remodeled food preparation areas, service areas, and restrooms. They want to approve selections of interior finishes and equipment. They are employed by the state and will interpret state codes.

Hospitality manager This professional will coordinate the design team and keep them on track with the concept and budget. He or she will be the final decision maker and/or represent investors, developers, or board members of the company. The manager will follow every detail of the plan and may involve other company personnel, including the purchasing agent.

The Design Project

Once you have a well-defined concept and you have selected your design team, you can begin on the new or remodel project. Every project is different and will require a different number of members on the team, depending on what is to be accomplished. For a simple remodel project, it is possible that all you need is an interior designer, as they can provide lighting plans, some interior architectural plans, as well as materials and finishes. Beware of the do-it-yourself approach. A perfect fabric for a doctor's office may not be perfect for a hotel lobby. The style of a chair perfectly appropriate in a business hotel may not be appropriate for a theme restaurant. Even if all that is needed is a carpet replacement, there are different commercial performance tests and safety issues that the designer can address for you. The designer will then specify a carpet specifically for your use, and then you can purchase it from any source. Using a professional will almost always save money because the margin for error is reduced and your resources are expanded.

Basic Design Elements

Color Color trends change dramatically every decade, but the psychology of color remains constant. Warm colors like yellows, oranges, and reds excite our passions, make us hungry and energetic, or they can make us feel cozy, cocooned in a warm glow. Warm colors can make a space seem smaller. Cool colors like blues, greens, purples, and pastels relax us and are peaceful and restful. Cool colors tend to widen a space, so we perceive it as bigger than it really is. Color has such a strong effect on us that it can affect our feelings and affect how our physical bodies function. For example, rose tones have been known to lower blood pressure, reds and oranges make us hungry. Color can create a dramatic fast-paced atmosphere or a passive place where we want to linger. Color can communicate to guests the intent of the hospitality establishment.

Flow This includes elements like traffic flow, use of lines and direction in patterns, and design transitions from one space to another. The flow affects how equipment will be placed, adjacencies of rooms and functions, or how one hallway transitions into another. Vertical lines are strong and sophisticated, horizontal lines are relaxing, and curved lines create a harmony, an almost maternal rocking motion when they are used as patterns in wallcoverings, as part of the traffic flow in the layout, or as a design element or characteristic of the furnishings. Flow helps hospitality patrons understand how to move from one space to another, it makes work more efficient, and it helps guests understand the concept you are creating.

Style These are characteristics that pull a visual presentation together. It can be a period style and can be defined as a room designed with characteristics from the Victorian period or from the reign of Louis the 14th. It can also mean an artistic style such as contemporary or traditional. Often style includes a portrayal of good taste that is associated with a particular look. That means to create a particular style, florals might be appropriate, but certain colors would not be fitting. Style may also govern other artistic elements including proportion, pattern, and rhythm.

Design Considerations

Each part of the hospitality establishment has different design considerations and priorities. In some areas, safety and function come before beauty. In other areas, pure drama is the most important element. The right interior design for your concept can allow guests to perceive the value of your services much greater than the competition. Some specific design considerations are as follows.

The guest room The guest room influences the perception of all the hotel's facilities. Guests spend more time in their room than anywhere in the hotel. Universal design is of primary importance, as rooms should accommodate the physical needs of a diverse group of people. Trends for guest room design are moving toward lots of texture and high comfort, including padded headboards, feather bedding, plump throw pillows in velvets or chenilles, and spa showerheads. Room design can be more fluid than other areas in a hotel, as accessories can be changed frequently.

Food/beverage service areas (includes dining areas, bars, and meeting rooms/banquet areas) Design concepts in these areas portray to guests the type of service offered and even the pricing. Design characteristics for fast food include easy maintenance, elements that encourage fast turnover, and lots of energy (see chart below). Some restaurants soften the hard edge of fast food design by adding plants, skylights, and play areas. Contrast this environment with tableside dining that creates barriers for privacy and provides a high-level of comfort that makes guests want to stay. Theme restaurants are not just about food but also about creating an experience. Theatrical food and beverage areas allow guests to "see the show" from all areas. Open kitchens may be part of the show, as are animatronics, displays, and videos. Trends for food and beverage areas run from casual and trendy European styling to the nostalgic craze from the '40s and '50s. Multitasking, including eating, drinking, and socializing, has now expanded to include computer graphics, games, and Internet surfing all while you are still at the table or bar.

Common areas (including corridors, elevators, stairways, lobbies, public restaurants)—The hallways in any hospitality establishment are not only the primary circulation areas, but also the escape system. The design must actually point the way in the form of directional patterns, handrails, and colors. Illumination of the walls and floors is also primary importance, as long narrow dark hallways trigger negative emotional responses. Trends include hallways wide enough to accommodate clusters of furniture and handrails in contrasting colors.

The number of seats in a restaurant dictates the number of restrooms. Good restroom design is a way to communicate goodwill to guests by adding colorful tiles, easy to clean beautiful wallcoverings, flowers, and makeup areas. Certainly, the appearance of cleanliness is part of good design. Trends include auto flush and the use of stalls as advertising centers.

Lobbies communicate the identity of the establishment to guests, as well as provide adjacencies to all other public areas. Guests are encouraged to

Fast Service Restaurant	Table Service Restaurant
Bright warm colors	Soft, peaceful colors/trendy special effects
Bright overhead lighting	Low level lighting with some lighting specifically for mood or atmosphere
Short seat depth and upright back on chairs	Long seat depth/angled back
Non-padded or partially padded seating	Thickly cushioned seats and back
Hard surface, low-cost floors	Multisurface flooring including carpets, tile, wood
Limited noise reduction	Finishes chosen to reduce noise including wall fabrics, linens, carpets, ceiling treatments
Line stanchions, condiment stations, open beverage dispensers for self-service	Wide aisles to accommodate waitstaff, tableside cooking, tray stands

socialize, transact business, and linger for whatever the reason. Typically, there are changes in materials, lighting and signage, and lobby areas as directional cues to other main areas of the hotel. Trends for design include a multitude of textures such as glass, wood, and even concrete mixed with fabrics, leathers, and metal. Custom designs are often used in flooring such as logos created with tile or carpet, exotic lighting, and high ceilings.

Designers, researchers, and manufacturers are constantly working on ways to benefit the hospitality industry with new finishes and materials. Wallcoverings have been developed so that the pattern and color runs all the way through to the backing. That way, if a child in a hallway gouges the wallcoverings, the blemish is minimized. New wallcoverings can also stand up to sprays of bleach and chemicals, which are everyday occurrences in food service areas. Carpets have been developed with new backings that will not allow coffee or wine stains to seep through to the subfloor. New fibers in the pile of the carpet can withstand heavier traffic than ever before and have allowed warranties to double the life of the carpet. New technology in fabrics includes Crypton, the "super" upholstery fabric that stands up to moisture, staining, and has bacterial resistance and is available in suedes, prints, and metallics. If your bar and lobby coexists, a spilled drink on furniture is no longer a problem. Ceiling materials can bounce the sound back to an audience from the speaker in front of the room or absorb sound waves so that they don't interrupt the guest on the next floor.

The entire interior design industry is committed to making the hospitality experience more efficient, more beautiful, more exciting, and more profitable. Your design choices communicate to the guest your commitment to his/her enjoyment and pleasure. Good design will keep guests coming back.

Web Sites

American Institute of Architects (AIA): www.AIA-online.org
American Society of Interior Designers (ASID): www.asid.org
The International Facility Management Association (IFMA): www.ifma.org

Name_____ Date_____

Chapter 28 Review Questions

1. How does an interior designer create the "effects" associated with walking into a restaurant or hotel?

2. What are several of the goals associated with interior design?

3. Does the design of a business effect the guests' level of comfort?

4. What is the starting point for the design team?

5. What are four of the challenges faced by the design team?

6. What does the interior designer do?

7. Describe the role of the following members of the design team:

    a. Architect

    b. Interior or Designer

    c. Electrical Engineer

    d. Contractor

    e. Acoustical Engineer

f.   Interior Plantscapers

g.   Commercial Kitchen Designers

h.   Health Inspector

i.   Hospitality Manager

8. What does the contractor do?

9. Why are acoustical engineers important in a hospitality business plan?

10. What does the Commercial Kitchen Designer review before creating his/her plan?

11. What is the major role of the hospitality manager to the design team?

12. How can using an interior designer save money for the operation?

13. How does color communicate to guests?

14. What are warm colors?

15. What impact do warm colors have on guests?

16. What are cool colors?

17. What impact do cool colors have on guests?

18. How does traffic flow impact the guests?

19. How do the following "lines" influence design:

    a. Vertical

    b. Horizontal

    c. Curved

20. What is period style?

21. What is artistic style?

22. What are the current design trends in guest rooms?

23. What does the design of food and beverage areas portray to the guests?

24. What are three design characteristics of fast food restaurants?

25. What are three design characteristics of fine dining restaurants?

26. What are "common areas" in the hospitality industry?

27. Why is lighting important in the common areas?

28. How does the design of common areas impact guest safety in case of an emergency?

29. What are the current design trends in lobby areas?

30. What are three new finishes and/or materials that were designed to aid the hospitality industry?

31. What is Crypton?

32. Why would ceiling materials be important in a large conference hotel?

Chapter 29

International Hospitality

Obelisk
Luxor, Egypt

Corbis

POSTAGE
PAID

Paul D. Rompf
Duncan R. Dickson
University of Central Florida

Have you thought about working overseas temporarily or on a more extended basis? Are you unfamiliar with hospitality and tourism career prospects and opportunities overseas? Do you have questions on how to best prepare yourself for international employment? If you answered "yes" to the above questions, you are not alone. Thousands of students annually express an interest in obtaining employment in another country, and many fulfill that goal.

An international business career is a realistic option, especially for those who have management skills in hospitality and tourism. Travel is a global phenomenon and the World Tourism Organization (WTO) reports that tourism is a very important source of foreign currency earnings and employment for both developed and developing countries. Many highly recognized U.S. firms—McDonald's, Best Western, Hyatt, Disney, and KFC to name a few—long ago recognized the growth potential of foreign markets and aggressively expanded overseas. Intense competition across industry segments in the U.S. continues to drive international expansion by both U.S. firms and other multinational companies. Earnings from international operations frequently account for as much as 50 percent of a multinational's gross sales and profits.

Globally, most travel is described as "domestic" or within country, in contrast to crossing a border between countries. Both local residents and international travelers drive an increasing demand for travel-related services. Fulfilling the demand fuels an expansion in service facilities (lodging facilities, food service facilities, recreational, and entertainment venues—both natural and man-made—and transportation facilities), creating employment opportunities.

Domestic and international travel has experienced almost continuous growth in the past decades, contracting slightly during economic downturns and acts/threats of war or terrorism. Business travel, especially to distant destinations where a firm has ongoing operations, is typically more affected than leisure travel by these events. The WTO reported adjusted world tourism arrivals declined only .6 percent in 2001 compared to 2000, a consequence of both economic and terrorism factors. The decline was not evenly spread around the globe, as some countries experienced gains while other countries experienced arrival declines approaching 25 percent.

International Employment Opportunities

If permanent employment upon graduation is the objective, your best employment strategy with international employment as an ultimate goal is to obtain a job with a U.S. multinational company (e.g., Disney, Marriott) or with internationally owned firms (e.g., Sodexho, ACCOR, Holiday Inns) that have a presence in the U.S. In truth, the route to an international career usually begins with employment in U.S. properties, as you further develop your skills and knowledge and climb the management hierarchy. Rarely is a newly hired employee fresh out of college in the U.S. sent abroad.

For citizens of a foreign country in which a U.S. firm may be penetrating for the first time, a reverse flow is frequently observed. The local nationals customarily do not have the familiarity and necessary knowledge base of the firm's business operation. As a result, the local management team is sent to the U.S. for extended periods to develop and then take those skills back to their home country. U.S.-based opening management teams, flown in from the U.S., regularly support property openings in the host country as well.

Potential Impediments to International Employment

The availability of jobs in other countries and your ability to obtain a job that you may be qualified for in a foreign country are not one and the same. Political barriers, relocation costs, language barriers, and the potential for culture shock are the more prominent realities a multinational firm must address when sending staff to a foreign country. As a result, the selection of the "right" persons for overseas assignments becomes paramount for the firm.

Many (probably most) countries, the United States included, place severe restrictions on the employment of foreigners. In some instances, it is a matter of self-pride, but economic and social issues are at the forefront. If qualified citizens within a country have the necessary skills and are available for employment by the multinational firm, local legislation and regulations may require a "national" (local citizen) be hired over an "expatriate" (foreign citizen). Regulations governing the employment of expatriates are subject to change and vary from country to country.

Expatriates, such as American citizens working abroad, may be employed in a foreign subsidiary when the availability of and/or quality of nationals are not sufficiently satisfied by the employee pool in the country. Those subsequently selected by a firm for foreign employment have extensive familiarity with the business practices and systems of the firm, usually have appropriate language skills, and may have international experience. Furthermore, successful expatriate workers are multiculturally aware, sensitive, and tolerant of other cultures and customs.

Foreign employment visa fees, the transportation of staff members (and family) and personal belongings, and assistance in the establishment of new households cost a firm several thousands of dollars (tens of thousands is not unusual) per employee. This is an upfront cost usually occurring before the employee actually performs any substantive work for the firm in the foreign country. These same costs will be repeated when the employee returns to the U.S. As such, the economic costs of sending an employee overseas are a deterrent to many firms.

One merely needs to travel across the U.S. to experience subtle "cultural" differences (e.g., language, social, religious, political, and legal) between geographic regions. If you have previously traveled overseas or crossed the border to Mexico or Canada (especially Quebec), you will have an even greater sense of the diversity that exists from country to country. The reality is that it is not unusual for a foreign employee to find it difficult to adjust to a new environment that is quite different from his or her own upbringing.

The Dickinson College Career Center Web site lists several questions for a student to self-evaluate his/her readiness for an international employment experience. If you answer "Yes" to the following, you will at the least demonstrate an appropriate attitude consistent with overseas employment:

1. Do you like to travel and enjoy new experiences?
2. Are you interested in people from different cultures?
3. Do you easily adapt to change and are flexible?
4. Do you speak another language or are interested in learning another language?
5. Do you have patience and perseverance in interacting with people from diverse cultures?
6. Do you enjoy a wide variety of ethnic-centered foods?

Positioning Yourself for International Employment

Employers, in evaluating a potential employee, consistently look at the total applicant record. That is, "How has the individual performed academically?" "What leadership experience, if any, is evident?" And, "What related industry experience does the candidate possess?" A multinational company may desire to view all management candidates as potential international placements, and experience in, with a demonstrated understanding of, the international business environment becomes a strong plus to advancing an international career.

A realistic, two-sided perspective is required if a student is to be successful in obtaining overseas placement with a firm. Duncan Dickson, formerly with Walt Disney World who has responsibilities with several organizations for both domestic and international recruitment and training, is more candid regarding candidates for international placements. A multinational recruiter looks for:

1. A proven ability to speak a second language,
2. A history of travel,
3. A study abroad program in a non-English speaking country, and
4. A strong rationale of why an international assignment will be beneficial to both parties.

How do you overcome a seemingly 'no-win situation,' international placement appears to require previous international experience? Capitalize on Dickson's viewpoint and consider studying abroad (and possibly working abroad) during your college studies.

An Internet search with Google using 'international employment' as the search terms will produce several million hits. There is a wealth of information and advice available to you. Employment services are also listed, and most, if not all, will charge a fee. Rather than exploring your options with unknown people and firms, first investigate the formal and informal employment services that are available through your university. Whether you seek temporary or permanent employment overseas, it is strongly recommended that you only use an employment service when and if recommended by your university's career placement services or by a faculty member in your program of study.

University-level Services

Just about every university has a placement office, and you will usually find a cooperative education division as well. These departments provide differing levels of employment assistance, typically acting as a central contact point for those seeking employment, as well as those looking for employees. Local part-time jobs, internship or externship placements (the terms are used interchangeably from institution to institution), cooperative education administration and placement services, and job placement assistance upon graduation may be provided through a central department or through specialized university departments. You will frequently observe a separate section providing advice and possibly assistance in obtaining overseas employment.

College and Departmental Options

A trend toward 'internationalizing' hospitality and tourism curriculum is very evident across the United States. A feature consistently associated with this is the signing of articulation agreements and student exchange programs between universities around the globe. The agreements enable and facilitate the option for a student to typically spend a semester studying at a university in another country while fulfilling degree requirements at his/her own institution. Many, if not most, international exchange agreements are college or program specific. Frequently, a faculty member is assigned the duty of coordinating the exchanges in addition to his/her other responsibilities. A student, as such, may view the process as less formal than a central university unit, but the outcome will be the same: a pathway to an international educational experience.

The experiential component (e.g., job experience requirement) of hospitality and tourism management programs may pay an added dividend when studying overseas. Governments, such as the United States and Australia, view the experiential component of a degree program more leniently, in contrast to a general request for foreign employment. You may find that you are able to satisfy a legitimate foreign work requirement in conjunction with your degree. This may include part-time work placement while taking a full-time course load, or it may permit in-country employment for up to a year without course work. The latter typically requires sponsorship by a firm in the country and is subject to change, as well as varying from country to country.

Conclusion

Aspirations of students to work overseas are realistic, as are the opportunities. This is in spite of foreign governments typically placing a greater priority on their citizens' employment and growth options in comparison to citizens from foreign countries being able to find work. Multinational firms with a presence in the U.S. are both the most fruitful path and potential source for an international career. However, rarely is a newly hired employee fresh out of college in the U.S. sent abroad. A career-building alternative is to develop international credentials and experience by studying abroad during your college years.

Your university, as well as faculty and supporting staff in your program of study, should be the first information resources you explore. Studying abroad during your college studies can be a strong enhancement to your international career growth and opportunities. A further option may exist for you to work in a foreign country as part of your studies. Finally, spending more than a casual holiday in a foreign setting will begin to answer the personal questions as to whether you truly are adaptable to working in culturally diverse environments.

References

Brooks, Kate S. (2002), *Web Guide to International Employment*, Retrieved December 26, 2002 from http://www.dickinson.edu/departments/career/international.html.

Frangialli, Francesco (2002, November 12), *Statement by Francesco Frangialli, Secretary-General of the World Tourism Organization*, Third meeting of the Tourism Recovery Committee, Retrieved December 26, 2002 from http://www.world-tourism.org/.

National Association of Colleges and Employers (2002), *Planning Job Choices 2003: A guide to the job search for new college graduates (46th Edition)*, Bethlehem, PA: NACE.

Chapter 29 Review Questions

1. Who/what is the WTO?

2. What does the WTO report regarding future job prospects for international employment?

3. What is a primary driver for U.S. businesses to expand overseas?

4. What changes in domestic and international travel actually occurred during 2000/2001?

5. What is the growth pattern of domestic and international travel?

6. What do the authors suggest as appropriate employment strategies to move overseas?

7. What is the typical flow of people when a U.S. firm is entering a new country for the first time?

8. What are some of the challenges one might expect when sending staff to a foreign country?

9. Who is a "national?"

10. Who is an "expatriate?"

11. What is a traditional rule related to hiring nationals over expatriates?

12. What are the employment conditions which are most favorable for a U.S. citizen to secure a job abroad?

13. List at least five of the characteristics you would need to be successful abroad.

14. What language skills should you acquire if you want to work abroad?

15. What are the economic costs to a company associated with sending a person abroad to work?

16. How do most individuals adapt to their new environment?

17. List the sought after traits of potential candidates cited by one experienced, international recruiter.

18. How does a student without international experience gain an edge?

19. How can the university placement office assist you?

20. How do the international student exchange programs between universities typically work?

21. Why is it more likely to secure employment abroad if it is tied to an academic program?

22. What is the most fruitful path a student might take for an international career?

Chapter **30**

Management Consulting

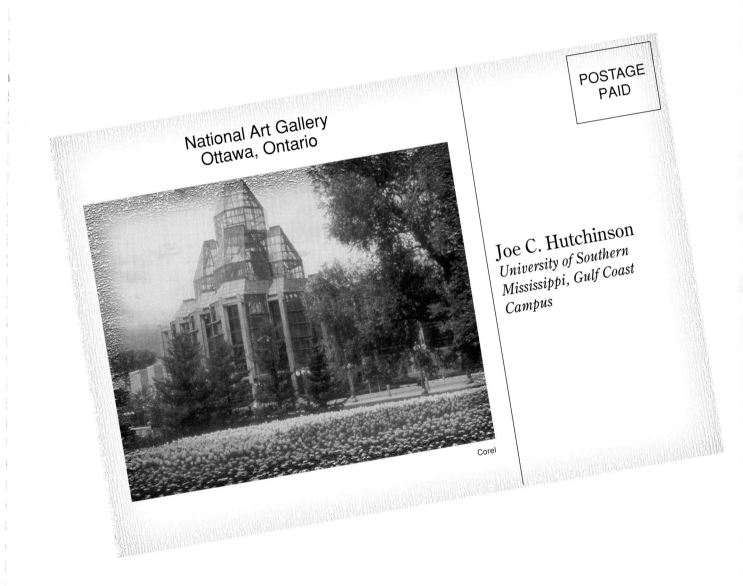

National Art Gallery
Ottawa, Ontario

POSTAGE
PAID

Joe C. Hutchinson
*University of Southern
Mississippi, Gulf Coast
Campus*

Corel

Introduction

The consulting industry is a rapidly growing segment in the service sector of the U.S. economy. Consultants offer a wide range of professional services to clients in many different fields. A consultant may be any individual who has a specific area of expertise and is compensated for providing advice or other services to a client. The client may be represented by an individual, a group of persons, or an organization that compensates the consultant in exchange for the advice or other services received.

Hospitality management consulting is an industry-specific form of consulting that may be included under the broader umbrella of business or management consulting. Management consultants often focus their services in specific functional areas, such as general management, human resources, marketing, management information systems, operations, administration, and finance/accounting. Most management consultants who serve clients in the hospitality industry also serve clients in numerous other industries. A hospitality management consultant would be a consultant who serves only hospitality industry clients and provides services in one or more functional areas.

Hospitality organizations may hire an external consultant because specialized expertise may be unavailable within their organizations to complete the specific tasks within the necessary time frame. For example, consultants may be hired to design a food service facility or to conduct a hotel feasibility study. Even when an organization has adequate internal expertise to complete the necessary tasks, an outside consultant may be hired because of the sensitive nature of the issues involved, the objectivity provided by an outsider, and/or the reputation and credibility of the consultant or the firm that he or she represents.

This chapter provides an overview of the management consulting profession. Topics discussed include the types of management consulting firms, the nature of the work, the consultant's lifestyle, consulting skill requirements and personality traits, ethics and professional development, and the consulting career.

Types of Management Consulting Firms

Management consulting firms may be classified according to a number of characteristics, such as their size, level of specialization, industries served, geographical location, or types of clients/industries that they serve. Consultants who provide services to clients in hospitality organizations are often found in the following types of firms.

General Management Consulting Firms

These firms provide general management consulting services to international clients in many different industries. Consultants in these firms may be referred to as generalists who provide a broad range of services to their clients and tailor their services to the specific needs of each client. The better-known international firms that provide general management consulting services to a diverse base of clients include McKinsey and Company; Booz Allen & Hamilton; and Arthur D. Little.

Management Consulting Divisions of Certified Public Accounting (CPA) Firms

Large international CPA firms that have a consulting presence in the hospitality industry include PricewaterhouseCoopers and KPMG Peat Marwick. The consulting divisions of these firms have formed specialized hospitality industry consulting practices. Hospitality consultants in these firms focus primarily on the lodging industry, particularly with respect to hotel development.

Functionally Specialized Firms

A number of consulting firms may serve clients in the hospitality industry and many other industries by providing their expertise in a specific functional area. Specialists in these firms focus on their narrow area of expertise. For example, a firm that specializes in management information systems may develop the system requirements for a large hotel.

Industry-Specific Firms

Some firms serve only the management of organizations that are in the hospitality industry. These firms often provide specialized consulting services to their clients by focusing on a specific industry segment (i.e., food service industry), an industry subsegment (i.e., full-service restaurants), and/or a specific functional area in certain industry organizations (i.e., facilities/equipment layout and design in food service operations). PKF Consulting is an international consulting firm that serves the lodging industry, whereas Cini-Little International serves clients in a wide variety of food service operations. There are also a large number of small firms and sole practitioners who specialize in the layout and design of kitchen facilities. In fact, most consultants who specialize in hospitality industry consulting work for either small firms (2 to 10 employees) or operate as sole practitioners (one-person firms).

Internal Consultants

External consultants serve clients of different hospitality firms, whereas internal consultants serve only one hospitality organization. These consultants may be on the payroll of the organization or they may serve on a contract basis exclusively with that one organization. These individuals are often referred to as "troubleshooters" or "field consultants" and perform many of the functions that external consultants perform. Most large restaurant and lodging chains have in-house personnel who provide operational support and assistance to both company-owned and franchised units of those organizations.

The Nature of the Work

Although the work of a consultant varies significantly among individuals and firms, there are three major steps in the consulting cycle that are common to most consultants: marketing, the consulting engagement, and administration.

Marketing

The marketing of consulting services is usually designed to build the reputation of an individual or a firm as a leading expert in a specific area. Every consulting firm, irrespective of size, must generate and sustain enough work to stay in business. Marketing in consulting involves the direct or indirect solicitation of new clients and/or efforts to generate additional business from existing or previous clients. Forms of indirect marketing include active membership in trade associations, serving on industry boards and panels, writing books and articles, making conference presentations, or conducting workshops and seminars. More direct forms of marketing would include advertising, direct mail, and meetings with potential clients.

The Consulting Engagement

Each new consulting project is typically referred to as a consulting engagement. Most engagements begin with an initial client meeting to discuss the scope and nature of the client's needs. The consultant may have responded to a phone call or a Request for Proposal (RFP). An RFP is a document, frequently used by government organizations, that outlines the nature of the work requested and other project details. Following an initial client meeting or the receipt of an RFP, the consultant often prepares a formal proposal. This proposal will clarify the details of the engagement by outlining the project background and objectives, the approach and work plan that will be used to complete the engagement, the final deliverables that will be provided to the client (i.e., oral presentations, written reports, etc.), and other project details (i.e., project fees, billing procedures, timing, qualifications of consultants, etc.). After completing all of the work steps outlined in the proposal, the consultant usually presents a final report to the client, in addition to an oral presentation discussing the findings and recommendations outlined in the report.

Administration

Consultants must perform other duties in addition to soliciting clients, writing proposals, meeting with clients, and completing consulting engagements. A number of administrative tasks must be completed in every consulting firm. In large firms, there usually will be a project manager who directs the work of the consultants on the project, maintains an ongoing dialogue with the client, and ensures that payments for services are received in a timely manner. These consultants may also be responsible for establishing a project budget and ensuring that each consulting engagement is completed within the allocated amount of time and dollars. Larger firms have support staff to perform necessary administrative and clerical tasks within the firm (report production, telephone calls, graphics, copy services, payroll, benefits, professional development, taxes, etc.). In small firms or sole proprietorships, consultants typically will be responsible for completing all relevant administrative tasks required to operate the business.

The Consultant's Lifestyle

There is no common lifestyle shared by all individuals in the consulting profession. The lifestyle of a consultant may differ significantly from one firm to another. Factors that may influence a consultant's lifestyle include the size of the firm, the type of services provided, the geographical area covered, and the industries served. For example, sole practitioners may shape their own working conditions to match their desired lifestyle by limiting travel, selecting only certain clients to serve, determining their own work hours, setting their own fees, working out of their own home, or working part-time. Conversely, consultants in large firms usually have little input into the services they provide, the hours they work, the type of clients they serve, the fees they charge, or the geographical locations where they work.

The consulting profession may be very rewarding for certain individuals. Consultants have the opportunity to help and influence others, and may derive a great deal of satisfaction from making a positive contribution to both clients and society. There is also the potential of high earnings, status, and respect. Many consultants thrive on the constant new challenges they are faced with and the opportunities to learn so much in a short period of time.

Despite the many rewards of consulting, there are lifestyle trade-offs involved. Although these job benefits are enjoyed by some consultants, the actual working conditions are usually much different from what they appear to outsiders. Most consultants are required to meet difficult project deadlines by working long hours under intense pressure to complete their tasks. The consultant must become absorbed in these projects and may be required to spend days, weeks, or months of sustained focus on a project until problems are diagnosed and appropriate solutions are generated. This lifestyle can be physically and mentally fatiguing.

Travel demands and uncertain living conditions also present a challenge for most consultants. Significant amounts of a consultant's time may be spent in travel. This often requires an individual to spend weeks at a time away from home. Although a sole practitioner may have greater control over travel demands, most successful independent consultants will be required to travel frequently over a wide geographic area.

Consulting Skill Requirements

The skill requirements of a consultant will vary according to the nature of services provided, the industries served, or size of the firm. However, there are a number of skills that are required for all consultants. These skills are discussed next.

Technical Skills

All consultants must have a certain level of expertise in a particular industry, function, or technique. However, it takes more than just experience, education, and skills to be a successful consultant. All consultants must have the unique ability to translate their knowledge base into applications that provide value to their clients.

Communication Skills

The ability to communicate both orally and in writing is one of the most critical skills needed to be a successful consultant. All consultants must communicate with other individuals on a regular basis. This communication may take the form of telephone conversations, meetings, interviews, presentations, or written proposals and reports. Consultants must have the ability to convey information clearly and professionally through every step of a consulting engagement.

Interpersonal Skills

The relationship between the client and the consultant is critical to the successful completion of all consulting engagements. The consultant must have strong interpersonal skills that create a mutual sense of trust and openness with clients. This requires that the consultant remain sensitive to the client's needs and feelings.

Administrative Skills

In addition to performing the tasks of a consulting engagement, a consultant may be required to maintain regular communication with clients, review the work quality of other consultants, keep projects within budgeted hours and costs, and manage the client billing and collection process. As a sole practitioner, these responsibilities are magnified, because one individual is responsible for completing all project tasks and managing the business.

The consultant must have strong interpersonal skills to be successful.

Marketing and Selling Skills

A consultant's ability to market and sell a firm's consulting services is essential to the promotion to upper-level positions in a large firm. To build and sustain a viable consulting business, a firm must maintain a strong relationship with existing and previous clients, while continually adding new clients.

In large firms, there is usually a progression that occurs in terms of a consultant's skills development. New consultants are typically hired on the basis of their technical expertise. An individual will usually first work on technical-related tasks relevant to his or her expertise. After this stage is mastered, the consultant will progress into a supervisory role. In this capacity, more emphasis will be placed on communication, administration skills, and interpersonal skills. As the consultant advances in the firm, he or she will become more involved in marketing and sales.

Personality Traits

Although a consultant may meet the skill requirements to complete all necessary tasks effectively, certain personality traits are necessary to pursue a career in the consulting profession. The following personality traits are usually required for all consultants, irrespective of the work settings.

Ambition and Self-Motivation

A consultant must have a high desire for personal success and must be internally driven, as there is often little outside motivation or direction. This requires an individual to have the initiative to start and complete tasks in an effective and efficient manner with little oversight and guidance.

Ability to Work with Others

A consultant is required to work with other consultants, clients, and employees of a client's organization on an ongoing basis. Thus, the individual must be able to get along with others and enjoy participating in a team-oriented process.

Self-Fulfillment

Despite the many benefits that a consultant may provide to his or her clients, their contributions often are unrecognized. Consultants usually receive few tangible forms of personal recognition (i.e., certificates, awards, etc.) for their accomplishments. This requires the individual to have a strong sense of self-fulfillment.

Mobility, Flexibility, and Tolerance for Ambiguity

Because most successful consultants serve clients dispersed across wide geographic regions, the traveling demands can be rigorous. Further, the nature of projects and the work settings may change on a regular basis, with roles and client problems not well defined. An individual who does not have the mobility to travel extensively, the flexibility to shift directions on short notice, or the tolerance to work in ambiguous situations may have difficulty coping with the challenges of consulting.

Energy Level and the Ability to Work under Pressure

The numerous demands and challenges of the consulting profession provide a great deal of excitement but also require high and sustained levels of energy. Most consultants must be able to work long hours on a regular basis. Projects often must be completed under significant pressure to meet multiple deadlines and to satisfy prior commitments made to clients. Although individuals may enjoy the challenges of consulting, it is difficult to maintain such a demanding pace over a sustained period of time.

Self-Confidence

Consultants must be confident in themselves, and they must be able to instill in their clients a strong sense of confidence in them. This often requires an ability to deal with rejection and failure due to lost proposals, mistakes, or a client's unwillingness to accept their recommendations. A consultant must overcome these barriers and continue to move on confidently to each new engagement with a fresh start.

Ethics, Certification, and Professional Development

Unlike many other professions, there are no governmental regulations, certification requirements, or codes of ethics that universally apply to all consultants. Because consulting applies to all fields, it is not possible to have one general licensing procedure. However, most major professional consulting associations and large consulting organizations have a code of ethics that outlines the consultant's responsibilities to the client and to the public.

Consultants are often faced with a number of ethical dilemmas that are not regulated by law and are not that obvious. Some ethical issues common to the consulting profession include confidentiality, conflict of interest, objectivity, and professional involvement. Specific examples of the type of ethical dilemmas consultants are often faced with include:

- The client seeks assistance for services outside the consultant's scope of competence.
- The consultant has an existing relationship or other interests with the client that would influence his or her objectivity in completing the work.
- The client requests the consultant to manipulate the results to favor the client's position.
- The client requests that the consultant omit, conceal, or revise certain information.
- The client requests that the consultant obtain proprietary information from a former client.

Professional development opportunities are available to enhance and refine an individual's technical expertise and consulting skills. Because technical skills can become obsolete quickly, successful consultants stay current by attending workshops, seminars, lectures, and professional meetings. These skills are further updated by reading current books, periodicals, and newspapers. To improve their consulting skills, consultants may attend professional association consulting skills workshops. Large consulting firms usually conduct their own in-house training to further enhance the consulting skills of their professionals.

Consulting as a Career

The consulting industry is anticipated to continue to outpace the growth of the U.S. economy by a wide margin. This provides a bright outlook for those individuals who desire to pursue a career in management consulting. Consulting can be a rewarding profession for individuals at all ages and career stages, such as recent MBA graduates, individuals in midcareer, retirees, or part-time consultants searching for other outlets to use their skills. The appeal of a career in consulting has continued to grow, as an increasing number of individuals enter the field to utilize their knowledge, skills, and experience.

Individuals who are considering a career in management consulting should take a personal inventory of their interests, skills, and personality traits. Although a person may desire a career in consulting initially, a more thorough examination of the skill requirements, lifestyle, and personality traits of successful consultants may reveal a lack of compatibility with a person's actual needs and desires. However, an individual's talents, interests, and personal situation may change a number of times during his or her career. As these changes occur, each individual should reevaluate his or her fit with a consulting career.

There are many different career paths that people take to become a consultant. These paths depend on a number of factors, such as age, education, experience, interests, and skills. Many sole practitioners have begun consulting careers after being laid off as part of company downsizings, restructurings, or mergers. Conversely, MBA graduates who lack the experience, skills, or capital to start their own firm often seek positions with national or regional consulting firms or as internal consultants to large companies. Even in these situations, it is usually desirable to have at least five years of management experience to establish credibility among clients. The expertise demonstrated through business management experience and the knowledge gained through education and other professional development opportunities should serve as assets for those interested in pursuing a career in management consulting.

Chapter 30 Review Questions

1. Define "consultant."

2. Describe the profile of a "management consultant."

3. Describe the profile of a "hospitality consultant."

4. When is it most likely for a hospitality business to hire a consultant? List three situations.

5. How are management consultant firms classified?

6. Define "generalist."

7. In which hospitality segment is one most likely to find a CPA consultant?

8. Describe the role of an internal consultant.

9. For whom does an internal consultant most likely work?

10. What are the three major steps in the consulting cycle?

11. What is the goal of the marketing phase?

12. What are several forms of direct marketing?

13. What are several forms of indirect marketing?

14. What is an RFP?

15. What are some of the administrative duties of a consultant?

16. Who performs the administrative duties in a large consulting business? In a sole practitioner's business?

17. What are five of the factors that influence a consultant's lifestyle?

18. How does the lifestyle/workstyle vary between the sole practitioner and the consultant who works for a large firm?

19. What are the rewards associated with a consulting career?

20. What are the drawbacks associated with a consulting career?

21. List the skills required for working as a consultant. What is the progression of skills from the newly hired consultant stage to that of being more experienced?

22. What types of communication skills do consultants need?

23. Why are communication skills particularly important?

24. How do interpersonal skills influence the building of trust with the client?

25. What personality traits are important for success as a consultant?

26. Why is "tolerance for ambiguity" important to a consultant's success?

27. What are some ethical dilemmas common to consultants?

28. What are the projections for careers as consultants?

29. How do consultants stay current in their area of expertise?

30. How many years of work experience does one need before embarking on a career as a consultant?

Chapter 31

Meeting and Event Management

Trevi Fountain
Rome, Italy

Corel

Catherine H. Price
*University of
Southern Mississippi*

POSTAGE
PAID

Evolution of Meeting and Event Management

The meetings, incentive, convention, and exposition (MICE) industry is young, relative to the hospitality industry as a whole. Its historical development closely parallels the development of the airline industry. Prior to 1960, individuals traveling to conventions either drove or traveled by train, both of which took excessively long times. With the introduction of the Boeing 707 in 1958 and transatlantic flights between New York and London, the airplane provided an affordable and fast alternative to trains and automobiles. The start of the "jet age" provided a huge stimulus to both business and leisure travel.

As the industry began to grow, the demand for lodging and meeting space increased. Intense construction of hotels and convention centers began in the 1970s. This was further fueled in the 1980s as a result of a major economic boom in the United States, favorable tax incentives to investors, and expectations of higher demand. The newer hotels were designed to meet the needs of this new "convention" market segment and the convention attendees. Features added to attract conventions were removal of interior posts, barrier-free space, flexible walls, blackout window treatments, and improved lighting. John Portman created the concept of the atrium hotel lobby, popularized by Hyatt. The purpose was to create a more open environment, especially for the increasing number of women travelers. Prior to the emergence of the new "convention hotel," meetings were primarily held in hotels that were designed for weddings and gala social events. The interiors were dark heavy wood, decorated in heavy brocades of garish colors, and massive chandeliers with elegant but poor lighting. The new, light, and open designs were a significant and positive industry change.

It was during this same period (1970–1980) that governmental entities began to recognize the economic importance of the MICE industry. Cities began to build a totally new type of facility for the single purpose of hosting large conventions and expositions. Convention centers continued to expand, with the largest in 1999 offering approximately one million square feet of flexible meeting space. More recently, expansions have been reassessed as the result of a slow down in the economy.

Because of the proven economic impact of the MICE industry, the development of convention centers is expected to experience a quick recovery and continue expansion worldwide.

In the '70s and '80s, the excess in room inventory caused by overbuilding of hotels proved advantageous to meeting professionals, who found hotels offering low rates and many incentives to book the association's convention at their property. This type of business environment is called a "buyers market," which is a time when the customers have a purchasing advantage. By 1995, the hotel industry had experienced a strong recovery in both occupancy and rates. The economic environment placed hotels in a strong "sellers market" position, which is the time when the seller has the advantage. In this type of environment, it was often difficult for convention managers to find hotels that were interested in their business. The general strategy of hotels was to market first to business travelers willing to pay higher rates and secondarily to the convention managers who were interested in lower to moderate rates. Contracts also had increasingly stringent clauses requiring convention managers to reserve (block) the correct number of guest rooms or face heavy penalties. These performance and attrition clauses are highly debated and hotly negotiated elements of the site selection process. The economic environment is likely to create a more equitable environment between buyers and sellers.

The MICE industry today is recognized as a substantial business activity for corporations and associations. It is also an important market segment for suppliers of services to these customers. In 1995, the Convention Industry Council (CIC) estimated total United States spending on conventions, meetings, expositions, and incentive travel at $82 billion. By 1999, the CIC reported growth of over $100 billion, a 20 percent increase in less than five years. Worldwide, these figures are even more staggering. Today, tourism is ranked as the number one industry in the world. When comparing business and leisure travelers, the two primary market segments of tourism, the business traveler/convention attendee spends approximately 50 percent more than the leisure traveler. For this reason, great emphasis has been placed on attracting meetings and conventions to cities all over the world.

Professional Associations and Publications

Professional associations have provided the foundation for the development of the industry historically, and they are spearheading the transition into the future. As the industry has grown, numerous professional associations, trade publications, books, and Internet resources directed to the industry professionals have emerged. Vendors and suppliers, from hotels to software developers, have become partners in providing the special needs and technical expertise required to conduct professional events.

The industry has grown and prospered without the benefit of industry standards. Try to imagine following a recipe if no one agreed on how much milk is in a quart or how much butter is in a pound. This lack of accepted industry standards has created confusion and limited the effectiveness of communications for the industry as a whole because of inconsistencies in job titles, job responsibilities, industry terminology, and standards. This is an important challenge for the future of this profession and one that will not easily be accomplished. As certifications, such as the CMP, which certifies practitioners as a "certified meeting professional," or the MMP, which certifies practitioners as a "meeting management professional," are increasingly required of industry professionals, the need for standardization will increase. Technology also demands standardization. Today the Convention Industry Council has formed a committee to explore standards in selected areas of the industry.

Professional Associations

More information on these and other major professional associations can be found at the following web site: http://www.hospitalitynet.org/web/index.htm.

Convention Industry Council

In 1949, the Convention Industry Council was founded as an umbrella organization for four professional associations primarily representing hotels, convention bureaus, and association executives. Their purpose was, and continues to be, to address professional concerns of all industry groups and, more recently, to offer certification of meeting professionals, which provides the designation CMP (certified meeting professional). According to the CIC, their membership now consists of close to 30 national and international organizations representing more than 81,000 individuals, as well as 13,000 firms and properties.

European Meetings Industry Liaison Group

The European alliance of the CIC is known as the European Meetings Industry Liaison Group, which is comprised of the following five groups: International Association of Conference Interpreters, the International Congress and Convention Association, the International Association of Professional Congress Organizers, Meeting Professionals International, and the European Federation of Conference Towns.

International Association of Professional Congress Organizers

The International Association of Professional Congress Organizers (IAPCO), founded in 1968, is headquartered in Belgium. It represents professional organizers and managers of international and national congresses, conventions, and special events. It has members from 52 companies, as well as individual members. The dominant member representation is from Europe, but there are members from Australia, the United States of America, Canada, Latin America, and the Middle East. They publish a quarterly newsletter and periodically a series of guidelines covering major aspects of industry best practices. Three recently updated publications are: *Guideline for Cooperation between the International Association, Organizing Committee and the Professional Congress Organizer; How to Choose the Right PCO;* and *Meeting Industry Terminology: A Unique Aid.*

International Congress and Convention Association

The International Congress and Convention Association (ICCA), founded 38 years ago, is headquartered in the Netherlands. The ICCA has very strict guidelines that require members to conduct meetings on at least four different continents. It has members from approximately 100 countries, which include hotels, convention centers, convention and visitors bureaus, professional congress organizers, travel agents, airlines, and other industry-related service companies.

European Federation of Conference Towns

The International Federation of Conference Towns (IFCT) was founded 35 years ago. Like ICCA, it has very specific membership guidelines, which require cities to have: (1) conference facilities that can accommodate at least 300 participants, (2) proper equipment, (3) traditional meeting services, (4) satisfactory hotel accommodations for at least 300 participants, (5) necessary transportation, (6) a team of experts in conference organization, and (7) proof that it has hosted, in a satisfactory manner, at least five international conferences during the previous three years. They publish a membership directory *(EFCT Directory)*, a newsletter on current industry developments *(Destination Europe)*, their history *(EFCT Thirty-Five Year On)*, a report on an annual survey of the European Market *(Report on Europe)*, and a brochure on the European Masters in Conference Management.

International Association of Convention and Visitors Bureaus

The International Association of Convention and Visitors Bureaus (IACVB) originated in the United States, but has a growing number of international members. Each of the member Web sites may be accessed from the IACVB home page (www.iacvb.org). The most commonly used services of CVB are their destination information services, supplier networks, and housing assistance programs.

Professional Convention Management Association and Meeting Professionals International

The Professional Convention Management Association (PCMA) and Meeting Professionals International (MPI) are two of the major professional associations for industry professionals. They provide strong education programs and have excellent publications and resources. *Convene,* PCMA's monthly publication, includes a Web-based archive of articles from 1996 to the most current issue. MPI's major publications are the *Meeting Professional,* published monthly, and *Meeting Europe Newsletter,* published quarterly.

Foundation for International Meetings

The Foundation for International Meetings (FIM), established in 1983, is focused exclusively on MICE industry organizations that conduct international meetings. FIM offers many educational travel opportunities and a unique trade mission program to link members with their counterparts in other countries.

American Society of Association Executives

The American Society of Association Executives (ASAE), headquartered in Washington, DC, was founded in 1920. Today, it has more than 25,000 individual members who manage leading trade, professional, and philanthropic associations, which represent approximately 10,000 associations, and serve more than 287 million people and companies worldwide. ASAE also represents companies that offer products and services to the association community.

Industry Publications

In addition to those publications emerging from professional associations, there are private publishers. Adams Business Media/Meetings Group, in the United States, publishes six trade magazines in the meeting/convention/incentive industry, each targeting a specific market niche. They are: *Association Meetings, Corporate Meetings & Incentives, Medical Meetings, Insurance Conference Planner, Religious Conference Manager,* and *Technology Meetings.* In addition to the publications, MeetingsNet is an online resource that archives articles from all of the magazines. Also published in the United States are *Successful Meetings, Meeting News,* and *Meetings and Conventions.* Each offers free subscriptions to qualified meeting industry professionals. Completion of an online survey about meeting practices is required.

Meetings Market

Industry Structure

There are two components of the industry structure: (1) buyers of services often referred to as customers and (2) suppliers or vendors. The individuals who are actively involved in the full range of processes required to initiate, plan, conduct, and evaluate meetings and events are technically customers. Those who sell services to these customers are a highly diverse group of specialists that provide for-profit products and services to these customers.

Customers fall into three broad industry groups: (1) meeting and convention managers, (2) incentive and special event producers, and (3) tradeshow or exhibition managers. Meeting and convention management activities are most often associated with conferences, seminars, conventions, training programs, and new product introductions. Each of these has a strong focus on education. Conventions are held annually for association members and, in addition to education have special events, expositions, and other professional activities. Incentive programs, usually sponsored by corporations, are reward-based programs for the top 1–2% of employees and product distributors that have consistently met corporate performance goals. They utilize resorts or exotic venues and usually have a very large budget. Special events, which include sporting and recreational activities, theme food and beverage events, and tours, are most often defined by a strong focus on social interaction. When included as a part of a MICE event, there are usually theme dinners, spouse or children's tours, or other activities that highlight the local area. An expanded view of special events includes fairs and festivals, Super Bowls, the Olympics, inaugurations, parades, fireworks displays, and other types of large public events. Tradeshows and exhibitions, a booth-based display of products and services, are defined by their marketing focus. Four types of expositions are: industrial, wholesale and retail tradeshows, professional and scientific expositions, and public or consumer shows.

Private product expositions are usually associated with association conventions such as medical meetings. Public expositions are stand-alone events that are open to anyone who pays the entrance fee. The success of American companies depends not only on the quality of products and services they produce, but also on their ability to market and sell those products and services in an increasingly competitive business environment. Since the creation of the Trade Show Bureau, now known as the Center for Exhibition Industry Research (CEIR), 20 years ago, they have repeatedly documented that companies that use exhibitions to bring products to market are able to do so in half the time . . . at half the cost . . . with half the effort. According to the 2000 CEIR Industry Report, for companies with sales of over 50 million U.S. dollars, exhibitions rank as the third-largest marketing expenditure behind sales promotion (#2) and advertising (#1), moving ahead of expenditures for sales force management and direct marketing.

Although each of these is considered an event, and each one may have all three components, the type event, as described above, is defined by its primary focus—education, reward, social interaction, and marketing. A commonality of all three is that they are planned for groups of people rather than the individual tourist or business traveler. They are also held for a limited time period, from a few days to two weeks. This is in contrast to an attraction, such as Disneyland, which is a permanent event.

Types of Organizations That Host Meetings

Corporations and associations are the two major types of organizations that host meetings. Corporations host large numbers of small meetings, such as board of directors meetings, sales training, and incentive or reward types of meetings. Because the corporation requires certain individuals to attend the meeting as well as paying the expenses, they can be very specific about the numbers, costs, and meeting space requirements. In contrast, attendance at professional and trade associations is voluntary and may vary depending on the attractiveness of the location, the time of year, the program content, and whether the attendee's employer is reimbursing the costs associated with attending the meeting. Planning association meetings requires a longer lead time because of the marketing that must be done to attract attendees. Association meetings are larger than corporate meetings for the most part and meet on a regularly scheduled basis, such as the "annual" convention. The SMERF market (see the chapter on Hotel and Lodging Operations) represents another category of meeting hosts. These are non-profit organizations, such as federal and state governments, universities, and churches. They are often low budget and prefer to meet when the demand in a city is lower because rates will be lower. Their attendees must use personal money to attend the meeting, which makes them more cost conscious. The individuals who plan these meetings are more likely to be inexperienced volunteers rather than professionally trained convention managers.

Association Convention Managers

Associations are organizations for members of a particular professional or trade group. Examples of such associations are: the American Medical Association, the American Bar Association, and the American Society of Chemical Engineers. There are thousands of professional associations listed in the Encyclopedia of Associations. Association conventions are usually held annually and have three major objectives: (1) to provide continuing education to their members, (2) to provide networking activities for conference attendees, and (3) to provide opportunities for leadership development. It is the responsibility of the convention manager to see that each of these objectives is met during the three to four days of the convention. To accomplish this, the convention manager has many diverse tasks from selecting the city and hotel for the meeting to program design, speaker selection, marketing and promotion, registration, and special-event management. Specifically related to networking, the social component of the program, a variety of different activities (special events) are offered, such as children and spouse programs, theme parties, golfing or other recreational activities, and dine-arounds. The implementation of special events requires hiring many different types of suppliers, which may include florists, transportation companies, caterers, audiovisual companies, and security. The convention manager may know that they want certain types of activities/events, but may be unfamiliar with the specific opportunities available in the area. The local special-events management companies are invited to present proposals of activities and costs to the convention manager. One company will be selected to handle the events that require local expertise. This company will work closely with the convention manager in implementing the selected activities.

Corporate Meeting Managers

Corporations conduct two primary types of meetings. Incentive travel is a reward type of travel that is specifically reserved for individuals, often employees, who have provided exceptional contributions to the profitability of the company. An example of this is the 100 Percent Club sponsored by IBM that is made up of sales staff and managers who have exceeded the sales goals set for the individual or department. These "high performers" are rewarded by travel to an exotic place with their every need and desire anticipated and fulfilled. The sales/incentive program is promoted throughout the year to motivate employees to reach their goals. Often the winners, accompanied by spouses, are picked up in limousines at their homes, flown first class to the destination, met by greeters and luggage handlers, and taken again by limousine to a five star resort for three to five days of fun-filled activities. They are wined, dined, entertained, and pampered royally. A special-events firm is hired from the local area to implement the plans made by the incentive travel planner. The same types of events are planned for both association conventions and incentive meetings, but the extravagance is much greater with the incentive groups.

Convention Management Activities

The individual with responsibility of organizing a special event is called the event organizer or meeting manager/professional. This person must be a highly skilled manager not only in keeping all activities and costs on track, but also in motivating and communicating with the numerous outside experts (suppliers) that are required to host a successful event. Following is a partial list of the tasks that ultimately become the responsibility of the event coordinator:

- Administrative and operating procedures
- Dates and timing of the event
- Theme/décor selection
- Site selection
- Budgeting and financial management
- Technology management
- Marketing (design, printing, distribution)
- Media relations
- Sponsor recruitment
- Transportation (parking, traffic control, VIP)
- Registration
- Lighting, sound, special effects
- Food and beverage/catering
- Entertainment
- Photographer
- Safety and security
- Permits and licenses
- Insurance

Some corporations offer exotic vacations as incentives to increase sales.

For each of these tasks, one or many companies may be required. For example, to fully decorate the site, the following suppliers may be required: a florist, which may also provide balloon art; a theme props rental company, which may also handle costumes; often a different company is required for rental of tables, chairs, linens; yet another rental company will handle tents; technicians are required for lighting, sound, and special effects; other companies will provide catering, signage, favors for the guests, transportation, and entertainment; marketing requires graphic designers, printers, and mailing houses; permits, licenses, and security will likely require a stop at several governmental offices. Each of these suppliers must be interviewed and have references checked, contracts negotiated, clear communications established regarding their specific areas of responsibility, and methods established for monitoring costs.

Convention and Special-Events Management Companies

Very often corporations and associations do not have sufficient staff or expertise to plan their meetings and special events. In such cases, they may hire an outside expert to assist with all or selected parts of the meeting. The term commonly used for this is outsourcing.

Prior to the appearance of destination management companies, limited services were provided by bus companies, known today as ground transportation. Meeting planners needed to move attendees from one location to another and soon began to ask these companies for additional services, such as catering, entertainment, decorations, florists, and rental companies. As the need for these services increased, a new type of company developed—destination management companies (DMC)—to handle the non-transportation needs of groups visiting their city. Because this became a very profitable type of business, other companies entered the special-events market. These companies have also expanded their markets to include local events such as weddings, fund-raisers, parades, and numerous other types of public and private events. Today, destination and special-events management is a very integral part of the hospitality industry. There are many exciting careers in this field for individuals with strong organizational and creative skills.

There are several types of companies/organizations that provide special-events management services. Depending on the event, one or more of these entities can work together to produce the event, although one will probably be assigned the primary responsibility. Following is a list of the five primary types of companies that provide convention and special-events management services.

Special events management companies have expanded to include local events such as parades.

1. Destination management companies
2. Independent meeting management companies
3. Travel management companies
4. Special-events professionals, public relations firms
5. Government entities and tourism offices

Destination Management Companies

Destination management companies (DMCs) are private companies that offer a range of services primarily for inbound customers, such as meetings, conventions, and incentives. The corresponding European service provider is known as a Professional Convention Organizer (PCO). Their primary responsibility is to expose their clients to the full range of opportunities available in the surrounding area; to prepare a proposal detailing the preferred events and costs; and on selection, to organize the special events for the convention attendees. These companies are familiar with the history and culture of the area and knowledgeable about suppliers of services required to conduct elaborate special events. Once selected as the DMC for the inbound group, they will organize the event, secure the site, obtain permits, and hire the appropriate suppliers such as the caterer, decorators, bands, and entertainment.

Independent Meeting Management Companies

Independent meeting management companies are similar to DMCs, although they provide services to both inbound and outbound clients. The primary market for these companies however is outbound groups. A group headquartered in Denver will have meetings, conventions, and incentives all over the United States and many internationally. When the independent meeting planner is conducting a meeting away from their home city, they are likely to hire a DMC in the host city. Again, this is because destination management requires experts from the local area. When the independent planner is in their home territory, they will provide services to inbound groups to maximize their profitability.

Travel Management Companies

Large travel management companies, such as Carlson, set up destination management departments as a part of their larger travel services product offerings. Although the independent DMCs and meeting management firms are much like the "mom-and-pop" restaurants and hotels, the large travel management companies are similar to national chain operations.

Major Event Producers

Major event producers are another type of destination management company. These companies design and produce sophisticated and often highly technical events, including fireworks displays such as the Fourth of July fireworks show in Washington, DC, parades such as the Macy's Thanksgiving Day Parade, sporting events such as the Super Bowl and Olympics, and political events such as the Democrat and Republican National Conventions and Presidential Inaugurations. This type of company usually works with large public events that require closing of streets, traffic management, and waivers of public ordinances. These are often high tech, high visibility, and many have components that could be dangerous without proper precautions. Clearly, a different level of technical knowledge is required to organize extravagant events of this type. These companies also offer the traditional types of events required for conventions and incentives, but that often is a secondary market.

Special-Events Market

Special events are extremely important to the attendees of meetings, conventions, and incentive programs. They encourage networking among attendees, build camaraderie within the group, and provide memories that last for years. Often special events during a convention are the most memorable part of the program and give status to the sponsoring organization. The companies that provide destination services are usually highly creative and imaginative. Their focus is on festivity and amusement. Even in serious settings, such as opening sessions at conventions and product introductions, creativity is important in capturing the interest of attendees. Entry into the special-events job market is often through private catering companies, hotel sales and convention services positions, large travel companies, and independent meeting management firms. Students may contact their local convention and visitors bureau to identify companies offering these services in their local area.

Major events producers design and produce sophisticated and highly technical events.

Special-Events Markets

When discussing special-events management, there are five primary markets, each of which have many submarket segments. The most common, from a tourism perspective, are those events that bring new dollars into a community—corporate and association incentives, meetings, and conventions. Many companies offer expanded services to specialized markets; therefore, it is important that all types of special events be considered. Listed below are the five primary special-events markets and the types of events included in each.

1. Corporate events—Incentive programs, product introductions, building openings, recognition events, anniversaries and retirement, groundbreaking, topping off, and ribbon cuttings
2. Meetings and conventions, Expositions—Opening ceremonies, gala dinner dances, opening receptions, awards ceremonies, theme events, tradeshows, and expositions
3. Public events—Parades, fireworks displays, festivals, fairs, inaugurations/swearing in ceremonies, holiday observances, military ceremonies, and sporting events
4. Retail events—Grand openings, promotions, celebrity appearances, and seasonal promotions
5. Social/Private events—Weddings, anniversaries, graduations, reunions, funerals, memorials, births, Bris or christening, Bar/Bas Mitzvahs, charity balls, runs, and auctions

Emerging Trends

There are many developments that will shape the MICE industry, but two of the leading factors are changes in communication systems, most specifically the Internet with its diverse applications, and the changing character of nations into a global community. The Internet provides an easily accessible format for virtual meetings and exhibitions, video conferencing, and online education. This connection to the cyberworld from the home or office makes Europe, Asia, and America as easily accessible as your local tourist office. Major corporations have already begun the process of globalization; now smaller organizations and individuals can equally participate in global integration.

Many organizations are addressing the question of whether the new meeting venue, the Internet, is a friend or foe. A recent and proactive study conducted by the Professional Convention Management Association advises professionals in this industry to focus on "what the technology allows, not the technology itself." They further suggest that once an infrastructure is in place and products that are valued by consumers are available, the demand for the new products will develop at an explosive rate. There is no indication that the demand for face-to-face meetings will disappear or even diminish, but the demand for new and improved types of training in alternative formats will increase.

References

Goldblatt, Joe Jeff. (1990). Special Events: The Art and Science of Celebration. New York: Van Nostrand Reinhold.
Price, Catherine H. (1998). The Complete Guide to Professional Meeting and Event Coordination. Washington, D.C.: George Washington University Press.

Name_____ Date_____

Chapter 31 Review Questions

1. Discuss the trends in building convention centers regarding number and size.

2. What is the economic impact of the meetings, incentive, convention and exposition (MICE) industry?

3. Explain the need for increased standardization in meeting and event management.

4. Name at least five professional associations for the convention industry.

5. Name at least five industry publications.

6. Identify the two components of the meeting and event industry.

7. Explain the key activities associated with the following industry groups:

   a. Meeting and convention managers

   b. Incentive and special event producers

   c. Trade show and exhibition managers

8. Describe the main differences between association meetings and corporate meetings.

9. Discuss what is involved in "incentive travel."

10. Delineate the major responsibilities of the event coordinator.

11. Describe the functions of a destination management company.

12. Compare independent meeting management companies with travel management companies and major event producers.

13. What are at least four entry points into the special events job market?

14. What are the five primary special events markets? Give two examples of types of events that could be included in each market.

15. Identify at least two trends for the meetings, incentive, convention and exposition industry.

Non-Commercial Food Service

Bessborough Hotel
Saskatoon, Saskatchewan

Corel

POSTAGE
PAID

Daryl V. Georger
Mercyhurst College

Introduction

Non-commercial food service management is one of the fastest growing segments of the hospitality industry. It is also known as Institutional Management, Volume Feeding, and often Contract Food Service Management. The many components of this industry segment have made it somewhat resistant to economic downturns and therefore attractive to "start up" companies, as well as established corporations.

Definition

It has been said the term non-commercial was coined because this segment of the industry is usually contracted by a host company not related to food service. Since many host companies subsidize food service, profitable food service is not a motive. As with most commercial ventures, profit is paramount. Since this was not the case, the term non-commercial food service was developed.

History

Non-commercial food service management, as we know it by definition, dates back to ancient times. Slaves building the pyramids were fed and given drink by others assigned to the task. Laborers building the nation's railroads were fed hot meals in order to maintain peak performance. During the industrial revolution and throughout the world wars, U.S. factories fed employees who sometimes worked double shifts to keep the economy and war machine running at a blistering pace. Today, non-commercial food service touches most industries, governments, persons, education, recreation, and health care in most parts of the world.

Scope

The scope of the non-commercial food service segment of the hospitality industry is extensive and always changing. Non-commercial food service categories include:

Business and Industry
Communication Companies
Service Organizations (i.e., insurance, financial)
Manufacturing

Correctional Food Services
Federal Facilities
State Facilities
Regional Facilities

Airline and Transportation
In Flight
Terminals

Sports and Recreation Food Service
Stadium/Arenas
Theme Parks
National Parks
Zoos
Aquariums
Olympic Games
Racetracks
Amusement Parks
Convention Centers
Conference Centers

College Food Service
Faculty Clubs
On Campus Catering
Concessions
Convenience Stores
Student Meal Plans

Support Positions
Contract Sales
Marketing
Purchasing
Management Information Systems
Accounting and Finance
Human Resource Management
Cost Containment

Special requests are no longer uncommon in today's airline food service.

School lunch programs are offering an increase of choices of a la carte foods.

Each non-commercial food service category component offers the same positions found in most commercial food service operations. Positions available include: general manager, manager, assistant manager, executive chef, sous chef, and accounting.

Career Advantages

Non-commercial food service is incorporated in so many segments of the world's economy that it has been difficult to satisfy its need for food service professionals. Advantages of a career in non-commercial food service are:

- Regular work hours averaging 40 hours per week
- More job satisfaction and less boredom as non-commercial food service companies have many divisions and recommend crossing the divisional boundaries (i.e., college feeding to correctional feeding)
- Job security since many of this industry's segments are resistant to downturns in the economy (i.e., correctional feeding)

- Opportunities for creativity to satisfy the most demanding clients
- Strong salaries with bonus
- Long-term relationships with clients with benefits of the host company (i.e., earning an MBA at the university under contract)
- To work in a location of the employee's choice. There are so many non-commercial food service companies operating all over the world it is easy to find a desirable position in a location of the employee's choice.
- Accelerated promotions and advancement

Conclusion

Many opportunities abound in the non-commercial food service segment of the hospitality industry. Offering a quality of life not often found in other segments of the hospitality industry, non-commercial food service positions are becoming more and more popular with young food service professionals. When deciding on a career, it is a segment of the hospitality industry which most definitely must be considered.

Chapter 32 Review Questions

1. Summarize the history of non-commercial food service.

2. Describe at least three different venues for non-commercial food service.

3. List three positions likely to be found at a non-commercial food service.

4. List six career advantages to non-commercial food service that appeal to you.

Chapter **33**

Quick Service Operations

Sky Dome
Toronto, Ontario

Corel

POSTAGE
PAID

Nancy Swanger
Washington State University

As today's hospitality student, you have grown up with industry icons like McDonald's, Pizza Hut, Subway, and Taco Bell being an integral part of everyday life. You have never known a life without fast food restaurants. Quick service restaurants (QSRs) and visits to them are so commonplace in today's society (the average QSR user eats 6.2 dinners from fast food/pizza restaurants each month[1]) that their existence is often taken for granted. However, nearly one-third of all adults in the United States have worked in the restaurant industry at some time during their lives.[2] Specifically, one of every eight Americans has worked at McDonald's.[3] This segment of the restaurant industry provides endless opportunities for the student serious about the business.

History

Quick service restaurants got started back in the 1930s and 1940s with White Castle, A & W, and Dairy Queen; however, it wasn't until the 1950s when Ray Kroc met the McDonald brothers that the face of the restaurant industry was forever changed. Kroc was not a restaurateur; he sold milkshake machines. In fact, he sold milkshake machines to the McDonald brothers for their fast food hamburger restaurant in San Bernardino, California. The fact that their concept often needed to be able to produce up to 40 milkshakes at a time caught Kroc's eye, and because the brothers had no desire to expand, they sold Kroc the rights to the name and system they had developed.

In his early days with McDonald's, Ray Kroc established the standards of quality, service, cleanliness, and value (QSC & V) that to this day, serve as the benchmarks for others in the quick service industry. Because of his early jobs in sales, Kroc fully understood the importance of a first impression. Kroc was always meticulously groomed and carried that standard forward with the employees of his own company. Today, McDonald's is the most recognized brand in the world.[4]

Quality, service, cleanliness, and value have become synonymous with today's quick service restaurants. In a recent study of students on the campus of Michigan State University, the number one factor influencing which fast food restaurant they patronized was cleanliness.[5] Friendliness, price, speed, consistency, menu variety, and location followed, in that order. Merely having QSC & V guarantees a quick service restaurant operator nothing; however, lack of them almost surely guarantees failure. What separates the winning restaurants from the others is hospitality—the delivery of genuine, caring, personable service to the guests from each of the employees.

Characteristics

Quick service restaurants are identified based on some common characteristics. They include limited menu, service style, size, location, and check average.

Limited menu QSR menus typically center on a common menu theme—pizza, tacos, burgers, submarine sandwiches, chicken, etc. Although many chains have expanded menu offerings to attract a larger customer base, most can still be identified by their core menu. For example, Arby's has added chicken choices to its line; however, roast beef remains its signature product. Items are generally prepared in less than five minutes and use a few key ingredients in multiple combinations for the appearance of a broader menu.

Service style Customers inside the restaurant generally place their order at the counter prior to sitting at a table or booth. The meal is usually paid for before it is prepared and eaten and is often picked up from the same counter where the order was placed. The restaurant business is very labor-intensive, and as a result, many operators have converted to self-service drink stations and condiment bars in an effort to reduce the number of employees required per shift.

Drive-thru windows provide a convenient way for customers to enjoy their favorite fast-food meals without ever leaving their cars. In the most recent report of the *QSR* Drive-Thru Time Study con-

[1] From business wire. (2000, November 7). *Dick Wray Executive Connections, 3,* (24) 2.
[2] National Restaurant Association (2000). *Industry at a Glance* [Online]. Available Internet: http://www.restaurant.org/research/ind_glance.html
[3] A & E Television Networks (1996). Ray Kroc: Fast Food McMillionaire. In *Biography.* New York: New Video Group.
[4] A & E Television Networks (1996). Ray Kroc: Fast Food McMillionaire. In *Biography.* New York: New Video Group.
[5] *QSR.* September 2000.

ducted by g³ Mystery Shopping, Chick-fil-A had the best overall ranking, beating out Wendy's by just one-tenth of a point. The survey measured the following attributes: speed, order accuracy, menuboard appearance, and speaker clarity.[6] The demand for convenience by customers has seen a modification of service style to include take-out and delivery options at many locations. Pizza has been delivered to the customer's door for years, but recently, chains like KFC and Subway have experimented with delivery in certain areas of the country with success. The challenge with both take-out and delivery is in maintaining the quality of the product while in transit.

Size The size of the QSR can vary; however, those including seating generally accommodate less than 100 patrons. Because of the need for speed and efficiency, unit layouts are designed to maximize productivity and reduce unnecessary steps for the employees. Operations can range from small, single employee carts or kiosks to large freestanding units with a drive-thru and inside seating, which may require double-digit numbers of employees per shift.

Location As the number of people working has continued to climb, the demand for convenience has also risen. Quick service restaurants are located where the consumers can access them easily. As America moved to the suburbs in the 50s and 60s, so did fast food. Units can be free standing, part of a strip mall, in a convenience store, inside the mall, at the airport, inside a grocery or department store—virtually anywhere traffic patterns have dictated a need. Because the reasons for choosing a quick service restaurant are not the same as those for choosing a special occasion or destination restaurant, location is key. The current trend which favors take-out food puts those restaurateurs with the most desirable locations in the best position to compete.

Check average Generally, prices in QSRs are lower than those found in full service restaurants, and as a result, quick service restaurants depend on high seat turnover to generate the necessary volume. In the late 1980s and early 1990s, Taco Bell turned the industry upside down with the introduc-

tion of its value menu. All items were less than $1, and many were priced at 49, 59, or 69 cents. To remain competitive, other quick service restaurants soon followed, and value menus, meal deals, and daily specials remain a part of most major chains today. As a result, check average can be pretty low (less than $5) in comparison to other segments of the food service industry.

QSR Categories

Quick service restaurants are classified, and sometimes compared, based on the category they represent. Those categories may include sandwich, pizza, chicken, seafood, and snack.

Chain Operations

The key to success in quick service operations is consistency—consistency of product, consistency of service, and consistency of facilities. One of the ways this is achieved is through tight controls established by the chain's corporate headquarters. Because the vast majority of quick service restaurants are part of a chain, a brief discussion of what that means follows:

Defined

According to Jaffe (1995), a chain is defined as "any single restaurant concept with two or more units in operation under the same name that follow the same standard operating procedures."[7] Many of the chain operations franchise their business format. This allows the business owner (franchisee) to use the name, logo, recipes, system, products, and marketing of the particular chain (franchiser).

Advantages

One of the biggest advantages of being involved with a chain is that because the concept has been tested and proven, the risk of failure is greatly reduced. When nearly 40 percent of all new businesses fail within the first year and about 75 percent fail within the first five years of operation, buying into a system can be very beneficial. According to the U.S. Department of Commerce, less than 5 percent of franchised businesses fail within the first year.

---

[6] Tutor, L., Navigating the Loop. *QSR* (October 2002) pp. 41–59.

[7] Jaffe, W. (1995). Chain operations in the hospitality industry. In R. Brymer (Ed.), *Hospitality management: An introduction to the industry* (pp. 94–108). Dubuque, IA: Kendall/Hunt.

Quick service operations can range from single employee carts to large units with inside seating.

Other advantages include help from the franchiser with site selection, design, and possibly, financing. The purchasing power of a chain is greater than the purchasing power of a single operator, helping the franchisee to keep costs and quality under control. Systems of budgeting, inventory control, and accounting are generally available for immediate use by the new franchisee.

Costs

The costs involved in franchising include the franchise fee (usually between $7,500 and $50,000), development costs (sometimes up to $1 million), royalties (usually between 3 percent and 8 percent of gross sales), and advertising fees (usually between ½ percent and 5 percent of gross sales.)

Franchise fee The franchise fee is a sum of money paid to the franchiser for the rights to use their system. This fee includes training in the system and a copy of the company's operations manual. This manual includes all the information necessary for the franchisee to operate the business and its contents are invaluable to the new owner or manager. As part of the franchise agreement and included in the franchise fee, the parent company may also send an "opening team" (a group of employees trained in operations and new store openings) to assist the franchisee during the critical first days of operation. Once the restaurant is open, the franchiser may send people to inspect the store on a regular basis to make sure the franchisee is adhering to the chain's standards and offer any necessary support.

Development costs Development costs are those associated with the land, the building, the furnishings, and the equipment necessary for operation of the restaurant. There can be a huge variation in these costs, depending on the particular situation. For example, will the land be purchased or leased? What are the current land values or lease rates in the area? Is this a remodel of an existing building or a new structure created from the ground up? Is there a level of décor packages available from the franchiser based on price or is there a standard, one-price package required for all units? Is the required equipment very specialized and unique to the concept or is the equipment more generic and easily purchased? Although these considerations are by no means complete, you can see that many factors contribute to the development costs of the restaurant.

Royalties Royalties are monies paid to the franchiser at regular intervals once the restaurant is open for business. Generally, the amount due is calculated as a percentage of gross sales for the period.

Advertising fees Monies for national and regional/area advertising are calculated and collected in the same manner as royalties. These fees are used to create and produce promotional materials and buy media, as examples, to help drive sales for the chain. Many times, each restaurant will also set aside an additional percentage of gross sales to support local store marketing efforts.

The Role of the Manager: A Personal Perspective

It can be argued that the unit manager is the most important factor in the success of a quick service restaurant. The following focuses on the three areas of the manager's position felt by the author to be most critical—their focus on selection, their role in training, and their influence on the environment.

Selection

One of the biggest challenges facing this industry is in finding quality employees. As mentioned earlier, this is a very labor-intensive business, and finding enough people to fill all the available positions is almost impossible. Even with the tight labor market, it is imperative the unit manager be very selective about the employees. Managers must "hire the smile and train the technical." A manager can teach a new employee how to make a sandwich or take an order, but he/she cannot teach the person how to smile and be nice to people.

Unit managers must be familiar with all legal and human resource issues involved in hiring; the process must be defined and implemented for each prospective employee. Having said that, it is important to remember that each new employee must "fit" with the other members of the staff. Because the success of the restaurant is based upon the efforts of the team, it is essential to keep the chemistry of the team in balance.

Standards of grooming and behavior must be addressed in the employee handbook and discussed during the interview and orientation sessions. The unit manager must "walk the talk" and always provide the example. Selecting the right people makes the manager's job much easier and sets the stage for building positive employee/guest relations.

Training

The time spent by the unit manager training the employees is vital to the long-term success of the business. Too many times new employees come to work, it is busy, and they are left to flounder on their own or told to follow so-and-so and do what they do. The best training programs are structured in their content and are scheduled during non-peak times to allow for maximum attention to the trainee. Taking the time to teach the new employee right the first time saves the manager from having to go back and try to correct established bad habits.

Training is not a one-shot deal; effective managers are constantly coaching even their veteran staff members for improved performance. Winning managers are continually raising the bar for productivity and performance through on-going training and feedback.

Environment

It is the job of the manager to create an environment in which the employees feel motivated. A survey conducted by Rice (1997) found the unit manager to be the most critical element in employee

satisfaction.[8] To help ensure employee satisfaction, it is important that the manager prove competency, show interest, and be sincere.

Prove competency Employees need to know the unit manager is on top of things. The manager does not necessarily have to be the best at every single position in the restaurant; however, they need to be good enough to hold their own and able to teach the position to others. Effective managers never ask an employee to do something that they are not willing, or able, to do themselves. One advantage to starting at the entry level and working up is the knowledge gained along the way about how the entire operation functions. Managers must demonstrate their ability.

Show interest Great managers get to know their employees as people. They build relationships with them that foster trust and loyalty. One way to do this is to spend some time with new employees on their first day doing a task where it is possible to chat while working. A good icebreaker question involves the employee telling the manager about his/her family. Usually, family is a topic people are comfortable with, and it generally leads to other discussion topics such as interests or hobbies. During these informal visits, attempts are made to connect the new employee to others on the shift with whom they may have things in common. Great managers know their people.

Be sincere Managers with credibility avoid saying things to employees they don't mean. Employees know phony praise and false promises. Honesty and integrity are everything when it comes to managing people. Character leads by example.

Recent Trends

The past two years have fared well for quick service restaurants in comparison to other segments of the hospitality industry. The weakening economy had already begun to take its toll on the hotel and airline industries prior to September 11,

---

[8] Rice, G. (1997, January). *Industry of choice: A report on foodservice employees.* (Available from The Educational Foundation of the National Restaurant Association, 250 S. Wacker Drive, Suite 1400, Chicago, IL 60606).

2001, and their recovery since has been very slow. However, because we have become a nation that is used to dining away from home, we may have scaled back our choices but have continued to eat out. While fine dining and upscale eateries have taken a hit in sales, the quick serve segment has been able to maintain and even show sales increases in certain areas.

Events currently in the news that may have an impact on the industry include the use of irradiated and genetically modified foods, banning the use of latex gloves in certain states, minimum wage hikes, and the infamous obesity lawsuit. (While the lawsuit was dropped because class-action status was denied, the negative press that was generated may have some lingering effects.)

As KFC celebrates its 50th anniversary this year, many quick service restaurants are making improvements they feel are necessary to enhance their own longevity. Those include upgrades to facilities such as new designs, remodeling or rebuilding of older units, improved signage, and updated décor options. New menu items are being added that provide the delicate balance of high quality products at a good value. The Market Fresh Sandwich line at Arby's is one such example.

Conclusion

What are the opportunities for you in quick service restaurants? As an industry, quick service restaurants will do sales just over $115 billion in 2002, according to the National Restaurant Association, which represents about 1.3 percent real growth over the year 2001.[9] It has been estimated this segment of the industry will need about 150,000 new unit managers by 2005. These unit managers will earn between $25,000 and $40,000 and be eligible for bonus compensation equal to an additional third of their base salary.[10] This bonus is often centered on goals in relation to sales volume, food/beverage/labor costs, customer count/ticket average, and profit. What other industry allows young people in their 20s the chance to be responsible for hundreds of thousands of dollars (even millions of dollars) in assets and sales? The opportunities are endless—go out and be great!

---

[9] National Restaurant Association (2002). *2002 Restaurant Industry Forecast* [On-line]. Available Internet: http://www.restaurant.org/research/forecast_sales.cfm

[10] Shingler, G. & Ludwick, J. (1995). The quick service (fast food) segment. In R. Brymer (Ed.), *Hospitality management: An introduction to the industry* (pp. 417–422). Dubuque, IA: Kendall/Hunt.

Chapter 33 Review Questions

1. What is the value of the first impression? Who in QSRs realized this first?

2. How did Ray Kroc get involved with the McDonald brothers?

3. Rank the following items in order of importance to you:

   a. Menu variety

   b. Location

   c. Cleanliness

   d. Value

   e. Friendliness

   f. Price

   g. Speed

   h. Consistency

4. What are the common characteristics of QSRs?

5. What are the attributes of a successful drive thru restaurant?

6. What new brands/items are moving into the delivery business?

7. Which food item was the first to utilize the delivery concept?

8. What are at least three factors that have contributed to the growth of QSRs?

9. Which brand was the first to offer "value menu" items? What year was this?

10. What are the categories of QSRs?

11. List at least two examples in each of the categories of QSRs.

12. What are the advantages to operating a chain QSR?

13. What items does a new franchisee get in return for his/her payment of the franchise fee?

14. What are at least five of the factors that contribute to the development costs of a franchise operation?

15. List the different fees associated with owning a franchised QSR?

16. What is meant by "hire the smile and train the technical?"

17. What are the critical aspects of the manager's duties?

18. Discuss the advantages and disadvantages of hiring "like" people?

19. Why is it important to consider the "right fit" with the team in hiring new employees?

20. Why is training important?

21. Give several examples of how a manager can "prove competency." Why is this important?

22. List three current trends that are impacting the QSR industry segment.

23. What are the employment opportunities for QSR management?

Chapter

34

Real Estate

Neuschwanstein Castle
Bavaria

POSTAGE
PAID

John M. Stefanelli
Karl J. Mayer
University of Nevada,
Las Vegas

Corbis

One of the advantages of working in the hospitality industry is the availability of a wide array of career options. Although most of the jobs are in operations (that is, production and service positions), several staff positions are available for persons who want to be in the hospitality industry but who are not interested in operations. For example, support staff positions exist in hospitality accounting, purchasing, inventory control, human resources, data processing, and real estate.

Many avenues can lead to working in a staff role. Some people enter these positions while going to school. Some move into them upon graduation. Others move into them only after working in several operations positions. A few find themselves thrust into these jobs through a combination of circumstances. An internship, if your program of study offers one, is often an excellent way to explore whether a staff position will be an interesting and rewarding career option for you.

Hospitality real estate offers interesting and rewarding career opportunities. Several hospitality firms employ real estate specialists, such as market analysts, location analysts, and lease negotiators. However, you do not have to be employed by a hospitality company in order to work in this field. You could be an independent appraiser or work for a lender, private investor, or real estate brokerage firm. The purpose of this chapter is to identify and discuss the options available for those who are interested in a real estate career in hospitality.

Typical Hospitality Real Estate Positions

Several career options relate directly or indirectly to the hospitality industry. Persons wishing to work in this area may find employment with real estate departments in multi-unit hospitality corporations, appraisal firms, real estate brokerages, business brokerages, site selection firms, vacation-ownership firms, and lending entities. The skills needed to perform well in hospitality real estate are very diverse and depend upon the specific area of emphasis. These areas are discussed next.

Company Real Estate Representatives

Many large, multi-unit hospitality corporations employ a real estate director and one or more real es-

tate representatives. These persons are usually responsible for the following activities:

1. Performing location analyses; i.e., evaluating real estate sites to determine whether the company should construct new businesses in these locations;
2. Evaluating existing business locations from the perspective of acquiring and managing the business that is situated there;
3. Working with a variety of external agents; for example, negotiating lease or purchase agreements with brokers or owners; and,
4. Interfacing with the company's legal, construction, operations, and financial personnel.

Company real estate representatives typically travel a great deal. It is usual for them to be on the road four days a week. Such extended travel, however, is necessary to evaluate a site properly. If insufficient time is spent researching a location, the company may make a rash decision. Since location is a critical factor influencing a hospitality property's success, it is very important to make good, well-informed site-selection decisions.

Appraisers

Real estate appraisers are employed to render estimates of value. They are trained to value real estate (i.e., land and buildings); furniture, fixtures, and equipment (FFE); collectibles and artifacts; and going-concern businesses.

Commercial lenders, investors, sellers, insurance companies, contractors, attorneys, accountants, pension funds, and other entities with a financial stake in a project engage appraisers. For example, before a commercial lender, such as a bank or savings and loan, can lend money, it must have the collateral appraised by an independent appraiser it selects. A hospitality firm that needs to borrow money to build a new property must pay the cost of the appraisal needed to satisfy this regulatory requirement.

Some appraisers specialize exclusively in the hospitality industry. The major one, Hospitality Valuation Services (HVS), was founded in 1980. HVS has offices in New York, San Francisco, Miami, Dallas, Chicago, Phoenix, and Denver in the United States, as well as offices in eight other countries. Although its array of client services has expanded in recent years, HVS's major focus is the appraisal of lodging properties.

It is unusual, however, for individual appraisers to specialize in hospitality because there may be insufficient work available to make it a full-time job. Generally speaking, appraisers tend to specialize in a particular category and not in a particular industry. For instance, a business valuation specialist who appraises restaurants will typically appraise related businesses, such as taverns, liquor stores, bakeries, and food marts.

In other cases, appraisers may be part of a larger consulting practice. The firm Ernst & Young is representative of these types of appraisers, and has consultants who are specifically designated to serve the hospitality industry through its Real Estate, Hospitality and Construction Group. Besides their appraisal work, these firms also conduct a wide variety of other assignments designed to assist their client companies.

In addition to appraisal assignments, appraisers usually counsel clients. For example, a motel owner may hire an appraiser to estimate the most likely sales price for the property. He or she may also ask the appraiser to suggest things the owner could do to make the motel more attractive to potential buyers. In this role, the appraiser is required to draw upon his/her considerable expertise in the real estate field to make sound recommendations to the property owner.

Lastly, over and above an appraising or counseling role, some appraisers also get involved with real estate sales, property management (such as overseeing a shopping center complex), and loan brokerage (such as helping clients search for and secure the most favorable debt financing available). It is important to note, however, that in all aspects of appraisal work, it is essential for appraisers to render objective, unbiased advice. To do otherwise would severely impair their reputations.

Real Estate Sales

While property owners are free to sell their properties without help from other professionals, most prefer using a third party to represent their interests. The same is true for potential buyers. Thus, brokers play a valuable role by serving as an intermediary in a real estate sales transaction.

Several brokerages specialize in the sale of lodging properties. For example, there are consortiums of brokerages in the United States that account for a majority of all lodging properties sold nationwide.

A brokerage office may also specialize in the sale of restaurants, taverns, liquor stores, and other similar hospitality businesses. In large cities, it is not unusual to find offices that deal exclusively with the sale and purchase of restaurants or tavern operations.

Persons working in a sales office generally are in business for themselves; that is, they are independent contractors. Their livelihood depends on the amount of property sold, in that their main (and most often, only) source of income is sales commissions generated when deals are concluded.

Some sales associates represent sellers and some represent buyers. Few represent both parties because doing so may be a conflict of interest.

While sales commissions are their primary source of income, some sales associates prefer to operate as independent consultants. In the typical sales transaction, the seller pays the commission, which is then divided among the relevant sales offices that helped consummate the deal. However, some salespersons work strictly for hourly fees and are paid regardless of the outcome of a transaction. In effect, they sell their time and are compensated accordingly.

A day in the life of the typical real estate sales associate finds him or her showing property to potential buyers, gathering pertinent data, suggesting appropriate sales and purchase strategies, recommending alternative financing arrangements, estimating the most likely sales prices, organizing and completing deal-related paperwork, negotiating contract terms and conditions, and shepherding the deal to ensure that it stays on track and is finalized.

It should be noted that the role of a real estate sales associate is evolving due to the impact of technology and growth of the Internet. The Internet is making it possible for companies to circumvent intermediaries and "go direct" to potential buyers and sellers on a worldwide basis. Although many aspects of being a real estate sales associate will not be affected by these developments, students who are interested in this area should carefully explore the impact of these trends on the future of working in a real estate sales position.

Business Opportunity Sales

A business opportunity is an ongoing business located in leased real estate facilities. The owner typically sells the furniture, fixtures, and equipment

(FFE); leasehold improvements (i.e., interior finishing of the leased premises); the business's name and reputation; and perhaps some other types of assets, such as inventory or a valuable liquor license. The business opportunity purchase usually includes everything but the real estate.

A business opportunity brokerage is very similar to the typical real estate brokerage. While business brokers do not normally sell real estate, they do sell businesses that must be transferred to buyers. In effect, the work performed by business sales associates parallels almost exactly that performed by most real estate sales associates. Additionally, like the role of the real estate sales associate, this intermediary role will likely be evolving due to technology and the Internet, so students should be mindful of the potential impact of these trends on future careers in this area.

Site Analysts

Some research firms, real estate brokerages, and business brokerages provide location analysis for persons or firms unable or unwilling to do the work themselves. These companies typically maintain computerized databases that can be adapted to suit any need or answer any question. Their reports help clients make sound real estate and business decisions.

Some hospitality firms prefer to contract out this type of work to independent firms because it is more economical than maintaining their own real estate divisions. This concept is known as outsourcing. However, even those large hospitality companies that have real estate divisions are apt to use an outside firm on occasion because it is not always feasible for them to study every potential site.

Vacation Ownership Sales

A vacation-ownership firm is in business to sell long-term vacation packages to guests. They sell "slices of time," in that they normally sell a guest the right to use a vacation apartment, hotel room, or condominium for a specified time period per year (usually two weeks) for several years (usually seven to twenty years) at a specific property.

Guests who prepay for these vacations usually have the option of swapping their time at one location for comparable time at other vacation locations that are part of a time-share exchange network.

Normally the guest pays a small fee for this exchange privilege.

In most cases, the prepaid vacation is an economical alternative to paying for vacations every year. Usually the guest needs to pay only a relatively modest maintenance fee each year in order to defray the cost of routine repairs, remodeling, and so forth.

At one time, these "time-share operations" had a seedy reputation. Most of them were high-pressure sales operations that generated numerous consumer complaints. However, while a few of these boiler-room operations probably still exist, generally speaking the industry is considered quite aboveboard today. This is due primarily to the involvement of major lodging firms such as Disney and Marriott in the field. Their participation has legitimized the industry. Today, this sector represents a growth area in the hospitality field. It offers excellent opportunities for hospitality students who are interested in the variety of careers available in vacation ownership sales.

Lenders

Many lenders are active in hospitality finance. Lenders provide the discretionary capital that allows new properties to be conceived and developed, or existing properties to be refinanced. The major players include the following organizations:

1. Life insurance companies that specialize in financing lodging properties;
2. Pension funds that invest in lodging properties or lend to them;
3. Banks and savings and loans that make real estate and business loans to qualified hospitality operators;
4. Government agencies (such as the Small Business Administration) that make direct loans or guarantee loans made by a third party; and,
5. Leasing companies that will construct a property and/or provide all necessary equipment and lease these assets to a hospitality operator on a rent-to-own plan.

Lenders must qualify potential borrowers. Before recommending a loan, the lender must ensure that there is a high probability that the money will be repaid in a timely manner. Lenders must perform "due diligence," which means that they must evaluate a borrower's credit worthiness, character, reputation, capacity to repay, business skill, and collateral.

Lenders who are heavily involved in hospitality finance may employ real estate experts on their own staffs to perform these functions. For example, DePfa Bank AG (Deutsche Pfandbriefbank) is a German-based institution that has a specialized hotel financing team. This team has financed first class hotels all over Europe and the United States, including properties such as the Plaza Hotel in New York City and the Adam's Mark Hotel in Dallas. In other cases, a lending institution may outsource these tasks to appraisers or consulting firms on an as-needed basis.

Desirable Background for Hospitality Real Estate Positions

If these career opportunities seem exciting, you should begin to prepare for them now. It is never too early to select the right college courses and work experiences most likely to give you an edge when applying for this type of work.

These positions are very academically oriented, in that a great deal of research, writing, and computer skills are needed to succeed. You should take college courses designed to develop and enhance these skills. You should also take a basic real estate course, real estate investments course, and real estate appraisal course. These classes will give you the best perspective of the industry, as well as highlight the various career opportunities that may exist in your local area. Accounting and finance courses are also necessary. At the very least, you should take the basic accounting and financial principles classes. Generally, however, additional finance courses are necessary to acquire the techniques needed to prepare the types of research projects you will encounter.

Computer literacy is a must. You should be very familiar with word processing, database, and spreadsheet software. In addition to working with your own computer files, you must be able to use the computerized databases most offices subscribe to. For instance, a real estate sales office usually subscribes to a computerized multiple listing service, or MLS. Sales offices also typically use services that provide demographic data and updated lists of lenders and their current loan terms and conditions. The number of service firms offering these data has expanded significantly in recent years in order to meet the industry's ever-increasing demand for information. Also, geographic mapping software is now available with such detail that a user can examine a potential site on-screen before ever leaving the office for a site inspection.

Computer literacy is also needed to efficiently access information available on the Internet. In recent years, there has been an explosion of real estate information that can be downloaded off the World Wide Web. This information could include such things as local market data and newspaper reports, national economic trends and conditions, financing availability and terms, and federal and state guidelines for site development activity. Thus, a broker, appraiser, or real estate director can now obtain a great deal of pertinent information without ever leaving the office. However, since real estate is inherently a localized business opportunity, there is no substitute for on-site visits by a trained real estate professional.

Many real estate positions require licensing or certification, or both. For instance, if you want to be an appraiser, you will likely need a state license as well as certification from a nationally recognized appraisal association.

Finally, you should acquire a reasonable amount of operations experience before tackling one of these staff positions. If you want to work in a hospitality company's real estate division, you should have a basic understanding of how the company's food or lodging units are operated and managed. This provides the perspective needed when wrestling with decisions that can make or break your employer's bottom line.

Your Future in Hospitality Real Estate

Research and experience have shown that for every four people graduating with a degree in hospitality administration, one of them leaves operations within one year, or leaves the industry entirely. Interestingly enough, for every four who leave operations or the hospitality industry, one of them ends up in some type of financial management career. In a nutshell, then, the odds are about one in eight that you will end up in one of the careers discussed in this chapter.

Hospitality is a people industry, and so is real estate. The skills, education, and work experience you have already earned and will earn in the future will qualify you for many types of careers. Take the time to explore the many options that are available.

Hospitality is a field that can accommodate many career interests and many different backgrounds. If you choose a career in hospitality real estate, you can be assured that many exciting challenges and new opportunities will lie ahead.

Name_____ Date_____

Chapter 34 Review Questions

1. What types of support positions (non-operational) exist in the hospitality industry?

2. List five real estate related job opportunities in hospitality.

3. What are the typical duties of a real estate representative in the hospitality industry?

4. What is a location analysis?

5. Why is a location analysis important?

6. Who does a real estate appraiser work for? List at least three opportunities.

7. Why must a real estate appraiser remain unbiased?

8. How do brokers get paid?

9. Who do brokers represent?

10. What impact is the Internet having on real estate positions?

11. What is a vacation ownership?

12. What is the current reputation of time-share operations? How does it compare to the past?

13. Describe what it means to "qualify" a borrower.

14. What college courses could help you prepare for a career in hospitality real estate?

15. What types of computer skills do real estate professionals need?

16. What are the functions of a real estate director and representatives who work for large multi-unit hospitality corporations?

17. How does the site selection impact the future of the business?

18. In what types of counseling do appraisers sometimes engage?

19. Explain the concept of "independent contractor" as it applies to persons working in real estate sales. How are these people usually compensated?

20. What type of businesses might be involved in conducting a site analysis?

21. List the types of organizations that are most active in hospitality finance and are major lenders in this industry.

Resorts

Royal Albert Hall
London, England

Corel

Michael J. McCorkle
Richard Stockton College
Albert J. Moranville
East Stroudsburg University

Introduction

People generally travel for business reasons, for pleasure, or sometimes for a combination of business and pleasure. Americans take over 300 million pleasure trips annually, and of this number, approximately 27 million trips are for vacations at resorts. The resort traveler is interested in getting away from daily life, being entertained, and relaxing.

This chapter will look at the history of resorts, the differences between traditional lodging operations and resort operations, and the evolution of the resort industry to the present state of development. Although traditional lodging organizations, such as hotels, motels and resorts, have many similar characteristics, resorts have the additional characteristic of being a tourism destination that provides extensive recreational facilities. This article will also provide the student with an understanding of the basic working of the resort hotel and the resort industry.

A Brief History of Resorts

Resorts and resort hotels are generally found in areas offering exceptional scenery, natural resources, recreational opportunities, lodging facilities, relaxation, and pleasure. The growth of the American resort closely followed the pattern of traditional hotel growth and was tied to the development of technology, especially transportation technology. The original settlers in America inhabited the Atlantic coastal regions. As the population moved inland, transportation methods changed to accommodate the inland movement. The appearance of river steamboats, stagecoaches, and finally the railroads created the need for various types of lodging facilities, including hotels and resorts. According to author Chuck Gee, "The real development of the American resort hotel came with the expansion of the railroads. At this period in history the many spas and mineral springs attracted thousands of people yearly. It was a natural development that outstanding resort hotels should locate in the areas served by rail. In fact, in several cases, those hotels were built and operated by particular railroad lines."[1]

Resorts offer scenery, recreation, lodging, relaxation and pleasure.

Major growth in the number of resorts in the United States came in the nineteenth century. Some of the more famous early American resorts were the Green Brier in White Sulphur Springs, West Virginia (1863); the nearby Homestead in Hot Springs, Virginia (1832); The Mountain View House, Whitefield, New Hampshire (1865); the Ponce De Leon, St. Augustine, Florida (1865); The Grand Hotel, Mackinac Island, Michigan (1887); and many others built and operated in the Catskill Mountains of New York, the New Jersey seashore and the Pocono Mountains of Pennsylvania.

Distinguishing Characteristics of Resorts

One of the distinguishing features of the resort property is the guest-market that is served. Unlike the business traveler, who stays at a lodging property as a necessary part of business travel, the resort lodging guest is seeking leisure pursuits and

---

[1] Gee, Chuck Y. *Resort Development and Management.* Lansing: Educational Institute, 1996, 37.

other recreational activities the resort has to offer. Secondly, whereas the business traveler generally desires to be close geographically to the business facility being visited, the location of the resort property is not as critical to the success of the leisure traveler. The third distinguishing factor is the nature of the lodging expenditure. The dollars spent for a resort vacation are discretionary dollars. Discretionary dollars are those that the consumer has a choice to spend or not to spend. During periods of positive economic activity, the typical consumer will plan for a resort vacation and elect to spend dollars for the opportunity to relax and have fun. Business trip expenditures, on the other hand, are not of a discretionary nature, and funds must be spent in the normal course of conducting business activity. Thus, resort financial success is impacted by what is termed *demand elasticity* to a much greater extent than is the commercial hotel.

Other distinguishing characteristics include typically high quality food service, high service expectations, seasonal demand variability, a variety of recreation facilities, special maintenance requirements, and even environmental demands. The nature of resort service is that it must be very personal. Many resort hotels pride themselves as providing a family-type environment where personalized service is part of the package offered to the guest. Research has shown that to create loyal, repeat resort customers, excellent service must be provided on a consistent and continuing basis.

Resorts typically have a *high season*, in which business demand is at its greatest. A *low season* is the opposite, and during this period, the lowest business demand is experience. The high season for a winter resort was during the winter months when skiing, ice-skating, sledding, and other winter activities took place. The high season for the summer resort was in the warmer months when swimming, golfing, horseback riding, tennis, sun, and surf activities took place. Although many, if not most, resorts are more year-round oriented today, there still exist seasonal fluctuations in which business demand decreases and staff adjustments must be made, as well as changes in other operations-oriented activities in order to deal with lower revenues and earnings. Often, resorts require the largest number of employees when the labor pool is the smallest.

Because resorts are generally located in rather isolated areas, employee housing often becomes problematic. Housing is not always available in nearby communities, and resorts must plan and provide housing for employees. Construction, provision, and maintenance of employee housing requires a substantial expenditure on the part of the resort. Commercial hotel properties, which are usually located closer to more heavily populated areas, generally don't experience the same type of demands.

The last unique feature of resort hotels is the requirement for recreation facilities. This aspect of resort operations may be the most important factor leading to financial success. Commercial hotels may, and often do, have a limited number of recreational facilities, such as indoor or outdoor swimming pools, workout rooms, and so on. The early resorts did not have extensive entertainment or recreational facilities. The principal activities consisted of dining, walking, climbing, horseback riding, swimming, sitting, reading, and enjoying the scenery. Dinner was served early in the evening, and it was not unusual for guests to retire by 10 p.m. Times have certainly changed, and the foundation of the modern resort is the provision of a wide variety of activities that will keep guests occupied and happy. Most resorts are associated with certain types of activities, such as golf resorts, skiing resorts, tennis resorts, seaside resorts, mountain resorts, fishing resorts, health spas, and more. And of course, resorts combine a large number of guest-oriented recreational activities, as well as entertainment activities, such as live music, dance bands, and popular entertainers.

Organizational Structure

The organizational structure of a typical resort is not dissimilar to the organizational structure of the typical hotel. Many of the activities found in a lodging property will also be found in a resort property. The personnel positions in both types of lodging properties may be delineated as line or staff and front-of-the-house and back-of-the-house. The resort facility has a third type of position involved with guest leisure and recreation services that is not generally found in hotels. The organizational structure and the relationships therein are unique to a particular resort. There is no "one size fits all" structure for hotels or resorts, and each property generally develops the structure that will best serve its needs.

In the lodging industry, most operational activities are organized along functional lines. Typical front-of-the-house functions are rooming activities, guest relations, and guest services. These activities are considered front-of-the-house because they generally occur in the presence of the guest. Back-of-the-house activities, on the other hand, consist of production and support operations that aid the front-of-the-house employees who serve the guests. These activities do not normally take place in the presence of the guest. Additional resort operations include: sports and recreation, health and wellness, entertainment and social activities, and other structured and nonstructured guest-oriented activities.

Guests in the typical commercial or transient hotel have their own schedules and time frames that are often dictated by their business objectives. When recreation or entertainment activities are scheduled for such guests, it is to help the business guest fill in time between business meetings and other appointments. Activity planning in the resort hotel becomes a management concern and function. Guest activities for both daytime hours and nighttime hours have to be planned. For this purpose, the resort hotel generally retains a staff of recreation-trained and oriented employees who work with the recreation or social activities director. The size of the resort will dictate the number of staff members needed and also the responsibilities of the director. There are actually three specific areas in which activity planning and management are required—recreation, social, and entertainment activities. In larger resorts, where recreational activities are a major revenue center, recreation is a separate function. In smaller properties, recreation, social, and entertainment activities may be combined.

The resort hotel offers a wide variety of services to its guests and is distinguished from the commercial hotel in the number and type of services offered, as well as the manner in which the services are delivered. The core of the resort concept in a successful hotel is the creation of an environment in which the promotion and enhancement of a feeling of well-being and enjoyment is created and maintained. To meet customer expectations, the resort hotel management group must create a culture that values the delivery of high-quality service in a professional, personal, and guest-friendly manner.

Vacation Ownership

During the last half of the twentieth century, the traditional American lodging industry continued to evolve as it has throughout its long history, and new types of properties were developed in response to various demands and opportunities. Some of these new types are:

Lodging Properties

Traditional	Non-traditional
Beach resort	Time-share resort
Mountain resort	Convention resort
Ski resort	Condominium resort
Health/fitness resort	Casino resort
Golf/tennis resort	Multi-resort complex
All-season resort	Mega-resort

Both traditional and non-traditional resorts offer overnight accommodations. There are, however, many differences between traditional and non-traditional lodging properties. Some of the basic differences are as follows:

- Non-traditional lodging have three categories of users: the guest, the owner, and the owner's guests, whereas traditional lodging establishments have only the guest-user.
- Non-traditional guests normally have a minimum guest-stay days.
- Non-traditional lodging units are furnished by owners, not the lodging company.
- In non-traditional properties, general managers must deal with multiple owners.
- Non-traditional property general managers generally report to a board of directors who are not hospitality professionals.
- Non-traditional properties may be governed by the Law of Innkeepers, as well as federal and state real estate laws, and Securities and Exchange Commission regulations.
- Non-traditional lodging property general managers must operate while there are many owners on the property.
- Because non-traditional lodging units usually have kitchens, there are usually no food and beverage facilities available at non-traditional units.

Non-traditional lodging may be divided into three specific groups: whole-ownership condominium resorts, interval-ownership properties, and a third much smaller segment, condominium hotels. We will briefly review the condominium hotel segment, but our main concentration in this section will focus on the whole-ownership condos and interval-ownership condos.

The main purpose for condominium hotels, which were largely built in the 1970s, was for tax purposes. In the early 1980s, the Economic Recovery Act of 1981 created a vehicle for investment tax write-offs that provided fuel for building hotel condominium properties. With the Tax Reform Act of 1986, such lucrative tax advantages were rescinded, and the hotel condo building boom came to an end. According to authors Robert Gentry, Pedro Mandoki, and Jack Rush, "Few, if any, new ones [condominium hotels] have been built since 1986." [2]

Whole-Ownership Condominium Hotels

This non-traditional lodging property is made up of residential units owned by individuals, and common areas owned jointly by the owners of the residential units, the owners' association, or by the developer of the resort. A whole-ownership condominium resort is a method of subdividing real estate into units and common elements; it has little to do with the construction or design of the complex or structure. This type of condo is sold outright and the owners generally have year-round occupancy. In addition to residential units, the whole-ownership condo property may also have a number of units that are owned by the developer, a management company, or other unit owners and are rented commercially.

Interval-Ownership Properties

This model of non-traditional resort property is often called "fractional-ownership properties, vacation-ownership resorts, or time-share properties." Time-share condominiums began originally as an alternative to renting hotel rooms, a way to save money on hotel stays. Property developers reasoned that instead of selling a customer an entire condo unit, why not sell one-twelfth (a 30-day period) of a unit or one-fiftieth (a 7-day period) of a unit. The advantage to the customer was the guaranteed use of the unit purchased for the particular time purchased. In other words, the customer would be assured of getting the block of time wanted when it was wanted. Over the years, as hotel room rates doubled or tripled, the investment in the interval-owned would appear better and better. Also for the economy-minded group of customers, who cannot afford the price of a whole condominium unit or those who desire a variety of vacation experiences, the interval-ownership model provides a way to achieve one's personal vacation goals. For yet another group, a more affluent group of interval-ownership purchasers, the objective was practicality, that is, why make a $50,000 to $100,000 condo investment when the unit might be used only one or two weeks a year? Thus, there are a variety of reasons for purchasing an interval-ownership condo.

Ownership

What does the interval owner actually own? There are a number of ownership plans beginning with the *condominium plan*. Under this plan, the owner may purchase an interval of one week in unit one. If the property sells 50 weeks in each unit during the year, the aforementioned buyer owns 1/50th of unit one. A second type of ownership structure is termed the *undivided interest plan*, in which the owner buys time in the entire property. For example, in a 100-unit property the buyer would own 1/5,000th of the collective units of the property. The owner of a vacation-ownership or interval-ownership property does not actually purchase a whole unit as one would when buying into a *whole-ownership* condominium resort. The purchaser actually buys an interval of times, which may or may not be tied to a specific condominium unit, or even one particular property. Vacation-ownership condominiums are either deeded or nondeeded properties. If the purchase is for a deeded property, the purchase is a real estate purchase, and a deed accompanies the sale. A transaction for a deeded property is a real estate purchase and is subject to various real estate laws. The term of a deeded purchase is generally 30 to 40 years or for perpetuity.

[2] Gentry, Robert A., Mandoki, Pedro and Rush, Jack. *Resort Condominium and Vacation Ownership Management: A Hospitality Perspective.* Lansing: The Educational Institute, 1999, 10.

The high season for a winter resort is during the winter months.

Interval-Use Plans

There are different plans that govern the ownership and the use of the interval unit. Use plans explain the interval buyer's access and occupancy rights are usually part of the buyer's purchase agreement. Use plans vary between properties and may vary at the same property. One such plan is the *fixed week/fixed unit plan,* which provides the purchaser with the same week period in the same unit each year. A *seasonal float plan* may not include a fixed week, rather a week is available during a specified season (i.e., in-season or off-season). And there are other plans that may allow the interval owner to split the weeks that he or she has purchased.

Vacation Clubs

A recent variation on the interval-ownership model is the vacation club, which offers a high degree of flexibility to the interval owner. These plans allow the owner to use their purchased time at any one of a number of properties. The system is administered using a *point system.* A certain number of points are assigned to such variables as in-season weeks and off-season weeks, two bedroom versus three bedroom, geographic location of the particular unit to be used and so on. Although a number of well-known lodging companies are involved in the time-share market, approximately 90 percent of time-share resorts are still owned by independents.

The Time Share Industry

The time-share industry has grown rapidly and is an important component of today's resort and lodging industry. Many of the major American hotel companies, including Marriott, Hilton, Inter-Continental, Disney, Ramada, Holiday Inn, Westin, Sheraton Hyatt, and others, have entered the industry.

Research into vacation trends has revealed that people are taking shorter but more frequent vacations, and that greater flexibility in choosing vacation time and location are desired. These factors suggest a very positive future for the success of interval ownerships, vacation clubs, and other variations of the basic time-share theme.

Chapter 35 Review Questions

1. What does the resort traveler typically desire?

2. Compare and contrast hotels to resorts.

3. Where are resorts usually located?

4. What factors affect price consideration of hotels and resorts?

5. List five characteristics of resorts.

6. How does the "season" (high or low) impact a resort?

7. What are "front-of-the-house" positions?

8. What are "back-of-the-house" positions?

9. Who oversees and operates the recreational aspects of a resort?

10. What type of recreational facilities are you likely to find at a resort?

11. List three of the oldest resorts in the U.S.

12. List six of the categories of resorts.

13. Compare and contrast traditional and nontraditional resorts.

14. What are the industry segments of nontraditional lodging?

15. What are the different types of ownerships available for vacations?

16. What is an interval use plan?

17. What are the advantages to the consumer to purchase an interval-ownership property?

18. What areas of the resort industry are likely to flourish in the future? Why?

Chapter

36

Restaurant Operations

Outdoor Restaurant, Chateau Lake Louise, Alberta

POSTAGE PAID

C. E. Vlisides
University of New Haven

Corel

The restaurant business is a challenging and unique profession. The challenges come from two main components: unskilled labor and perishable products. These two crucial issues cause restaurateurs to seek individuals that are motivated by their abilities to react to many different factors that cannot be planned for in advance. The satisfaction of working in the restaurant industry comes from the inherent joy one receives when making others happy.

There are two recognizable styles of leadership: proactive and reactive. Defining these terms are not difficult, practicing them is. Proactive leadership means that the one in charge forecasts what will happen. Forecasting can include, but is not limited to, the volume of business, safety and sanitation measures, or the ordering of food and supplies. In essence, proactive management attempts to thwart any issues that may negatively impact the operation before such an occurrence takes place.

Reactive management is the opposite of proactive. A leader is forced to come to a reasonable conclusion that will avert a negative action and lessen its impact on the operation. For example, a customer falls in your restaurant and requires immediate attention to be made comfortable. They need to also know that you are personally concerned about their welfare.

It is in the nature of the restaurant business that reactive management skills are as important as proactive skills because of the two crucial items mentioned before. Careers are made or broken on how well your leadership style accommodates these two principles.

Classifications of Restaurants

The selection of which restaurant classification you choose does make a critical difference in your career advancement possibilities. There are several different classifications. The Quick Service Restaurant (QSR) has been examined and discussed in detail earlier in this book. A second classification is the specialty quick service restaurant. These are specialty QSRs that specialize in coffee or sandwiches, such as Krispy Kreme doughnut shops or Mr. Goodcents submarine sandwich shops. A third classification is that of coffee shops. These are operations that provide all three meals per day. Breakfast, lunch, and dinner items appear on their menu. The fourth level is that of dinner house. A dinner

house operation usually operates through two meal periods, lunch and dinner. The last classification is that of a luxury or fine dining establishment. This operation is usually open for dinner only and is very formal in its types of service and food. There will be more detailed examples of these types of restaurants later in this chapter.

The National Restaurant Association claims that 11.6 million people are currently employed in the restaurant industry (2002). The restaurant business continues to grow on a yearly basis and more restaurants are being built. The devastating effects of September 11th, 2001 had negative implications to most of the hospitality industry. However, the restaurant segment continues to grow as more and more people are eating outside their homes (Orilio, W. 2002).

Types of Service
Quick Service Restaurants (QSRs)

The classification of the restaurant profession is dependent on the type of service the operation desires. A rule of thumb is that the less formal the service, the quicker the food is delivered. Therefore, QSRs create limited menus and develop architectural styles that allow for a quick turnover of customers. The key to their profitability is the volume of customers served. The higher the customer count, the more revenue is generated. The more revenue that is generated leads to greater profitability. As a note, revenue is based totally on sales. Therefore, QSRs require a heavier flow of customer traffic through their doors.

Quick Service Specialty Restaurants

The classification of specialty QSRs is new to the industry. The segmentation of QSRs has created this category. As reported on the A&E network *Food Show* in December 2002, these operations have limited their menu offerings to a few specific items. The customer can pick and choose what they desire, and their orders are filled most rapidly. Variations of the items that are available may be offered, but only to what the operation can provide.

For example, Dunkin Donuts specializes in coffee drinks and a limited number of pastries and bagels. Customers are most generally aware of the menu choices before entering the door. Dunkin Donuts operators know that their prime business

Menu items, service, and ambiance combine to meet the needs of restaurant customers.

hours will be early in the morning. Therefore, the bulk of their employees and products are consumed at that time. Managing a QSR or specialty QSR is not easy. Customer satisfaction, employee efficiency, and product quality are keys to success.

The same can be said of Mr. Goodcents, a submarine sandwich shop found mostly in the Midwest. The principles are still the same. In this case, customers order their food choices and the amounts they desire to be placed on a roll. Each item placed on the sandwich is weighed, and a price per ounce determines the cost of the sandwich. The customization of each customer's sandwich makes Mr. Goodcents unique. The same principles of this type of operation hold true as described in the QSR chapter.

The largest of these chains is Subway. This is a global operation that has 17,514 units in 70 countries (Subway, 2002). The cost per unit is dependent upon its size, location, and regional construction costs. Estimates to own one of these units range from $70,000 to several million dollars, as underscored by the units operating near Times Square in Manhattan, New York City. The responsibilities of a unit manager are very well described in the QSR chapter.

Coffee Shops

The coffee shop concept is not one to be taken lightly. Each of us has been at Denny's or Big Boy restaurant. The type of service that is used to deliver the food is performed by a server who waits on each customer. This is a key difference from the QSR operations. The interaction between the customer and the server is critical because the

customer's perception of service makes this an experience that is either enjoyable or not. Therefore, the selection of servers who can interact with people is absolutely critical.

The type of menus found in the coffee shop are larger and more expansive than that of the QSRs. This requires managers to seek out, hire, train, and motivate individuals that can create, prepare, and present food within the confines of a standardized recipe. Coffee shops generally try to get the food from the time the order is taken to the table in 10 minutes at breakfast time, 10–12 minutes at lunch and 15–20 minutes at dinner. These are rules of thumb that have been learned from 25 years in the restaurant business. Of course, some menu items may take more time or less time, depending on the customer's desire.

Because there is more food variety on the menu, there are more specialized requests. These requests oftentimes determine the success of the coffee shop. All customers have the right to request what they wish to be served. The successful operator makes most of those desires come true. This level of customer expectation and perception of the operation separates the good from the best. It is easy to be perceived as good; it is difficult to be perceived as great. It is most difficult to remain being perceived as great.

The coffee shop is open more hours and more days per week than any of the other concepts. They offer more variety of menu items and offer them any time of the day or night. They rely on their hours of operation and their diverse menu to bring in their revenue. They have increased expenses because they have more employees than QSRs. Therefore, their menu prices are higher, because the customer is getting more service and more food choices.

Dinner House

The dinner house concept is fashionable and can be the most profitable. The impact that the dinner house restaurant segment has had on the entire American dining experience is quite remarkable. The largest dinner house chain in America is Red Lobster with nearly 700 units (http://www.redlobster.com, 2002). The Olive Garden Restaurant chain continues to grow with nearly 500 units. Darden Restaurants, Inc. owns both of these chains. The reason they are named Darden is because Mr. Bill Darden created the original Red

Lobster concept and restaurant. Each unit within the chain generates approximately $4–5 million per year. The total revenue between these two concepts is then approximately equal to $5.85 billion per year. The responsibility of a general manager and his or her subordinate management team is obviously heavy.

Each unit is constructed at an average cost of between $2 and $4 million dollars. This does not include any of the inventories that are needed to supply the restaurant for its initial operation. Having opened two units in Las Vegas, Nevada and Houston, Texas, it was a very interesting experience. There must be coordination among the architect, the general contractor (who is in charge of construction), and the operator. The two restaurants were remodeled from former restaurant operations and so they needed to look and "feel" like currently operating Olive Garden restaurants. The reason for this is that the customers from the East knew from their experiences what to expect from the new operations in the West.

Las Vegas was especially important because as a destination point for travelers and conferees, the expectation for nation-wide acceptance of this chain was critical. The selection of the management team and their training was done in a meticulous fashion. Management teams were pre-selected to open Olive Garden units in the western U.S. Orlando was the selected training site, as it was the area that Olive Garden first opened and subsequently succeeded. Therefore, their operating and training systems were proven to be successful. To secure restaurant chain continuity, the training was done in operating units, as well as the corporate training headquarters.

The training proved to be invaluable, as those who participated in the intense management-training program were certified as qualified Olive Garden managers. It is noteworthy that not all participants were successful, and many were eliminated from the program before anyone left Orlando. That was just the beginning because after training, the management teams were sent to their opening sites.

Construction Complications in Houston

The completion of construction had to be overseen. The experience of being in the Orlando units was needed to secure the same environment in Las Vegas and Houston. Construction does not often match with architectural plans because remodeling took place after each of the units was originally built. The architects in Orlando had no knowledge of the remodeling that took place before the building was to become an Olive Garden. The general contractor was forced to make decisions that were inherent with property. A prime example would be that either the cook's line would be two feet wide or the server's aisle would be less than three feet wide.

The architect was called immediately to help remedy the situation. The results took several weeks to resolve. While the ultimate resolution to this problem was found, it pushed back the opening date and cost over $40,000 to remedy. The purpose of this example is to underscore the necessity of leadership within the industry. Someone has to make decisions that affect organizational resources. These resources include fiscal, physical, and human, which are considered assets of an organization. Each leadership decision, on whatever level, affects these assets. Good decision-making skills are a necessity within the restaurant profession at all levels and classifications.

Luxury and Fine Dining Segment

There will always be the need for fine and luxurious dining. This segment of the restaurant industry generally caters to those who can afford it. Normally, these dining establishments are open in the evening and on special holidays. They may cater to specific clientele, as seen in a previous chapter. The type of service and menu must meet or exceed customer expectations and enjoy an excellent recommendation in the form of word-of-mouth marketing made by customers. These recommendations are crucial for this type of operation's long-term success. Each detail of the operation must be overseen, as it is essential that nothing is overlooked. Of course, this argument may be said of each of the other previously mentioned segments. However, it is imperative in this restaurant segment. You may be thinking to yourself, why?

A Perception Ruined

Simply put, the reason is because the customers pay top dollar and expect top of the line service and products in an exceptional environment. As an illustration to this point, a visit was made to a fine city club that will remain unnamed. Upon entering the club, you received a warm and personable greeting from the door person; one could feel their feet sink into the plush carpet. The foyer was elegant with richly decorated hand-carved oak wood panels, staircase, and front desk area. The tile was marble and the chandeliers were made of exquisite imported crystal. The paintings that hung from the walls were original oils by well-known artists. The entire building was immaculate and the service was outstanding.

Upon entering the sanitized restrooms, one could not help but see the luxurious accouterments that were in place. Gold spigoted faucets on marble sinks. More original oil paintings and other accent pieces were to be marveled by all who saw them. The linens were thick and fresh, laid out so everyone who entered would be assured of receiving a fresh towel. This entire experience was beyond compare, until one looked at the soap dispenser. It was totally out of place. It was plastic, and the 79 cent price tag was still on it and could be viewed by all. That one item destroyed the perception of exquisite surroundings and left the patrons with the perception that if this was done, where else were cost-saving measures occurring?

It is the attention to small details that make or break any restaurant operation. Cleanliness, uniforms, plate presentations, personnel selection, floor and wall coverings, music selection, interior and exterior lighting, interior and exterior landscaping, purveyors, bar and food menus, and more. Each of these items must be specified clearly and concisely for operational uniformity and conformity. These become expected standards of operation for the restaurant unit or chain.

Fine operations will deviate very little from established standards because their patrons expect quality and consistency in service, atmosphere, and product. To deliver that kind of quality and consistency every time requires vigilance by restaurant leadership.

Selection of Personnel

As mentioned earlier in this chapter, one of the critical issues that face restaurant managers/leaders is the selection of people that will impact their business operation in the near and distant future, especially the front line people that take care of the customers. Within the restaurant industry, it is common that these are the least paid employees and yet have the most interaction with the customers. Therefore, the selection of these individuals is critical to the long-term success of the operation. When opening the Las Vegas Olive Garden in 1986, 1,800 people were interviewed for 108 positions. When the operation was running at peak efficiency, the number of employees dropped to eighty-eight. These remaining individuals stayed with the operation for a longer than normal period of time.

When Houston opened its Olive Garden in the Baybrook Mall, the same scenario was needed. It began as a larger unit, as its seating capacity was nearly 300. The number of individuals interviewed was over 2,200 for 135–140 positions. These statements are actual activities and counts which are made to underscore the need for the creation of a team of employees that will meet or exceed your customer's perception of quality of service.

Conclusion

The restaurant profession is a most honorable one that demands individual excellence. Personality, decision-making skills, and the inherent joy of making other people happy are necessary skills. Can you make a good living and earn enough money to enjoy a wonderful lifestyle? Yes. In a survey done of 23 corporate and partnership restaurant operations, the average number of years to make it to senior level management was 11.2. If you are in charge of an organization that employs over 1,000 people, your earnings will exceed 6 figures (Vlisides, 1993). The ability to influence and impact many peoples' lives from either a customer or employee standpoint is incredible.

References

Darden Restaurants. Giving Today, Investing on Tomorrow. Retrieved December 18, 2002. http://www.dardenusa.com/community/df2001/df2001.pdf

National Restaurant Association, (2002). Forecast material. [http://www.restauarant.org]

Orilio, W. (2002). Hospitality bubble may have burst, but aim of operators still should be customers first. *Nation's Restaurant News; Vol. 36,*(49). December 9, 2002.

Red Lobster: Our Company. Fact Sheet [*http://www.redlobster.com/discover/our_company/fact_sheet.asp*]

Subway, Inc. (2002). Company website statement. [*http://www.subway.com/development/*]

Vlisides, C. E. (1993). *Personal Value Systems of Senior Corporate and Partnership Restaurant Managers and Higher Education Program Implications.* Denton, TX: University of North Texas.

Name _____ Date _____

Chapter 36 Review Questions

1. What are the two major challenges of the restaurant industry?

2. What obstacles do these two challenges pose to restaurant managers?

3. Why do people enjoy working in the restaurant business?

4. Define proactive leadership.

5. Define reactive leadership.

6. Why are both proactive and reactive leadership skills needed in the restaurant business?

7. List the five classifications of restaurants described by the author.

8. Identify two examples of restaurants in each of the five classifications. If possible, cite restaurants in your area.

9. What does it typically cost to own a Subway restaurant franchise?

10. Define the characteristics of a coffee shop.

11. Define the characteristics of a specialty QSR.

12. What are the challenges associated with managing a coffee shop?

13. Define the characteristics of the luxury and fine dining segment.

14. Why is detail management important in fine dining?

15. List at least eight detail areas that need attention in a fine dining restaurant.

16. What does the author describe regarding interviewing many candidates in order to hire the right "team" for a restaurant?

Chapter

37

Senior Services Management

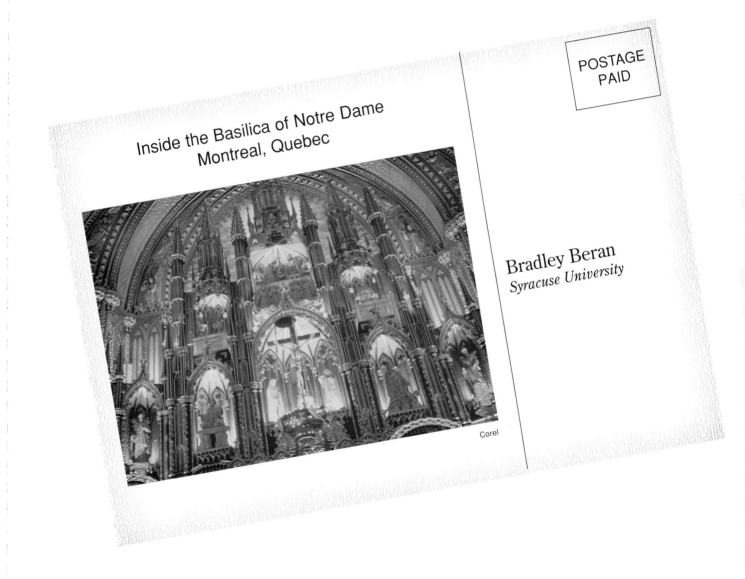

Inside the Basilica of Notre Dame
Montreal, Quebec

POSTAGE
PAID

Bradley Beran
Syracuse University

Corel

According to the 2000 Census, 34.4 percent, or 96,944,389 people are at least 45 years old, 21 percent, or 59,266,437 people are at least 55 years old, and 12.4 percent or 34,991,753 people are at least 65 years old. The largest single segment of the population, baby boomers, is getting ready to enter retirement age. This group has living needs, demands, and desires that are being filled by senior living centers. People who no longer have the ability and/or desire to maintain a self-owned residence, want greater flexibility, and/or fewer responsibilities during their golden years are looking to senior living centers to meet their residential and personal needs.

Senior living centers are residences that offer a multitude of services depending on the needs and desires of the residents. At the extremes, minimal services include housing and indoor and outdoor maintenance and repair similar to apartment living, while maximum services provide full medical and personal care, transportation, and more are available to residents in need of the most assistance. As the services increase, so does the cost to the resident. The level of services identifies the type of living center.

Independent, Assisted, and Full Care Centers

These centers have progressed far beyond institutional-style nursing homes. Independent and assisted living centers are new or completely remodeled facilities designed to be comfortable, attractive, efficient, and convenient apartment-style residences. They are typically well landscaped with flower gardens, atriums, and other amenities that offer a high quality of life and emphasize family traditions.

Independent Living Centers

Independent living centers offer the fewest services and the lowest cost and are for the most independent senior residents. Typical services at this level are lawn care, snow removal, and similar outdoor maintenance. Other services often include a community center and/or recreation center, food services/catering/restaurant/home replacement meals, and laundry services.

An example of high-level services at the independent level, Marriott offers independent full service communities. Services provided are exercise and wellness programs, outings to local events and attractions, on-site entertainment, programs and activities, fine dining, landscaped grounds, and weekly housekeeping and linen service.

Independent living center residents are generally in good health with few limitations and not interested in the responsibilities of home maintenance and costs. They typically own a car, are quite mobile, and come and go as they please. They need little to no assistance in living. These centers are usually set up as apartments and often come fully or partially furnished.

Assisted Living Centers

Assisted living centers offer more services, at greater costs, to residents who are not capable of fully living on their own, but do not need full care. The degree of care, services, and cost varies depending on the needs of the resident. In addition to the services offered by independent living centers, assisted living centers also generally offer assistance with medications, meal preparation and/or feeding, personal care (shaving, showering, dressing, etc.), ambulatory care, transportation, and, to a lesser degree, medical care. Some assisted living centers provide specialty care for residents with Alzheimer's and other debilitating, non-communicable disease. Coordination with physician and pharmacy services is provided.

Services available for assisted living are usually offered in one of three ways. A resident may select from a menu of services and pay a fee based on the number of services selected. Another option allows a resident to select one of several service programs, each offering more services, at different costs. Finally, an assisted living center may offer only one set of services at one price. Usually, these centers are full service operations.

Marriott Assisted Living Centers services include three meals per day served in a restaurant-style setting, health and wellness assessments, scheduled transportation, activities programs, weekly housekeeping and linen service, and personalized levels of care based on each resident's needs.

Residents of assisted living centers usually do not drive, need varying degrees of assistance due to medical, physical, or mental conditions, and may be in declining health. Typically, the longer these residents stay at a center, the more services they require as they age. These centers are often set up as apartments or as group units with a central common area and bedrooms for eight to twenty residents and several units per center.

Full Service Living Centers

Full service senior living centers are most commonly known as nursing homes. These centers provide full service for those seniors least able to care for themselves. All services are provided for these residents. Services include all meals, housekeeping, laundry, feeding, personal care, medication, and other services. Medical personnel are on staff, including Registered Nurses (RNs), Licensed Practical Nurses (LPNs), and Certified Nursing Assistants (CNAs). Doctors are on call, and pharmacy services are provided.

Marriott's nursing homes offer 24-hour nursing, post-hospital care, post-surgical care, physician and pharmacy coordination, family counseling and other support services, and emotional and physical health and well-being.

Residents of nursing homes can only provide minimal care for themselves. Some cannot provide any care for themselves and some may be bedridden. These centers are usually set up as rooms, private or semi-private, with common areas for recreation, meeting, and dining.

Respite Care

Many assisted living centers offer respite care. This is a short term, temporary use of assisted living center resources and services. Respite care is designed to fill the needs of a senior who may need assistance in recovery from surgery, injury, or other ailment and only needs temporary assistance during recovery and rehabilitation. Respite care lasts from one week to a few months and is usually billed by the day and/or week. Typical services for respite care include three meals per day, laundry and housekeeping services, and other services, as needed depending on each situation.

Multiple Service Centers

Usually a living center will not specialize in one style of service, but rather offer multiple levels of service. It is not uncommon to find a living center offering a full line of services ranging from minimal services for independent living to full assisted living services and, in some cases, full nursing care services. Think of the list of services as a sliding scale. At one end are minimal services provided for independent living centers, at the other end are full nursing home services. As residents age and their abilities decline, providing more services affords a company the opportunity to care for a senior through any and all stages of life, health, and ability. Essentially, as a person's faculties decline, more services are needed, and they begin moving from one end of the sliding scale toward the other, stopping when the level of service meets their needs. As a result, this keeps a stable resident population and maintains a consistent occupancy rate within the community.

The Nature of the Work in Senior Living Centers

Living centers have needs and challenges that are a blend of many other hospitality operations.

- Like hotels, living centers are 24 hours per day, 7 days per week, every week of the year. Similar services include housekeeping, laundry, and sometimes room service.
- Like private clubs, the members, in this case the residents, are the same group of people all the time. This creates challenges to keep menus interesting and activities exciting. While many centers include meals in the cost of services, in some independent living centers residents are free to use, or not use, the on-premise restaurant as they choose.
- Like an event planner/activities director, residents are offered activities that are interesting, enlightening, challenging, and entertaining. Since the residents seldom change, there is a constant challenge to create excitement and avoid the boredom of the "same old thing" in activities.
- Like a full service caterer, special events and holidays require special services, menus and meals, decorations, and more.
- Like a nutritionist, meals must meet dietary needs of the residents. Some of them are very specific regarding spices, flavors, fat content, and more. Others are on more general diets.
- Like a restaurant, all of the challenges to operations are here. Culinary arts and food preparation, servers, linens, sanitation, inventory, menu planning, cost control, and other similar restaurant management tasks are required.

- Like a resort, landscaping, mowing, snow removal, gardens, flowers, walk-ways, and other grounds maintenance must be done.

Positions in Living Centers

Positions in living centers are as varied as the nature of the work. Living centers can provide jobs in many different areas of interest, many of which are hospitality related. Some positions include:

Administrative
> Executive director
> General manager
> Regional director (for multi-unit operations)
> Purchasing director
> Information systems
> Business director
> Marketing

Food Service
> Food and beverage director
> Catering manager
> Nutritionist
> Executive chef
> Station chef
> Cook
> Dining room manager
> Host/Hostess
> Server

Residence
> Director of residence services
> Activities director
> Housekeeping manager
> Housekeeper
> Facility maintenance
> Grounds keeper

Some senior living centers have administrative and staff positions that require residency. Since these are 24-hour operations and the homes of the residents, resident positions provide accommodations, and resident employees are expected to live at the center as part of the job requirement and compensation package. This type of arrangement puts the resident employee "on-call" virtually 24 hours. The idea behind resident employees is to create a family type environment between the residents and the resident staff.

Market Outlook

The 2000 census lists 1,720,500 residents in nursing homes. Some estimates state that a senior living center capable of housing 600 residents must be built each week for the next 40 years to fill the expected demand. By 2010, it is projected that there will be 36,818,000 Americans aged 65 or older. By 2020, the estimate increases to 47,338,000 and to 81,999,000 by 2050.

Private companies are building and/or completely renovating apartments and other buildings into senior living centers to begin to meet the demand. The Federal Government is also expanding the market for living centers. In order to reduce costs while still providing services, seniors who meet certain eligibility criteria are encouraged to consider assisted living centers instead of more expensive nursing home care. To accomplish this, Medicare has developed the PACE program. PACE also has an option that allows qualified seniors to receive assistance while remaining in their own homes.

The Marriott Care Management Program assesses the right level of care for each resident.

From the Medicare Web site:

Program of All Inclusive Care for the Elderly (PACE)

PACE is unique. It is an optional benefit under both Medicare and Medicaid that focuses entirely on older people who are frail enough to meet their state's standards for nursing home care. It features comprehensive medical and social services that can be provided at an adult day health center, home, and/or inpatient facilities. For most patients, the comprehensive service package permits them to continue living at home while receiving services, rather than be institutionalized. A team of doctors, nurses and other health professionals assess participants needs, develop care plans, and deliver all services, which are integrated into a complete health care plan. PACE is available only in states which have chosen to offer PACE under Medicaid.

Several Web sites and other forms of assistance in selecting a senior living center and/or determining the level of service needed are available. Assisted Living On-Line offers complete and free consulting and advice to families considering senior living center alternatives. They can be visited at: http://www.aplaceformom.com/index.html

Assisted Living On-Line also offers an evaluation form to assist in determining the level of services and care needed. It can be found at: http://www.assistedlivingonline.com/apfmassessment.asp

Ownership

Senior living center residents do not own their apartments. They are tenants who contract for the space and services they receive. Senior living centers have several types of ownership. Some are owned by religious orders, such as Menorah Park, which is owned by the Jewish Orthodox. Religious based living centers are operated for members of their religion, and costs can be subsidized by the religious organization. Charities and foundations, such as the Bethesda Living Centers owned by the

Bethesda Foundation, also own and operate living centers. Like religious owned living centers, resident fees are often subsidized to some degree. Residents generally meet certain criteria to belong to these living centers, such as income guidelines, specific medical needs, etc. Private companies and corporations, such as Sunrise Assisted Living, Inc. and Marriott, form a third type of ownership. These are usually for profit companies supported by private investment. Government agencies also own retirement centers; however, this type of ownership is declining and most often was limited to nursing homes. As local and state governments cut costs and move toward the privatization of services, many community owned senior centers are being sold to private concerns or closed.

For more information, please visit any of the sites below providing information and services for seniors, or do an Internet search on your favorite search engine for "Senior Living Centers."

Medicare Nursing Homes http://www.medicare.gov/Nursing/Overview.asp

Medicare Nursing Home Alternatives http://www.medicare.gov/nursing/alternatives/PaceSites.asp

Sunrise Assisted Living http://www.sunrise-al.com/homepage.asp

Menorah Park Center for Senior Living http://www.menorahpark.org/entryway.html

Life Care Centers of America http://www.lcca.com/

American Senior Living Centers http://www.aslc.net/

Bethesda Living Centers http://www.bethesdalivingcenters.com/default.htm

Southern Living Centers http://www.southernlivingcenters.com/

Marriott Senior Living Centers http://www.marriott.com/senior/

Hallmark Senior Communities http://www.hallmarksenior.com/

References

Assisted Living On-Line (2002) http://www.aplaceformom.com/index.html
Bethesda Foundation (2002) Bethesda Living Centers on-line http://www.bethesdalivingcenters.com/default.htm
Marriott Corporation (2002) Marriott Senior Living Centers on-line http://www.marriott.com/senior/
Menorah Park (2002) Menorah Park Center for Senior Living on-line http://www.menorahpark.org/entryway.html
Sunrise Assisted Living, Inc. (1999) Sunrise Assisted Living on-line http://www.sunrise-al.com/homepage.asp
U.S. Department of Health, Education and Welfare (2002) Medicare on-line http://www.medicare.gov
U.S. Department of Commerce (2002) Census Bureau on-line http://www.census.gov

Chapter 37 Review Questions

1. What are the general goals of seniors?

2. How many people in the U.S. are more than:
   a. 45-years-old

   b. 55-years-old

   c. 65-years-old

3. What is the range of services provided by senior living centers?

4. Describe the interior design "look" of independent and assisted living centers.

5. What group of seniors does the independent living center attract?

6. What types of services are offered by the independent living centers?

7. What group of seniors does the assisted living center attract?

8. What types of services are offered by the assisted living centers?

9. What are the three traditional ways one can arrange for services from an assisted living center?

10. What are the characteristics of those individuals interested in assisted living centers?

11. What group of seniors does the full service living center attract?

12. What types of services are offered by the full service living centers?

13. What are the characteristics of those individuals interested in full service living centers?

14. What is respite care?

15. Draw a sliding scale as the author describes. Label it based on the continuum of care available to seniors, and the costs associated with each level.

16. Describe seven ways senior living centers offer the same services as other traditional segments in the hospitality industry.

17. List at least four positions in the senior living center.

18. Describe the residency requirement of some positions.

19. What are the advantages and disadvantages of living on-site?

20. What are the future projections of senior living centers?

21. What is PACE?

22. What services are provided by PACE? To whom?

23. Describe four types of ownership of senior living centers.

24. Does the senior typically own his/her own dwelling?

25. What is the trend regarding government owned assisted living in the U.S.?

POSTAGE PAID

Westminster Bridge and Big Ben
London, England

Corel

Patrick T. Tierney
San Francisco State University

Growing demand by both domestic and international tourists and the complexity of the travel industry have lead to an increasing desire by many travelers for highly specific travel information, help in making their travel plans, and convenient packages of travel services. Out of these needs have evolved travel agencies and tour operators, and most recently electronic travel agencies relying on Web sites and online reservations. *Travel agents* within an agency act to match the travel desires of leisure and business travelers with the most appropriate suppliers of tourist services. Agencies do not normally own the means of production, that is the lodging facilities, restaurants, or attractions that will be used by travelers, but act as agents for the suppliers. *Electronic travel agencies* have developed from the Internet revolution and communicate entirely via Web sites and e-mail. They do not have physical locations where clients can go, but they employ extensive databases, online booking technology and are open seven days a week and 24 hours per day.

So what do traditional travel agencies provide: Information to plan a trip; they arrange an individualized, coordinated itinerary; and secure tickets for transportation, lodging, receptive services, resorts and cruise lines and recreation attractions. Traditional travel agencies play a key role in the travel industry, accounting for over 65 percent of all airline ticket sales worldwide during 2000 and over 85 percent of all cruise sales (PhoCus Wright 2001).

Tour operators organize complete travel programs for groups or individuals to every continent, by all modes of transportation. Perish the thought of tour operators only offering sedate sightseeing to groups of senior citizens in busses, today there are a vast array of tour itineraries and formats that appeal to youthful and mature audiences alike. Tour operators are different from travel agents and individual suppliers in that they plan, arrange, and market pre-established *packages* at a *set price* that include, to varying degrees, transportation, lodging, educational opportunities, recreation, meals, and entertainment. Many, but not all, tour companies operate substantial portions of the tour package. They make their profit from operations, markup and/or buying other accommodations, meals and necessary services at discount rates. Through volume buying power they can offer competitive rates. The importance of the tour industry is underscored by the fact that residents of the United States and Canada spent a total of approximately $166 billion on packaged tours worldwide (National Tour Association 2001).

Travel Agency Management

In 1867, Thomas Cook introduced the first hotel coupon and started the travel agency business. The modern travel agency era really began with the advent of the airline industry in the 1960s. Since that time, the number, roles, and types of travel agencies have mushroomed. Some travel agencies specialize in one type of travel service, while others, as exemplified by the country's largest travel agency conglomerate, American Express, are active in multiple markets. Over 85 percent of travel agencies today are considered small independently owned businesses.

Types of Travel Agencies

Corporate agencies Those agencies who specialize in serving business clients, often with little or no walk-in clientele. They cater to corporations on the telephone or through e-mail, often working under contracts which provide for exclusivity, but also require the return of a portion of the normal travel agent commission, or on a fee-based arrangement. They rely heavily on revenue from airline tickets, hotel rooms, and rental cars.

Leisure agencies Tourists going on vacation are the primary clients of this agency. Clients have traditionally gone to the agency office to discuss options and to look at brochures and videos. This business relies heavily on cruise sales, resort packages, airline tickets, rental cars, tours, and hotel room sales.

Wholesalers These organizations sell primarily to travel agents and not to the general public. They organize and promote specific types of travel services, but do not operate the tours or facilities. Wholesalers contract with suppliers for blocks of tickets or rooms in anticipation of future sales.

Specialized leisure agencies A growing trend in the travel agency business are shops that specialize in one category of leisure product, such as cruise or dive agencies, or in one region of the world. By limiting what they sell, these agents can become experts on unique products, services, and destinations.

Incentive travel houses These agencies develop customized programs for corporations who offer incentives for high employee productivity by providing deluxe travel rewards. They setup and administer reward contests, inform eligible staff and contract with suppliers. Incentive agencies earn their profits from supplier commissions and management fees.

Consolidators These are businesses that purchase large blocks of airline seats or cruise berths at a substantial discount and resell them to travel agents or the general public for a lower than normal fare. They may also have contracts with certain airlines for larger commissions on certain routes. Consolidators, also known as "Bucket Shops," advertise to the public in the travel sections of metropolitan newspapers, while others deal exclusively with travel agents.

Electronic travel agencies As a result of the Internet revolution and communication advances, a growing number of companies sell travel products entirely via Web sites. There are no human travel agents to talk with, and they do not have physical locations where clients can go, but they employ extensive databases, online booking technology. Some electronic travel agencies are independently owed, like Travelocity (www.travelocity.com), while others are owned and/or controlled by the airlines, such as Orbitz (www.orbitz.com). Initially, these businesses only offered airline tickets, but now they offer a wide range of travel services and have moved aggressively into booking hotel rooms.

How Travel Agencies Get Paid

Since travel agencies do not own the facilities or equipment used to operate destination services, they are paid only when they make a sale. Payment is in the form of a commission, based on a percentage of the sale price, or increasingly payment is by an additional ticketing fee. The cost of the agent commission is built into the sales price so in the past it did not cost the consumer more to use the travel agent than if they went direct to the supplier. Commissions historically have been about 10 percent for airline tickets and other services, but on February 9, 1995, Delta Airlines announced it

would pay travel agents no more than $25 on any one-way domestic ticket or $50 round-trip. Since then, all major U.S. airlines have discontinued paying commissions on domestic flights altogether. The main exception to this no commission policy is where the airlines and large travel agencies have a preferred-provider contract that allows for a small commission. In contrast to the airlines, Carnival Cruise Lines announced at the same time it would increase its travel agent commission from 10 to 12 percent. The end result has been that more travel agencies are seeking other sources of revenue besides the sales of airline tickets, such as commissions from cruise lines, tours, resorts, and international air carriers. In fact, many travel suppliers offer agents *over-ride commissions* of an additional 2–5 percent to encourage group sales or introduce new travel products or services. A large number of agencies have diversified and are starting to develop and market their own tour packages. Still, other experienced agents charge *hourly fees* for the time they spend developing complex customized vacation packages. A *ticketing fee* from $15–$25 in addition to airline ticket price is being charged customers by an increasing number of agencies. Even electronic travel agencies are charging a ticketing fee. For example, Expedia.com has a $5 ticketing fee, but they show it in the ticket price, rather than as a separate charge. Another way to increase profits has been by reducing their operational costs through increased automation (as exemplified by electronic travel agencies). Lastly, more travel agents are quoting lower fares to consumers than can be found on the Internet by becoming or using consolidators.

Certainly one of the most desired benefits of being a travel agent is discount travel to destinations worldwide. Suppliers wanting to promote new travel services are often willing to provide familiarization trips at little or no cost to agents. Airlines, cruise lines, and resorts provide very low cost tickets or ticket class upgrades. An inclusive five day stay at a new resort in Brazil for only the cost of taxes, for example, is a unique opportunity available to travel agents. These benefits tend to make up for the rather low wages that travel agents receive, which average about $30,000 per year for an agent with three years of experience. Some agents are paid a monthly salary, some only commission, others a combination of these. So persons considering becoming a travel agent must weigh their financial goals against the excitement and low cost of travel that are available to agents.

From the outside, a travel agency in your neighborhood appears to be a lucrative, if not glamorous, business. But increasing competition from larger agencies with volume discounts and lower overhead, electronic travel agencies, the Internet (see following section), elimination of airline commissions, and generally increasing costs of doing business have resulted in low profitability, distressed sales, and business failures, especially small independent neighborhood companies. To increase profitability, some agencies have joined consortiums, groups of agencies that combine strength to negotiate lower rates for clients and higher commissions for their agencies. A member agency is often required to use a limited number of *preferred providers* who have contracts with the consortium. With such contracts, the agency must offer a fare quote from their preferred supplier first, but can sell from any supplier the consumer wishes.

Automation and Certification

Precise and accurate information on schedules, availability, and rates is critical for a travel agent to know, but the scope and amount of information on the global travel industry is overwhelming. Therefore, computerized databases are a basic tool of the travel agent. Global Destination Systems (GDS), such as Apollo, Sabre, World Span, and Amadeus, list over 12 million fares, a quarter of which are updated daily. These systems were started by airlines and, at one time, carried just airline schedules and inventory, but today they have become full scale travel information systems that also contain lodging, tours, and attraction information. Effective data search and ticketing with a GDS are critical skills for agents.

In order to be able to issue domestic tickets, an agency must be approved by the Airlines Reporting Corporation (ARC). This organization is an association of U.S. airlines who facilitate funds transfer and ensure that travel agencies have experienced management. For sale of international airline tickets, a travel agency may also be approved by the International Airlines Travel Agent Network (IATAN), who has similar responsibilities to the ARC. These licensing agreements limit the number of companies that can sell travel to legitimate businesses and help protect the consumer from fraud.

Individual travel agents must show proper identification in order to receive travel discounts and promotions. The most accepted form of credential is a photo identification card issued by IATAN. Some travel agencies, but not all, require that their senior agents be a Certified Travel Counselor (CTC). The later credential, issued by the Institute of Certified Travel Agents, is awarded to persons who pass rigorous examinations and have five years full-time experience in a travel agency.

Although the full-time in-office travel agent will continue to be the backbone of any travel agency, there are a growing number of Outside Sales Agents (OSA) who are affiliated with the company, but are independent contractors, not employees. The OSA provides her/his own office and telephone and pays employment taxes, but shares commissions with their affiliated agency.

Information Revolution and the Internet

Travel agencies no longer have exclusive access to the myriad schedules, fares, and destination information that are found in a GDS. The Internet is a global network of computers with many sites dedicated solely to travel services. The electronic travel agency Travelocity (http://www.travelocity.com), for example, contains an easy-to-use program for booking reservations on most domestic flights for a $5 booking fee. It also has content on destinations, an area where viewers can ask questions about travel providers, and a shopping "mall" with specialized travel merchandise for sale. Suppliers have also embraced the Internet as a way to lower their travel sales distribution costs. Hilton Hotels, for instance, was one of the first lodging chains to place all of its properties worldwide on the Internet (http://www.hilton.com). Travelers themselves, especially business travelers, have gone directly to supplier Web sites, by-passing the middle organization. Obviously, this type of free service is in direct competition with some of the services that both traditional and electronic travel agencies have provided. The travel agency business is now undergoing a radical transformation due to changes brought on by the Internet and air carrier payment policies.

But the Internet revolution is also threatening other "middle men," and it is leading the push towards a more direct consumer-supplier link. For example, in January 1999, Delta Airlines announced that it will require anyone not booking directly with only the Delta Web site to pay a $2.00 per ticket surcharge. Subsequently, Delta and other airlines have backed off requiring surcharges, but instead are offering lower priced "Internet only" fares to drive traffic to their Web sites. If more suppliers follow this trend and many more consumers start using the Internet to book directly, it could mean radical changes in the travel services sales and distribution system in the future.

Tour Operator Management

The most basic functions of a tour operator are to bundle together a *package* of travel services, offer it at a fixed price, and provide some or all of the services during a tour itinerary. Describing exactly what a tour operator offers can be tricky because there are many types of tours. Below is a listing of the most common tour formats.

In a *group tour*, clients travel with a number of individuals sharing similar interests and have the potential for substantial savings and unique opportunities. *Escorted tours* offer a professional guide who remains with a tour group for the entire package. This escort takes care of travel problems that may arise and usually is knowledgeable about the culture and natural history of the area being traversed. A fully *inclusive tour* provides everything that a traveler will need for a set price, except for shopping, gambling, and personal needs. This type of tour is the most convenient since the escort facilitates and pays for all included services.

An *independent tour* or *FIT* is a travel package which normally includes some lodging and a rental car or train pass. It can also include airline tickets and specialty recreation activities, like rafting trips or attraction admissions. The traveler is independent when it comes to travel and must get from destination to destination on their own by driving a rental car or catching trains and busses.

A *fly-drive package* is a common tour in the U.S. and includes flights, motels, and a rental car. Mass marketing companies, such as Pleasant Hawaiian Holidays, specialize in this type of tour. Such a package allows the traveler to enjoy volume discounts but have the freedom to travel where they wish in between specific meeting dates.

Types of Tour Operators

The escalating demands of sophisticated travelers and the competitive nature of the travel industry has resulted in the tour operator business becoming more specialized with many types of tour services. Some companies engage in only a narrow niche of the tour market, such as Adrift Adventures, a whitewater rafting outfitter in Jensen, Utah (www.adrift.com), while other large organizations, such as Maupintour (www.maupintour.com), operate tours throughout the world via multiple transportation modes. To further confuse things, some air carriers and travel agencies also act as tour operators. Described below are the most well recognized types of tour operators.

Wholesale tour company Arranges and promotes tour packages, but sells them primarily to travel agents or international tour operators, and not to the general public. They often do not operate any portion of the tour. Marketing to the travel trade is one of the strengths of this type of firm. Revenues come primarily from markup of tours they represent.

Receptive operator This type of company, also called a ground operator, may meet and greet groups at airports, make arrangements for lodging, and shuttle them to the lodging at one particular destination. They also frequently offer foreign language interpreters, sightseeing tours, or step-on guides.

Specialty travel tour operators Organizations that possess highly specialized equipment and guides for unique tours, such as diving, rafting, biking, and photography programs. Tours may be geared towards adventure and risk activities, nature or eco-tourism, skills development, or simply sightseeing in unique settings. Clients are often younger than for other tours, averaging 40 years old.

Motorcoach tour operators These companies own and operate deluxe motorcoaches holding up to 52 passengers, with some costing over $250,000. Sightseeing via a motorcoach is still the most popular and economical tour both domestically and internationally. Operators may provide long distance or local tours, with and without narration. Some motorcoaches have two levels for sightseeing and sleeping on-board, others have bars and gambling tables.

Types of Jobs with a Tour Operator

Tour escort/guide The tour guide job provides exciting opportunities to enter the travel profession and for a career traveling the globe. This occupation can require the skills of a teacher, entertainer, accountant, doctor, and psychologist. Tour conductor and guide schools provide training and certification to get a start in the field. Guides lead everything from adventure travel, like rowing a raft through the Grand Canyon, to sightseeing tours in the wine country of Italy.

Operations manager This professional manages the logistics of equipment and staff scheduling, as well as coordination with other suppliers. This person must also be proficient in budgeting. He or she works primarily in the office and not on the road.

Tour planner Designing a new tour, contracting with appropriate suppliers, testing the itinerary, and costing the program are the duties of a tour planner. This person must be in touch with changing client wants and supplier status. Such a position usually involves a balance between business travel and office work.

Sales and marketing manager He or she works with key trade industry and client accounts, and develops promotions directed at consumers. They must be very familiar with company services and the competition. Personal sales skills are very important in this position.

The Future of Travel Agencies and Tour Operators

Despite being battered by global changes in the marketplace, travel agencies and tour operators will continue to offer needed services to business and leisure clients in the future. Undoubtedly, there will be consolidation through attrition and independent agencies joining consortiums. Travel agencies must shift away from their traditional dependence on domestic airline ticket sales and look for more profitable opportunities as consumers are better able to book flights directly and revenues from commissions decline. More agencies will rely on outside sales associates to reduce employment costs and enlarge their reach in the marketplace. The shear magnitude of travel services available

and the need for expert advice will continue to push small agencies to specialize and large firms to hire agents who are experts in a segment of the industry.

But despite the poor economy in 2001–2002, the decline in airline travel after the tragic events of September 11, 2001 and increasing pressure from airline Web sites, travel agencies have not been replaced by the Internet. In 2000, airline reservations made over the Internet accounted for less than 25 percent of all bookings (PhoCus Wright 2001). However, many agencies are not growing, except electronic travel agencies. Most industry analysts agree that there will be continued consolidation in the industry, but traditional travel agencies will not disappear if they add value through personalized service, learn to manage information sources, such as the Internet, to their advantage, and conduct business in new ways. Many people with Internet hookups simply do not have the time or desire to conduct an extensive search of the Internet, and these folks will continue to look to travel agents for assistance with lengthy and expensive travel plans. Others will still value the specialized expertise that experienced agents possess. The Internet also has the potential to save agencies money. The days of agents simply being "order takers" are nearly gone and they are being quickly replaced by true *travel consultants*.

Tour operators will need to design new tours that cater to changing customer demands, such as family travel, more independence, and participation. Aging of the population will provide expanding opportunities for senior travel, served by new and exciting tour programs. Demand for eco-tourism and other specialty travel tours are predicted to experience rapid growth. But managers will need to contend with increased access restrictions and regulations. They must develop ways to assure clients their deposits are secure and satisfaction guaranteed.

Both travel agencies and tour operators will have to reduce overhead and increase profitability. Enlightened travel agency and tour operator managers still see substantial future business opportunities, although the way they conduct their affairs will need to evolve to keep pace with changing consumer demands and technological changes.

References

American Society of Travel Agents. *Conversation with Corporate Office,* December, 2000.

National Tour Association. 2001. *2001 Packaged Travel in North America.* Lexington, KY.

PhoCus Wright Inc. 2001. "21 Million Americans Usually Buy Travel Online." Press release at http://www.phocuswright. com/press/release.html, dated November 6, 2001.

Name _____ Date _____

Chapter 38 Review Questions

1. What are the services provided by travel agencies?

2. What are the services provided by tour operators?

3. How is a tour operator compensated?

4. How is a travel agent compensated?

5. Describe the following types of travel agencies. Who is the target market of each?

    a.   Corporate Agencies

    b. Leisure Agencies

    c. Wholesalers

    d. Specialized Leisure Agencies

    e. Incentive Travel Houses

    f.   Consolidators

    g. Electronic Travel Agencies

6. What has happened over the last ten years related to the commission paid to travel agents from the airlines?

7. What has happened over the last ten years related to the commission paid to travel agents from the cruise ship industry?

8. Who/what is relatively new competition for travel agents?

9. What are the advantages of being a travel agent?

10. What are familiarization trips?

11. What is a GDS?

12. Describe the licensing and certification options available for travel agents.

13. What are the airline companies and hotel companies doing to draw business to their Internet sites and away from the travel agent?

14. What impact has the Internet had on travel agencies?

15. What impact is the Internet likely to have on travel agencies in the next decade?

16. Describe the following types of tour operators. Who is the target market of each?

   a. Wholesale Tour Company

   b. Receptive Operator

c. Specialty Travel Tour Operator

d. Motor Coach Tour Operator

17. Describe the following positions likely found in a tour operator's business.

a. Tour/escort guide

b. Operations Manager

c. Tour planner

d. Sales and marketing manager

18. Why is today's travel agent often (maybe better) described as a travel consultant?

19. What future demographic trends are likely to impact travel?

Glossary

A la Carte—Every item on the menu is priced independently, including side items and salads

AAHOA—Asian American Hotel Owners Association

ABC—The Alcoholic Beverage Commission; the state agency that enforces restrictions on methods and hours of operation, records and expansion, concerning the sale and service of alcohol

Academic Freedom—The educator has the right to teach as he/she sees fit

ACF—American Culinary Federation

ACPHA—The Accreditation Commission for Programs in Hospitality Administration; evaluates and awards accreditation to four year programs

Aft—Rear of the ship

AHLA—American Hotel and Lodging Association

AIA—American Institute of Architects

Ambiance—The overall décor, sound, lighting, and furniture of an establishment

Americans with Disabilities Act—A law that calls for "reasonable" accommodations for both employees and customers who are functionally challenged; became law on July 26, 1990

Amusement Parks—A collection of rides and food stands located in one central area; most of the time each ride requires its own ticket or admission fee

Anti-gaming Advocates—Those individuals who protest against gaming, and try to deter people from voting for gaming

Appraisers—Professionals who are trained to value land and buildings, hired to render estimates of value

Apprenticeship—The European model for training chefs, where a chef gains employment and through the tutelage of the chefs on premises, hones one's skills and progresses through the ranks of a single kitchen

ARDA—American Resort Development Association began in 1969

ASID—American Society of Interior Designers

Assisted Living Centers—Centers for senior citizens that offer more services and moderate costs (medications, meals, transportation); designed for the senior residents that cannot fully live on their own, but do not need full care

Associations—A body that is made up of individual, organizational, and allied or affiliated members, who are drawn together to promote and develop a specific industry through a variety of services (including continuing education) and benefits to the membership

ASTA—American Society of Travel Agents formed in 1931

Audit—Another individual checking the cash handling often of a subordinate

Autonomy—The ability to work well and productively yet primarily alone; make decisions with little to no supervision

Bacchus—The Roman god of wine and indulgence

Back-of-the-House—Refers to positions whose worksite is removed from the customers view

Bag drop—A location where golf assistants help golfers unload golf bags from their cars and place them in waiting golf carts

Balance Sheet—Measures the flow of money, showing a business's net worth; it shows total assets, total liabilities, and owners equity; shows the performance of a business at a snapshot in time

Balance—A delicate mixture of your time spent at work and off; one needs to spend enough time at work to succeed and achieve personal goals, but time off work is important to maintain good health and get sufficient exercise and rest

Base Fee—A percentage of total revenue paid by the host organization to the management company; trends show these are declining

Bed and Breakfast Inns—Started in the early 1800s as overnight stays in private homes

Benefits—Traditionally a motivational tool, though now often expected; often includes health insurance, vacation pay, sick time off with pay, dental insurance, retirement, 401K plans, etc.

Berth—A sufficient distance for maneuvering a ship; also a place to sit and sleep on a ship

Blind Spot—"When you don't know what it is that you don't know"; can be a handicap to people in their careers, especially if there is limited feedback

Bow—Front of the ship

Brand Identification—The symbol or trademark of a company which consumers recognize, such as the swoosh of Nike or the golden arches of McDonald's

Branding—Taking a known brand, like McDonald's or Pizza Hut, and opening that facility in a hospital, B&I, or school

Brokers—A professional who serves as an intermediary in a real estate sales transaction

Cages—Mini banks within a casino

CAHM—The Commission for Accreditation of Hospitality Management; evaluates and awards accreditation to two year programs

Capital—Money used to build a new business venture, or make long-term improvements

Captain—The top leader, person in charge, of the ship

Captive Foodservice—Where the customer has little or no choice in his/her decision to pay for and consume the food services; examples are elementary schools, hospitals

Career Fair—An event where many recruiters come together on a college or university campus to meet and interview students for employment opportunities—often internships and entry-level management

Cash Handling Procedures—The proper way an employee is trained to handle cash transactions

Catering—The service of food for a group of people coming together for a reason, may be on-premise (at the site where the food was prepared) or off-premise (when the food is prepared at one location and served at a different location)

Chains—Often referred to as multi unit operations; a business with three or more separate outlets bearing the same name, concept style of service and systems of operation

Chief Purser—The position responsible for accounting, personnel services, and the concessions

Chief Steward—The position that is responsible for the dining room and food services

Chips—Small round plastic disks used in lieu of money

CHRIE—International Council on Hotel, Restaurant, and Institutional Education

CIC—Convention Industry Council, founded in 1949; provides the CMP (Certified Meeting Planner) designation

City Clubs—Establishments that are in urban areas, and cater to the businessmen or women, provides dining services and occasionally athletic events

Civil Rights Act—A law signed in 1964 which prohibits discrimination on the basis of race, color, religion, sex, or national origin

Classification by Location—The lodging industry can be classified many ways including the location of the property: City Hotels, Suburban Hotels, Highway Hotels/Motels, Airport Hotels

Classification by Price—The lodging industry can be classified many ways including the price likely to be paid for one night stay at that property: Luxury and Deluxe Hotels, Midmarket and Commercial Hotels, Budget and Economy Hotels

Classification by Service—The lodging industry can be classified many ways including the degree of services to be found at that property: Luxury Hotels and Resorts, Deluxe Hotels, Midmarket Hotels and Commercial Hotels, Full Service Hotels, Limited Service Hotels, All-Suite Hotels/Extended Stay Hotels

Classification by Unique Characteristics—The lodging industry can be classified many ways including the types of facilities: Bed and Breakfast Hotels, Casino Hotels, Convention Hotels, Residential Hotels, Resort Hotels

CLIA—Cruise Line International Association

Club—A group of persons organized for social, literary, athletic, political, recreational or other purposes

CMAA—Club Managers Association of America formed in 1920

Coffee Shops—These restaurants provide waiter/waitress service, larger menu variety and service takes longer; open more hours and more days of the week than any other restaurant concept

Coles Ordinary—The first American tavern, opened in 1634; the term "ordinary" soon changed to "inn"

Commercial Kitchen Designers—Professionals who provide planning and drawings of commercial kitchens, and specify equipment

Communication Skills—The ability of one to spell well and clearly, and write succinctly and correctly

Comparative Negligence—Where a jury or judge must determine the percentage of fault applicable to the parties in a negligence action in order to apportion financial liability

Comps—Free enticements given to gamblers while in the casino to encourage more or repeated play at a later date; usually includes free meals, room nights, or special event tickets

Conceptual Skills—The ability to see the company or department as a whole and understand how the different parts work together

Connectivity—The fact that many business systems or units are now connected electronically, and can communicate with relative ease, regardless of geographic location

Consolidation—Often the result of buy-outs and takeovers, several (what were) independent businesses are merged together within the same company

Consolidators—Businesses that purchase large blocks of airline seats or cruise berths at a substantial discount, and resell them to travel agents or the general public for a lower than normal fare

Consultant—An individual who has a specific skill set or area of expertise and is compensated for providing advice or other services to a client

Contract Management—When a mutually binding legal document has been negotiated between the operator who furnishes management services and the owner who pays for these services

Contractors—The professional builder of the project

Control—Comparing the performance of employees in a workforce against the objectives and goals that have been set by the company

Controlling the Money—The focus of casino management; securing the flow of cash; uses computers, accounting departments, security and surveillance

Convention Hotels—Those hotels with added features such as the removal of interior posts, barrier-free space, flexible walls, blackout window treatments, and improved lighting

Conversion Rate—The percentage of web visitors that actually buy a product online

Core Menu—The main "signature" item line of a restaurant, such as pizza, hamburgers, roast beef

Costs—The outflow of dollars

Country Clubs—Hospitality establishments that provide elaborate social events, offer dining, pool, tennis and golf

Creativity—The leading core characteristic that research has shown is vital in determining success or failure of an entrepreneur; the ability to create innovative ideas sets one business apart from the others

Cruise Director—The position that is responsible for securing and procuring continuous entertainment for the ship

Cruise Ship Market—A major segment of the travel and tourism industry, which has increased more than 800% from 1970 to 2000

Cultural Attractions—Anything made by humans that draw people to it; sites set up to preserve or further the culture of the community

Customer Relationship Management—Software that enables the company to track customer's preferences, enhancing their hospitality experience and ultimately increasing the customer's loyalty to the brand

Daily Fee Course—These are golf courses that are privately owned, but open to the public, and require a fee be paid for each round of golf

Development Costs—Those costs associated with the land, the building, the furnishings, and the equipment necessary for operation of the restaurant

Dinner House—Waiter/waitress service is provided, more upscale, menu variety and better service is received, open for lunch and dinner

Dionysus—The Greek god of wine

Direct Marketing—Sales force reaches potential customers through personal interactions and increasingly through technology

Discretionary Dollars—Those that the customer has a choice about spending; vacation and resort revenues are typically from a person's discretionary dollars

Distribution Services—The chain of operational products that are produced, handled by a middleman, then delivered to the operator

Domestic—Within the country

Dram Shop Laws—Laws that impose penalties on the establishment if guests leave intoxicated and are involved in an accident

Drop—Total amount of cash plus the value of the markers (credit slips) the casino takes in

E-Business—Companies that expand the use of technologies to include all major stakeholders in their business: customers, employees, management, government, business partners, bankers, suppliers/vendors, and stockholders. The focus is on synergy, integration and collaboration.

E-Commerce—Focuses only on the customers and suppliers and the transactions with them that occur online; is concerned with enabling and successfully completing sales transactions online efficiently

86ed—When the operation has run out of an item; a slang term

Emergency Maintenance—Breakdowns that are unpredictable, and often expensive; requires immediate attention of maintenance and engineering

Empowerment—Where a contemporary leader has created the organizational work environment in which staff members are trained in necessary skills, and management delegates a certain degree of power and decision making authority to the employees, often on the front line; to establish ownership in the position and organization, and ultimately better achieve the company's goals—usually improving guest service; management must support the decisions made by the staff members

Energy Management—The effective management that monitors both consumption and costs of energy, and climatic conditions

Enterprise Resource Management—Inventory management software that manages information across the enterprise so that the same information is available to all parties

Entrepreneur—Someone who starts, manages, and assumes the risks and rewards of a new business enterprise; he/she also strives to achieve business growth and possible expansion into new markets or geographic locations

E-Procurement System—When purchasing transactions are conducted in an electronic environment, such as the Internet

Equity Clubs—Those facilities owned by their membership, are non profit; oldest form of clubs

Ethics—A set of principles that managers apply when interacting with people and their organizations; fair and equal treatment, truth, lack of bias, consistency, and respect of others

Expatriate—A foreign citizen

Extended Stay—A segment of the lodging industry, which accounts for most of the new construction of properties built from 1998–2001; consumers want the luxuries of home in space and design

Fabricators—These companies take one or more manufactured products and "assemble" them or add more "value" by creating a new product; sometimes called processors

Fast Food—The traditional name for QSRs, limited menu, counter service, so the consumer is served their food very quickly

Feedback—The exchange of words, used often to provide praise, or constructive remarks

FF and E—An abbreviation for furniture, fixtures, and equipment

Fine Dining—Dinner only typically, very formal waiter/waitress service; often used for special occasions

Fiscal—Financial; often used as "fiscal year" for financial records

"Fit"—What you and potential employers want to know—do your values line up with their organization, and how successful will you be in their work environment

Food/Beverage—One of the four major subdivisions of hospitality and tourism, this segment includes taverns, restaurants, bars, catering and vending

Food Cost—The cost of the food being prepared

Food Quality—The utmost expectation of a chef, food quality must taste good, be appealing to the eye, and appeal to the specific customers of the business

Foursome—A term used to describe the golfing party; usually four people

Franchise System—Comprised of properties that have the same name and design, but are owned and operated by different parties; this group is characterized by tight performance standards; and where the franchisee pays a fee to open and operate a unit

Franchise—Owned by an individual (the franchisee) who pays for the rights to operate, including the operating systems, standardized policies and procedures, and agrees to maintain the performance standards of the larger group (the franchisor)

Franchising—The process of selling a "prepackaged" brand of restaurant or hotel to an entrepreneur for a fee

Full Membership—Entitles a member to full use of the club, all amenities during any hour of operation

Full Service Living Centers—These centers are more commonly known as nursing homes, they provide full services (medical, personal care—bathing, etc.) for senior citizens who cannot care for themselves, high cost; designed for the most needy senior resident

Fusion—The blending together of two traditionally different styles

Gaming—The industry built around gambling; casino industry; generates huge money for state government

GCSA—Golf Course Superintendents Association of America

Generalist—One who provides a broad range of services to their clients

Golf 20/20—The golf industry's initiative committed to growing the game of golf

Golf Professional—The head of the golf department; oversees the pro shop, gives lessons, manages golf tournaments, usually is PGA certified

Golf Superintendent—The professional who is educated in agronomy and oversees the care of the golf course and surrounding property

Grill Room—An informal dining facility in the club house where golf attire is appropriate

Gross Registered Tonnage (GRT)—A classification for ships which gauges the volume of public space; the greater the GRT the greater number of passengers it can carry

Halfway House—A small food and beverage facility that serves food between the "front nine" holes and the "back nine" holes of golf

HAMA—Hotel Asset Managers Association

Hard Products—Products sold online, often outside the hospitality industry, which must be physically shipped to the buyer, such as chemicals or apparel

Haute Cuisine—A high-end, lavish style of cooking, elegantly prepared and served

High Rollers—People who gamble large amounts of money at the tables, the target market profile of a casino

High Season—When demand is at its peak

Hospitality—An environment of friendliness, warmth, cheer, graciousness, and conviviality

House—The particular casino; chips from one casino may not be used at another casino

Hub-and-Spoke System—A system created by the airlines after deregulation, where a carrier has a "hub" in certain cities in which most flights pass through

Human Resource Management—The management of people, who work for the organization, includes recruiting, training, maintaining extensive records, and ensuring all workforce laws are adhered to

HVAC—The heating, ventilation, and air conditioning system; delivers heating and cooling on demand while maintaining the proper humidity and air quality

IAAPA—International Association of Amusement Parks and Attractions founded in 1918

ICCA—The International Congress and Convention Association founded in 1965

IFMA—The International Facility Management Association

Impersonal Marketing—Sales force reaches potential customers through marketing promotional tools such as advertising or public relations

Incentive and Special Event Producers—Usually sponsored by corporations are reward-based programs for top employees; utilize resorts, tours, and recreation facilities, with a high degree of social interaction

Incentive Fees—A fee based on performance improvement(s) after at least a year, usually a percentage of the amount over a specific goal, paid by the host organization to the management company

Income Statement—Also known as the profit and loss report; although the format may vary it includes a record of accounts including: total sales, cost of goods sold, gross profit, expenses, taxes, and net income

Independent Living Centers—Centers for senior citizens that offer few services and the lowest cost (lawn care, housekeeping); designed for the most independent senior resident

Independent Operations—Owned and operated by an individual or group of individual investors; owns one or two operations and enjoys greater business decision making freedom than that of the franchisee; a person who maintains a limit to the size and scope of the business operation; the owner directs a business that has no affiliation with any other facilities or operations

Indirect Marketing—Sales force reaches potential customers through wholesale intermediaries, such as tour operators or meeting planners, who in turn sell to retail travel agencies or the customer

Institutional Foodservice—A term no longer used, now called contract food services

Intellectual Capital—The combined knowledge of all knowledge workers (employees) working to improve a business, thinking outside of the box

Interior Designers—Professionals that design interior spaces involving materials, finishes, colors, space planning and layout

Intermediaries—These are distributors, wholesalers, suppliers, dealers, purveyors, and vendors that buy products from manufacturers and sell them to hospitality and tourism providers; sometimes called middlemen

International Exchange Agreements—Articulation agreements between two schools or universities that allow its student to attend the other school, in a different country, and receive credit toward graduation

International—Outside of one's home country; within many countries

Interpersonal Skills—The ability to understand people and work well with them on an individual basis and in groups

Interval-ownership Properties—Property developers sell a fraction of a designated space, such as a 30-day slice or 7-day slice of a condominium

Job Analysis—The process to determine the tasks and skills necessary to complete the job

Job Descriptions—A tool used to identify the purpose, duties, and conditions under which jobs are performed

Job Design—Determines how the job is organized, and how it can be planned to provide both productivity to the organization and job satisfaction to the employee

Job Specifications—The qualifications, knowledge, and skills necessary to perform the position

Just-in-time—When an item of inventory (food, airline seat, hotel room) becomes available just before the next consumer wants to rent/buy it; ultimately reduced capital is tied up in inventory

Knowledge Worker—A person who knows how to access, where to search, and how to get base knowledge in real time

Labor Intensive—The business or industry that employs a large number of employees to provide customers with a product or service

Labor Relations—Specialized area of the law devoted to unionized workplaces

Leadership—The influencing of others to channel their activities toward reaching the goals of the business

Learning Organization—A business that encourages (and often rewards) learning, accessing new information, and applying it towards achieving the company's goals

Lease—A legal document outlining usually the rental of space from a landlord

Leisure Activities—Entertainment, attractions, recreation, cruises, gaming, and shopping

Lido Deck—A deck that offers informal activities such as indoor and outdoor buffets

Liquor Liability—State laws that govern the selling of alcohol and its licensing

Lodging—One of the four major subdivisions of hospitality and tourism, this segment includes hotels, motels, resorts and vacation ownership

Low Rollers—People who play the nickel, dime, and quarter slots; only gamble a small amount of money

Low Season—The lowest business demand time

Macro View—A perspective outside the immediate geographic location of the business to include any company or customer that may do business with them online; understanding the large scope of the competitive environment

Management Control System—Records to track the costs of the operation; can document the responsibility and accountability for all items

Management—The process of getting tasks accomplished through people

Manufacturer—Sources of the product supply; sometimes referred to as "growers"

Manufacturing Economy—Businesses that contribute to the gross national product (GNP) that are manufacturing in type—such as the automobile or chemical industry

Marketing Mix—A blending of several inducements designed to create and keep customers

Meeting and Convention Managers—These professionals are most often associated with conferences, seminars, conventions, training programs, and new product introductions; events with a strong focus on education

Mega-Ships—Those ships built in the very recent past that are extremely large and offer amenities similar to a resort

Member—Regardless of type of club, each is made up of members, who have applied for and been accepted into membership

Mentor—Someone who is experienced in the business that one can talk to for advice and counsel; usually not one's immediate supervisor

Merit Pay—Providing increased wages based on an employee's performance that is at or above expected levels

MGM Grand Hotel and Theme Park—The largest resort in the world, and the dream of pioneer Las Vegas hotel developer, multimillionaire, Kirk Kerkorian

MICE Industry—Meetings, Incentive, Convention, and Exposition Industry

Mid-ship—Middle of the ship

Military Clubs—Cater to enlisted men and women and the non-commissioned officer; provides a social outlet, often has golf

Moments of Truth—Any time a guest comes in contact with anything that represents the operation; may be positive or negative

Motel—Also known as a motor hotel, provides a room and parking available near the room as many motels did not have uniformed staff or bell persons; flourished as the Interstate highway system grew

MPI—Meeting Planners International

Multiculturally Aware—A person who is sensitive and tolerant of other cultures and customs

Multinational Company—A business with locations in more than one country

Multiple Service Centers—Centers for senior citizens that offer all types of service centers—Independent Living, Assisted Living, and Full Service—at one site or campus

Municipal Course—Golf courses that are owned and operated by a tax supported entity, such as a city or county, open to the public

National—A local citizen

Natural Attractions—Nature's beauty; often protected by the government or special interest groups

NCA—National Club Association

Negligence—The area of the law that attempts to define who is legally responsible for a particular accident and to make that person, or entity, pay for the reasonable costs of the accident victim

Net Income—All of the inflows of dollars, minus the outflows of dollars

Networking—The process of meeting and getting to know other people; usually people with similar interests and share information that is beneficial to all parties, often making contacts for future employment opportunities

NGF—National Golf Foundation

Non-Commercial Food Service—Those food services that are in businesses whose primary function is not food and beverage (schools, hospitals, businesses, or universities); profit is not always a motive

NRA—National Restaurant Association

Occupational Safety and Health Act—Mandates safety regulations and practices at the federal level, so that businesses in the U.S. provide a safe property and safe work environment

Onsite—The operation of services within the physical structure of the host organization

Operations—The day-to-day managing and running of the business; great career opportunities for people who get fired up by the day to day contact with customers and the myriad of challenges and surprises that arise in the business

Organizing—The efforts involved with determining what activities are to be done and how employees are grouped together to accomplish specific tasks

Owners Equity—The portion of the assets that the company owns

PACE—Program of All Inclusive Care for the Elderly, developed by Medicare, provides comprehensive care for the elderly

Paradigm Shift—The changing environment, when the notion that "we always did it this way" no longer is sufficient, and often for growth or survival, a company must change the way it is doing business

Paradigm—An environment, example, pattern

Partnership—Owned by two or more people

Pathological Gambler—Problem gamblers who get caught up in trying to win the jackpot and stay too long; less than 2 percent of the population is at risk

PCMA—The Professional Convention Management Association

People Person—In the hospitality business one is surrounded by people: employees and customers; a manager must be able to communicate effectively with individuals in the different roles of subordinates/superiors and guests

Performance Clause—A clause in the contract that states if the management company does not perform to a pre-agreed upon level the owner has the right to terminate the contract

Performance Standards—Guidelines created by a franchisor to ensure consistency in products and customer service experience in each operation, regardless of franchisee

PGA—Professional Golfers' Association

Phoenicians—Among the first real travelers

Physical Plant—The facility in which the products or services that guests purchase are created, delivered, and generally consumed

Picea—The earliest known version of today's pizza, consumed by Roman soldiers during the approximate year of 1000

Pineapple—Not only a delicious fruit, but now recognized as the international symbol of hospitality

Placement Office—An office on most colleges and university's campuses that help students develop resumes, practice interviewing skills, and can assist with job searches

Planning—The establishment of goals and objectives and deciding how to accomplish these goals

POM—An accounting abbreviation for property, operation and maintenance accounts

Port—Left side of the ship

Ports of Call—Cities that cruise ships enter into and dock so their patrons can visit the city

Ports of Embarkation—Cities from where cruise ships take off (embark) on their voyage

Practice Range—An area near the pro shop and first tee to practice hitting golf balls

Pro Shop—A small retail establishment, boutique style as it is highly specialized in golf apparel, equipment, and tools for the game

Proactive Management—The leader forecasts what may occur within the business such as volume of business, safety issues, ordering supplies as to not get caught off guard or unprotected

Professional Associations—These associations hold meetings and conventions often annually and are a major source of revenue for the MICE Industry

Professional Certification—Offered through associations in a specific area or field, usually a culmination of work experience, continuing education, and passing a comprehensive examination. It validates one's knowledge and demonstrates one's commitment to lifelong learning, and the industry.

Professional Development—Continuing education in a specific industry, often in the form of seminars, workshops or distance education

Project Design Team—A group of professionals who are brought together because of their individual and varying skill sets to create a new facility or remodel an existing one

Project Manager—One who directs the work of the consultants on a project, maintains an ongoing dialogue with the client, and ensures that payments for services are received/paid on a timely basis

Promotions—Short term inducements such as coupons or drawings for free prizes

Proprietary Clubs—Those owned by a corporation, company, business or individual; they are for profit businesses

Prove Competency—A QSR manager should be able to work in each position to prove to his/her employees he/she has a working knowledge of the operation; they do not need to be the best at each job

Publicity—Unpaid communication about the firm or its products

Purchasing Agent—Someone who works for the hospitality business who purchases and receives the products

Purchasing Economics—The purchasing of products in larger volume to gain substantial discounts, then redistributing these products to the units

Putting Green—A putting surface used by golfers to practice putting

QSR Location—Where people can easily access them; virtually anywhere traffic patterns have dictated a need; suburbs, malls, grocery stores

Quality Assurance—Specific operating standards that must be met, often enforced through regular inspections

Quick Service Restaurants—A very large segment of the restaurant industry, which provides a limited menu, counter service, yet prepares the food quickly; often used interchangeably with "Fast Food," though many would argue these terms are not synonymous

Ranger—A person who monitors the pace of playing golf, and may tell a foursome to speed up if need be

Rating Services—The two primary services in the U.S. are the American Automobile Association (AAA) and Mobil Travel Guide. These businesses rate restaurants and hotels on specific criteria to render judgment on its property level of services to the guest; consumers who are seeking consistency while traveling use these

Reactive Management—Being able to "think on your feet" and react well to changes and unpredictable events, such as a slip and fall accident

Real Estate Representative—A person who works for the hospitality firm that specializes in real estate transactions including site location and analysis

Real-time—Current time, immediate

Recreation Services—A department typically found in a resort hotel that manages the recreational facilities and possible youth programs at the resort, such as golf, tennis, horseback riding

Recreation—One of the four major subdivisions of hospitality and tourism, this segment includes festivals, parks, gaming, and attractions

Referral Associations—Comprised of properties that have the same name and design, but are owned and operated by different parties; this group is characterized by greater owner autonomy. Benefits include international marketing and a central reservation system, while maintaining the independence of an individual hotel

Refrigeration Systems—A system that maintains the temperature of a space by removing any heat that enters the space

Regional Carriers—Those airlines which operate within a certain geographic area or region

Representative—A company that provides advertising services and books reservations for independent hotels; receives a commission on each reservation it books, but imposes no quality assurance standards on its properties

Respite Care—Short term, temporary use of assisted living center resources and services

Retention—Keeping employees employed; the best method to enhance retention is an atmosphere of fair treatment, where employees enjoy working, where they feel they make a difference and are rewarded based on their own individual performance

Revenue—Money flowing into the business

RFP—Request for Proposal; a document that outlines the nature of the work requested and other project details

Routine Maintenance—General upkeep, occurs regularly, requires little skill

Royalties—Monies paid to the franchisor at regular intervals once the franchised business is operating

Sales—The inflow of dollars into the business

Saloons—America's first bars, they provided the community a place to spend leisure time and even hold trials

Sanitation—A key component to any kitchen, employees must be trained in safe food handling practices to prevent food poisoning and meet heath code requirements

Scheduled Maintenance—Initiated by formal work order and attempts to meet a known need in an orderly and timely manner

Security—The task of protecting people—both guests and employees, and protecting assets

Self-managed Teams—A group of employees, often with technical skills, which work as a team to accomplish the company's goal(s) with little or no close supervision

Self-op-self operating—The parent company chooses to take full responsibility and operate the integrated services (food, lodging) themselves

Service Economy—Businesses that contribute to the gross national product (GNP) that are service oriented in type—such as the restaurant or lodging industry

Service—The reason why private clubs exist; members receive high-end, personalized service at their club

Slots—Games that include slot machines, video poker, and other computerized games; the 25-cent slot machine is the most popular

Small business—Currently accounts for 9 million self-employed Americans, this segment created more than 63 percent of all new jobs, and is responsible for 43 percent of the Gross National Product (GNP)

Social Membership—Entitles a member to limited use of a country club, typically dining, pool, and tennis, but not golf; reduced initiation fee and dues structure

Soft Products—Digital products that hospitality companies sell online such as airline tickets that lend themselves well to online distribution channels

Sole Proprietorship—Owned by one person

Special Events—Food services at specialty events such as outdoor concerts, tennis or golf tournaments, or extensive events like the Olympics

Specialty Quick Service Restaurants—Very limited menu, orders are filled most rapidly, such as Krispy Kreme Doughnuts or Subway

Staff or Support—Those positions which exist to provide assistance to managers in operations; such as human resources, training, accounting, and marketing; without operations these positions would not exist

Staffing—Supplying the human requirements necessary to service guests

Starboard—Right side of the ship

Starter—A person at the starting location of a golf course who verifies payment has been received and gives any instructions for the course

Stern—Extreme rear of the ship

Super-service Industries—Telecommunications, information technology, and tourism, the three areas that futurist John Naisbitt stated would drive the global economy in the 21st century

Supply Chain Management—The management of information related to the flow of material along the entire production cycle

Support—Professionals that work in hospitality and tourism but not in operations

Surveillance—A department that operates above the gaming floor; utilizes hundreds of cameras embedded in the ceiling of the casino

Table Games—Any game played on a table

Tangible—Touchable, something that can be seen and felt

Task Force Team—A group of employees who come together to address and solve a specific task for the organization; often made up of one person per department affected by the task

Taverns—First found in the U.S. in 1770s, built in the colonies and became the focal point of the community

Technical Skills—The skills involving knowledge of and the ability to perform a particular job or task

Tee time—A reservation for a specific time to start a round of golf

Tenure—A faculty member has employment on a continuing basis

Terminal Degree—The highest degree offered in that field

Theatrical Food and Beverage—Areas that allow guests to see the show in the kitchen

Theme Parks—Strive to create a fantasy atmosphere that transports the visitor to another place and time; closed geographical boundaries exist with an admission price at the gate

Thinking outside of the box—Looking to other non-related industries or businesses to improve one's operation, taking another business's model and applying it to a similar situation to improve operations

Third-Party Liability—Imposes penalties on those who sell or serve alcohol when certain circumstances exist

360-Degree Evaluation—The most optimal method of performance evaluation, yet time consuming and costly; where the supervisor evaluates the employee performance as do the employees they supervise, peers, and customers

TIA—Travel Industry of America formed in 1941

Toque—The traditional tall white hat worn by chefs

Total Assets—The possessions of the business

Total Liabilities—What the company still owes on its possessions or has already used

Tour Operators—Professionals that organize complete travel programs for groups or individuals to every continent and by all modes of transportation

Tradeshow or Exposition Managers—Events where there are booth-displays of products and services, focus is on marketing

Travel Agents—Professionals within an agency that act to match the travel desires of leisure and business travelers with the most appropriate suppliers of tourist services

Travel—One of the four major subdivisions of hospitality and tourism, this segment includes railroads, automobiles, cruise ships, and airlines

Troubleshooter—An internal consultant, one who works for a single company but goes to different units as they have problem areas; also called a field consultant

Turnover—A term used to describe the cycle of when an employee leaves for any reason (fired or quit) and must be replaced; an expensive occurrence

Vacation Clubs—Similar to interval ownership, this plan allows for maximum flexibility as the owner earns points for the value of his/her time that is owned, and trades those points for space elsewhere

Vacation-Ownership Firm—A business focused on selling long-term vacation packages to guests; "slices of time," can be hotel room or condominium at a specific property

Value-added Relationship—The ideal relationship between an employee and his/her employer; mutually beneficial to both parties

Wage and Hour Law—Requires the employer pay at least a minimum wage, pay extra for overtime work, and pay for all of the work that was completed

Wastewater Systems—Systems that remove and sometimes treat wastewater (sewage)

WATS—Wide Area Telephone System—allows leasing of telephone lines which dramatically reduces the cost of high volume use

"We work, so others can play"—This motto depicts the type of work done in the hospitality industry, it often includes nights and weekends when a lot of other people are off work

Whole-ownership Condominium Hotels—These facilities are usually sold outright and the owners generally have year round occupancy

Word-of-Mouth Marketing—Recommendations from friends and relatives; far and away the best way to generate interest and business

Workers Compensation—State regulated insurance programs that are meant to compensate employees for medical expenses, lost wages, and rehabilitation costs that may be incurred as a result of work related injuries

Working Capital Management—The short-term management of what the company owns and what the company owes

"WOW"—A term coined by Tom Peters when describing a business that effectively thinks outside of the box to improve its core operation, and ultimately better reach its goals

WTO—World Tourism Organization

WTTC—The World Travel and Tourism Council

Yacht Club—Establishments near or on the water, activities center on sailing and boating, dining also available

Zoning—Regulations that specify how land might be used

Index

Darden Restaurants, 20, 29, 90, 345–46
Davidson Brothers, Inc., 19
Davis, Stan, 38
Day, Cecil B., 20
Days Inn, 20
Dedman School of Hospitality, 241
Delta Airlines, 363–65
Delta Express, 29
Delta Queen Steamboat, 216
Deluxe hotel, 261–62
Demand elasticity, 337
Denny's, 345
DePfa Bank AG, 331
Desegregation, in hotels, 20
Design. *See* Interior design
Destination management companies (DMC), 305–6
Destinations, cruise ship, list, 218
Development costs, for chain operations, 320
Dickinson College Career Center, 285
Dictionary of Hospitality, Travel, and Tourism, 90
Dining clubs, 205
Dinner house, 345–46
Direct compensation, 121
Direct sales force, 129–30
Director of golf, 251
Discount travel, 363
Disney, Walt, 21, 181, 284, 340
Disneyland, 181–82
Disneyworld, 21, 31
Distribution services, 231–38
    career preparation, 236
    intermediaries, 233–34
    job categories in, 235
    manufacturers and, 233
    network of, 232–33
    purchasing agents and, 235–36
Divisional areas, hotel/lodging operations, 266–67
Dollywood, 22
Domino's Pizza Distribution Corp. Services, 234
Dram shop suits, 172
Drive-ins, 18
Drop, defined, 195
Drury Inns, 93
Due diligence, defined, 330–31
Duquesne Club, 205–7

E

Eastern Michigan University, 162
Eatzi's, 22
E-business
    activities chart, 76
    benefits of, 74–76
    competition and, 74
    conversion rate and, 75

    cost reduction, 74
    customer convenience from, 74–76
    defined, 72–74
    functions, 76–77
    global reach of, 74
    model, 72
    operations streamlining, 74
    price reduction and, 74
E-commerce model, 72, 74
Economic Recovery Act, 339
Economics, golf management, 249
Economy hotels, 263
EcoTourism Societies, 21
Edgeworth Club, 205, 209
Education careers, 239–46
    ACPHA, 243
    CAHM, 243
    colleges, 241
    community colleges, 241
    compensation, 242–43
    culinary arts academies, 241
    curriculum vitae for, 241–42
    four-year programs, 241
    graduate programs, 241
    growth in, 240
    high school programs, 240–41
    lifestyle, 242–43
    NRA, 47
    opportunities, 46
    post-secondary programs, 241
    scope of, 240
    teaching load, 242
    tenure, 242
    training institutes for, 241
    two-year programs, 241
    universities, 241
    vocational/technical schools in, 241
Educational Institute of the American Hotel and Lodging Association, 268
EEOC (Equal Employment Opportunities Commission), 120
EFCT (European Federation of Conference Towns), 301–2
E-hospitality, 71–80. *See also* E-business
Electrical engineers, 274
Electrical system maintenance, 149
Electricity, 17
Electronic travel agencies, 363
Elevators, 16
Elks Club, 205
Emergency maintenance, 151
Employee loyalty, 120
Employment discrimination, law, 170–71
Encyclopedia of Associations, 46
Engineer's Club, 205
Engineering/maintenance, hotel, 267

Engineering systems, physical plant management, 149–50
Enterprise Resource Management (ERM), 76–77
Entrance fees, referral associations, 102
Entrepreneurial operations, 81–87
    characteristics of successful, 84–85
    defined, 82–83
    pros and cons of, 83–84
Environment, quick service operations and, 321
Equity clubs, defined, 208
Equity contributors, 110
Ernst & Young, 329
Escoffier, Auguste, 16
Escort, tour operators, 365–66
Escorted tour, defined, 365
Eta Sigma Delta (ESD), 53
Ethics, 173
    hospitality/tourism operations, 173
    vs. law, 173
    management consulting, 294
    management of operations, 141–42
Eurest Dining Services, 93
European Federation of Conference Towns, 301–2
European hotel, 265
European industry, 265
European medieval castle feasts, 14, 28
European Meetings Industry Liaison Group, 301
European training model, culinary industry, 224
Evaluation, human resource management, 121
Everglades Club, 205
Execu-Stay, 28
Expatriates, employment and, 285
Expedia, 363
Extended Stay America, 93
Extended stay hotel, 263
Extracurricular activities, 60–61

F

Facility description, club operations, 207
Fairfield Inns, 140
Fast service restaurant, interior design for, 276
Fazoli's, 90
Fee structures, franchising/referral, 102
Fermentation process, history of, 14
FFE (furniture, fixtures, and equipment), 328–30

Tools for Student Success

The CD-ROM included with this book contains files that correspond to each of the chapters. Within each chapter, you will find:

- Key Words with definitions
- Websites related to the chapter for further inquiry
- End of Chapter Review Questions to print out for homework assignments or use as study guides
- Slides that highlight key points of the chapter